Keepers of the Common Good

Keepers of the Common Good

The People, Opinion, and the Social Foundations of Constitutional Authority

D.J. GALLIGAN
University of Oxford

OXFORD
UNIVERSITY PRESS

OXFORD
UNIVERSITY PRESS

Great Clarendon Street, Oxford, OX2 6DP,
United Kingdom

Oxford University Press is a department of the University of Oxford.
It furthers the University's objective of excellence in research, scholarship,
and education by publishing worldwide. Oxford is a registered trade mark of
Oxford University Press in the UK and in certain other countries

Published in the United States of America by Oxford University Press
198 Madison Avenue, New York, NY 10016, United States of America

British Library Cataloguing in Publication Data

Data available

Library of Congress Control Number: 2024936967

ISBN 9780198907367

DOI: 10.1093/9780198907398.001.0001

Printed and bound in the UK by
Clays Ltd, Elcograf S.p.A.

MIX
Paper | Supporting
responsible forestry
FSC® C018072
FSC
www.fsc.org

In memory of my parents and other
Keepers of the Common Good of Vacy Plains

'The herd without a keeper strayed'
Walter Scott: *The Lady of the Lake*

Preface

In that period of relief and respite between finishing one book and starting the next, I came across a record of the Putney Debates held in St Mary's Church Putney in October 1647. The debates caught my interest and set off an enquiry that led, quite some years later, to this book. The weekly meeting of officers of the New Model Army, chaired by Oliver Cromwell, to which on this occasion a few civilians were admitted, turned into a convention on the constitution. One motion before the assembly stands out: 'all inhabitants that have not lost their birthright should have an equal voice in elections'. The purpose of the motion was to give the right to vote to the men who had fought and won the civil war for the parliamentary side. Colonel Rainsborough spoke in support, his words a lasting melody of constitutional memory:

> the poorest he that is in England has a life to live as the greatest he; and, therefore truly, sir, I think it's clear, that every man that do live under a government ought first by his own consent to put himself under that government.

Henry Ireton, Oxford-educated son-in-law to Cromwell, leapt to defend the existing order. The vote was rightly denied to those without 'an estate', a certain amount of property, for they 'have not a permanent interest'. They are entitled to protection of the law and to enjoy the liberties the law provides; but they have no place in deciding who makes the law. Cromwell added wisdom to the debate by describing such men as having 'no interest but the interest of breathing'. The outcome, hardly unexpected, was to deny the vote to the mere 'breathers'; the men who, although without property, had just fought and won a long and bloody war.

How an assembly of such officers and civilians, men of 'the middling sort', with much in common and united in war, could be so divided in their views of the constitutional order, is both intriguing and a mystery. How could it be that only a few were to have a say in who rules, while most were excluded, despite their major contribution to the constitutional cause? What kind of society lies at the base of such opinions; separates citizens according to property; is confident the few know what is good for the whole? The answers are to be found, not in imagining and resolving paradoxes, but in analysing the structure of society, the relationships and conventions, the sentiments and dispositions of the members. And so my enquiry began, the voyage of discovery launched, my purpose to discover the social foundations of constitutional authority, the Ithaca of the constitution.

Along the way, many debts have been incurred, many opinions taken into account. Alberto Febbraio, eminent sociologist of law and former Rector of Macerata University, in an early seminar pointed out that David Hume's concept of *acquiescence* was not enough to capture the relationship between the people and those in authority. What more was needed, he left to me to work out, which I hope to have done in the following chapters. Special thanks to Sir Stephen Sedley who introduced me to John Warr, whose ideas on the 'tyranny of form' have a prominent place in the text. Others who merit special mention are: Francesco Bilancia, Erica Charters, Christopher Decker, Bogdan Iancu, Monika Magyar, Daniel Smilov, Ruzha Smilova, Richard Clary, and Heather Allansdottir. From Daniel Bilak and Myroslava Bilak, models of courage and fortitude in the face of adversity, I have learnt much about the constitutional systems of eastern Europe. As a Jean Monet Professor at the Università degli Studi di Siena, I came to understand the legacy of Roman law, while becoming acquainted with *Buon Governo*, the frescos by Ambrogio Lorenzetti, painted in the 1320s, adorning the former council chamber of the *Palazzo Pubblico*, and featuring in the following chapters.

My colleagues at the Oxford Centre for Socio-Legal Studies have been a fertile source of comments, challenges, and suggestions over many years. Several of my very capable doctoral students were distracted from their own subjects by engaging with mine, while Christina Tang merits special mention for her supporting research. Thanks to Raghav Srinivas and Abinand Lagesetti for their generous contribution to background research. To them and many others, I record my thanks and appreciation. Also to Dr Jufang Wang, Ms Jinrui Ge, and Ms Yulin Song, who helped at various stages and gave order and form to the final version. To Ms Merel Alstein and her colleagues at Oxford University Press special gratitude for their guidance from proposal to completion.

Several members of the family have contributed to the enterprise. Dr Francesca Galligan, whose classical training and literary eye have been invaluable; Professor Daniel Butt for discussion and guidance on matters touching political theory; my *nipoti*, Evie Rose and Rowan Joseph, for performing so well the tedious task of compiling the bibliography. Last but not least to Martha Galligan for her support and endless patience.

D.J. Galligan
Oxford University
December 2023

Contents

PART II. CONSTITUTIONAL FIELD

Introduction

Observing how readily the people submit to constitutional authority, David Hume went on to say: 'it is on opinion only government is founded'.[1] How opinion enters into the relationship between the people and officials to influence action is at the foundation of constitutional authority. It is also the subject of this book. Opinion forms from sentiments and dispositions: the one a sign certain interests are valued, the other an inclination to action to protect and advance what is valued. For the social understanding of constitutions, the questions are several: what interests are at issue and why are they valued; how do the people make sure their interests are respected; how do they come to have opinion prior to, and a basis for assessing the constitutional order; how does their opinion count within it? My purpose is to enquire into these matters by studying the constitutional order from the point of view of the people.

Exiled to a small village in the far south of Italy in 1935, Carlo Levi records how the people, living in poverty and disease, regarded the state as alien and an enemy.[2] Northerners looked to the state to solve the *questione meridionale*, while to the peasants of the south the state itself was the obstacle to progress, an unbridgeable gulf, an abyss between them. It was not just that some interests were favoured over others; the problem ran deeper. Whatever form the state were to take, the peasants believed they would never have a genuine place within it, never be considered true members. They saw themselves as pre-Christian and, therefore, almost pre-human, their world shared with wolves and populated with spirits; a world foreign to that from which the Italian state emerged and the constitutional order formed. Between peasants and officials there was no social relationship, no bond of reciprocity or mutuality; they always would be treated more like beasts than humans, denied the respect due to the bearers of rights. The world of the peasants had its own foundation of purposes, understandings, and values, around which social relationships formed and a discourse developed to guide their actions.

Authenticity and *legitimacy* are concepts at the core of the discourse, the concepts on which the peasants' sentiments and dispositions take shape and actions are taken. Actions are judged to be authentic if they emerge from social relations among the people in advancing purpose. A petition to local officials asking that the narrator, a painter and writer but trained as a doctor, be permitted to treat them

[1] D Hume: *On the First Principles of Government*: Essay IV in *Essays Moral Political and Literary* (Indianapolis: Liberty Fund, 1985).

[2] C Levi: *Cristo si è fermato a Eboli* (*Christ Stopped at Eboli*) (1943) (London: Penguin Books: 2000).

Keepers of the Common Good. D.J. Galligan, Oxford University Press. © D.J. Galligan 2024.
DOI: 10.1093/9780198907398.001.0001

was authentic because it was founded on the purpose of communal life and relations among the members. Since that is the test of true *authority*, a natural law arising from the same foundation is legitimate. The petition was an authentic and legitimate act of authority, the refusal inauthentic and illegitimate. Innate in the communal life of the peasants is a discourse, a set of ideas and values to guide their own actions; a foundation from which to judge actions from outside and institutions such as the state imposed on them.

The community of Gagliano may seem a long way from the constitutional orders of the twenty-first century, at least from those broadly democratic, in which all are included and all are respected. The peasants, isolated and remote in a barren land, displayed a wisdom as to the nature of society and a constitutional order, regardless of time and place. A wisdom captured in three words, *peoples precede nations*, the words of Susan Reynolds writing later that century, who might have cited the peasants as a perfect case. Peoples form communities, settle social relations among themselves, and develop a discourse to guide collective action for common purposes. If the state be among the institutions formed and empowered to advance purposes, it rests on the same foundation and is expected to function in accordance with the discourse, by which it may be monitored and judged. The *contadini* of Gagliano, despite the strangeness of their world, understood the nature of society, the foundation of purposes, the need for collective action pursued through social relations and guided by a discourse of ideas and values, moderated by natural laws and conventions. Just as peoples precede nations, purpose guides action, a lesson of universal appeal.

The foundation of purpose serves as a base-camp from which to explore, examine, and evaluate all that occurs within or is imposed from without, including the constitutional field fenced around it. That hinterland of understandings is present in every community, from the peasants of Gagliano to the yeomen and yeowomen of Vacy Plains, from the freemen of Pennsylvania to the ranchers of Shasta County. In resistance, rebellion, and revolt, resort is had to the same hinterland of ideas, values, and language, an alternative to and reasons for rejecting prevailing ideas, language, and values. The discourse of the people is likely to be smothered or obscured by an order imposed from above or from outside, and justified by a different discourse. Yet the discourse survives ready to be called on when needed, even by those living in conditions of severe oppression, whether slaves, serfs and indentured labourers, or the Calibans under the heel of a Prospero. All retain or construct an alternative sense of social life from which to view and gauge the present. The foundation common to all, from the free to the enslaved, is a sense that human endeavour, individually and collectively, has a purpose for the pursuit of which social relations are entered and communities form, institutions created and nations built. The means to purpose are many and diverse from one field of activity to another, one community and nation to another, but the foundation is firm, constant, and shared. To enquire into purpose, the social relations formed, the understandings and the discourse, is the point of reference from which to study the place of the people in a constitutional order.

The parable of the peasants is on one narrative no more than a curiosity of time and place. Constitutional orders are now constructed on a different base. *We the people*, each individually and collectively, are the core, the *sovereign* authority that makes the constitution or *consents* to what others make. We exercise sovereignty by entrusting government to *representatives* acting on our behalf and with our *consent*, even becoming us. After centuries of struggle from beginnings not too distant from those of the peasants, where the people had no place in the constitutional order, other than the feet to bear the weight of the body politic, or mere 'breathers' without property, admitted on sufferance, the people have become the foundation on which the order is constructed. The order is given organic wholeness and inherent harmony based on consent, the actions of officials being by definition taken with the consent of the people. Relations between people and officials are settled and fenced off from relations among the people, transcending social, economic, and political differences. The trouble is, the pleasing narrative depends on *fictions*, on the submerged subjunctive, the *as if* style of argument: as if the people were sovereign, as if they were a corporate body, as if they consented, as if representatives become them.

Mention of fictions draws attention to *form*, the tendency of constitutional discourse to substitute form for substance. John Warr, writing in 1642 as civil war loomed, charted the seemingly unstoppable slide in human affairs from principle to form.[3] The 'divine principle' is 'the clear light, equity, reason and understanding of things themselves, abstracted from all human constituted forms'. When principle is restored, all 'stand on even ground, in a perfect level, coordination and parity'. Until then, 'civil darkness' prevails. The 'darkness is within', consisting of ignorance of principle and 'on idolising of the form'. Whatever yoke is imposed by form is but 'a badge of our inward darkness'. All settled forms 'keep us in subjection to others'; 'use and custom' are 'the servants of usurper form' and have 'inured the world to bondage'. The people accept this either because they know no better or are 'unwilling to bear the cost of deliverance', and after all, 'power is sweet to those who have it' and 'not easily wrested or extorted from them'. The outward form is 'tenacious and a lover of itself, and labours to maintain itself upon the stilts of its own power'. Form emerges from 'the covert and shadow of equity', which it claims to serve. Form is at first a faithful servant of equity and reason; but over time 'proved false to its master, and set up for itself'. Form 'lays heavy burdens on its followers, to cow down their spirits and keep them in subjection'. Among civil forms the constitutional order is prominent. Civil forms 'are not the substance, but the outside only and appearance of that equity and reason which they ought to represent'.

[3] J Warr: *A Spark in the Ashes: The Pamphlets of John Warr* (eds) S Sedley & L Kaplan (London: Verso, 1992). The quotations in my text are taken from *Administrations Civil and Spiritual*, the first pamphlet.

Despite the power of form, 'true reason' is 'a traitor to the outward form'. It will in time 'eat out our own darkness and overthrow the form', or rather perfect the form, for ''tis the perfection of the shadow to expire into the substance'. The form that conforms to the first principle and 'gives out justice and judgement in a measured proportion' will survive. A constitutional order designed according to the first principle 'will free rulers from the bondage of form and will guide the use of power of some over others'. The danger is that constitutions, and laws made under them, serve not reason but lust, greed, and ambition. This is not to reject form, for form properly designed and managed is necessary in the conduct of human affairs and may serve the first principles of equity and reason. Form has a place in the field, not as a permanent plant, 'a standing rule', but as 'a temporary help in advancing the people's interest'. The people's 'purest civil intent' is freedom, the enemies 'privilege as well as prerogative', both 'encased in the womb of darkness'.

Behind John Warr's lyrical prose and prophetic warning lies a live and lasting feature of social relations: the interaction between form and substance, the tension, and the danger. Form brings to substance order, is necessary for certainty and stability, the setting and realizing of expectations, doing justice by giving what is due. Yet, form is prone to uncouple from its foundations and assume its own power, to be 'a yoke' that 'inures us to bondage'. Warr admits the need for form, that 'it can give out justice and judgement in a measured proportion', but does not tell how a balance is to be kept between the virtue of form and the tyranny, how form can remain loyal to its master equity. Nor is the master alone without stain, or so palpably virtuous, for equity without form occupies its own 'womb of darkness', threatens its own tyranny. Equity unadorned and unmediated, being as long or as short as the sleeve of the bearer, the foot of the judge, the fickleness of fortune, poses problems of its own while raising the same risk of bondage. Between the two, no perfect balance is to be found for there is no measure to guide design and action. Instead, the value of each has to be worked out; how each contributes to the purpose of social relationships, while showing respect for the parties and the values guiding and moderating action. The relationship in all its variations we shall see running through the following chapters.

Fictions deflated and form deposed, the true relationship between the people and officials appears looking anything but whole and harmonious. Now complex and variable, the terrain is uneven with groups and sectors competing for attention and influence, while the power of rule is hard to contain. From the people's point of view the sole purpose of the constitutional order is to protect and advance their well-being. But beyond a common core, which aspects of well-being; how to select among competing views of well-being; and how to make sure officials use power for that purpose? The focus in the following chapters is the place of the people in this field of rough-and-tumble, tug-and-scramble. How do the people get into the field and, once in, what room is there to engage in the processes of governing and influencing outcomes; what means are available to keep officials under watch from leaders at one end to administrative agencies at the other; how are the people to hold power to purpose?

As if this were not enough to cope with, the people have to face other structural features of a constitutional order. Contrary to the narrative of *we the people*, normally the people rather than create, have to confront a constitutional order established and entrenched, or the recent handiwork of a few whose own interests shape the design. The order in place has its own ends and means, its own logic and method, while being open to outside influence. It is presented as the work of the people, adorned with pleasing images, yet turns out to be a foreign field where the barriers to the people's entering are high, their reaching the centre ruled out. The other feature to confront is the link between the constitutional order and the wider social order, where relations among the members are uneven and the economic and political orders a constant influence. The detachment and autonomy of the constitutional order, much admired in the narrative of *we the people*, the separation from the underlying social order, turns out to be wishful thinking. The constitutional order can never be sealed off from the surrounding social relationships, intermingling of the two unavoidable. And finally, if we were to ask why bother with a constitutional order and agencies of state so laden with risk and licensing danger; why not rely on collective action grounded on social relations and directed to purpose? The answer is that some aspects of purpose can be achieved only or best by investing power in the agencies of state. How to gain the advantages while discounting the costs is for the people the critical issue.

In this setting, my study of the people in the constitution takes place. It divides into three parts: *foundation*, *field*, and *form*.

Part I lays the *foundations* for enquiry into the place of the people. Starting with David Hume's asking why people accept the power of the state, the study enquires into purposes of social action guided by Adam Smith and Giambattista Vico, especially the latter for proposing a science of society. Drawing on these ideas, and after identifying several patterns of opinion among the people, I propose a model of social action. A model based on the purpose of advancing civility and humanity, from which follow ideas of well-being. The next stage is to show how the model relates to the social structure, the main features of which are briefly described: interests and purpose; the sequence of action; relations, spheres, and fields; types of power and the kinds of action by which the people influence the use of power; and finally, how to use the model to analyse the constitutional order.

Part II introduces the constitutional order, here depicted as a *field* of action reasonably discrete and separate, but interacting with other fields of action. The people armed with a sense of purpose and knowing the lessons of Gagliano, are introduced into the field, shown the lay-out, the several forms and methods of cultivation, the matters to manage if purpose is to prevail and well-being served. The features are identified, the field charted and mapped, the conflicts and tensions bought out. Two *registers* of discourse, the *upper* and the *lower* are examined, the concepts of sovereignty, consent, and representation scrutinized.

Part III singles out three *forms* or models of rule: rule by princes, the people ruling themselves, rule by representatives. Each model is analysed to uncover the social foundations, and to consider the appeal and practical application of each. The place of the people in each form of rule is examined; the patterns of opinion, sentiments, and dispositions aroused by each; the potential to protect and advance their interests assessed. The instabilities are identified and the limitations from the people's point of view recorded. A fourth model of rule is proposed, drawn from a pattern of opinion that emerges. A pattern based on the evidence of history: the experience of persons, groups, and sectors confronting the constitutional order; the reasons some give for rebelling against it; others trying to make sense of it, accepting the need for it and wanting to be engaged, like keeping watch over it. On this empirical base a fourth model is constructed, a frame through which to make sense of experience, a fresh understanding of the place of the people in the constitution, a place designated *the keepers of the common good.*

My purpose throughout is to provide a social understanding of constitutional authority from the perspective of the people. It is neither a work of abstract theory nor a normative prescription of how a constitution should be. The method is to centre on social relationships as the units of society, around which social spheres form, partly from within, partly from without, to guide and moderate sentiments and dispositions. The metaphor of a field is used to depict the constitutional order as a distinct area of activity. The perspective is that of the people, their sentiments and dispositions, opinion in Hume's terms, towards the constitutional field, how the field can serve their interests, the obstacles to confront. The study is not designed to tell the people how they ought to act or what their place in the field should be. My aim is to enquire into episodes of history and experience, to find and extract a sense of purpose at the base of human endeavour, the realization of which relies on individual effort and collective action, the constitutional order one field of activity. Guided by Vico, his theory and his maxims, history and the patterns of opinion of the people are my sources of evidence, while keeping in mind that history, including constitutional history, is a foreign field but one, again following Vico, we must try to know. Several characters of William Shakespeare, some good some bad, take the stage from time to time, not only to enliven the narrative but for the wisdom they display of matters constitutional.

PART I

FOUNDATIONS

Social Foundations of Constitutional Authority

I
Hume's Philosophical Eye

1. 'It is on opinion only that government is founded'

The social understanding of constitutions centres on the relationship between rulers and ruled, between government and the people.[1] Reflecting on the relationship, David Hume, wrote:

> Nothing appears more surprising to those who consider human affairs with a philosophical eye, than the easiness with which the many are governed by the few, and the implicit submission, with which men resign their own sentiments to those of their rulers.[2]

Raw power is on the side of the governed, for 'the governors have nothing to sustain them but opinion. It is on opinion only that government is founded.' Opinion vests or accepts government in the hands of a few. The people suspend their own judgement on matters of moment and surrender their natural liberty to the decrees of others. Self-restraint is the critical action. It is both negative and positive: negative in not acting as one otherwise would, positive in acting where one otherwise would not. Why do the people submit and restrain their actions in favour of the few? The answer lies in opinion, on how opinion of the many is moulded and shaped to conform to the rule of the few. Hume gives two reasons for self-restraint. One is the ends government serves, the other the people's natural inclination to accept the order of rule that happens to be in place. One looks to outcomes of government, the other to the process leading to outcomes.

The logic is plain. The people want certain social goods, some to serve their needs, others to add to the utility of their lives, delivery of which requires power vested in the state and exercised through its agencies.[3] Hume wrote of 'the general advantage reaped from government'. A critical phrase on two counts. One is to assume a social relationship between the people and officials that is more than command and obedience; the other to define the purpose of government within the relationship. Put simply, the people gain and value the advantage from having

[1] For explanation of this point of focus, see M Weber: *Economy and Society* (Berkeley, London: University of California Press, 1978) (eds) G Roth and C Wittich, p 51.

[2] D Hume: *On The First Principles of Government: Essay IV* in *Essays Moral Political and Literary* (Indianapolis, Liberty Fund, 1985) Referred to as *Essays.*

[3] The terms *needs* and *utility* come from G Vico: *The New Science* (1744) (London: Penguin Books, 1999)

Keepers of the Common Good. D.J. Galligan, Oxford University Press. © D.J. Galligan 2024.
DOI: 10.1093/9780198907398.003.0001

a system of government in place. Hume goes on to say the people know that once in place, one government is likely to be 'equally advantageous with any other'. The general advantage flows from having government whatever form it takes. And because the right to property 'is of moment in all matters of government', the general advantage includes, even is based on the protection of property.[4] Hume takes his place in a familiar line of political and legal thought explaining and justifying the power of the state and the need for government. Earlier accounts spoke of the common good as the guiding goal, meaning the good of society as a whole and the good of each of its members, to which security of person and property are essential. Contemporary accounts use other language to express the same ideas, with a shift of emphasis from the common good to the interests of each person. HLA Hart's rules necessary for a society's survival, the minimum content of natural law as he calls it, have their roots in the Humean approach.[5] Hedley Bull summarizes the general advantage as the protection of life, the keeping of contracts, and the stable possession of things.[6] Such social goods are elementary and primary. Elementary in that associations of persons without them would hardly qualify as a community, let alone a nation;[7] primary in being the foundation on which other social goods are based. As societies progress, develop, and prosper, the range of social goods widens and others are added: a higher standard of living and personal liberty; protection of a range of interests, forms of social welfare, and rights derived from a notion of equality, to name just a few. Aspects of each over time come to be regarded as essential to social cohesion and conducive to personal well-being. The contemporary state is expected to be active in the supply of social goods, and its power used to set and enforce standards across a practically limitless range of social relationships, from employment to the environment, from how to do business to the duties of parents. Progress is not inevitable and is easily reversed, the range of social goods narrowing rather than broadening.

2. Justice as a social good

In addition to such benefits, Hume proposes another kind of social good, less tangible but more fundamental. As a society develops, its members 'establish political authority, in order to administer justice'.[8] Notice the change in language. Power is

[4] Hume: *Essays*, p 33.
[5] HLA Hart: *The Concept of Law* (Oxford: Clarendon Press: , 1961), Chapter IX.
[6] H Bull: *The Anarchical Society* (Oxford: Oxford University Press, 1977), p 4.
[7] Deidre McCloskey sums it up: 'most societies have always enforced property rights. It is what we mean by society': D McCloskey: *Bourgeois Equality: How Ideas, Not Capital or Institutions, Enriched the World* (Chicago: University of Chicago Press, 2016), p xxiii. This is generally true, but overlooks societies that do not have property rights.
[8] Hume: *Essays*, p 37.

transformed into authority, suggesting it is given and held for distinct purposes, and is to be used according to settled standards and procedures. Hume continues:

> We are—to look upon all the vast apparatus of our government, as having ultimately, no other object or purpose but the distribution of justice.[9]

The doing of justice must be part of the general advantage of government, although whether it merits quite such a defining role is debatable. The relationship between justice and other social goods is as follows. Justice has two main senses, one as a foundation on which to build a social order, the *dynamic*; the other that burdens and benefits be distributed according to the terms of the social order once in place, the *protective*. And since the social order consists of sets of social relations, justice enters into and constitutes a component of each set. Hume uses justice in the second, narrower, almost procedural sense. Justice requires the parties get what is due according to the terms of the relationship and the rights to property within it. Justice and property are, to use Hume's word, *artifices*, that is socially created rather than in some way natural. Both are essential to the existence of society; both are expressed in and dependent on social conventions. The notion of property makes sense only within sets of social relations where justice is the guardian. Justice is the convention or understanding by which a possession, such as land or goods, is regarded as mine or yours, from which it follows that rules and procedures are needed for its protection.[10] Social life in its rudest form is on this account based on property.[11] As Gerald Postema writes: property makes possible 'social cooperation and productive combination of efforts beyond the narrow circle of the family'.[12] And because cooperation depends on and results from social relations, justice is embedded in cooperation. Hume makes the case for justice within social relations as a primary social good, the delivery of which is one of the main purposes of the power of the state, the system of government, and the constitutional order.[13]

Among the dimensions of justice a few points need be noted. First, justice is not restricted to property, but is inherent in and critical to almost all social relationships. Relationships depend on reciprocity, on the parties mutually respecting the entitlements acquired and the obligations incurred within them. Justice is the guardian that oversees the distribution of burdens and benefits according to the terms of the relationship. To do justice is to give each party what is due, where what

[9] *Ibid.*

[10] D Hume: *Treatise on Human Nature* (ed) LA Selby-Bigge (Oxford: Clarendon Press, 1988) (*Treatise* first published 1739), Book III Part II.

[11] G Postema: *Bentham and the Common Law Tradition* (Oxford: Clarendon Press, 1989), p 84.

[12] *Ibid.*

[13] Among many accounts of special benefit, see R Hardin: *David Hume: Moral and Political Theorist* (Oxford: Oxford University Press, 2007) and G Postema: *Bentham and the Common Law Tradition* (Oxford: Clarendon Press, 1989).

is due depends on the terms of the relationship between them. In this way justice as fair treatment, perhaps a plainer notion, is inherent in social relations, directing how each party is to treat the other. A second point is that agencies of government in exerting control over social relationships, whether already in place or created by them, have to engage with matters of justice, which means following suitable procedures to reach the stated outcomes.[14] The third point is to distinguish between doing justice within a given social relationship, and using justice to modify the terms or create new relationships. Justice within a relationship Adam Smith refers to as a negative principle guarding one from injury and demanding redress where injury occurs. Justice in this *protective* sense is individualized, making sure each person is treated in accordance with the terms of a relationship. Such protection is central to people's expectations of government, of how officials are to settle disputes whether between private parties or with an agency of government. Protective justice enters the logic of state power in two ways, as a social good itself and as a standard guiding the distribution of other social goods within relationships. The value of protective justice will become clear as the thesis of this book unfolds and the link is made to the concept of juridical equality.[15] The last point is to return to justice as a *dynamic* force, as the basis for forming or re-forming social relations. Being not only the guardian of entitlements within social relations, justice is the reason for modifying relations or forming new ones. How a parent should treat a child or an employer the workers, the policeman a suspect or the court an accused, to take just a few cases, have origins in the customs and conventions of the time. Yet, often such relations are regulated by law on grounds laid by ideas of justice. Justice as a dynamic principle can be put to more ambitious ends, to censure the social order and to urge revision of the terms of settled social relations. Disparities of property, wealth, and status are open to criticism on grounds of justice and the power of the state enlisted as the instrument of change.

The two senses of justice, justice as a *protective* principle within relationships and justice as a *dynamic* force for social change, are at one level of analysis separate and distinct. The party who goes to court to protect a property right invokes the protective principle, claiming what is due within the settled order, and is not expected to make arguments for its overthrow. The dynamic side of justice is the rallying cry for changing social relationships, the distribution of power, property, and status within them. At a deeper level they share common ground. Both are about how each person is to be treated, the entitlements each has or expects to have, the terms and conditions of social relationships. From that common base their paths

[14] For a study of the two aspects of justice and their relationship, see DJ Galligan, *Due Process and Fair Procedures: A Study of Administrative Procedures* (Oxford: Clarendon Press, 1997).

[15] Individualized justice, justice as a protective principle, weighs heavily in, has a special place and importance in, the people's acceptance of government. Such importance helps to explain why even despotic rulers are likely to provide means of redress by way of courts and similar institutions broadly adequate and easily accessible. Discussed later in Chapters X and XI: *Princely Rule*.

diverge. Constitutions normally are laid on top of a settled social, economic, and political order. They normally have nothing to do with, occupy a different conceptual space from, deeper questions about the distribution of power, property, and status. And yet the dynamic side of justice offers a stand, a point of reference always available from which to assess social arrangements. The two sides cannot be kept wholly apart but overlap and intersect. The deeper issues, just below the surface and out of sight, have a habit of turning up and edging their way into constitutional discourse. Relations between the two, the two faces of justice, is a theme running through the theatre of matters constitutional.

The purpose of constitutional authority is to deliver to the people goods they value. Since delivery means overseeing the distribution of burdens and benefits within social relations, notions of justice and fair treatment are engaged. A dread of unjust treatment ranks high in the order of social harms, at times higher than the social good seems to merit. That helps explain why the administration of justice is a critical feature of government, why it is a social good in itself, a critical element in successful coordination. Even a system of authority scarred by imperfection is likely to provide to some degree the institutions and agencies for doing justice.[16] Hence Hume's claim that as long as a system of constitutional authority respects and upholds the elementary justice of social relations, it will retain the support of the people. That overstates the value of justice within social relations. The more accurate judgement is that protective justice, respect for justice within social relations, is a condition of the people's acquiescence, neglect of which leads to distrust and, if grave enough, to their seeking redress elsewhere. Protective justice, a necessary condition, is not always sufficient. Justice can be subversive as well as protective, and the appetite for justice, once whetted, barely notices the borders between the shallows and the deep, the protective and the dynamic. The people's appeal to justice in its dynamic mode we shall see in later chapters diligently digging around the edges of the constitutional field.

3. Utility of the state

The needs and utilities of life are plain enough, the wish to secure and advance them universal, so we might ask why rely on the state to provide them? The power of the state is one of many forms of power, each of which sets and enforces standards of behaviour for a segment of social relations.[17] The issue for Hume was to give reasons for the people's self-restraint in the face of state power, to explain their acquiescing in the decrees of government, rather than invoking that raw power to

[16] Discussed in DJ Galligan: 'Ally or Enemy, Friend or Foe' in *The Courts and the People: Friend or Foe?* (ed) DJ Galligan (Oxford: Hart Bloomsbury, 2021).

[17] Further on power, see Chapter III:6.

act on their own initiative. If aims can be met and purposes fulfilled by the people themselves, then why exercise self-restraint, why acquiesce in the power of the state? Hume makes no bones about the need for government:

> A small degree of experience and observation suffices to teach us, that society cannot possibly be maintained without the authority of magistrates, and that this authority must soon fall into contempt, where exact obedience is not paid to it.[18]

Tangible benefits follow. One is the 'general advantage' without which there can be no 'peace, nor safety, nor mutual intercourse'.[19] The other is the advantage particular to each person of property being protected, perhaps because, as Hume contends, property is the foundation of all government, or at least because property weighs heavily in the formation of opinion.

To assess the advantage of a constitutional order and the power of the state, we need first to sketch the structure of society.[20] Society is constituted by people entering into relations with each other, some informal, others formal. Relations range through the personal and voluntary to others over which we have no choice, including family, school, and work, and extend to relations between citizens and officials. Lives are lived within such relationships, which we form and foster, as Hume puts it 'from necessity, from natural inclination, and from habit'.[21] Society consists of networks of relationships intersecting and overlapping, sometimes mutually reinforcing, at other times competing and conflicting, each bringing a degree of order and regularity to a segment of human activity, some a matter of choice, others thrust upon us. Relationships are structured and the terms settled at several levels, by the parties themselves, by social spheres of rules and conventions, and by law. The dimension of social relations of present interest is the power to co-ordinate collective action for common purposes. Relationships are an expression of collective power, of the parties coming together to exert control over an aspect of life whether social, political, or economic.[22] To coordinate means to create a pattern of regularity where otherwise diverse opinions and actions would prevail, breeding uncertainty and instability. By compliance with common standards of action, whether by agreement, convention, or law, order replaces disorder, shared attitudes and expectations emerge and in turn are strengthened by practice. The point of coordinating actions is to achieve common purposes, which range and vary from the rearing and education of children, to building an efficient workplace

[18] Hume: *Essays*, p 33.
[19] *Ibid* p 37.
[20] A more complete account of the structure of society is given in Chapter IV: 5.
[21] Hume: *Essays*, p 37.
[22] Social spheres are explained more fully in DJ Galligan: *Law in Modern Society* (Oxford: Clarendon Law Series Oxford University Press, 2007), Chapter 6.

and protecting the environment, to respecting the law. Each relationship is a form of collective action to coordinate a segment of life in pursuit of common purposes.

Hume's emphasis on the state could suggest neglect of the power of informal and spontaneous social relationships in coordinating collective action. Questions are raised about some of the alleged advantages of state power over other forms of collective action.[23] Robert Ellickson, after a vigorous critique of 'state centralism', shows how the ranchers of Shasta County are able to coordinate relations among themselves, to set standards and devise processes for resolving disputes without reference to the state.[24] The yeomen and yeowomen of Vacy Plains manage the affairs of a farming community on the basis of common understandings and mutual support, with the state vaguely in the background. Elinor Ostrom examined the empirical basis for 'self-organizing and self-governing forms of collective action' and concluded they are often more effective than the state.[25] In many areas of life an all-powerful state is neither the only nor the most effective means of coordination.[26] It is enough to note two points. The people have many ways of organizing themselves for collective action, each shaping, guiding, and regulating, among which the power of the state is just one. The other point is that the effectiveness of each form of collective action depends on variables to be identified and assessed through empirical enquiry. In some cases the state turns out to be the most effective, in others action at lower levels are more promising. Joint action by the state and a segment of civil society is potentially effective, while sometimes any of several routes would lead to a successful outcome.

The claim that society cannot be sustained without the authority of the state may now be assessed.[27] The case rests on the state's capacity to coordinate and organize beyond that of other forms of association. The state's advantage is being able to set standards, marshal the resources for implementation, and create agencies for enforcement. It sets standards across society from sustaining social order and protecting persons and property, to cover practically any area of activity. It has the resources to empower agencies to enforce the standards and to resolve disputes arising from them. The power of the state is plain enough but why is it needed? Why are the powers of civil associations and informal relationships not enough for a people to live together and prosper? The answer is the state in common with justice has two faces, one negative and *protective*, the other *dynamic* and positive. The first is familiar, the second often overlooked, while both are critical to constitutional authority. The need for the state's protective role is well-known. Thomas

[23] E Ostrom: *Governing the Commons: The Evolution of Institutions for Collective Action* (Cambridge: Cambridge University Press, 1990); R Ellickson: *Order Without Law: How Neighbours Settle Disputes* (Cambridge Mass: Harvard University Press, 1991).

[24] R Ellickson: *Order Without Law* where the claim of *legal centralism* is challenged.

[25] E Ostrom: *Governing the Commons.*

[26] Hobbes's idea of the state having absolute power has been a strong influence.

[27] Here I follow an earlier analysis: DJ Galligan: *Law in Modern Society*, Chapter 12.

Hobbes states the case: if 'security and well-being are the ends of human life', a claim few would contest, then 'it is a dictate of reason that ordinary men trade submission for protection'.[28] Security and well-being are at risk because people work to advance their own interests, 'seeking their own ends', which is bound to lead to conflict and division. The power of informal or spontaneous social relations is not strong enough to suppress the conflict and smooth the division. Some interests will prevail over others, putting at risk the security and well-being of all. From the 'calculations of endangered men' the need for the state is the compelling conclusion. In short, we need the state to keep the peace, to prevent one faction from oppressing another, to guarantee the safety of person and property.

The dynamic capacity of the state, less acclaimed or documented, deserves equal place. It takes several forms. *One* is the power to take the initiative in defining and supplying social goods, not just to protect those that flow from informal social relations, but to create a new order of benefits broadly defined as social welfare. The benefits relate to such matters as health and education, unemployment and pensions, and much else. The kinds and quantities naturally vary from state to state, some providing much, others little. Whatever the kind and however bountiful, the positive provision of social goods in the form of welfare is a common and valued feature of modern states. A *second* expression of the dynamic function is to guide society towards ends and values, to intervene in and reshape social relations, even to create and design new ones. The state has the power to insert into relationships ends and values otherwise lacking or undeveloped, and in this way lead as well as respond to opinion. Notions of equity and fair treatment, substantive and procedural, while implicit in social relations are bolstered by the state's inserting exacting standards. The agencies of state are often ambitious and vigorous in advancing values, against discrimination and inequality, respect for the environment, and safety of workers, to name a few cases, all aimed at improving the lives of its people. The *third* dimension of the dynamic role is the state's power to intervene in and control private relationships, to curb the actions of some sectors in order to empower, encourage, and assist other sectors in their efforts to improve their position. By regulating areas of activity the state reins in the power of some to enable others less powerful to engage, and by engaging better to secure and advance their interests. This dynamic side of the state, the capacity not only to protect what is in place but to enable the people at all levels of society to improve their lives, is essential to a well-working social order.

It would be wrong to conclude from this outline that the state stands above and apart from the formations of civil society. The lines sharply drawn to display the state's power now have to be smudged and softened to capture the fullness of

[28] T Hobbes: *Leviathan* (ed) N Malcolm (Oxford: Oxford University Press, 2012); see further PA Rahe: *Against Throne and Altar: Machiavelli's Liberal Republican Legacy* (Cambridge: Cambridge University Press, 2008), p 319.

relations between the two. *First*, despite its superior power spread through a web of agencies, the state is still only one among many spheres of authority, each capable of coordinating a segment of social relations. The interaction between the two, agencies of government and civil associations, is a major variable ranging from harmonious cooperation, to competition, to outright conflict. How interaction between the two works out in practice, how conflicts are resolved, has been the subject of empirical research that would guide further analysis and the design of models of relations between the agencies of government and civic associations.[29] *Secondly*, power is a resource, an instrument to advance interests, the power of the state a most valuable resource. A resource for which persons, groups, and sectors compete in the hope of exerting influence and gaining favour. *Thirdly*, moderate influence and favour easily and often give way to the state falling under the control of more dominant persons, groups, or sectors, whether by tradition or by design. In the drive for advancement the spectrum is wide, from mild and subtle influence, to collusion to capture, where the state becomes the instrument of certain interests and an arm to suppress rivals.[30] Whatever the degree of domination by some over others, the tendency is to clothe the power of the state in images and ideas of universal appeal, draped in a constitutional cloak fastened with a clasp of bewitching discourse. How to release the clasp, reach beneath the cloak, and hold a moderate balance among competing interests is a task the people face and a subject at the core of a constitutional order.[31] *Fourthly*, against the benefits of state power are to be set the dangers. Power has innate qualities. One is to expand and encroach beyond its boundaries; another to be used for purposes other than those authorized; another still to be used oppressively. All are the natural companions of the power of the state; all wait in the wings ready to pounce and do their mischief; all are matters to be addressed by the constitutional order.

To conclude, the case Hume makes for state power remains intact, but needs to be developed and refined. The power to protect social goods is valued for being effective and potentially more effective than other social relationships. Whether the two goals are realized depends on many factors. The record suggests that despite lapses and abuses, the state has proved to be an invaluable source of benefits, not only in making secure person and property, but in providing other services, advancing other interests valued by the community. The utility of the state includes the provision of social goods, forms of welfare, and a capacity to regulate social relations, all to enable the people to improve their lives. The capacity of the state to supply the three sets of social goods is a prominent feature of a constitutional order, as appears time and again in later chapters. The benefits are plain, the

[29] On issues of institutional design, see *The Theory of Institutional Design* (ed) RE Goodin (Cambridge: Cambridge University Press, 1996).

[30] Now known in strongest form as *state capture*, a modern name for an ancient practice.

[31] For Hume's view of the relationship between dominating sectors and the power of the state: see Notes.

risks equally so. The first signs of a constitutional order start to show, a first glimpse caught of the issues to be faced and how they are to be resolved. Above all we begin to realize that Hume's portrayal of the people acquiescing, restraining their actions in return for benefits, is only the first brush-stroke of a deep and dense portrait of constitutional authority.

4. 'Antiquity begets the opinion of right'

The other main reason for the people resigning their own sentiments to those of their rulers is the inclination to acquiesce in the system of authority in place.[32] 'The attachment which all nations have to their ancient government' Hume calls the *right to power*:

> Antiquity always begets the opinion of right. The people once accustomed to obedience, never think of departing from the path, in which their ancestors have constantly trod.[33]

Well, people do think of departing from the path of their ancestors and at times depart. Apart from that, how is it that 'antiquity always begets the opinion of right'? The answer relies on several strands of argument. Let us look first to Adam Smith, Hume's younger contemporary, who put the case simply and appealingly. Smith calls it the 'principle of authority': 'everyone naturally has a disposition to respect an established authority and superiority in others, whatever they be'.[34] The young respect the old, the children their parents, while all respect 'those who excel in power and strength'. Whatever the 'foundation of government' may be, it is sustained by a natural respect for authority. Each of us is 'born and bred under the authority of the magistrates', who demand the obedience of all, to which most willingly submit. We see the 'propriety of submitting to them as to a father'. And, it ought to be added, their expectation of submission is backed by the threat of punishment.[35]

The natural respect for authority is born and nurtured within social relationships. The power of one to control another, a feature of the most formative relationships, is justified by the ends served. Experience of a multitude of relations fosters sentiments and dispositions of respect for authority whatever form it takes. The claim is reasonable but care must be taken not to claim too much. A general

[32] For more on the basis of authority, see DJ Galligan: 'On Constitutional Authority' (Valedictory Lecture, Wolfson College Oxford, 2017).

[33] Hume: *Essays*, p 33.

[34] A Smith: *Lectures on Jurisprudence* (eds) RL Meek, DD Raphael, and PG Stein (Indianapolis: Liberty Fund, 1978), pp 318, 405.

[35] *Ibid* p 318.

disposition to respect authority detached from particular relationships is likely to be weak and contingent. The disposition follows from a sentiment, which seemingly self-supporting, is in practice aroused and its strength determined by the ends served and the interests advanced by authority. Since authority is tied to purpose, the strength of the sentiment of support depends on what the ends and the interests are and how well they are served. The authority of the state is respected because the general advantage, in Hume's words, is to serve the people's interests and advance their well-being. The sentiment of support is likely to vary in strength according to how well that purpose is achieved. It is not that the people scrutinize every action of the state to test whether it is for their well-being. If the system as a whole be to their advantage, lapses and losses are tolerated, unless a point is reached where the benefits are so few nothing is gained.

It helps to insert two more concepts into the equation, *convention and social spheres*.[36] Once a system of authority is in place, once the people see the general advantage and acquiesce, a convention of compliance comes into being. The word *convention* brings ambiguity. It comes from the French *convenire*, meaning to convene, to come together. The coming together ranges from mere habit or practice at one end to a binding rule at the other, with shadings in between. The people's coming together in support of the constitutional order begins as a convenience but soon becomes compelling. Convention here means a social rule. Between the reasons and the action, a rule is inserted requiring acquiescence in government. It is no longer a matter of each person judging whether the general advantage is enough to warrant acquiescence and, if not, whether to withdraw it. The people now have a duty to follow the rule, a duty sustained by a combination of the advantage gained, the critical attitudes of others, and the threat of sanctions. The concept of a *social sphere* now enters the scene. A social sphere consists of the perceptions, standards, and sanctions that form around each social relationship. Those between people and officials are encased in social spheres dense and demanding, at the core, an expectation of obedience by the people regardless of how much they benefit from the general advantage of government; an expectation backed by sanctions. To Hume's account of the relationship, the two reasons for the people's acquiescence in government, is to be added as a third reason the coercive quality and the threat of punishment.

To this simmering pot where respect for authority is born and braised, another ingredient has to be added, a reservation entered. If the ends of government no longer were met, the people's interests no longer served, the case for respect would crumble. It might linger on because a social institution, a set of relations and spheres once established acquires an autonomy of its own, a detachment from

[36] Among many accounts of special benefit, see R Hardin: *David Hume: Moral and Political Theorist* (Oxford: Oxford University Press, 2007) and G Postema: *Bentham and the Common Law Tradition* (Oxford: Clarendon Press, 1989).

its roots and the reasons for it, strengthened in this case by force to sustain it. The respite is short-lived. A social relationship failing in purpose, and a social sphere unanchored in practical moorings, sooner or later sink. No matter how hard it is for the people to withdraw acquiescence or renegotiate the terms, solutions eventually are found and action taken. Or in desperation resort is had to the raw power held in reserve to come together to oppose, to resist, even to rebel. The logic shifts from acquiescence to coercion, from an order all respect to one which all are forced to obey.

Hume has shown the positive side of constitutional authority. Government contributes in essential ways to the needs and utilities of the people, and in return wins their acquiescence and respect their favourable opinion. The two together are the foundation of constitutional authority, of consensus among all as to the need for government, and the social harmony that follows. There is however a third, less positive side to add, a side barely mentioned by Hume. The coercive nature of authority opens a door onto another dimension of constitutional order and social relationships, one marked by dissent and disharmony, where two features stand out. One is the competition among persons, groups, and sectors to gain influence over the agencies of government; the other is the intermingling of relations between the people and officials on the one hand, and relations among the people on the other hand. The first is a sign that behind the imagery of consensus and harmony lies a social order marked by competition and conflict, where some are more powerful than others and prosper, while others only manage. The second is a sign that the constitutional order, although presented as a set of social relationships between the people and officials, discrete and distinct, is in reality intertwined with social relationships among the people, which despite all efforts cannot be wholly separated. The central issue for social enquiry is how a constitutional order copes with the opposing features, how from conditions of conflict and competition a system of rule can be constructed to win the acquiescence and support of the people. Into that social world we now enter to examine and understand better the place of the people.

Notes

Self-restraint

On self-restraint as a critical concept in social understanding: DJ Galligan: *Law in Modern Society*, pp 278*ff*. According to Hobbes: 'The final Cause, End, or Designe of men (who naturally love Liberty and Dominion over others) in the introduction of that restraint upon themselves, (in which we see them live in Common-wealths,) is the foresight of their own preservation, and of a more contented life thereby': T Hobbes: *Leviathan*, Volume I, p 254. The opposite of reasoned self-restraint is the mindless mob. A major theme in constitutional discourse is the inability of the people to exercise reasoned self-restrain, and hence the need for rule by one or a few. See further Chapter IV:7 herein.

The opposite view, developed in later chapters, is well-stated by Giovanni Lottini, writing in the late sixteenth century: 'in popular states, men of the lowliest condition—those to whom one would pay no attention as individuals—make many wise, praiseworthy decisions as a group.—the whole people becomes—a very intelligent man, with many memories, many eyes, and many hands': G Lottini: *Avverdimenti Civili* (Bologna: G Mancini, 1574), p 185. For discussion: VI Comparato, 'From the Crisis of Civil Culture to the Neapolitan Republic of 1647: Republicanism in Italy between the Sixteenth and Seventeenth Centuries' in *Republicanism: A Shared European Heritage* (eds) M Gelderen and Q Skinner (Cambridge: Cambridge University Press, 2002), p 169.

All governments are equally advantageous

Hume's point is that government means a set of officials and agencies capable of providing that 'general advantage'; who they happen to be is of less interest. Whether and to what extent this rather contentious claim be justified is a recurring theme of this book.

Unable to provide the general advantage

The lesson of the Soviet Union in its last years is instructive. Officials and agencies became unable to provide the general advantage, leaving the people to seek benefits by other means. The situation is analysed in: AV Ledeneva: *Russia's Economy of Favour: Blat, Networking, and Informal Exchanges* (Cambridge: Cambridge University Press, 1998). See further: DJ Galligan: 'Legal Failure: Law and Social Norms in Post-Communist Europe' in *Law and Informal Practices: The Post-Communist Experience* (eds) DJ Galligan and M Kurkchiyan (Oxford: Oxford University Press, 2003).

Being able to provide the general advantage is a necessary condition of government, a threshold to meet in order to constitute government. Above the threshold, form matters. The form of government in the sense of how it is constituted influences, even determines the course it follows, the policies it decides, and the way it treats the people. Hume acknowledges this in other passages, especially in *Essays*

Moral and Political, III: 'Politics a Science'. Forms of government are examined in Part III of this book.

On the alliance of private interest and public power

Hume writes: 'where the original constitution allows any share of power, though small, to an order of men, who possess a large share of the property, it is easy for them gradually to stretch their authority, and bring the balance of power to coincide with that of property. This has been the case with the house of commons in England.' *Essays Moral Political and Literary*, p 35.

On justice

On justice as the foundation of society, Hume writes: 'All men are sensible to the necessity of justice to maintain peace and order, and all men are sensible to the necessity of peace and order for the maintenance of society': *Essays Moral Political and Literary*, p 38. Emile Durkheim captures the centrality of justice to social relations: justice 'is the necessary accompaniment of every kind of solidarity. It is necessarily encountered wherever men live in common, whether this results from the social division of labour or from the attraction of like for like': E Durkheim: *The Division of Labour in Society* (London: Free Press, 1984), p 77.

In the pre-modern state, government was concerned with 'maintaining *folkright*', which meant to maintain each man's rights. The king in Anglo-Saxon England is *mundbora*, meaning the principal function of reigning is to administer justice, to see that the people are not denied justice: JEA Joliffe: The *Constitutional History of Medieval England* (London: Adam and Charles Black, 1937), p 27*ff*. Default on justice is the ground of rebellion: p. 159. Notice that none of the three makes the distinction between the two faces of justice, the protective and the dynamic.

Power of the state

JH Strayer gives an illuminating account of the early formation of the state and explains the centralization of power in England. By 1200 England had 'permanent institutions run by professional or semi-professional officials'. Issues over land rights were settled in the King's courts, and the power to impose direct taxes was established. Strayer shows the link between the strengthening of the state and the growing sense among the people that the state is necessary for human well-being: *On the Medieval Origins of the Modern State* (Princeton: Princeton University Press, 1970). An earlier work, Jollife's *The Constitutional History of Medieval England*, charts the gradual change from the *folkmoot* of Anglo-Saxon society in which the king is *mundbora*, charged with ensuring that people are not denied justice due to them, to the king's being responsible for the general peace: pp 27*ff*, 113*ff*.

Social conventions

Hume explains the nature and place of social conventions in *Treatise* Sections 3.2.2.11; 3.2.6.6; 3.2.2.22, the argument well-outlined in TL Beauchamp's Introduction in D Hume: *An Enquiry Concerning the Principles of Morals* (Oxford, New York: Oxford University Press, 1998), p 37 (referred to as *An Enquiry*). He draws from Hume this definition: 'Conventions are rules that almost all members of society follow in almost all circumstances': p 37. Hume writes of conventions: 'by convention be meant *a sense of common interest*; which sense each man feels in his own breast, which he remarks in his fellows, and which carries him, in concurrence with others, into a general plan or system of actions, which tends to public utility': *An Enquiry*, p 172. Hume goes on to say that justice arises from human conventions.

Among the many accounts of social conventions, I mention just two: R Hardin: *David Hume: Moral and Political Theorist* (Oxford: Oxford University Press, 2007 and J Elster: *The Cement of Society* (Cambridge: Cambridge University Press, 1989). Elster writes: 'Most social norms are simply to obey and to follow, compared with the canons of rationality which often require us to make difficult and uncertain calculations. The operation of norms is to a large extent blind, compulsive, mechanical or even unconscious': p 100. Elster goes on to modify this statement, but the general tenor remains accurate.

Elinor Ostrom defines social norms as follows: 'Norms—reflect valuations that people place on actions or strategies in and of themselves, not as they are connected to immediate consequences.—If the norm is shared by others, the person is also subject to considerable social censure for taking an action considered to be wrong by others.': *Governing the Commons*, p 35. My argument is that conventions are best seen as occurring within, a critical part of social spheres, which have a cognitive, normative, and regulatory character: see Chapter IV:5.

On the nature of rules and rule-following, HLA Hart's account remains authoritative: *The Concept of Law* (Oxford: Clarendon Press, 1961). For commentary and amplification of rules and rule-application: DJ Galligan: *Law in Modern Society*, Chapters 3, 4.

On Hume's method

JW Danford describes Hume's method as follows: 'Hume's great philosophical contribution was epistemological, all knowledge of the world or of "matters of fact" ultimately rests on the experience and perceptions from what Hume liked to call "common life".' Danford adds: 'Hume recommends taking our bearings from "common feeling and our most unprejudiced notions"': 'Getting Our Bearings: Machiavelli and Hume' in *Against Throne and Altar: Machiavelli's Liberal Republican Legacy* (ed) PA Rahe, pp 112–13. This basic idea is enlarged in Chapter IV herein, where I propose a sequence of action from purpose to interest to action.

II
Praise, Fictions, and Beyond

1. In praise of Hume

Hume's philosophical eye prepares the way for enquiry into the social foundations of the constitutional order as viewed by the people. Not the first to put relations between the people and officials at the core, Hume deserves praise for an account subtly different from others. After noting 'the easiness with which the many are governed by the few and the implicit submission' or 'acquiescence',[1] and how they 'resign their own sentiments to those of their rulers', Hume introduces *opinion*. On the opinion of the people government is founded. To concede that the people's opinion counts is a subtle but seminal shift in describing their relations with officials. Acquiescence is tied to opinion. Opinion is shaped by well-being, by how adequately well-being is served by government; the better served the firmer the opinion, and the stronger the inclination to restraint and support. Relations with officials now have a dynamic quality, not just bare obedience but a quality enabling mutual engagement, the people to make known their interests, officials to take notice.

The shift from submission to acquiescence brings to mind two metaphors of constitutional order: one a *fortress*, the other a *field*. A fortress the people have no choice but to enter to find a constitutional order walled against the outside world and ruled rigidly within.[2] The governors decide what benefits to grant inmates, who in return are expected to obey the rules, the threat of punishment a powerful incentive. What happens outside, where persons, groups, and sectors compete to advance their interests, where discord is normal and consensus has to be achieved not imposed, within the fortress is of no constitutional concern. A field by contrast casts a different image. The field is more open, fenced not sealed, allowing the people's engaging with officials and having some say in cultivation. And, fences being permeable, relations within the constitutional field are not wholly cut off from relations among the people outside. Within the field, relations between people and officials, and to an extent among the people themselves, have to be worked out in practice rather than cemented in advance. The relationships are contingent and variable, subject to fortune and circumstance, appetite and will, as well as purpose. The line between social, economic, and political action on the one

[1] Hume describes the 'implicit submission' as *acquiescence*: *Essays*, pp 469–70.

[2] Warr seemed to have the *fortress* in mind in writing: 'open the iron gates and knock off the bolts': *A Spark in the Ashes*, p 79.

Keepers of the Common Good. D.J. Galligan, Oxford University Press. © D.J. Galligan 2024.
DOI: 10.1093/9780198907398.003.0002

hand, and the constitutional order on the other hand is less fixed and ever adjustable. The result is a relationship between the people and officials, the one trying to keep the power of the other to the purpose of advancing well-being. A constitutional order forms and develops; an order in which the people potentially engage and have influence on outcomes.[3]

Hume's essay *Of the First Principles of Government* marks a shift in approaching the constitutional order, simply stated but profound: the people as the aggregate of persons are not mere subjects to be ordered around but citizens with opinions that count. On that base I now proceed to construct a social account of the constitutional order from the perspective of the people.[4] But first a note of caution and clarification. While I have found in the essay an account of the people's place in the constitutional order, a more cautious reading might find Hume himself poised between the metaphors of the fortress and the field. He combines a claim and a concession that seem at first sight to be contradictory. The people 'resign their own sentiments to those of their rulers' and 'implicitly submit'; yet, 'it is on opinion only that government is founded'. How can the people give up their own sentiments to rulers and at the same time their opinion count? Hume's wording holds the clue: opinion is sentiment and disposition under another name. Sentiment is aroused by interests the people value, which taken together constitute well-being. The disposition to action is aroused and has two parts, one to accept rule, the other to influence rule, the first leaning towards a fortress, the other edging into an open field. The fortress-image follows from Hume's claim of one government being 'equally advantageous with any other'. It matters not who governs; there is no need for the people to engage and none is conceded. However, once opinion counts, the fortress-image fades and a field opens up where both sentiments matter: submission to gain the 'general advantage' of government, security, and protection; the wish to advance other interests the people value, other aspects of well-being government has the potential to advance. How the two sentiments, seemingly at odds, are reconciled to result in effective government is the riddle to be resolved in charting the place of the people in the constitutional order. The fortress-image fades but stays just beyond the border looking over the field, the constitutional order, tempting the people back to the security and certainty on offer.

Other features of Hume's account merit notice. First is the separation of experience from ideals. Hume observes social relations as they are rather than how they *ought* to be according to the opinion of one or another. His account is descriptive not prescriptive. The two forms of enquiry have different purposes, make different assumptions, and conform to different logics. Idealist accounts have a place in social understanding only if they enter into the people's reasons for action, a point to

[3] *Fortress* and *field* are here used as metaphors, terms to describe situations to which they are not literally applicable. They might qualify as ideal types as defined by Weber.

[4] For similarity with Max Weber's approach, see Notes.

return to shortly. Another feature is Hume's scepticism of fictions, ideas invoked to give content and meaning to the relationship between rulers and ruled. The people remain for Hume the aggregate of persons rather than an abstraction; there is no pretence of a social contract and no need to conjure up consent; sovereignty and representation cloud rather than clarify and are of no practical use. A final feature of Hume's account is that, normally, the people confront a constitutional order already in place, of which they are neither the authors nor the principals for whom officials are agents. There may be occasions where they have a hand in constitution-making, engage in the design, but in general the constitutional order is confronted rather than constructed. Hume takes it for granted and looks beyond the coercive side to show the benefits of acquiescence. On that note we part company with Hume, although he is never far away, keeps an eye on the field, and reappears from time to time to correct corruption of practical reason and to deflate flights of fancy from practical purposes.

Construction proceeds at several stages. The social relationship between people and officials, the foundation, has to be developed and deepened along several lines. One concerns the benefits the people want from the relationship, the question being which among all potential benefits they expect government to provide and for what reasons. The answer draws us down to the common purpose of human endeavour, then to consider the practical process of rendering purpose into action, while noting obstacles along the way. The next stage is the design of the field of constitutional action, the officials and agencies and the powers of each, the discourse of ideas and values on which the design rests and action taken. The people enter almost as strangers, the field already laid out, the tasks before them daunting: how to put the agencies of government to work for their benefit; how to restrain officials and keep power to purpose; the measures open to them to influence and guide power to serve their interests, and the limitations. The last stage concerns the forms of rule, the social base, the gains and losses, all gauged from the people's perspective. In building such an edifice on Hume's bare base, for both architecture and inspiration I turn to Adam Smith (1723–90), Hume's younger friend,[5] and Giambattista Vico (1668–1744), a solitary but profound voice from Naples,[6] while the spirit of Niccolò Machiavelli (1469–1527) and lesser spirits are never far away, at times mocking and scoffing, at times wise. Before burying ourselves in theories from eighteenth-century Scotland and Naples, one feature of constitutional discourse stands out, hinted at above, and best dealt with at once. The discourse of constitutional authority in expressing relations between the people and officials is

[5] A Smith: *The Theory of Moral Sentiments* (1759) (London: Penguin Books, 2009) and *Lectures on Jurisprudence* (eds) RL Meek, DD Raphael, and PG Stein (Indianapolis: Liberty Fund, 1982).

[6] G Vico: *New Science: Principles of the New Science Concerning the Common Nature of Nations* (1774) (London: Penguin Books, 1999) (referred to as *New Science*).

steeped in abstractions and fictions. And although Hume found no need for them, they so saturate the discourse it is prudent to see what is at stake.

2. Concepts of constitutional discourse

Ideals about how a constitutional order ought to be constructed, what relations between people and officials ought to be, are to be separated from ideas embedded in constitutional discourse. My aim now is to enquire into the nature of such ideas, the concepts on which they are based, and the purpose they serve. But first a note on *ideals*. While normally outside social understanding, ideals may enter into the people's reasons for action. The pattern of history on one view is just that, the people holding on to an ideal of ruling themselves as the best way of advancing well-being, and to that end devoting much effort. The ideal of self-rule becomes a purpose the people pursue, gives rise to an interest they value, and for the realization of which they take action. How and to what extent the ideal of self-rule in practice entered into the people's reasons, influenced sentiments and dispositions, and led to action is an empirical matter and a theme of later chapters. That ideal is best seen, not dominating, but as one row of stitching in the fabric of practical action, a row present but visible to varying degrees from one epoch to another, at times a reason for action, at other times absent from the discourse. The point for now is to note how an ideal can enter into practical reason and influence practical action. *Ideas* within constitutional discourse are different. Ideas are made up of concepts that give meaning to actions. A discourse of ideas is innate in a constitutional order, the function to express social relations between the people and officials.[7] That social relationships be explained and justified is normal, indeed required by conventions of human interaction and mutual respect. Such ideas are meant to shape the way the parties, people, and officials view the constitutional order, the sentiments and dispositions that form, the actions that follow. Whether in practice the people admit such ideas into their reasoning and trim actions to match depends on the evidence.

The task now is to enquire into ideas embedded in constitutional discourse, drawing mainly on English history while aware that a similar discourse, with origins in the Roman tradition, underlies other constitutional orders in Europe and beyond. The *body politic* stands out in depicting the constitutional order, with *consent* and *representation* in support. The *sovereign people* later emerged and gave rise to *we the people*, who enter a *social contract* in which we consent to the constitutional order in place; and even if we do not agree to a social contract we *consent* to rule by a few *representatives*. Constitutional discourse historically and presently

[7] Some *ideals* are likely to be included in the wider category of *ideas*.

abounds with such ideas, which under scrutiny turn out to be abstractions and fictions, forming part of a discourse detached from experience. My aim now is to understand the origin of such ideas, the function, and the need.

A constitutional order emerges out of and is shaped by the social structure, absorbing and reflecting relations as to status, economy, and power. The path may meander and fragment, be overgrown and hard to track, yet reach the right destination. History and experience show the tendency of select persons, groups, and sectors to acquire superior status, economic advantage, and political power. The constitutional order is designed and the form of rule refined to sustain and fortify the social order. The people as an aggregate of persons pose a problem. The raw power at their disposal is a threat from which the social order has to be protected, a way found to smooth the passage to willing compliance, a process to which the constitutional order contributes. Instead of starting with the people, attentive to their needs and utilities, the constitutional order begins with the social structure and works backwards to the people. They have to be persuaded that although their place in the social order be low, they are valued and they benefit from the constitutional order. The positive purpose has a negative side, fear of the people's unleashing the raw power to which Hume refers. Despite the inequalities and disparities, the social order and in turn the constitutional order have to be presented in a manner acceptable to all, that in Bolingbroke's phrase being 'the measure of our submission'.

But why, from the people's perspective, is it not enough that person and property are protected, harmony, stability, and peace cultivated? Hume thought that would satisfy the people, regardless of who governs and the vulgarity of their sentiments. Yet, history and experience teach that the defects of a social order dominated by select sectors are plain and bound to weigh on the opinion of the rest, rendering the order unstable. The protection of interests and the allocation of benefits are unequal, some doing well, others managing, most eking out a meagre living on the margins. The security of even basic entitlements is uneven and precarious, justice denied as often as done, abuse and oppression common at the hands of officials and private parties. The people are restricted in their actions and have limited freedom to improve their lives, to better secure needs and to enhance utilities. The strength of their compliance turns on three variables: the level of goods provided by government, just treatment when wrong is done, and room to better one's lot in life. A people content with the benefits and safe from abuse and oppression, is a people disposed to restrain its actions and support the system in place. As the level of each drops, discontent sets in, unrest is rife, raw power at hand to offer resistance, outright rebellion a last resort. The pattern appears to be that the three variables influence the sentiments and dispositions of the people and the actions they take. The higher the level of all three, the stronger the sentiment of support and the disposition of self-restraint. The lower it drops, the deeper the discontent and the more ardent the ruling sectors have to be in finding ways to justify the system and win support. Images are created and ideas invented to cultivate in the people sentiments and dispositions of support. The first signs show of a distinct discourse, a register of ideas with language to match, partly describing and partly justifying the constitutional order. Appeal is made to the *body politic*, in which all have a place and all benefit from the harmony, stability, and unity that result. Authority comes from above, safe in the hands of the prince who knows the purpose of ruling, knows how to sustain the good health of the body politic and promote in fatherly fashion the good of all organs, including the feet, the common people. The prince in time gives way to rule by a few, the body politic loses appeal as the people raise their voices and demand a better life and a say in ruling. Other ways had to be found to explain and justify the rule of a few, while maintaining the social, economic, and political order.

Hume as historian charted the changes.[8] The English civil war of the mid-seventeenth century had shown the fragility of settled forms in the face of discontent. Members of parliament made the claim, original at the time, that being elected by the people, albeit a small percentage, gave the House of Commons added authority in relation to king and peers.[9] For the people to acquire a voice in the affairs of state, even if muffled and filtered through representatives, marks a shift in constitutional thought and practice, signals a redesign of the constitutional order. Barely audible at first, the voice once heard was bound to grow louder; the people to become more confident in their claims at all levels of the social order, including the constitutional. By Hume's time a century later, society had altered in critical ways. The bonds of the rigid social order had loosened and social relations were being redefined. A sense of the free and individual person was emerging and a freer economy growing. The easing of restrictions on movement allowed labour to be more mobile and opened the way for enterprise and initiative, aided by restricting or removing the state's monopoly in fields of economic activity. The people for their part were laying claim to new rights and liberties, including rights to engage in the process of governing, nurturing in some the ambition to govern themselves. As society moved from one of strict social bonds and hierarchical order to social fragmentation and the freedom and division of labour and enterprise, in Durkheim's terms from mechanical to organic solidarity, the constitutional certainties of the old order came into question.[10] An observer like Hume could put aside conventional constitutional discourse, dispense with abstractions and fictions, and ask with a philosophical eye, why the people accept the authority of the few? What practical reasons have they for acquiescence? The approach,

[8] D Hume: *The History of England* (1778) (Indianapolis: Liberty Fund, 1983).

[9] See further DJ Galligan: 'The People, the Levellers, and the Constitution' in *Constitutions and the Classics: From Fortescue to Bentham* (ed) DJ Galligan (Oxford: Oxford University Press, 2014).

[10] E Durkheim: *The Division of Labour in Society* (London: The Free Press, 1984).

while well-founded, leaves unexplained why abstractions and fictions continued to be invented and their function in constitutional discourse.

3. People as an abstraction, a corporate entity

A prince, wrote Machiavelli, 'can never secure himself against a hostile people';[11] to survive, he needs their favour and support. A lesson lost on Coriolanus, whose contempt for the citizens of Rome, whose love he 'prized' as 'the dead carcasses of unburied men/that do corrupt my air', cost him dearly.[12] Even a prince as seasoned as Richard of York is frantic to know what the common people think of his plan to seize the throne.[13] But how do a prince or a few win the support, even affection of the people, the 'nerve and life' of the nation? What routes are open other than material benefits? The answer is to give the people a place and status of a special kind in the constitutional order. The discourse moves from material well-being to a plane of ideas, images, and language. The gains are intended to be twofold. One, the power of rule, is justified by appealing to images with which the people identify, and to ideas and values they share; the other, the people, are presented as having a place in the origin, the discourse, and the conduct of constitutional authority. These ideas amount to a distinct mode of constitutional thought, prompting a matching discourse, an upper register, based on a set of concepts about the social order, social relationships and social spheres, and the purpose of the constitution.[14] The upper register, the nature of the discourse and the contribution to constitutional understanding, is the subject of later chapters; the purpose now is to ask the point of casting the people as an abstraction, a corporate entity.

Early versions of the upper register project an image of the body politic by analogy to the body natural, where each sector of society is an organ with a place and function, from the prince as the head to the people as the feet. Attention shifts from the coercive side of ruling, softening the reality of power and summoning images of harmony, unity, and stability, on which the good health of the body depends and from which all organs benefit. The prince, the brain, not so much wields power but prudently and wisely draws on the means to good health innate in the body itself. A body politic in good health serves the common good and the good of all its members.[15] The people, naturally the feet, become restless, throw off false images and the bonds of servitude, aspire to a position more noble, want to improve their

[11] N Machiavelli quoted in E Benner: *Machiavelli's Prince: A New Reading* (Oxford: Oxford University Press, 2013), p 131.

[12] W Shakespeare: *The Tragedy of Coriolanus*, Act 3: 3: 125.

[13] W Shakespeare: *Tragedy of King Richard III*, Act 3: 5: 66.

[14] The upper register is explained more fully in Chapter VII.

[15] John of Salisbury: *Polycraticus* (c.1159) (ed) CJ Nederham (Cambridge: Cambridge University Press, 1990).

lives, and claim a share in governing. Conflict sets in and the image of an organic whole loses its appeal. Other ways have to be found to tame the native power of the people, to stem the surge for political influence, the demand for more attention to their well-being, and a fairer share of material goods. The solution is to enter the people into the constitutional order in a new way by casting them as the source of authority, then rendering them powerless. Among the strategies to that end, two stand out. One is to accept that the power of the ruler flows from, is authorized by, and bears the name of the people. The idea of the people as the source of authority becomes the foundation of discourse. 'We The People', the opening words of many constitutions, proclaims the people to be the authors.[16] Even if those words are not used, in many texts the idea is implicit. The other strategy is to replace the body politic with the people as a *corporate entity* acting through *representatives. Representation* takes on a special meaning, not as agency acting on instructions from the people, but a select few who are substitutes for the people. A few who know what is best for the people, how to advance and protect their true interests. It is then a subtle shift from the few being substitutes for, to becoming or embodying the people.[17]

The concept of the people changes to match the shift. The people as the aggregate of individual persons is displaced by an abstraction, the *corporation of the people.*[18] The distinction between the real person and an abstract concept has a long history in constitutional discourse. The prince was held to have two bodies, one real and personal, the other an abstraction.[19] And just as the prince in representing the realm became its embodiment, so representatives became the people. The House of Commons relied on the distinction to invent the sovereignty of parliament in the late eighteenth century, the purpose to counter demands by the people for a presence in governing.[20] If representatives become the people, the real people are defined out of the discourse and consigned to the constitutional wilderness. The shift from the real to the abstract means resort to ideas removed from actual social relations and separated from real entities. The *people* is a classic case. They are the flesh and blood persons who enter social relations, the aggregate of whom constitutes the community and the nation. At the same time the *people* is an abstract concept, a mental construction severed from reality. Just as the political order earlier had been re-conceived to become the body politic, and just as the prince

16 Around one quarter of national constitutions begin: 'We The People'; many others express the same idea indirectly. For further analysis of the source of modern constitutional authority, see Chapter VI.

17 *Representation* is examined in Chapter XIV.

18 In Latin, the *universitas*, a concept passed down from Roman law and used in many contexts. Italian universities are still presented as *universita' degli studi.*

19 Discussed in EH Kantorawitz: *The King's Two Bodies: A Study in Medieval Political Theory* (New Jersey: Princeton University Press, 1981).

20 Pasi Ihalainen provides an authoritative analysis of the parliamentary debates: P Ihalainen: *Agents of the People: Democracy and Popular Sovereignty in British and Swedish Parliamentary and Public Debates 1734–1800* (Leiden & Boston: Brill, 2010).

symbolizes the realm, the people now become a corporate entity.[21] The ideas are appealing. The people are *sovereign*, the source of constitutional authority, and set the terms, which they then put into practice through *representatives*. The people in this abstract sense have a central place in constitutional history and discourse. The reality is different. From the concession that the people are the source and centre of constitutional authority, no practical results follow. The power to exercise authority vests in a few, while the people are left to engage only on the margins. They at best have limited say over who rules and weak influence over how they rule.[22] Nevertheless, outside and regardless of the formal discourse, the corporate notion of the people and their fictional place in the constitution, the real people find ways to win a share in governing, to better protection of rights, and the liberty to improve their lives. The route is far from straight or even; the gains of one generation easily lost by the next. The force of abstractions by now is largely spent, yet lingers in the background, hovering around practical matters of constitution, at times swooping to make its presence felt, as later chapters relate.

4. Fictions and the submerged subjunctive

Hume thought 'the general advantage' gained by a system of government, fortified by dispositions of respect and to avoid sanctions, enough to explain the people's acquiescence in constitutional authority. Yet Hobbes and Locke, with whom Hume shares some common ground, thought more be needed to justify the power of the state. All three agree on the purpose of government being to provide the people with social goods. For Hobbes, civil society comes into being 'on the basis of a calculation of advantage',[23] the securing of which requires coordination to deal with the confusion and dangers of the state of nature, and to create notions of right and wrong.[24] Locke's reasons are similar: to avoid 'the inconveniences of the state of nature' and to preserve liberty and property, which are subject to 'uncertainties and constantly exposed to the invasion of others'.[25] Here the alliance ends, with Hobbes and Locke adding conditions for the people's compliance. Hobbes, to strengthen the practical case for compliance, moves to another mode of discourse, one based on fictions. His account has three parts: an effective constitutional order needs a

[21] Origins of the corporate entity are discussed in DJ Galligan: 'The People, the Constitution, and the Idea of Representation' in *Social and Political Foundations of Constitutions* (eds) DJ Galligan and M Versteeg (New York: Cambridge University Press, 2013), pp 134–56.

[22] A distinction is drawn between people as a collection of individual persons and the people as an abstract or corporate entity. The distinction is of importance in constitutional understanding, as shall be shown later in Chapter VI. Other texts are more nuanced: the people are the source of constitutional authority, authority itself vests in the nation, the organs of government exercise authority.

[23] Quoted in P Rahe: *Against Throne and Altar: Machiavelli and Political Theory under the English Republic* (Cambridge: Cambridge University Press, 2008), p 308.

[24] *Ibid* p 273.

[25] Locke: *Second Treatise*, p 88.

sovereign without limits on power; compliance depends on the people's consent; and consent is conveyed by covenant among them. In order to rescue the people from the state of nature and to protect their interests, government needs unlimited power. The *Democratical Gentlemen* are mocked for thinking a ruler of limited power could protect the people. Hobbes invents a sovereign who acquires the natural power of each person to protect themselves and their property. The transfer of a power critical to the very identity of a person requires consent, which the people give by agreeing among themselves that each person cede to the sovereign their natural power and liberty. The sovereign's actions become the actions of each person. Compliance is certain, for it would make no sense to contest or contradict one's own actions or to impose limits on oneself in governing.[26]

The place of consent in constitutional discourse is still taken for granted, witnessed in symbols and rituals, and tirelessly asserted without much attention to what it means. Beneath the surface simplicity, consent is a complex concept, as shown in Chapter VIII. For now two points are enough to note. First, one soon notices an ambiguity between *consent as a positive* act of agreeing to something and consent as *consensus* in the sense of shared sentiments about something. Hobbes and others insist on consent in the positive sense, then rely on a fiction to show it is given. Hume saw no need for the concept. Positive consent could be inferred from acquiescence but adds nothing of its own, merely describing an action complete for other reasons. A second point is whether consent as a positive act is a necessary condition of the people's compliance. For Hume plainly not, while for Hobbes it is essential because of what is at stake. On his account, each of us has by nature liberty and power prior to the social relationships into which we enter. Government can be effective only if the people give up their natural power and liberty, which they may do only by consent. The people convey consent by entering into a covenant with each other; or in the absence of a covenant, they act *as if* there were one. They conclude that the best way of understanding social relations among themselves, and with officials, is to act as *they would act were there* a covenant.[27]

That leads to fictions, by Touchstone so deftly defined. A quarrel between two persons, having defied the power of seven justices to settle, can be patched up and lying avoided with an *if*:

> as if you said so, then I said so, and they shook hands and swore brothers. Your 'If' is the only peacemaker; much virtue in 'if'.[28]

[26] For references to Hobbes, see Notes.

[27] Sheldon Wolin remarks how Hobbes and Locke, and others, showed how a constitutional order could be based on consent yet kept safe from popular rule: *Tocqueville: Between Two Worlds* (Princeton and Oxford: Princeton University Press, 2001), p 69.

[28] W Shakespeare: *As You Like It*, Act 5: 4: 95*ff*.

In the words 'much virtue' is much wisdom. Pretend *x* to be the case, then act as if *x* is the case. A statement by Locke catches the soul of a fiction: 'the people give right to Civil Government to employ their force for the execution of the judgements of the Commonwealth which are their own judgements'.[29] The phrase 'which are their own judgements' is not a conclusion logically drawn from what goes before. It makes sense only if the words *as if*, as if they were their own judgements, are inserted. For judgements of the Commonwealth to be the people's judgements, a premise has to be added along the lines: according to a set of ideas about constitutional authority, the actions of government officials are deemed to be the judgements of the people. The same reasoning applies to consent: if the people comply with the decrees of government, the people are deemed to have consented. Once we look, the discourse of constitutions bristles with fictions: as if the people were a corporate body; as if the prince were to embody the realm; as if representatives were the people; and as if the constitution were made by the people. These are just a few of many cases. Fictions are not confined to constitutions but find their way into all dimensions of life. To say much of life is lived on fictions would not be a distortion; in the constitutional context, they are rife. The submerged subjunctive tells all. The subjunctive tense properly used alerts the reader to the claim being hypothetical and dependent on an undisclosed premise, a feature retained in the true heirs of Latin, although largely lost in colloquial English. Despite the contention of the *Oxford English Dictionary* of the subjunctive practically being obsolete, it remains in good stead and when used properly serves a profound purpose. The subjunctive in point here, the *as if* form, is a signal that appeal is being made to a premise unstated, the purpose to define the relationship between the rulers and ruled. The premise is either that the actions of rulers are the actions of the ruled or that the ruled have consented to them. If the pretence be accepted, the conclusion follows.

5. Social function of constitutional fictions

What then is the social problem to which fictions in constitutional discourse are the solution? The answer has three parts: the nature, the function, and the effect. Derived from the Latin verb *fingere*, to pretend, a fiction is an invention; an act of imagination, a pretence that something be the case when it is not; the feigned existence of a state of things. Giorgio Bassani describes a garden in Ferrara belonging to the Finzi-Contini family, a place of love and despair in 1930s Italy, as the race laws tightened around Jewish communities.[30] The location is given, the layout

[29] Locke: *Second Treatise*, Section 88: 325.

[30] As depicted by G Bassani in: *Il giardino dei Finzi-Contini* (*The Garden of the Finzi-Contini*) (Milan: Mondadori, 1976).

described in detail, the garden brought to life in the mind of the reader; yet all is an invention of the author. Constitutional fictions are far from the garden of the Finzi-Contini, but just as much inventions. Social relations between rulers and ruled is the context into which fictions insert features that are not there. Just as we know what a garden is, we know the meaning of concepts of constitutional discourse, such as sovereignty and consent, representation and the people. And just as there is no garden in Ferrara, so the features signalled by such concepts do not exist in the constitutional field. The people are an aggregate of persons, not a corporate body; the few take action on behalf of the people, in some sense represent the people, but do not become or embody them. Sovereignty is ascribed to the people but has no practical effect in their relationship with rulers. The people could, but in practice do not, enter into a contract either among themselves or with a few, by which they assign their natural power to the few.

The question is why go to all this trouble. That novels be based on fictions, on creating an imaginary world, is the nature of novels; why constitutional discourse should be so infused is not so plain. Sifted from history and practice, the purpose is to present relations between the people and officials in a particular way, the logic of *as if*, the submerged subjunctive the means. As if the people were a corporate and sovereign body, which officials represent or become; as if the people had entered a contract conceding power to officials or otherwise consented; as if the relationship were that of a body to the health of which all contribute as one organ or another. The constitutional order, the basis on which officials govern, is built on such features as if they were real and present. The reality is fictions serve as instruments of power, a means by which power moves from the people to officials.[31] By deeming themselves to be substitutes for the people, representatives lay claim to the power of the people. By deeming itself to embody the people, the parliament acquires the power of the people. By pretending the people have consented to rule, officials consider themselves authorized to govern in the name and with all the powers of the people, and with their agreement to whatever be done. In setting the terms of the relationship between the people and government, fictions bear a heavy load. The assumption is that power granted by or agreed to by the people is justified power. Why does power in constitutional affairs have to be justified or, to be more accurate, why do rulers feel the need to justify their power to the people? The answer noted here and expanded later has two parts. Social relationships occur within social spheres of perceptions, rules, and sanctions, among which, under certain conditions, are notions of mutual respect among the parties from which arise rules of interaction. The people and officials normally consider the constitutional order to be subject to such conditions, among which is mutual respect. Each person has a status, an entitlement to be treated with respect, from which follows a duty to

[31] On power, see Chapter IV:6.

justify the power of one over the other. The will of the ruler is not enough and has to be justified.[32] The other reason is fear of the people, fear of the raw power to reject rule. If the people consider rule justified, they are disposed to restrain their own power and give support. Appeal to fictions, to the *as if* style of argument, is one means of justification.

The nature and function of fictions is now clear, but do they mean anything to the people? Do fictions enter into the people's reasons for action? If the people in fact were to consent by act or inference to rule by a few, they would be disposed to accept and support a constitutional order built on that base. Where there is no actual consent, the usual case, fictions are meant to fill the gap. If the people pretend a covenant has been concluded with others, even though it has not, or that they have anyhow consented, or that representatives embody them, then the pretence enters into their reasons for action, shapes sentiments and dispositions, and induces compliance with authority. But are the people aware of the fictions of constitutional discourse? If they are, do they take any notice? The answers are stated in brief to be expanded later. First, whether or not the people even know of the fictions depends on the evidence from one constitutional order to another and from one fiction to another. Secondly, even if the people know of the fictions of constitutional discourse, a separate question is whether they admit them into their reasons for action or to influence their understanding of relations with officials. Thirdly, and critically, the people have their own view of the purposes of a constitutional order, the reasons officials have power, and relations between them. Such view is prior to the official constitutional order, normally lies dormant, often only dimly perceived and rarely proclaimed. Yet, when need beckons, it provides a hinterland of ideas and values on which to draw, as we learnt from the peasants of Gagliano. There, we caught a glimpse of a lower register of constitutional discourse, overlapping and intersecting with the upper register, but separate. A register of ideas arising from the elemental purposes of human endeavour; a register by which to view and judge the constitutional order descending from above.[33] The lower register guides the people in their approach to fictions. Provided government serves their well-being, secures and advances their interests, the fictions of the upper register are of no practical consequence and harmless. If the fictions be used to silence the people or to justify actions against their interests, the people have in reserve the discourse of the lower register as a means of resistance. Just what that means in practice, and the power of the lower register, we shall see as the chapters unfold.

[32] On interaction and mutual respect, see J Watts: *Henry VI and the Politics of Kingship* (Cambridge: Cambridge University Press, 1996), p 59; see further W Brown: *Undoing the Demos* (New York: Zone Books, 2015), p 206.

[33] The *lower register* is analysed in Chapter IX.

Let us return lastly to the need for a sovereign without limits on power. A critical part of Hobbes' theory, the reasoning is as follows. The natural power each person has to protect interests is without limits. And since the sovereign is constituted by becoming each person, it follows that the power the sovereign acquires from each person is without limits. Half hidden in the theory is an empirical dimension, the claim that in order to protect the people the sovereign needs power without limits. Historical experience suggests the opposite. Limitations on the powers of government do not prevent it from discharging both protective and enabling functions. The purpose of limitations is to protect and advance other social goods and values not mentioned by Hobbes. Nor does Hobbes take account of the dangers of a sovereign with unlimited power; dangers the protection against which is a critical purpose of the constitutional order.[34]

6. Beyond Hume

Now that the site has been cleared, the construction of a constitutional order can proceed along the lines set out at the start of the chapter. The standpoint is that of the people: how they view the constitutional order, what they expect from it, and how to involve themselves within it. That means digging down to identify the purposes of human action, charting the interests that result, then asking how the constitutional order contributes. Several factors guide the enquiry.

First, the people enter the constitutional field, form relations with officials in order to gain benefits, and in return acquiesce. Around the core other features are to be added. One, acquiescence, depends on the opinion of the people, which is conditional on their expectations being met to a reasonable degree. The other, officials need power, but power creates risks of misuse. The people soon realize that to be confident of even moderate benefits, and to reduce the risks, governing has to be conducted in certain ways and under certain conditions. Just what ways and conditions, they learn from reflection and experience.

Second, prompted by intuition and tutored by experience, the people realize that in order to be sure of gaining the benefits, they need to be engaged in the processes of governing; although what that means in practice has to be worked out between them and officials. The people see emerging from history patterns of rule, with matching patters of opinion, grouped roughly as rule by one as the prince, rule by a few as representatives, and the people trying to rule themselves. Each has some appeal, but they are sceptical and want to know more about the strengths of

[34] Considered further in Chapter XII. See further D Acemoglu and JA Robinson: *The Narrow Corridor: States, Societies, and the Fate of Liberty* (London: Viking, Penguin Books, 2019).

each, as well as the defects and drawbacks. None they feel quite catches their place in the constitutional order or captures the spirit of relations between them and officials, and among themselves. They keep an eye out for other ways of defining such relations, which then would help in defining their approach to the practical processes of governing.

Third, the people notice the efforts made to present the constitutional order as transcending the social and political domains. Having seen how fictions and abstractions are invoked to aid and mask the process, the people are on guard. They see the distinctiveness of social relations within the constitutional order and the need to keep them apart from other sets of relations. Yet, they know the borders are neither precise nor rigid, that the constitutional field allows other sets of relations to enter, if not through the gate then under the fence. They are well aware that behind the imagery of consensus and harmony, the constitutional field itself is an arena of competition and conflict among interests, all striving to influence the course and outcome of government.

Fourth, once the constitutional order is perceived as purposive, the people forming social relations with officials to achieve purposes, the enquiry deepens. If we are to understand the process by which to achieve the purposes of the constitutional order, we must study the nature and structure of society and how collective action can be directed to and effective in achieving purpose. One matter to explain is the sequence from purpose to action and how it applies to the constitutional order. Another is what means the people have to hold officials to purpose, the kinds of actions available to them. And finally there is more to say about the lesson learnt from the peasants of Gagliano that a community, a people, has a hinterland of ideas, language, and values, rooted in social relations and manifest in daily practice, from which to guide and gauge the actions of officials.

Notes

Abstract entities

Weber explains abstract entities in this way. Abstract entities 'have a meaning in the mind of individual persons, partly as something actually existing, partly as something with normative authority. . . . Actors thus in part orientate their action to them, and in this role such ideas have a powerful, often decisive, influence of the course of action of real individuals': *Economy & Society*, p 14. This account does not quite match my own. Whether abstract entities, and we should add ideals, 'orientate action', that is, enter into the reasons for action, is an empirical contingency, not a necessary outcome.

Hobbes and the people

It is interesting to note Hobbes' conception of the people. They begin as the multitude, a mass of individual persons, and end as united in one person, the sovereign. The actions of each are 'directed according to their particular judgements, and particular appetites, they can expect thereby no defence, nor protection, neither against a Common enemy, nor against the injuries of one another'. In order to overcome these defects the multitude enter into a covenant among them to create a 'Common Power, to keep them in awe, and to direct their actions to the Common Benefit'. That means conferring all 'their power and strength upon one man, or upon an assembly of men, to bere their Person'.

'This is more than Consent, or Concord; it is a reale Unite of them all, in one and the same person.' When this is done, 'the Multitude so united in one Person is called a COMMON-WEALTH'. Common-wealth is defined, the essence: 'One Person, of whose Acts a great Multitude, by mutuall Covenants one with another, have made themselves every one *the* Author, to the end he may use the strength of them all, as he shall think expedient, for their Peace and Common Defence.' *Leviathan*, Chapter XVII, pp 254ff.

Fictions

The Garden of the Finzi-Contini. Once I went to Ferrara in search of the garden. The author's directions are clear, streets are named, landmarks noted. Enquiring at shops along the way, I was reassured. Having arrived where the garden was meant to be, I found neither a garden nor any sign there had ever been one. I asked at a nearby kiosk selling trinkets. With an amused or perhaps bemused look, the proprietress replied: 'Signore, soffre di una grand illusione. Il gardino dei Finzi-Contini non esiste, non esisté mai. Non esisté mai che nella mente dell'autore.' I still wonder about the shopkeepers' nodding me on and assuring me I was heading the right way.

Fictions and the submerged subjunctive

Much has been written on fictions, and much of what is written is obscure. Bentham devoted energy to the issue and wrote at complex length, which Gerald Postema has valiantly set out to explain: *Bentham and the Common Law Tradition.* Philip Schofield's more recent writings have done much to make Bentham accessible: *Utility & Democracy: The Political Thought of Jeremy Bentham* (Oxford: Oxford University Press, 2006). More recently, KA Appiah: *As*

If: Idealization and Ideals (Cambridge, Mass: Harvard University Press, 2018), with a review by Thomas Nagel (*New York Review of Books* 2018).

A last word

Ludwig Wittgenstein took enquiry into language and fictions to a new height: 'Language disguises thought. So much so, that from the outward form of the clothing it is impossible to infer the form of the thought beneath it, because the outward form is not designed to reveal the form of the body, but for entirely different purposes': *Tractatus-Philosophicus* (London: Routledge & Kegan Paul, 2nd edn, 1971), p 35. Fictions are an 'outward form—not designed to reveal' the (form of) the body, the substance.

III
Foundations of Social Understanding

1. From philosophy to social understanding

The philosophical eye cold in gaze and clear in vision begins with the people and asks why they restrain their actions and defer to officials. The explanation is one of common sense, prompted by the needs and utilities of the people and how the state can contribute. That is the reality behind the ideals, abstractions, and fictions commonly encountered in constitutional discourse. Around this segment of experience may be assembled a social understanding of constitutional authority. The task now is to complete the assembly by integrating the reason for acquiescence with the wider context of personal and collective endeavour. The advantage of government, and the relationship between people and officials, are placed in a social setting and new lines of enquiry launched, one down to the deeper sources of human action, the other up to the social relations and institutions they support. The enquiry proceeds at two levels: one follows the fragments Hume left as to the nature of a constitutional order;[1] the other probes the purpose of collective action and considers how the people in pursuit of purpose perceive and handle the order.

Hume assumes a constitutional order already established, rulers empowered, a system of government in process. How all this came about and whose interests are served are neither disclosed nor noteworthy. All that matters is that the people acquiesce in return for benefits. We are curious to know more about a constitutional order where relations between officials and the people reduce to one giving the other receiving. The images of a fortress and a field aid the enquiry. Imagine the constitutional order as a field of activity, fenced off from other fields, laid out by the few in charge and run by the agencies of government.[2] The people are told they will gain certain benefits by entering, provided they accept the lay-out, ask no questions, and comply. They gain in return security of person and property, maybe basic welfare, and some room to improve their lives by their own actions. Whatever rights accrue are respected; if not, redress is provided. The people have no say in the design of the field and only marginal influence on how it is managed and cultivated, or what the benefits are to be. In Hobbes' words 'they trade submission for protection'. If after hearing the terms of entry, some were to waver and prepare to leave, the welcome would take a nasty turn, the waverers told they have no choice but to enter and conform; to put themselves under government in Locke's polite

[1] Explained in Chapter II:1

[2] The idea of a constitutional field is developed in Chapter V.

Keepers of the Common Good. D.J. Galligan, Oxford University Press. © D.J. Galligan 2024.
DOI: 10.1093/9780198907398.003.0003

term, or more crudely to enter and obey under threat of punishment. They are guests by compulsion who benefit from the 'general advantage' of a constitutional order; guests who are expected to show gratitude by restraining their actions and acquiescing. The image of a field starts to look more like a fortress. Hume, on one reading, takes this to be the standard form of the constitutional order. The people are content with the benefits, security of person and property and not much else.

Despite the appeal of the fortress and the vigour of support, Hume hinted at another way of conceiving the constitutional order. Once the people's opinion matters, a different logic unfolds. The constitutional order opens into a field where the people are citizens not mere subjects; citizens who have a say in how it is cultivated and managed; where the relationship with officials is more than one of command and obedience. The issue for the people is how to approach the field, what to expect from it, and how to bring it about. They see the openings for influence; try to gain a foothold in the processes of governing; normally on the margins, occasionally more central, always precarious and liable to reversal. On rare occasions, fired by zeal for *freedom*, they take over and attempt to govern themselves. Such efforts are short-lived before the constitutional field returns to its normal state of being ruled by one or a few. The other factor, more subtle, is the cloaking of the constitutional order in ideas, language, and images aimed at making it more appealing to the people. The discourse at first is that of the body politic, which serves the good of all by creating wholeness, harmony, and stability. Later it is recast to position the people at the centre by inserting into the discourse concepts of authorship and sovereignty, consent and representation; concepts invented to explain and justify the constitutional order as if it were the work of the people. [3] They are alert to the submerged subjunctive and understand that in order to rule, the few must curb the power of the many by presenting them as being at the centre of the constitutional order. Despite the pleasing imagery, the people know their place in the body politic is not among the noble organs but down with the feet. They normally comply with the order in place, partly for the benefits, partly due to the conventions of respect for authority, and partly to avoid punishment.[4]

However, like the peasants of Gagliano, the people are able stand back to judge for themselves the merits of the order, their place in it, and how it could be different. Evidence gathered from history shows the people's musings to be several. One is to be realistic and accept as normal the constitutional order's being there looming over them. There are exceptions, occasions when they have a say in the design, but normally the order is solid and settled and not easily altered, their only hope to have some say in how it is run. Another, the people know many factors guide the design and influence the practice. They are sceptical of calls on the common good and know from experience the ties between select sectors, the constitution, and

[3] On ideas, abstractions, and fictions, see Chapter II.
[4] Explained in Chapter I.

government, a feature of social life to accept. A third, the people value the benefits they receive, security of person and property and not much more. They have heard Hobbes' warning of the state of nature, noted Hart's caution about society not being a suicide club, and how the state is the solution, all aimed at strengthening the case for the firm rule one or a few can provide. Finally, the people know that within the constitutional order, whether fortress or field, many aspects of their well-being, interests they value count for nothing in the processes of governing. The people are left with an image of the constitutional order more like a fortress than a field, an area walled off from their world, unconcerned for their aims and aspirations, into which they have no real choice but to enter.

Being walled not sealed, chinks appear and walls crumble, and open onto a field where there is room for the people to engage in cultivation, to bring fresh ideas and a new approach to social life, and in turn the constitutional order. Acting alone or together, the people have a sense of purpose lighting the path of action and paving the course of everyday affairs. They associate and form relationships of many kinds to achieve and advance purposes. The purposes can be broad and open or precise and narrow, at times stated at times implicit in action, some at the foundation of social life, others branching in many directions. The question is whether the range of actions alone and together have a common foundation, a set of ends the realization of which is the point of social endeavour. The peasants of Gagliano believed in such a foundation guiding their actions from the critical to the trivial; a foundation from which to understand and judge the Italian state. The same belief is shared by other communities small and large, evidence of which appears in the following chapters. Not purpose in the sense of a noble ideal the people ought to pursue; rather purpose they do in fact pursue, the underlying and unifying reason for action. Purpose in this sense is observed in practical action and studied by gathering evidence of practical action, whether the peasants, the farmers and ranchers, or the people in rebellion. The aim now is to enquire into purpose, how it forms the foundation of human action and social relations, and then to return to show how purpose guides the people in entering and working the constitutional field.

2. Adam Smith on the purposes of social relations

The lines of enquiry into social relations and their purposes are twofold. One looks to social relations in general, the aims and intentions of the parties, and asks whether a core of common purposes prompts their formation, girds them together, and guides their course. The other is to narrow the enquiry to relations between the people and officials as part of the canvas of society, as one distinct social relationship yet connected to and interacting with others. We are brought back to the idea that somehow the power of the state has to be connected to the people more profoundly than mere acquiescence in return for benefits. The relationship has to be probed to find what forces brought it into being; how it advances the purposes of the people, is sustained over time, and copes with adversity. The enquiry opens with ideas from Adam Smith, teaching and writing in eighteenth-century Scotland.[5] Then to Naples where Giambattista Vico, occupying a modest chair of rhetoric, formulated in *La Scienza Nuova, The New Science: Principles of the New Science Concerning the Common Nature of Nations*, a science of society soon acknowledged to be original and seminal to social understanding.[6] Smith's pragmatic account of social relations fits well and supplies evidence to support Vico's theory of society.

Adam Smith, friend and in some ways successor, shared Hume's view of constitutional authority, but only as a foundation on which to build. It is as if Smith, having inherited the canvas with only a figure at the centre, takes up where Hume left off. Provided government meets the people's expectations, supplies basic social goods and acts with 'ordinary moderation and tolerable decency', the people give their support. If the expected benefits flow, the people have good reasons for acquiescing, reasons boosted by a disposition of respect for authority. No need to rely on fanciful theories of social contract; nor to invent idealist theories of justification; nor to insist the people must govern themselves. Governing is a practical matter for concrete ends, and it matters not much who governs as long as they govern tolerably well. Smith ventures beyond this familiar ground. That the people benefit is a critical element of constitutional authority, but for social understanding not enough. In enquiring into relations between the people and government, in entering the recesses of society, from the caverns to the crevices, Smith is struck by two main factors. One is the high level of cooperation and coordination among the people, and between the people and government. The other is the need to shift our gaze from government and its multiple forms to the people, to their understanding of social relations, of which relations with government is just one of many.

Social relations on Smith's account have two features in common. One is the people's natural disposition to 'truck, barter, and exchange',[7] the purpose of which is 'to render the conveniences and necessities of life more attainable'. Notice the general purpose is made more concrete, attached to conveniences and necessities. '[P]roviding of meat, drink, raiment, and lodging' are 'commonly reckoned the meanest of employments and fit for the pursuit of none but the lowest and meanest of the people'. Much of the energy and enterprise of a community is dedicated to that end. From the disposition to truck, barter, and exchange follows the division of labour, which in turn depends on and promotes a high level of cooperation

[5] Two main works of Adam Smith: *The Theory of Moral Sentiments* (original publication 1759) (London: Penguin Books, 2009); *Lectures on Jurisprudence* (delivered 1972–76) (eds) RL Meek, DD Raphael, and PG Stein (Indianapolis: Liberty Fund, 1982).

[6] Isaiah Berlin's talks on the BBC followed by publication were for many an introduction to Vico. See I Berlin: *Vico and Herder: Two Studies in the History of Ideas* (London: Hogarth Press, 1976).

[7] *Lectures on Jurisprudence*, p 328.

among workers. From the division of labour comes the 'opulence', the richness and wealth of a nation. The connection is made plain by comparing the labour of the single person, who has to do everything for himself, with the worker who can buy a 'linnen shirt' for a small portion of his wages, even though one thousand hands have gone into making the shirt.[8] The division of labour, the cooperation on which it relies, and the benefits it brings, result from and are necessary in supplying those conveniences and necessities, the well-being of the people. That is the primary purpose: to advance the people's well-being by securing their needs and improving their lives.

The other notable feature of social relations is that one may consider 'all the arts, the sciences, law and government, wisdom, and even virtue', all 'arts and businesses', tending to this one thing: to render well-being, to make 'the conveniences and necessities of life more attainable'. Social relationships of all kinds, spontaneous or planned, natural or artificial, voluntary or enforced, have purposes prominent among which is the seeking of social goods serving and satisfying the well-being of the people. 'In the great scramble of human society everyone scrambles to get as much as he can and keep what he has got.'[9] The force driving the scramble, such frenetic and consuming activity, is the urge of each to secure not just the needs of daily life, but to add goods and benefits enriching life. An end to which arts and science, law and government, wisdom and virtue, indeed the sum of human ingenuity and invention, are the necessary means. No need for an invisible hand, nor to search for deeper explanation. It is simply the case that much of human endeavour is directed at securing and improving the lot of the people. Other objectives are not ruled out, but the overriding aim and purpose of human action is to secure 'the conveniences and necessities' of life. Collective action is needed, for unless the people come together and coordinate their efforts, that linen shirt will not be made and life is bound to be barren and solitary. Social relationships of all kinds make possible cooperation and coordination that enable the people to achieve their purposes. A final point critical to the account is that 'law and government', the power of the state, the function of government, is one means among many, but a necessary means for achieving those purposes. Empowered to coordinate collective action towards desired ends and goals, government is part of and a partner in the scramble for well-being. So, although state power is prone to appear alien and imposed on spontaneous relationships, if properly understood, is wholly compatible with, an essential part of the absorbing and enduring endeavour for human betterment.

[8] *Ibid* p 339.

[9] *Ibid* p 263. Philip the bastard had earlier noted how, on the death of Prince Arthur, 'The life, the right, and truth of all this realm/Is fled to heavens, and England now is left/to tug and scramble': W Shakespeare: *The Life and Death of King John*, Act 4: 3: 145. Adam Smith would surely have approved of adding tug to the scramble.

3. Constitutional authority as part of human endeavour

We are now able to advance our understanding of constitutional authority. Despite appearances, it is not just the people's passive acquiescence in the power of the state. Nor is it that the people confronted with such power have to find reasons for complying. That might do on the philosophical plane but Adam Smith takes us beyond to the sociological. He does so by going back to the base of society, to the purposes of social relationships generally, and those between the people and government in particular. When approached historically and socially, that relationship turns out to be as indigenous, natural, and necessary, as central to the life of a community, as other relationships with which it shares a common foundation. For among the ends and purposes of human endeavour, one central and constant is that the people, individuals and groups, have certain needs and utilities, desire certain qualities of life, and take action to attain them. Collective action is needed, people coming together in relationships, some informal, others more formal, some established and long-standing, many spontaneous and temporary. All aimed at achieving common goals. Among the social relationships formed to attain desired outcomes, power is present and pervasive, dressed in colour or disguised in shades, at times bluntly displayed, at times subtle and subversive. Between the people and government, power is essential, some ends and purposes being most effectively attained by a certain kind of power entrusted to certain kinds of agencies. While the people for their part have in reserve and in reach that raw power with which we began.[10]

On this account constitutional authority is neither external nor alien but a partner to natural and spontaneous relations, integral and necessary to their endeavour. The agencies and institutions are entrusted with tasks not easily or effectively carried out by other means. There is room for opinion as to what those tasks are, how far beyond a common core they should go, how much power is needed, and how to control it. Debate about boundaries and the risks of power do not detract from or diminish the central notion that government as a network of agencies and institutions is an essential part, a necessary mechanism, in the people's achieving their purposes, securing and advancing their interests, their collective and individual well-being. From that foundation, social relationships arise and social action taken. There are other reasons for forming social relations, other aims and purposes of value, but securing and advancing well-being is at the centre of human endeavour and social interaction. This simple set of ideas Smith observes to be the foundation of social life, the social relations the people enter into, the social structures they erect, the institutions they invent, and most of all is the foundation of the constitutional order and the authority it confers.

[10] See Chapter I:4.

4. Vico's science of society

The canvas of social endeavour is filling up, the portrait of constitutional authority taking shape, the bare patches left by David Hume partly filled by Adam Smith. To finish the canvas and deepen the theory we turn to ideas from Giambattista Vico. Smith might have known of Vico, perhaps read the *New Science* and absorbed Vico's science of society, for there are themes common to both. By science, Vico means a theory in the sense explained, a set of concepts, a *philosophy* 'which contemplates reason, from which we derive our abstract knowledge of what is true'.[11] The method, the route to theoretical understanding, is that of *philology*, the gathering of evidence by grammarians, historians, and critics. The philologist armed with the philosopher's reasoning is the intrepid explorer, today's empirical researcher, gathering evidence across the totality of human experience: 'languages and deeds, including both domestic customs and laws, foreign wars, peace, pacts, travels, and trade'.[12] The purpose of such endeavour is to establish a scientific understanding of society in all its parts. We might pause to ask why in a study of constitutions invoke Vico? What is gained from a voyage through the course not only of human history but pre-human as well? The answer is that Vico's new science is comprehensive, embracing all aspects of human action and showing how they hold together. The new science deepens and strengthens the foundations of constitutional authority and the place of the people, with the aid of Adam Smith already laid. The enquiry must be kept short, drawing on just a few ideas from Vico's complex and ingenious science of society, while being aware of the risk of not doing it justice. I propose no more than a sketch of a theory of captivating interest in its own right, my purpose to show how it fits with and goes beyond Smith's account of constitutional authority.

Vico like Smith immersed himself in the long sweep of history. More than Smith he had an eye for theory, for drawing from history a theoretical framework for social understanding. The theory of society consists of a series of axioms stating ideas and concepts reached by studying the actions and intentions, the motives and purposes of human beings. Unlike the natural world where we are outsiders and which we never fully grasp, the social world is ours, we the insiders, society a product of our purposive actions. 'In history, we are the actors; in the natural sciences mere spectators.' Purposes are embedded in actions, the study of which over the course of history leads to knowledge of human beings, the relations they form, and the institutions they build. History is to be studied by paying attention to, documenting, analysing, and making sense of all human actions and events down to the most minute. This is the labour of the philologist who studies 'everything that depends

[11] *Scienza Nuova*, p 79. An approach similar to Hume on this point.
[12] *Ibid* p 79.

on human volition: for example, all histories of the languages, customs, and deeds of various peoples in both war and peace'.[13]

In examining actions we are guided by several ideas. One in Vico's words is 'a metaphysical conception of man's nature', which comes down to the rather simple idea that the human mind has a capacity to know what purposes are worthwhile and how to reach them. A capacity Vico calls, not so surprisingly, common sense. People face the same issues of life wherever they are and whatever the era. They have to decide where to direct their actions, which ends and goals to pursue and how to reach them, guided by an innate capacity and a native common sense. The metaphysical conception, the common sense, Vico attributes to divine providence. Tying the social nature of humans to divine providence, according to Vico, had not been done before. For social understanding we need not take that extra step, that theological leap. It is enough to observe that people do have an innate common sense, a natural disposition to determine what is worthwhile, what to seek, what to put aside. And despite sometimes being abused and misused, native common sense guides us though the course of life. At the end of *Uncle Vanya*, Sonia expresses movingly that native common sense: 'There is nothing for it. We must go on living, Uncle Vanya! We shall live through a long, long chain of days and weary evenings; we shall patiently bear the trials fate sends us; we shall work for others, both now and in our old age, and have no rest.'[14]

Humans are purposive beings who direct their ideas and actions to realize desired outcomes. This trait of human nature, 'driven by inner purposes', a sense of the ends worth pursuing, is central to the metaphysical concept of the human being.[15] The next stage in revealing the mysteries of the human mind is to identify those inner purposes, to ask: what are the ends for which humans strive to reach. The answer is that which is necessary and that which is useful, in short, needs and utility in Vico's phrase, or human well-being as proposed here. This idea is the motor of human action and the motive for human association. To advance well-being the people enter into relations with others. For the same reasons they settle on conventions and laws, and create institutions. They found nations for which they provide government and adopt a constitution defining its powers and responsibilities. If people were left to pursue only their private interests, 'they would live in solitude like wild beasts'.[16] By use of reason, by invoking common sense, people are led by that 'same self-interest to live with justice like *human beings* and to remain in society'.[17] People know that association, while serving the interest of each, imposes conditions on and restricts their actions. If they are to benefit from association, the people must restrain their own actions. 'To live with justice' deftly

[13] *Ibid* p 5.
[14] A Chekhov: *Uncle Vanya* (London: Heron Books, 1969).
[15] Berlin: *Vico and Herder*, p 27.
[16] Vico: *Scienza Nuova* , p 2.
[17] *Ibid.*

summons up a set of ideas about what it means to enter into relations with others, for justice, getting what is *due*, brings with it principles guiding and mediating association and the duty to moderate the pursuit of self-interest. Such self-restraint is worthwhile, a wise and natural course of action, for the point of the *New Science* is to show that 'the social nature is the true civil nature of humankind'.[18]

5. Social institutions

Fortified by such firm foundations, we now move from the human mind to social institutions and the origin of nations. Two ideas guide the enquiry: one that social institutions are the product of people's intentions and actions, the other that to understand social institutions we look to their origins. Vico frowned on philosophers for attending to nature rather than human affairs. Nature is the province of the creator, and only the creator is capable of full knowledge. The civil world is different. It is the creation of humankind, the work of the people themselves. 'For there can be no more certain history than that which is recounted by its creator.' It follows that 'the principles of the civil world can and must be discovered in the modifications of the human mind'.[19] In order to gain knowledge of social relations, the formation of nations, and the invention of government, we must look to the human mind. The second idea shows us how to do that. We return to origins, to the earliest social formations, examine their forms and purposes, and trace them through the course of history to the present. That is the task of the philologist, the empirical researcher, who gathers evidence from any source available, no idea, institution, or practice being too obscure or too trivial to escape scrutiny or offer reward.[20]

The fruits of philology are plain and plentiful. First, philology reveals how the common thread of necessity and utility runs through all such creations. The common sense of the people, spurred by necessity and nurtured by utility, leads them to create institutions and guides the form and shape they take. Institutions come into being 'for preservation of the human race'. Among institutions is 'a necessary harmony', 'which is the source of all the beauty of the civil world'.[21] Secondly, philology applied across cultures shows how all peoples face common problems, some mundane and pedestrian, some refined and sophisticated, others lofty and noble. They range from acquiring useful skills, such as producing food and wine, learning trades and herding animals, to those affording comfort and pleasure, adding to the quality of life, enhancing enjoyment and satisfaction. One

[18] *Ibid.*
[19] *Ibid* pp 129–30.
[20] Norbert Elias makes no mention of Vico, although his study of table manners as a route to social understanding fits well: N Elias: *The Civilizing Process* (Oxford: Blackwell, 2nd edn 2000).
[21] *New Science, Scienza Nuova*, p 129.

is architecture, another dancing, to which may be added endless others.[22] Culture, defined as 'the complete pattern of living', embraces all, while law, history, and literature contribute to the pattern of 'civility and humanity'. Philology does not neglect the darker edge of life, the aptitude for avarice, the disposition to dominate, and the urge to put self before all else. Each puts at risk the bonds of society; yet, all are attributes of the human mind, as innate as their arch-enemy common sense. They have to be managed and repressed for they cannot be eliminated. All pose threats to institutions and social relations, all inflame the inborn urge of self-interest. Each has to be confronted and contained if a people is to survive and prosper.

The final fruit of philology is to show that all peoples across history, facing similar problems of association, take similar measures to solve them and devise suitable social Institutions. Axiom 22 states that all peoples and nations grasp the substance of the same essential institutions.[23] By tracing institutions through the course of history, philological enquiry shows that from the brutish beginnings all share, each nation and each people develops the same primary social institutions. Vico's enquiry led him to settle on three: religion, marriage, and burial. Since all three are common to all peoples, they are the foundations of civil society, and so the base on which to build a science of society. All social institutions and social relations, however detached and distant they appear, have their origins in the three institutions. How then do we make sense of a claim so seemingly strange?

Early humans had recourse to religion and the divine as a way of taming their bestial nature and moving from a solitary to a social life. They knew from common sense, that innate quality of mind, that to make the move from solitude to society means entering into relations with others. That demands dampening the passions and rallying self-restraint. Entry of the two basic components of social life, relationships and self-restraint, marks the transition from a sub-human existence to the fully human. Marriage means a further 'moderation of the passions' to create families and bind them together. Children are reared to know the customs of social life, without which they would soon cause civil society 'to revert to the great ancient forest through which in their nefarious feral wanderings once roamed the foul beasts of Orpheus'.[24] Families come together for mutual comfort, protection, and support, which signals the start of civil society. At first 'left to tug and scramble', cooperation and coordination on the one hand, competition and conflict on the other hand, the need for a superior power vested with authority is soon apparent. And hence the beginnings of government and constitutional authority. Burial, signifying decency and respect for the dead, is another stage in advancing beyond mere association to a flourishing of culture and enriching of life.[25] Imagine a feral

[22] *Ibid* p 309. Vico apparently enjoyed dancing.
[23] *Ibid* Axiom 22, p 24.
[24] *Ibid* p 55.
[25] *Ibid.*

state in which dead bodies remain unburied 'as food for crows and dogs'. Such a vile custom would signify an absence of human sentiment. Vico cites with approval Tacitus' description of burials as 'the compacts of humanity', without which the barest fragments of humanity and association would be absent. In comparing his love of the common people with that of his love for 'the dead carcasses of unburied men', Coriolanus reaches into that feral world for the ultimate insult.[26] From such foundations relationships form, ideas develop, sensibilities refine, and institutions emerge to advance common purposes. On the foundation of religion, marriage, and burial, social life is based. The passage of ideas, customs, and institutions meanders among peoples, responding to local conditions and external forces; yet, the origins stay firmly anchored in the three founding institutions, the proof of which painstaking philology provides.

To be reminded of the logic: the science of society is built on the ideas and intentions of the human mind, which we know from the institutions humans create. The study of social institutions is then the route to social understanding. The same institutions are common to all peoples and so provide reliable evidence from which to construct a theory of society. Vico's two main contentions are worth repeating. First, the human mind, driving its keeper to discover or invent whatever is necessary and useful, comes to know the power of social institutions and the resulting social relations. Secondly, all peoples in their progress to civility and humanity create similar institutions. A distinction is drawn between the foundation of institutions common to all, and the expression which differs in detail from one people to another. The critical idea is that all peoples have the same common purpose, the same commitment to civility and humanity, to advance well-being, and to design institutions dedicated to that end, institutions in substance the same.

6. The natural law of peoples

The study of the shared nature of people and their institutions leads to discovery of the natural law of peoples, *il diritto delle genti*.[27] It is neither natural law in the philosophical sense nor law among nations. The natural law of peoples means the values common to all peoples and built into their institutions, the study of which shows a common and recurring pattern of formation and growth across societies, guided by the primary purpose of advancing civility and humanity. And if we ask in what sense is this a scientific discovery, the answer is in Axiom 144 which states that 'uniform ideas, born among peoples unknown to each other, must have a common ground of truth'.[28] Vico explains:

[26] *The Tragedy of Coriolanus*, Act 3: 3: 126.
[27] More often called *Natural Law of Nations*, which can be misleading. Vico uses *genti*, which translates well into English as *peoples*.
[28] Vico: *The New Science*, p 53.

> the natural law of the gentes had separate origins among the several peoples, each in *ignorance of the others*, and it was only later, as a result of wars, embassies, alliances and commerce, that it came to be recognized as common to the entire human race.[29]

The method is 'a severe analysis of human thoughts about the human necessities or utilities of social life'. These are 'the two everlasting springs of the natural law of the gentes'.[30] The new science of society is then 'a history of human ideas'.[31] Each of the three epochs, that of the gods, the heroes, and the humans, has its natural law, although here we need concern ourselves only with the human. It began when 'the first men began to think humanly'[32] the evidence of which is the creation of institutions, starting with religion, marriage, and burial. They are the route along which 'the people strive to escape their brute nature'[33] by cultivating humanity and civility, enhancing needs and utilities, in other words preserving human life and improving the quality of all dimensions. By following the signs suggested by such artefacts as language and myth, customs, laws, and literature, we see how peoples move from primitive beginnings to a humane and civilized society, the two forming and progressing together. The principles guiding that progress, giving content of the science of society, are expressed in a series of axioms, the study of which richly rewards the effort.

Caution is needed in assessing the natural law of peoples. First, it does not mean that the route of any *gente* to humanity and civility is straight or smooth. It is well-described as 'a tug-and-scramble' based on personal effort and collective cooperation, while provoking conflict among groups and classes, each struggling to gain advantage over others to achieve what it wants and to defend what it has.[34] Conflict among classes, especially between the many and the few, the plebs and patricians, lords and vassals, landlords and tenants, workers and bosses, is not only normal but an essential element in forming relations and institutions, and advancing well-being. Secondly, neither the ideal nor the reality is to reach a state of organic wholeness, harmony, and unity. No need to invoke the imagery of a body politic mirroring the body natural where all parts have their place and all work in unison to make the whole. Such images do not match the reality of division, discord, and distrust. The better concept, the more realistic aim, is *equilibrium*, the idea that for a people to realize its purposes a state of balance among persons, groups, and classes has to be struck and sustained. Not a balance once reached fixed for all time, but fluid and open to adjustment as sentiments form and conditions change. The

29 *Ibid* p 146.
30 *Ibid* pp 61–62.
31 *Ibid* p 62.
32 *Ibid* p 62.
33 Berlin: *Vico & Herder*, p 25.
34 On *tugging* and *scrambling*, see Notes.

balance is inevitably precariously perched, preserved only by effort and restraint, and soon lost in turmoil. Each people and each generation has to find a point of equilibrium, and then establish a constitutional order to guard it. Stretching across ancient Israel, republican Rome, medieval Europe, and modern notions of democracy, the possible points of equilibrium and the threats to each are many.

Thirdly, the warning is worth repeating that although each people begins with the same three institutions of religion, marriage, and burial, from there the paths divide. Sentiments and dispositions, social relations and institutions are born and bred by each people at varying pace, influenced by local factors and forces, some of human origin, others from external sources, all to the delight of the philologist in studying and comparing them. The natural law of peoples insists only that the ultimate purpose, the final motivation, the organizing principle is to serve well-being, improve the quality of life, and enhance civility and humanity. Finally, despite such unevenness among people, we shall see how on the common base some have erected ideas, relations, and institutions which have lasted over time and across peoples. Their origins in Roman ideas and Roman law, they have endured among European peoples and stretched far beyond. I refer to the notions of civic and juridical equality, and justice the offspring, based on and expressing an idea moderating relations among persons otherwise deeply unequal, and between persons and state power. We shall see as this study progresses how central the concepts of civil and juridical equality and justice are to the constitutional order.

7. Science of society to science of constitutions

Vico's science of society extends to the constitutional order as one segment.[35] By science he meant gathering evidence, drawing on the evidence to form concepts, using the concepts to give meaning to human action. Vico drew from the historical evidence the concepts of civility and humanity the advancing of which is the principal purpose of social relationships. Civility and humanity generate more specific interests, needs and utilities in Vico's terms, well-being in all its forms. The aim now is to apply this model of purposive action to the constitutional order. The people know aspects of well-being are best advanced by the institutions of government, which means entering the constitutional field, restraining their own actions, and entering relations with officials. The first stage of the enquiry is to examine evidence of the people's attitudes and opinions, their points of view towards the constitutional order, for ease of reference, the *patterns of opinion*. Reviewing the historical record, one soon notices among the people several patterns, each based on practical experience, each a set of understandings and expectations of the

[35] *Society* is analysed and defined in Chapter IV; here I use the term in the general sense of the totality of social relations and social spheres.

constitutional order. That leads to the next stage, drawing out concepts innate in the evidence and formulating models of relations between the people and officials. At the final stage, the models are used as frames through which to look back on and make sense of experience. This approach guides the enquiry through the following chapters.

Before examining the patterns of opinion, the idea of the people's being the authors of the constitutional order, an idea much repeated, needs to be considered and corrected. Let us return to Adam Smith who, in an account of the origins of the state, notices from the evidence how the solitary efforts of each person to advance their well-being are augmented by the collective power of social relations, the state being one of the many forms they take. In an age of hunters the state is not needed; government begins with the age of shepherds:

> Property makes it absolutely necessary. When once it has been agreed that a cow or a sheep shall belong to a certain person not only when in his possession but wherever it may have strayed, it is absolutely necessary that the hand of government should be continually held up and the community assert their power to preserve the property of the individuals.[36]

The people, far from being passive subjects, are the authors of government, 'assert their power to preserve the property' of each. And to that end they confer on a few part of their own power and authorize its use for certain purposes. The shepherds' appointing a few to protect their flocks shows they are the authors of government, which they *authorize* by granting power of rule to a few and setting the terms. The peasants of Gagliano held similar views. In rejecting the Italian state because it was neither authored nor authorized by them, they conceived of a state of their own making, serving the purposes of their community. The trouble is neither Smith nor the peasants realized that a state, even one created by the people themselves, once established tends to detach itself from its origins, sever its moorings, gain autonomy and independence, and become a resource sought after. Authorship and authorization are rendered irrelevant or sustained by fictions and of no use in understanding the constitutional order. The people in practice confront the state looming fortress-like over them, forcing them to shelter within, on terms set by the few. With that perception framing the enquiry, let us turn attention to the patterns of opinion among the people, to their understandings, expectations, and experience of the constitutional order.

The metaphor of a *fortress* promotes one pattern of opinion, that of a *field* another.[37] *Fortress* suggests the people accepting strong rule that serves some aspects of well-being, protection and security in particular. Outside the fortress lies the

[36] A Smith: *Lectures on Jurisprudence*, p 208.
[37] Introduced in Chapter II.

field, which the people consider more open to ways of cultivation, for their being engaged and having influence. In the people's opinion the field has the potential as an instrument to well-being in a fuller and more satisfying manner. Before exploring the field and charting the potential, there are other currents of opinion among the people to extract. One source to tap, a trickle not a torrent, approaches the constitutional order as a means to freedom, the freedom that comes with the people being in charge of their affairs and ruling themselves. Evidence is abundant of the three patterns in historical experience, running in parallel at some points and intersecting, at others confronting and competing, as will be seen in later chapters. Another pattern of opinion, less familiar but seminal to social understanding, appears when a community rejects and refuses to engage with the constitutional order. The rejection can be absolute or in part. To the peasants of Gagliano, the Italian constitutional order was so alien and an enemy to their well-being, they wanted nothing to do with it. Rejection is more likely to be partial, triggered by groups or sectors who, after bitter experience and persistent frustration, decide rebellion be the only route to well-being. The peasants and rebels are not to be confused with the anarchists, who display another pattern of opinion in denying the need for a constitutional order, considering their well-being better served without one. The peasants and rebels, knowing the value of a well-working order, reject the one in place because it fails both to respect their community and to provide for well-being as they expect. Other patterns of opinion may be drawn from the historical experience of communities and peoples. Each source of evidence reveals the opinion, the sentiments and dispositions, of persons, groups, and sectors as to the nature of the constitutional order, how it fosters purpose and contributes to well-being. My purpose in the following chapters, in summary, is to analyse the several patterns and the concepts implicit in them; to propose several models of the relationship between the people and officials; consider their appeal and their drawbacks, all from the point of view of the people; then to draw from the evidence a fourth pattern.[38]

The evidence from historical experience prompts two comments on the task and the obstacles. Persons, communities, and peoples begin with a common purpose of civility and humanity, from which follow notions of well-being, some common to all, others particular to time and place, legacies partly of history, partly of fortune. Each community settles on a sense of civility and humanity, forms a scheme of well-being at different levels, fixed with degrees of permanence and detail, which provide the reasons for action and the justification. The peasants of Gagliano in condemning the state had no need to invoke the deep foundation of purpose, for already in place were settled ideas of community, social relations, and social spheres to guide action and from which to view action. As the social

[38] For more on scientific understanding of society see Notes.

structure firms and matures, civility and humanity the foundation of purpose fade into the background but are never lost. Always there in reserve, a base to resort to, a source to consult in times of trouble, to inspire in confronting the unexpected; a base from which to view and judge ideas and practices within or from outside. The people approach the constitutional order within that framework of purpose.

The other comment concerns constitutional order. It is not designed as the people would wish, nor run as they would want, but nevertheless has the potential to advance their well-being. The system of rule being already in place is a problem. The grip of select sectors dictating the design and dominating the practice has to be loosened; officials weaned from undue influence of a few and coaxed to attend to the interests of all. The tendency of agencies to autonomy and independence has to be curbed, the risk of misrule contained. The task of confronting the fortress of state and guiding it to advance the people's purposes is daunting; but if well-being is to be advanced, there is no alternative. Daunted but not defeated, the people come armed with a sense of purpose, a set of priorities, a base of values, and a notion of how government can be a positive force in achieving the ends of social life. Given the formidable task of converting the fortress into a field, taming the power of the state and turning it to their advantage, and the risks, why not use other means of advancing purpose? The answer is plain and compelling. The agencies of state have the capacity to do things and achieve ends not easily done or achieved by other means, other forms of collective action, although just where the dividing line runs is disputed.[39] The utility of the state is worth repeating. Besides protecting person and property, the agencies have a dynamic role in delivering social goods, inserting values into social relations, and regulating private affairs to enable all to improve their lives. The issue for the people is how to ensure the power of the state is used to their advantage. How can the people break out of the fortress and open up the field? The *freedom* model proposes the people take over the field and govern themselves, to some the obvious and only solution. The appeal is plain but the drawbacks daunting, which explains why historically the model has been a minor theme in the mission of the people.[40] The only option left is to return to the *field*, to regard the constitutional order as an arena in which persons, groups, and sectors encounter each other, sometimes cooperating at other times competing, sharing some common grounds, contesting others. The tug is uneven, the scramble unbalanced, and yet despite all, effective and reasonably sound government can result. Success is never assured and achievement is variable; but the process can be charted, the dangers marked, and the traps disabled.

Signs appear in the course of the enquiry of a fresh understanding of the people's perception of the constitutional order, how they see their place within it, and their relations with officials. An approach subtle and still forming, yet grounded in the

[39] See the discussion in Chapter I.
[40] The *freedom* model, or the people ruling themselves, is analysed in Chapters XII and XIII.

people's sentiments and dispositions towards the constitutional order. An approach that on one hand registers the fortress, its permanence and persistence, and is aware of the guile of its agents, even when disguised as representatives; and on the other hand resists the temptation of freedom at all costs by ruling themselves. The evidence points to another way between the poles of perceiving and encountering the constitutional order, another pattern of opinion to be investigated. An intuition still to be defined and nurtured. Not to govern, but to be engaged in governing, and yet stand back from, and keep watch over the processes of governing. *Keeping*, an appealing image, suggests a distinct pattern of opinion among the people towards the constitutional field. As keepers the people try to make sure the constitutional order serves the well-being of all its members, individually and as a whole. What it means to the people in practice, and its potential, are given content in the following chapters by enquiring into the evidence, proposing a model, and then showing its place in the constitutional order. The enquiry, culminating in the last chapter, begins by noticing that, despite the forces ranged against them and the obstacles, the constitutional order has the potential to advance humanity and civility as they the people conceive it.

Before enquiring further, a brief return to Hume for a last reflection on the nature of the constitutional order, implied but unspoken. With the fortress framing the constitutional landscape and hints of the field in vision, we now see that Hume's account, despite a certain ambiguity, indeed captures the social reality. It is the people who are poised or perched, or to be more exact caught between the two, the fortress and the field. That they be caught, at times veering towards one or the other, trying to mark a steady course between the two, and just occasionally succeeding, is the social reality. Yet, the existence of the field and the potential being only hinted at, the task now is to enter and show how the peoples' aspirations and expectations beyond bare benefits might be met; how the processes of governing could contribute; how the relations between the people and officials could be redefined. Of being *keepers*, keepers of the constitutional field and the activities within it, appeals as a working title, the full meaning, the powers and responsibilities entailed, to be left till later.[41]

A final tribute to Vico who shows how to move beyond philology, beyond the practice and experience Smith documents, to a theory of society. He would have found Smith's account to be consistent with his own. Had he rested there, his place as an historian of ideas of originality would have been secure. His ambition knowing no such bounds, he went on to unearth the foundation of human action, from which human endeavour flows and by which it can be explained. Its essence should now be clear and is simply stated. Humans have by their nature a disposition

[41] For further explanation of theory, see M Weber: *Economy and Society* (eds) G Roth and C Wittich (Berkeley: University of California Press, 1968), Part 1; HLA Hart: *The Concept of Law*. For commentary, see DJ Galligan: *Law in Modern Society*.

to live well and to devote their energy and enterprise not only to securing their needs but to advancing all that adds to the quality of life. To achieve that purpose, social relations form and institutions are created, self-restraint is imposed and support given. Included among institutions is that of government, a set of agencies and officials, which by performing certain tasks and providing certain services contributes to the purpose of living well. In practice, in stark reality, the road to living well is not straight, but twists and turns, often leads nowhere, is plagued by pirates and prone to head in the wrong direction. Despite the dangers and the setbacks, the spirit to live well and securely is undaunted and advances can be made. The point of social understanding is to chart that passage, to plot the course of human relations and institutions, to show how it is that the menial worker can buy a linen shirt made by a thousand hands, how the arts and sciences can flourish even in adversity and add immeasurably to human well-being. And not least how the agencies of government are indispensable to the purpose of living well.

Notes

Theory and Experience

The social theory of constitutional authority proposed here begins with Weber. A few points of guidance:

(i) Social theory is a science concerned with the 'interpretive understanding of social action and therefore with a causal explanation of its course and consequences'.
(ii) The interpretative understanding or meaning of action may be the 'actual meaning' of the person acting or 'the theoretically conceived *pure type*'.
(iii) Pure type means the 'subjective meaning attributed to the hypothetical actor or actors in a given type of action'.
(iv) Explanation requires 'a grasp of the complex of meaning in which an actual course of understandable action thus interpreted belongs'. Understanding is 'the interpretive grasp of the meaning present in . . . a scientifically formulated pure type (an ideal type)'.
(v) A correct interpretation of action is reached 'when the overt action and the motives have both been correctly apprehended' and 'their relation has become meaningfully comprehensible'.
(vi) For social understanding 'the object of cognition is the subjective meaning-complex of action'.

Taken from M Weber: *Economy & Society*, pp 4–22. For more of Weber: *Politics as a Vocation* in Gerth and Wright Mills, pp 77–128.

RN Lebow catches the essence of Weber's account. Pure or ideal types are concepts with an empirical dimension. A concept is 'an analytical accentuation of aspects of one or more attributes of a phenomenon to create a mental construct that will never be encountered in practice, but against which real world actions can be measured'. He goes on to distinguish *ideal types from the* real world: ideal types give 'a picture of what a pure world would be like' and 'a benchmark for measuring how closely it is approached by real worlds': *A Cultural Theory of International Relations* (Cambridge: Cambridge University Press, 2008), pp 93–95.

Elinor Ostrom explains theory and the relationship to experience: 'Theoretical enquiry involves a search for regularities. It involves abstraction from the complexity of a field setting, followed by positing of theoretical variables that underlie observed complexities. Specific models of a theory involve further abstraction and simplification for the purpose of still finer analysis of the logical relationships among variables in a closed system': *Governing the Commons*, p 24.

For further discussion

S Eliaeson: *Max Weber's Methodologies* (Cambridge: Polity Press, 2002); M Weber: *From Max Weber: Essays in Sociology* (eds) HH Gerth and C Wright Mills, pp 55–74.

HLA Hart crisply states the relationship between philosophy, here the *concept of law*, and social understanding: although his analysis is 'primarily designed for the student of jurisprudence', he hopes that 'it may also of use to those whose chief interests are in sociology': *The Concept of Law*, Preface. I should go a step farther and say the philosophical analysis of concepts is not just of use to, but a critical element of, social understanding. A second point is worth noting. Hart 'raised questions which may well be said to be about the meaning of words'. That the analysis of words may reveal meanings of social importance is verified at several points in the following chapters. On this matter, Hart and Vico were fellow travellers. On Vico, see for instance Axiom 65: *New Science*, p 98. For further analysis, see DJ Galligan: 'Legal Theory and Empirical Research': *Oxford Handbook of Empirical Legal Research* (eds) P Cane and HM Kritzer (Oxford: Oxford University Press, 2010), pp 976–1001 and 'Concepts the Currency of Social Explanation of Law: A Review of the Later Work of William Twining' (2015) 35 *Oxford Journal of Legal Studies* pp 144–65.

Adam Smith and social relations

For Adam Smith's account of the division of labour and the role it has in meeting needs and improving lives: *Lectures on Jurisprudence*, especially pp

337–55. Further analysis of Smith's ideas relevant to the text and more generally: *The Theory of Moral Sentiments* (published 1759) (London: Penguin Books, 2009) and *The Wealth of Nations* (1776) (London: G Bell and Sons, 1925) especially Book III.

Vico's ideas and commentaries

Isaiah Berlin's essay catches the spirit of Vico and draws out the main ideas of the New Science in: *Vico and Herder: Two Studies in the History of Ideas* (London: Hogarth Press, 1976). Among the many commentaries, the following I have found helpful:

L Pompa: *Vico: A Study of the New Science* (Cambridge: Cambridge University Press, 1990).

J Goetsch: *Vico's Axioms: The Geometry of the Human World* (New Haven: Yale University Press, 1995).

Berlin sums-up Vico's *new science* in this way: 'a theory of history founded on a metaphysical conception of men's nature as driven by its own inner purposes': *Vico and Herder*, p 76. Purposes guide action: 'This kind of cosmic, purposive tendency, which moulds passions and desires into institutions and forms of social life in an intelligible pattern': p 75. Society is made by men and women; 'the principles of society are found within the modification of our own human mind': p 80.

Vico and the tug-and-scramble

We may wonder what Vico would have made of the image of a *scramble*, even more of the *tug and scramble*? His knowledge of Hobbes, Selden, and other English writers suggests he knew the English language. *Scramble* has several shades of meaning, perhaps the most apt for present purposes is: *to take part in a physical or other struggle to secure as much as possible of something from competitors*. The equivalent in Italian would be the combination of *gara, corsa, lotta,* none quite catching the spirit of a *scramble*. As for *tug*: to pull vigorously, in Italian, *tirare vigorosamente, strappare*; the noun: *uno strappo, una tirata*.

A sample of Vico's maxims

On common sense: 'Common sense is judgement without reflection, shared by an entire class, an entire people, an entire nation, or the entire human race': XII, 142.

On common ideas: 'Uniform ideas originating among entire people unknown to each other have a common ground in truth': XIII, 144.

On philosophy and philology: 'Philosophy contemplates reason, whence comes knowledge of the true; philology observes that of which human choice is author': V, 129 The same axiom shows how the philosophers failed by half in not giving certainty to their reasoning by appeal to the authority of the philologians, and likewise how the latter failed by half in not taking care 'to give their authority the sanction of truth by appeal to the reasoning of the philosophers': X, 138.

On scientific enquiry

Scientific enquiry begins with metaphysics, 'which seeks its proofs not in the eternal world but within the modifications of the mind of him who meditates it. And since this world of nations has certainly been made by men, it is within these modifications that its principles should have been found': *New Science*, p 74.

The state as necessary for human well-being

JH Strayer links the strengthening of state formation to the growing sense that the state is necessary for human welfare. And that to serve human welfare, concentration of power in the state is also necessary. To weaken the state is to threaten the future of society, from which it follows the state should take any steps to ensure its own survival: *The Medieval Origins of the Modern State* (Princeton: Princeton University Press, 1970), p 108. Strayer appears to support the fortress image of state.

On authority

In a commentary on the Digest of Roman law, Azo writes of rulers as *rectores*, which is to say officials whose authority is assigned not in the form of donation but as 'a matter of administrative convenience'. The people act for themselves and coordinate their relations to advance common purposes, but it is convenient and effective to assign some tasks to officials: P Azo: *Questiones et al*, quoted in Q Skinner: *Visions of Politics* Volume II (Cambridge: Cambridge University Press, 2002).

John Watts writes of medieval kingship: 'The royal dignity and majesty were primarily sustained not by the king's private resources, but by the communal power of his satisfied subjects. Both the powers and the interests of the king were tied to those of the *communitas*. Rule was less a force imposed by the king upon the realm than a reaction which his proper functioning elicited from it.' The king 'was the vehicle for a communal enterprise for the realization of communal interests': J Watts: *Henry VI and the Politics of Kingship* (Cambridge: Cambridge University Press, 1996), p 29. The point is that the ruler, having no interest other than the interest of those ruled, rules for the good of the people. It is tempting to think of the ruler as an agent appointed to do certain things on behalf of the people. This is accurate to a point but not wholly, for the ruler has plenary power, which means autonomy in deciding on action. The relationship between ruler and the people is more complex and nuanced than that between agent and principal.

IV
Purpose to Action

1. Sequence of purpose to action

The purpose at the foundation of human action, recovered by Smith and Vico in the recesses of history, is to advance civility and humanity, well-being of all kinds. The task now is to ascend to the surface and to consider how in practice purpose is turned into action. That means entering the structure of society to show how interests emerge, patterns of opinion form among the people, and action results. The enquiry has several stages: to analyse the sequence from purpose to action; clarify the concept of interest; examine social relations and social spheres, add a sketch of field and power; draw out the means the parties have to keep social relationships to purpose, the quintet of actions; and lastly, to apply the analysis to the constitutional order.

The sequence of action unfolds in this way: pursuit of a purpose generates interests; an interest gives rise to a sentiment; a sentiment gives rise to a disposition; a disposition leads to action. Each step in the sequence is contingent. Purpose is not necessarily pursued; nor an interest arouse a sentiment, nor a sentiment stimulate a disposition, nor a disposition result in action. For one step to follow from the one before, certain conditions have to be met. Take a simple case. Suppose you have several pens acquired over the years, much used now less so. You value the pens for a number of reasons. You have benefited writing with them, they are pleasing to hold in your hand, you admire their elegance. Plainly you have an interest in the pens, an interest that creates in you a sentiment towards them, a feeling of their value to you. The sentiment gives rise to a disposition to look after them. The disposition prompts action, to keep them clean and safe and in working order, to have them serviced and insured against loss and damage.

Slight variations alter the sequence. The pens have served you well but now are rarely used; they clutter the desk and maintaining them is an expense. You still have an interest in the pens, a feeling or sentiment of their value, and an inclination or disposition to look after them, although weaker than when they were in daily use. The sentiment wanes as time passes until the pens, edged to the back of the drawer, fade into fond memory. Except for one, an old Mont Blanc, the empress of fountain pens, which you prize and for which you still have a lively sentiment. Let the other pens gather dust, get lost, perish, but not the Mont Blanc still occasionally put to use and an object of affection. Your sentiment for this one pen, being as strong as ever, stimulates and sustains a disposition to take action to look after it and keep it in working order. Disposed to act to that end, you learn that the pen

Keepers of the Common Good. D.J. Galligan, Oxford University Press. © D.J. Galligan 2024.
DOI: 10.1093/9780198907398.003.0004

needs repairing, a specialist task and costly. Other bills await attention, the pen is not a priority, and you decide not to have the work done, the disposition to keep it in good order overridden by other dispositions more urgent. And so the Mont Blanc, still admired and valued, cannot compete with more pressing dispositions to act and is left to gentle decline. The tale of the pens contains an account of action, a logical sequence from interest to action, an account of general application, not least as we shall see in the constitutional context.

2. 'Reason is nothing but interest'[1]

The concepts of *interest*, *sentiment*, and *disposition* need to be clarified. The word *interest* has several shades of meaning deriving from its origins in Latin via French.[2] Interest as a noun means a benefit or advantage, something of value to the person. Some interests, the most obvious, confer tangible benefits or advantages: an interest in property, in being educated, in practising a profession, for instance. Other interests are less tangible, more matters of concern, things that engage attention. Some follow from ideas such as that children not live in poverty, a suspect not be wrongly convicted, free speech be protected. Others are tied to aesthetic experience and satisfactions, the beauty of nature, the piece of music, and the painting by Rafaello, even the skill of the batsman. The list could go on but enough has been said to show that *interest* means something valued by somebody for a reason, the focus here on interests relating to the constitutional order. What is valued is partly subjective according to the sensibility and preference of the person, and partly objective in being commonly shared. All have an interest in well-being, their own and that of others. To have needs met, the essentials of life provided, is the base of well-being on which we try to build a good life, one of fulfilment and enjoyment, success and satisfaction. Many things contribute, including friendships and relationships, art and literature, nature in all its forms, and much else. To have needs met and ways of improving the quality of life are together essential dimensions of well-being. We know others have similar interests to defend and extend, and normally we value their well-being as well as our own. All such matters of value, our own interests, the interests of others, and abstract interests generate matching sentiments that dispose us to take action for their support and cultivation.

The regard one has for the interests of another appears both indirectly and directly. Indirectly where advancing the interest of another is incidental to, an effect of advancing one's own; directly when the purpose, the reason for action, is to benefit

[1] James Harrington discussed in 'Machiavelli and the English Revolution'. See P Rahe `in *Machiavelli's Liberal Republican Legacy* (Cambridge: Cambridge University Press, 2006).

[2] The Latin origin is *inter-esse* meaning to be between, suggesting a tie between the person and something, a tie constituted by the person valuing the something.

another. Consider tipping. In one case you give no thought to whether the waiters are allowed to keep the tip, nor whether they want or expect it. You leave a tip out of habit or perhaps feel by convention an obligation. In another case, by generously tipping you act out of self-interest, taking action to ensure the waiters are attentive on your next visit. You are likely to have an additional reason. You know the waiters will benefit, that their interests are served by the gratuity. In satisfying your own interest, you advance the waiters' interests. If you were to meet one of them made redundant and in need, you would be moved by their plight and inclined to help, your intention to serve the distressed waiter's interest. You are bound to feel satisfaction at being able to help and at the gratitude shown, and in that sense your own interest is served. So, in one case you act wholly out of self-interest; in another, in order to satisfy self-interest, you benefit the interest of another; in a third, your reason for action is to serve the interest of another and perhaps consequentially your own.

That interests provide reasons for action is for Hume the key to constitutional authority. That an action *a* serve one's interest, or that the interest of another be advanced by action *a*, is a reason for the action. The equation is not quite complete. That you benefit from having an attentive waiter seems a good reason for a generous tip. There are, however, as shown above two more steps to take, two other concepts to insert to make the connection between interest and action. Having an attentive waitress makes my meal more enjoyable and is likely to create a matching sentiment. But suppose you neither care much what you eat nor whether the waitress is diligent in serving your needs or not. It is in your interest to have a waiter who gets the food to your table; but being absorbed in other matters, whether the service is good, the waitress attentive, is to you a matter of indifference. It just is your habit to tip generously for reasons no longer remembered; that is what people of your station in life do. Whether the waiter benefits or not is equally of no concern, creates no sentiment in a distracted soul. The reason for your action in this case is neither to advance self-interest nor that of another. The concepts of sentiment and disposition linking the two are missing, other than a weak sentiment born of habit. A sentiment leads to a disposition to act, but as noted not every sentiment creates a disposition to act; not every disposition to act leads to action.

There is another kind of interest to add, best called *abstract*. If you go to the city of Urbino, enter the municipal art gallery, amongst the wealth of art your gaze is drawn to a small painting, a portrait of a young woman. It beckons you even before you learn the artist is Raffaello. In looking at the portrait you are likely to feel pleasure and satisfaction, adding to your enjoyment of life. There is more to the encounter. You admire the portrait as a beautiful object, just as you admire Raffaello for having the talent to create such beauty. The same appreciation, the sense of something valued, is stimulated in all sorts of ways. The personality of another person, the architecture of a building or a work of literature, a piece of music or the beauties of nature, and many more. Each creates a similar sentiment of something valued. Our sense of value, of something being valuable and valued, is often aroused by less obvious objects and artefacts. I admire the Constitution of the Republic of Turkey for the way it expresses the concept of sovereignty, analytically accurate and rendered with elegance and economy. I hold the text in esteem regardless of whether it is in practice a sound constitution or contributes to a commendable system of government, or in practice advances the welfare of the Turkish people.

Other segments of social life arouse the same sentiment of appreciation and admiration, justice a leading case. That persons, whoever they are and whatever occurred, be treated justly is of value. It is of value to know that if the situation were to occur, I would be treated justly; it is also of value to me to know the same applies to others. That our interests are served by living in a society respecting justice creates a sentiment strong enough to stimulate a disposition to give encouragement and support. That does not exhaust the reasons for valuing justice. We value justice as a good, an abstract good, without needing to attach it to another. Other ideas, liberty among them,[3] are valued in the same way, create similar sentiments and dispositions, and prompt action. It is common among farming communities for one to help another, bale the hay, dip the sheep, harvest the wheat, without thought of payment or reward, prompted by ideas of neighbourliness, supported by an unspoken expectation of reciprocity. In each case, from the Raffaello portrait to justice to neighbourly farmers, the object or artefact, the idea or concept or practice is of value to me independently of my self-interest or yours. In addition to any practical benefits, each is valued as a good in itself, for its qualities, and so contributes to my or your well-being in that abstract sense. Each creates a sentiment of value, which may lead to a disposition to act in certain ways, to protect the portrait, to promote that concept of sovereignty, to help with the harvest, to stand up for justice. While that is one rather obvious reason for valuing such goods, there is another less obvious. The beauty of art, justice, and neighbourliness are elements of a civilized social order, contribute in Vico's terms to humanity and civility.

3. Sentiment, disposition, action

The word sentiment derives from the Latin verb *sentire* to feel. The verb is used transitively with a direct object, or intransitively meaning to feel with respect to or about something. The intransitive sense is here the more useful. The Latin verb found its way into English via the French *sentiment*. Amongst the subtleties of meaning, the most apt is 'what one feels with regard to something; a mental attitude of approval or disapproval'.[4] The idea of value fits well: the sentiment of interest

[3] Considered in Chapter XII:2.
[4] *The Oxford English Dictionary*.

here is a feeling that something is of value and is valued. Your interest in your own well-being is to your advantage; but more, it is something you value, something creating in you a certain sentiment. Sentiments have their own rules. Each person has a host of sentiments in the course of a day, some lasting others passing, the charting of which for just one person would be a daunting task. Sentiments vary in strength from the powerful and compelling to the faintly felt and lightly held. They come and go, even those seemingly central to one's being are liable to change and to adjust over time, while others are as fickle as one's mood. They need not form a harmonious whole, rather, around a settled core competition, inconsistency, even conflict are rife. A sentiment, even one firmly held and highly valued, does not lead inevitably to action or even to a disposition to action, the path from sentiment to disposition to action being strewn with obstacles and distractions.

To understand how one leads to the other we need to attend to dispositions. Its origins in the Latin *disponere* the transitive verb means to dispose of or to deal with, while the intransitive means being disposed towards something. The intransitive again suits the context. From the verb to *be disposed towards* something comes the noun *disposition*, which relates to a state of mind, an inclination to act.[5] The disposition to act follows from, is prompted by, a prior sentiment. Whether one leads to the other is contingent on two factors, one the strength of the sentiment, the other competing factors intervening. The sentiment your pens arouse is not strong enough to create a disposition, except for the Mont Blanc. If you think people should rise above adversity by their own efforts, your sentiment towards the plight of the redundant waiter would not prompt a disposition to help. To do so would prolong the adversity and so in your opinion not be in the waiter's interest. The difference between the two concepts is subtle and neglected but critical. Each signifies a state of mind, the one passive from which nothing flows necessarily, the other active in initiating action. The move from sentiment to disposition means a shift from the passive to the active, a shift without which there is no action. Dispositions share some of the marks of sentiments. Each of us has many, some long-lasting, others passing, some central to life, others peripheral. As with sentiments, dispositions differ in strength and power; they come and go, shift and change, some working in harmony, others in competition. And in the same way that a sentiment does not always stimulate a disposition, action does not necessarily follow from a disposition. Action results only if certain conditions, the nature of which depends on the context, are met. My disposition to help the waiter comes to nothing because I have no money on me or because I have none to spare. You might feel a higher degree would advance your career and after thinking about it you form a disposition to enrol next year. Until you fall ill and are unable to

[5] *Ibid.*

proceed, or because as the deadline approaches your disposition is dampened by the prospect of the hard work and the fear of failure.

Finally *action* where origins as ever are instructive. The verb *to act*, from the Latin *agere*, is an intransitive verb of motion fertile in meaning. Of most use here is the process of taking action, doing something for some end. In the Italian version *agire* means to deal with some matter, not act aimlessly but for a purpose. A purpose which, according to the sequence, is specified by the disposition and the prior sentiment. The sentiment of affection for your Mont Blanc gives rise to a disposition to act, to look after it, to keep it safe and serviced. To restate the logic of action: *purpose* gives rise to *interests*, which being valued by X generate *sentiments*, which may induce in X *dispositions* to act, which may lead X to take action. The four concepts combine to form the sequence of human behaviour. Our interests, the things we value, we want to protect and advance. We normally, but not invariably, value the interests of others being treated in a similar way. The logic of each situation is different, one serving my interest, the other serving the interest of another. But they are not as different as at first sight appears because, even in the case of direct altruism, I derive satisfaction from, have an interest in another's interests being served. Being altruistic enhances my quality of life and so my sense of satisfaction. The third category, that of ideas as interests, also has a place in the logic of action, for ideas give rise to sentiments and dispositions, from which action follows.[6] A model of social action is ready to assemble showing the sequence from purpose to action. We have learnt how peoples down the ages and across cultures have the common purpose of advancing civility and humanity, which includes fostering the well-being of all. Well-being consists of self-interest, interest in others, and abstract interests. The advancement of civility and humanity depends on the people, on their taking action. Action is the end of a sequence from purpose, to interests, to sentiments, to dispositions. The sequence is ready to be inserted into the frame of common purposes, the two together being essential in understanding social action and in forming a theory of constitutional authority.

4. Prudence, justice, and beneficence

In the *Theory of Moral Sentiments*, Adam Smith charts the sentiments binding people together. From his own enquiry into the foundations of social life, he settled on the concept of *moral sentiments* that guide and support the people's efforts in advancing well-being and improving society, including support for government. From Smith's account it is enough to draw an outline of how moral sentiments relate to the efforts of the people in forming stable and successful social relationships.

[6] *Ideas* in relation to action are discussed in Chapter II:2.

The sentiments guiding practical action are prudence, justice, and beneficence.[7] *Prudence* is essentially self-regarding, concern for one's own interests, one's own needs and utility. *Justice* is both self-regarding and other-regarding. It is in my interest to be treated justly and fairly, to have what is due to me, while equally it is in the interest of each other person to be treated in that way. I cannot coherently claim justice for myself without conceding the same to others. Justice, while a sentiment critical to social relations, is 'but a negative virtue'.[8] *Beneficence* means 'concern for the happiness of others'[9] and is other-regarding, prompting us 'to promote the happiness of others',[10] since each person by nature has an 'interest in the fortune of others'.[11]

The three sentiments make possible social relations and, in turn, society as an aggregation of relationships.[12] The sentiments, at one level innate to the human mind, at the social level have their origins in shared interests, from which arise dispositions to act prudently, justly, and with beneficence. The sentiments permeate social relations of all kinds, giving guidance and structure. We all share such sentiments, although how intensely they are felt and how consistently practised are variables. The higher the value placed on being prudent, just, and beneficent, the more forceful the sentiments and dispositions to action. The more firmly they are embedded in social relations, the more secure the social bonds and the more stable the community, qualities weakened by wavering commitment and endangered by its absence. The natural sentiments are confirmed, nurtured, and strengthened by practice, by being engaged in social relations. The sentiments enter into relations and shape ways of thinking; they serve as standards of right action learnt from the earliest age, their appeal backed by sanctions. Within social relations the three moral sentiments give rise to sentiments and dispositions suitable to the situation.[13] Prudence guides us towards courses of action likely to contribute to meeting our needs and improving our lives. The prudent person engages actively in social relationships, each of which helps in reaching a desired end.[14] Along the road to ends, justice moderates action by overseeing the distribution of burdens and benefits, protecting us from certain kinds of harm, and where inflicted providing redress. Beneficence bestows on each 'an earnest desire to render the

[7] The discussion of such flows through *The Theory of Moral Sentiments.*

[8] *Ibid* p 99.

[9] *Ibid* p 308.

[10] *Ibid* p 308.

[11] *Ibid* p 13.

[12] *The Theory of Moral Sentiments* may justifiably be read, and commonly is, as a normative account of moral principles. Here, it is the sociological dimension that is of interest, by which I mean the place of moral sentiments in social relationships.

[13] Piaget's study of childhood and how children acquire and learn suitable sentiments illustrates Smith's theory. See J Piaget: *The Moral Development of the Child* (New York: The Free Press, 1965).

[14] Utility includes, on Smith's account, not just tangible ends and outcomes but a host of qualities, *beauty* he calls it, such as the beauty of a building or a machine or a system of cooperation and coordination: *The Theory of Moral Sentiments*, pp 258 *ff.*

condition of our fellow citizens as safe, respectable, and happy as we can'.[15] The three sentiments combine to guide a community towards utility in the broad and generous sense of well-being; utility layered by intermediate goods and guiding values. The sentiments foster cooperation and coordination, mutual aid and support, concern and respect for others, an appreciation of abstract as well as tangible goods. They equip us with the means for successful social relations, to realize the well-being of all, and to give content to civility and humanity.

5. Social relations, spheres, fields

In asking how people engage in collective action, we encounter two approaches. One portrays society composed of individual persons striving by their own efforts to advance well-being. Each might decide to join with others in pursuing that end, but only if, judged by self-interest, that be the rational course to take. Much thought has gone into deciding under what conditions it is rational for such a person to combine with others and when to act alone.[16] An alternative is to begin not with the existential persona but the social, the person in a social setting, for after all as Montesquieu states 'man is born into society'.[17] Rather than the person deliberating on whether to join with others, each of us from the beginning is embedded in social relations. Social relations occur within a setting of social spheres, that is, ways of thinking, binding standards, and pressures to conform. We are from birth engaged in social relations and encircled by social spheres, each constituting and giving meaning to a segment of life, each exerting power over us. The combination of the two constitutes the structure of society. It is now time to say more about the three concepts and to show their place in the constitutional context.

The sentiments and dispositions we each have are partly personal and partly cultivated by social relations. The interaction between the personal and the collective varies in kind and intensity. A portion of our sentiments and dispositions, to borrow a word from Bourdieu, are *inculcated*, pressed persistently upon us by social relations. Another portion is a matter of personal preference and the capacity to form one's own judgement and exert one's own will. And a third where the two interact with social relations, confirming, cultivating, and strengthening a person's sentiments and dispositions, often fostering new ones, sometimes discarding and replacing the old. Confirmed in that the normal purpose of social relations is to serve the interests of the parties, to take action that advances in some way, major or minor, directly or indirectly, their mutual interests. Cultivated and strengthened by engaging with others, while directing them towards desired ends, the resulting

[15] *Ibid* pp 273 *ff.*
[16] For a review of the issues, see R Axelrod: *The Evolution of Cooperation* (London: Penguin, 1984).
[17] Montesquieu: *Spirit of the Laws* (Pleiade Edition, 1748).

restrictions on personal preferences made tolerable by the benefits gained. The terms are settled partly by agreement, partly by convention and practice, and partly dictated by law. Much of daily life is lived within and guided by social relations, although many actions are left to personal sentiment and disposition by chance or design, unbridled by relations with others. Social relations both stimulate sentiments and dispositions, and alter and adjust them according to the sentiments and dispositions of the parties, while being influenced by, indeed vulnerable to, external events and forces, some reinforcing some disrupting.

Each set of social relations occurs within a setting of understandings, standards, and sanctions. The concept of a *social sphere* catches the sense of this setting.[18] Social spheres have in common cognitive, normative, and regulative qualities. *Cognitive* in defining perception and ways of thinking about a matter; *normative* in setting the rules and conventions guiding action; *regulative* in imposing sanctions, from mildly critical attitudes to severe penalties. Each dimension complements and reinforces the others. The cognitive forms around and gives meaning to the subject matter, guides perceptions, and gives rise to sentiments and dispositions. Conventions and rules form, partly to add a normative edge to meanings and perceptions, partly to import values from the wider society. Both are reinforced by the pressure of sanctions, from mild to severe. Social spheres are loose and informal at one end, dense and formal at the other. They tend to go under other names, institution the most common, others embracing *practice, tradition*, and *network*. Social spheres vary in their density, in their force in guiding and constraining action, some tightly closed to variation or outside influence, others open and responsive to the sentiments and dispositions of those engaged, and to the flow of ideas and values from the wider environment. Social spheres guide action in both a positive and a negative sense, one enabling, the other restricting. They enable by supplying the means, the cognitive, normative, and regulative elements by which to achieve ends and purposes; restrict in constructing meanings and requiring compliance with standards. Some social spheres come and go, form and fade; others are stable over time, creating history and memory. Social spheres both guide action and are reinforced by action, and in that way are reflexive, last over time, and support continuity. Sentiments and dispositions lead to action; action reinforces sentiments and dispositions. Social spheres are dynamic and open to change, normally by degree and increment, sometimes abrupt and drastic.

Social relations and social spheres combine to form the structure of society. Action results from sentiments and dispositions, partly personal and partly cultivated, encouraged, and mandated within social relationships and social spheres.[19] The conduct of a seminar illustrates the interaction. The students enter with the common purpose of learning, prompted by a combination of interest in the subject

[18] *Social sphere* is explained more fully in DJ Galligan: *Law in Modern Society*, Chapter 6.
[19] A selection of authors and writings relevant to social relations and social spheres is given in *Notes*.

and need to pass the exam. They know the classroom is a space structured by modes of thought, settled standards, and expectations of self-restraint. The seminar begins with lecturer and students agreeing on ground rules: how the class be conducted; students to be prepared and ready to contribute; a break in the middle and end on time. Other conventions and rules are unspoken and taken for granted, some enabling some restricting. Guided by the purpose of the seminar, the students expect the lecturer to explain the issues, answer their questions, and treat them with respect and on an equal footing. They in return are required to be attentive, courteous, and appreciative. The lecturer is obliged to impart the knowledge needed to pass the exam, and expected to contain impatience at ignorance, conceal amusement at silliness, and be courteous. On the prohibitive side, no dancing on the desks, no wandering about, no overt flirting. The students are diverse culturally and ethnically, and come from all over, yet know the nature of a seminar, the purpose, the mutual obligations and expectations. They seem to know and to accept certain conventions and rules without their being stated. Such ways of behaving are neither agreed nor written down nor mandated by law. Yet, they are present and binding, breach met with adverse reactions by others, even being ejected from the class. The law is present: not to assault the lecturer or fellow students or make abusive comments or set fire to the classroom. And so the seminar proceeds on the basis of shared perceptions and understandings of the purpose and how to achieve it; rules some agreed, some implicit and assumed, some stated; sanctions hovering in the background. The social encounter among the students, and between them and the lecturer, is reproduced endlessly across the sweep of society embracing private relations and public.

That brings us to structure. What does it mean to talk of the structure of society? Even to ask in that way is misleading. It assumes an entity *society*, into the *structure* of which we now enquire. Suppose instead we ask what is meant by *society*. The answer is society consists of the aggregate of social relations and social spheres. Society is the structure formed by the totality of social relations and social spheres. Knowledge and understanding of society is gained by studying both sets; the more studied the more complete our knowledge. There are several stages. One looks to the nature and purpose of a relationship, the understandings of the parties, the terms on which it is conducted, and how it interacts with other relationships. The next stage considers the setting of meanings, standards, and regulation in which a relationship occurs. A third examines the interaction between a relationship and the setting. The scrutiny of social relations and social spheres leads back to the attitudes, understandings, and expectations of the parties, their sentiments and dispositions, at times mutually supportive, at other times competing and conflicting. Those of interest to constitutional authority are of two kinds. The secondary and more obvious is the relationship between the people and government. Secondary in the sense that it originates in and is a result of prior, primary relationships among the people. Rulers rule according to the terms of relations between them and the people, which terms derive from and depend on the underlying relations of status, economy, and power.

The structure of society is completed by adding one last concept, that of a *field*, the fertility and utility of which we have already glimpsed. The concept of field conveys the sense of an area of activity made up of social relations and social spheres directed towards common ends.[20] The primary meaning of *field* is a piece of ground traditionally bounded by fences or hedges. The concept extends figuratively beyond rustic origins to cover field of battle, to playing field, to any setting of social endeavour. Field fits well into the structure of society to indicate an arena of activity such as education and sport, religion and security, or the constitutional order. It is a way of grouping sets of social relations and social spheres that are reasonably discrete and distinct, but not wholly fenced-off from other sets. Structure is then layered with social relations at the base, social spheres encircling, sets of the two making up fields; the aggregate of fields constituting society. The concept of *field*, as we have already seen, fits well the constitutional order and figures prominently in the following account.

6. Power: 'then everything includes itself in power'[21]

The oligarchs of Florence in 1290 declared power is best left to 'the timely solicitude and careful meditation of prudent men privately consulted, whose decisions will, as a result of their wisdom and prudence, shine with the clarity of justice once they are made know to the general public'.[22] Notice the partnership of status, wisdom, and prudence. Men superior socially and economically, being by nature prudent and wise, are fit to hold power. Commenting on the union of social, economic, and political power, Matteo Villani enters a note of scepticism. Such men he remarks are capable of 'fostering the illusion' that they 'represented the common good of the whole community'.[23] Study of the constitutional order is from one point of view the study of power, the purposes and the distribution, how it is used and the risks. Power is common to social relations, a means to ends: power to rear the child and educate the pupil, get the job done and send the offender to jail.

The word power comes from the Latin verb *potere*: to be able to do or not do an act. Weber defines social power as having two qualities: one, the ability of a person or group to achieve their ends; the other, even if opposed by those subject to the

[20] On *field*, see Notes to the preceding chapter.
[21] W Shakespeare: *Troilus and Cressida*, Ulysses' speech to the Greek generals: Act 1: 3.
[22] Quoted in LM Najemy: *Corporatism and Consensus in Florentine Electoral Politics, 1280–1400* (Chapel Hill: University of North Carolina Press, 1982), p 13.
[23] M Villani: *Cronica di Matteo Villani* quoted in Najemy, p 215. In place of *illusion* we could insert *fiction*.

power.[24] The idea is sound but needs to be refined. Power is tied to ends, the means to ends, where the ends are variable, clear and defined on one side, subtle and refined on the other. For present purposes, ends are of two *kinds, force* and *influence*, the two critical concepts: power to force action and power to influence action. Officials have power not only to force obedience, but to influence the people in various ways by shaping sentiments and dispositions. *Force and influence* in many forms give structure to the relationship, in Hume's terms shape opinion. Power in blatant form brooks no opposition, tolerates no resistance. Often power acts by stealth not force, aimed at winning support rather than provoking resistance. One party influences the other by projecting an image of the social order composed of ideas and images of universal appeal. To these two qualities of power another has to be added. Power within a social relationship is sometimes one way, one party dominating the other, but normally power is shared, each party having some power over the others. The power of officials is patent, the people's less so, occasionally blunt but often nuanced, not obvious but effective. The very existence of a constitutional order depends on the people's restraining their raw power, even if it is rarely invoked. Short of that final act of force the people have powers of influence, some formally provided for, others naturally emerging in their relations with officials.

Let us now track several lines of power in the constitutional order. Between the two poles of power, one to command action and force obedience, the other to reject the system, sits the constitutional order. Within the bounds, power appears in other forms, wily and subtle, less blatant but just as virile, at times dictating at others influencing action. Who marks out and fences the constitutional field, who decides the layout within, involves power. The power to destroy lies with the people; the power to create is not so plain. On one view, the people confront a state already in place, their only power not to submit. Another reverses the order, the people preceding the state, its power their gift. [25] However winding and overgrown the path between the two, the state has its origins in and flows from the power of the people. This happens on the rare occasions the people design the constitution. Even then just how much is their work varies, often under scrutiny less than appears, and anyhow lapses with the next generation. Nevertheless, it is hard to find a constitution, ancient, medieval, or modern not proclaimed to be the work of the people. Soft power is now at work projecting the constitutional order as if the work of the people.[26] The people might be persuaded by the fiction and, as authors, think the constitution to be theirs and that, despite appearances, they are in charge. Aware of the fiction, they are likely to be sceptical. They know it is not the origin

[24] To this bare definition, additions and refinements have been added and argued about, see Notes: Power.

[25] See the account in Chapter III:7.

[26] Analysed in Chapter II.

that matters but how the constitutional order works in practice, whether their well-being is advanced.[27] Their main concern once inside the field is to use their own power to influence officials in the use of theirs.

Another display of power appears in relation to purpose, the notions of well-being, and in defining interests. Power works on two fronts, one in constructing a notion of the common good, the other in inserting ideas into relations between the people and officials. As to the first, the purpose of officials being empowered is said to be to serve the common good. But whose interests count and how are they ranked? The common good is a construction of ideas, language, and values, the selection of which is itself an act of power. How the selection is made and by whom are matters vital to constitutional authority. It could be the deliberate action of a person or group but normally is not directly attributable. The origins are found in social relations, where interests are ranked, ideas and values cultivated, and a discourse constructed. That can be abrupt after conquest or upheaval, but is more likely to be a long process originating in the interests of sectors, while over time the discourse transcends and appeals to the interests of all. Whatever the steps, however rough the terrain and obscure the passage, the result is a conception of the common good around which a constitutional order forms, a field cultivated according to settled social relations and social spheres. Power permeates the process, fostering in the people a sense of shared interest and breeding sentiments and dispositions to match, coercion ever in the background.

The other weapon of power in the hands of officials is resort to fictions. The power of fictions we have seen; how concepts of sovereignty and the people, consent and representation in the lead others in tow, transfer power from the people to officials.[28] Relying on the submerged subjunctive, fictions make it seem the sovereign people consent to power vesting in officials, by whom the people are represented. The virtue Touchstone found in fictions is for officials the passage to power. The upper register, formed around fictions, exerts power in two ways, one in constructing the discourse, the other in shaping the sentiments and dispositions of the people. Above a base of interests shared by all, the defining of interests and deciding the value are open to the sway of the upper register. Yet, power does not roam unresisted. The peasants of Gagliano drew on other interests, grounded in deeper ideas of well-being, likely to be half-hidden and unstated, yet a source of power. The power to generate an alternative register of ideas, language, and values with its own conception of the common good; the power to arouse sentiments and dispositions, and on occasions action. At the centre of the constitutional order sit

[27] Montesquieu distinguishes between the nature of government, which is in part how it came about, and the *principe*, 'the passions that cause it to function': Montesquieu: *Spirit of Laws*, Book III, Chapter 1. For commentary, see J Plamenetz: *Man & Society* (London: Longman, 1963). For *passions* read sentiments and dispositions.

[28] Discussed in Chapter II:5.

the two registers, each conveying a conception of relations of power between the people and officials, cooperating on some matters, competing on others.

This leads to further enquiry into the connection between ideas, language, and values at the constitutional level, the structure of society, and the place of power. Social relations and social spheres distribute power among the parties. A register of ideas, language, and values is devised to explain and justify the distribution. On that foundation a constitutional order is erected, which then affirms and reinforces the ideas and values. The pattern is common and persistent. A sector of society tends to dominate social and economic relations, the sustaining of which the sector regards as critical to the well-being of its members. All are in pursuit of well-being; all are encouraged to form, beyond a shared base, their own notion of what that means; and power follows in step. Again qualifications are to be entered. On the one hand, ideas, language, and values have other origins besides social and economic relations. On the other hand, other groups and sectors, while bowing to force, still have resort to that hinterland of discourse embedded in primary social relations and grounded in purpose. This alternative discourse can be rallied for frontal attack, but is more often a weapon of annoyance, an irritation urging and sometimes achieving small adjustments to the reigning order. For the constitutional field two conclusions follow. One, it is designed and planted according to the ideas, language, and values of select sectors of society.[29] The other, that although the constitutional order once formed is cast as an autonomous field separate from social and economic relations, the separation is only ever partial, the two ever intersecting and overlapping.

Inside the field the struggle over power continues. It is not a field of open competition, a free tug-and-scramble, nor a commons where all have the right to compete in advancing well-being. Rather a field fenced and gated, and restricted according to a view as to what matters are relevant to the constitutional order. The people enter a field laid out according to the interests, sentiments, and dispositions prevailing outside; a field in which the distribution of power among the people, and between officials and the people is settled. The outright competition for power is over, the winners awarded the field as the prize. And yet the field is fenced not walled and fences are permeable, enough to allow the people to bring with them the same urges and efforts they had outside to improve their lives. The blade of their power is blunted but has edge enough to enter whatever cracks appear in the constitutional structure and the processes of governing. The constitutional field remains, in Bourdieu's words a *field of struggle*,[30] each site inside marked by competing power between the people and officials, and among the people themselves. The parallel with justice is apt. Justice is stripped down to fit the constitutional form, although never wholly severed from the fecund parent, always in the

[29] M Weber: *Economy & Society*, introduction by G Roth and C Wittich, p lxix.
[30] D Schwartz: *Culture & Power* (Chicago: University of Chicago Press, 1987), p 121.

background eager to enter the field and exert its force.[31] The power of the people runs in parallel and the struggle for advantage continues within the constitutional order, both among the people and between the people and officials. Sometimes the struggle gets out of hand and the fence is torn down, the hedges levelled; just occasionally the displays of power lead to sound rule.

How common purposes can be born of competition and conflict is said to be the riddle of the constitution, the mystery of things as Lear would say. Riddles have solutions and mysteries can be unravelled. The solution lies in singling out the conditions under which the several fonts of power work together to reach common ends. Where officials use power to govern well, to discharge both the protective and the dynamic functions, and the people use theirs to share in the settling of ends, to guide officials towards those ends, support them in their efforts, and keep them under control. The alliance and its aims are easy to state but hard to achieve.[32] Sometimes the people and officials avoid the risks and coordinate action to produce government from which all gain. The constitutional order is the field where this takes place, where the many bubbling springs of power merge to form a current of equilibrium, where efforts are united enough to enable good and effective government as judged by the people. To understand how that is possible, to single out the conditions, we need to enquire further into relations between rulers and ruled, and among the ruled, to consider how they are constructed and presented and turned into action.

7. Quintet of actions moderated by a trio of sentiments

In explaining the nature of a commonwealth and the people's reasons for joining, Hobbes writes of 'the introduction of that restraint upon themselves' which they exert for 'their own preservation, and a more contented life thereby'. And to avoid 'that miserable condition of Warre'.[33] Restraint of the passions in the face of authority is neither blind nor a mere means to avoid punishment. The case is rational, practical, and ingrained, the logic worth repeating. The people want to advance well-being; some aspects depend on or are more easily attained by the authority of the state; authority is effective only if the people restrain their own actions. Restraint, on its face, is a negative disposition to abstain from action one might otherwise take. The positive aspect, less obvious but equally valuable, is to enable action in achieving purpose. Following the rules allows us to enter or create social relationships, which the state will uphold and enforce, whether to make a contract, acquire property, or practice a profession, a few examples. Self-restraint

[31] On justice, see Chapter I:2.
[32] See the discussion in Chapter I.
[33] *Leviathan*, Chapter 17, p 234.

on the part of the people, while a necessary condition of constitutional authority, is not enough to keep government to purpose.[34] Actions required of the people, in addition to restraint, are *support, engagement, vigilance, and censure.*

To show how, let us return to the seminar, to relations among the students, and with the tutor, where the purpose is to master the subject. The students know the rules, what they have to do, and what is not allowed. They know that self-restraint of both students and tutor is a condition of the class being well-conducted and the subject being learnt. Support is more elusive and shows in a multitude of ways, some trivial, others of weight, all together a condition of success. While restraint consists in being passive and attentive, support means positive action and takes many forms, some plain and obvious, others concealed and subtle. Being prepared by having read the set texts, grappling with the issues, and preparing questions and comments, each a small contribution to the success of the seminar. The many positive signs of support are matched by discipline in ruling out certain actions. The frowns of disapproval towards a student distracting attention from the subject, the words of the tutor, the seriousness of the discussion. The students *engage* by being prepared and answering questions, offering comments and entering the discussion. The seminar of silent stony-faced students, reliving in their minds the antics of last evening or dreaming of the next, is unlikely to succeed. *Vigilance* means being on the lookout, keeping purpose in mind and an eye on the others, teacher and students, for signs of their straying from purpose. Vigilance prepares the way for *censure*. The teacher who comes unprepared or is incoherent; who leaves out part of the course and consistently consults her phone, is bound to arouse in the students sentiments of disapproval and dispositions of censure, leading to acts from subtle hints to outright criticism. The student who repeatedly distracts others by muttering comments or disrupting the process in any of many ways is likely to attract at least the critical looks of others, at worst, to arouse their fury.

The dynamics displayed in the seminar are built into the structure of social relationships, not least between the people and officials. The primary action is that of officials' achieving purpose; the secondary action that of the people in keeping officials to their task. The people's actions, based on sentiments valuing good government and dispositions to act, consist of the quintet, the content of each action moulded around each site of power, each set of processes. The content and the intensity of the quintet, and each member, are dictated by each site of power, sometimes hardly needed, at other times critical in keeping officials to purpose. The next stage of understanding is to add to the sequence from purpose to action ideas of prudence, justice, and beneficence, and the sentiments and dispositions they promote in moderating purposive action.[35] *Prudence*, signifying worldly-wise

[34] David Bromwich commenting on Edmund Burke writes: 'Acquiescence will not do. There must be zeal.' D Bromwich: *The Intellectual Life of Edmund Burke* (Cambridge, Mass: Harvard University Press, 2014), p 375.

[35] Analysed in Chapter IV:4.

concern for well-being, is the main reason each student takes part in the seminar. Justice shows itself in several ways, in criticism, disdain, even anger for the student who disturbs and distracts others, the tutor who shows favouritism or dislike. *Beneficence*, the sentiment of concern for another, is ever on hand and displays itself in a multitude of ways. The student struggling to cope, suffering disability or other disadvantage, gets special attention from the tutor and support from other students. The one who shines, but with modesty, wins praise, and is in turn generous in sharing knowledge with others. The failings of human nature are ever present, among them jealousy of one for another, the selfish concerns to do well at all cost, the will to dominate and do others down, the vanity to show superiority, all the target of self-restraint but never conquered. And just as the poet found the whole world in a grain of sand, the social order is portrayed in a university seminar.

8. From description to theory

The parts are now in place to assemble a theory of society, the place of persons, groups, and sectors within it; the sequence from purpose to action; the means available to keep action to purpose.

First: the foundation is the natural law of peoples, the essence of which is the purpose common to all persons and groups, communities and nations, of attaining humanity and civility, and the notions of well-being that follow.

Second: Well-being generates in each person interests, some subjective to the person, some cultivated within social relations, others fostered by social spheres. Interests of three kinds: self, others, and abstract, intersect and overlap.

Third: Valued interests give rise to sentiments, from which dispositions to action can but do not necessarily follow. Both sentiments and dispositions are subject to the influence of social relations, social spheres, and external forces.

Fourth: Each person devotes time and effort to advancing well-being, with some success and much frustration. All learn the benefit of acting with others and enter into social relations with others for shared purposes. Some relationships are entered freely, some by necessity, some by compulsion. Relations intersect and overlap, sometimes inducing harmony and concord, at other times inciting disharmony and discord.

Fifth: The people learn the conditions for successful collective action: that mutuality and reciprocity are the fabric of association; that sentiments and dispositions of prudence, beneficence, and justice are necessary conditions; that passions are to be curbed and self-restraint exerted. They know cooperation is conditional, never certain or lasting, dependent on sentiments and dispositions of support and restraint.

Sixth: The people feel the power of social spheres, influencing sentiments and dispositions, moulding and guiding social relations. Power to create expectations and impose responsibilities, sometimes requiring positive action, sometimes demanding self-restraint, variable in strength from one situation to another and contingent on numerous factors. The force of social spheres can be intense and pervasive but not absolute. Nor should the concept of the socialized person be overdone, made too rigid, suffocating rather than enabling and inspiring.[36] The over-socialized person is as much a distortion of social reality as that of its opposite, the iconoclast free of social bonds.

Seventh: The more accurate image is of a combination of the two, each moderated by the other, the power of the social always guiding, sometimes dictating the actions of the individual person, who retains the capacity for critical assessment and detached judgement in the manner of an impartial spectator.

Eighth: A register, a discourse of ideas, language, and values tends to form and exert power over social relations and social spheres, yet is never total or exclusive of other registers and discourses grounded in other ideas, language and values more closely tied to the founding purposes of social life. Armed with this theory of social understanding, we are ready to enter the field of constitutional authority.

Ninth: The many ways and means the people have of influencing the cultivation of the constitutional field are contained in the quintet of actions, restraint and support for the one part, engagement, vigilance, and censure for the other part.

Notes

Action

The concept of action is of much interest in philosophy, social science, and psychology. From a vast literature, I mention just two. On the philosophy of action: S Hampshire: *Thought and Action* (London: Chatto and Windus, 1959), Chapter 3. From a broadly psychological perspective, R Harre and PF Secord offer a most perceptive analysis, with one slight reservation at the emphasis on rules to the cost of the more complex nature of social relations and social spheres: *The Explanation of Social Behaviour* (Oxford: Basil Backwell, 1972). On the sociological side, see the references below.

[36] DH Wrong: 'Oversocialized Conception of Man in Sociology' 26 (1961) *American Sociological Review* 183.

Social relations, spheres, and structures

Social relations and social spheres are analysed in my *Law in Modern Society.* On social relations: pp 35–36, 71–75, 122–25, 248–50, 324–25. On social spheres: Chapters 3, 4, 6, 10. On relations between social spheres and social relations: pp. 183–88.

The enabling or empowering quality of social relations and social spheres in achieving purpose is not to be overlooked. The enabling quality of both is a critical feature of collective action as appears throughout my text. HLA Hart's account of secondary rules as empowering remains a valuable source: *The Concept of Law* (Oxford: Clarendon Press, 1961), Chapter III. A Giddens makes the point well: 'the structural properties of institutions are not just constraints upon action, they are enabling': *Politics, Sociology and Social Theory* (Cambridge: Polity Press, 1997), p 196.

In conceiving and developing the concept of a social sphere, I have gained much from the ideas of others. Of special help are the following: N Elias: *The Civilizing Process* (Oxford: Basil Blackwell, 2000); D North: *Institutions, Institutional Change and Economic Performance* (Cambridge: Cambridge University Press, 1990); E Ostrom: *Governing the Commons: The Evolution of Institutions for Collective Action* (Cambridge: Cambridge University Press, 1990); D Putman: *Making Democracy Work* (Princeton: Princeton University Press, 1993); WR Scott: *Institutions and Organizations* (London, 1995); P Winch: *The Idea of a Social Science in Relation to Philosophy* (London: Routledge & Kegan Paul, 1958, 1990).

Habitus of Pierre Bourdieu

The defining feature of *habitus* is *disposition*: dispositions 'generate and organize practices', that is, connect mental states to action. Other concepts are invoked to convey the idea: cultural unconscious, habit-forming force, basic, deeply interiorized master-patterns, mental habit, and schemata of perceptions, appreciations, and action: discussed in D Schwartz: *Culture and Power*: *The Sociology of Pierre Bourdieu* (Chicago and London: University of Chicago Press, 1997), especially p 101. In other words: 'The habitus is a set of dispositions which incline agents to act and react in certain ways. The dispositions generate practices, perceptions and attitudes which are "regular" without being consciously coordinated or governed by any "rule"': JB Thompson: Editor's Introduction to P Bourdieu: *Language and Symbolic Power* (Cambridge: Polity Press, 1991), p 12. Thompson continues: 'Dispositions are acquired through a gradual process of *inculcation* in which early childhood experiences are particularly important.

The dispositions . . . are also *structured* in the sense they unavoidably reflect the social conditions within which they were acquired': p 12.

The similarities between Bourdieu's account of action and my own are plain; there are also differences. (i) Bourdieu's dispositions embrace both sentiments and dispositions; but they are conceptually different, need to be separated, and have different roles in action. (ii) The influence of social relations in forming dispositions is implicit in Bourdieu but warrants closer consideration and their power examined. (iii) The structure of society results from both social relations and social spheres. Field covers both; but social sphere is a distinct concept and has a place in structure. (On field, see notes below.)

Another seminal source is Anthony Giddens' *The Constitution of Society* (Cambridge: Polity Press, 1984) where structure is defined as: 'the properties which make it possible for similar social practices to exist across . . . spans of time and space and which lend them "systemic" form'. Which I take to mean continuity and orderliness. Notwithstanding the choice of terms and concepts, there is common ground between Giddens' account and mine, although again the separation of social relations and social spheres, and how they relate to each other, needs explanation. One point to add is that because social spheres and social relations vary in density, the *structural properties* follow suit, some 'deeply embedded' but others quite flimsy.

Douglas North's account of action and structure fits the text: 'Our theory must include not only the reasoning processes but also the processes that generate the actor's subjective representation of the decision problem, his or her frame': *Institutions, Institutional Change and Economic Performance* (Cambridge: Cambridge University Press, 1990), p 23.

Institution

Institution is often used to describe the social structure. Douglas North defines institutions as 'the rules of the game in a society or, more formally, . . . the humanly devised constraints that shape human interaction': *Institutions, Institutional Change and Economic Performance*. These 'regularized patterns of human interaction' are necessary to simplify complexity and enable people to realize common ends. There is, however, a tension inherent in the definition. 'Rules of the game' is an incomplete description of an institution. The 'constraints that shape human interaction' suggests there is more to it than rules but is not explained. Perhaps North intended this to include the cognitive and regulative dimensions, the capacity of an institution to mould ways of thinking, and the coercive side of sanctions. The 'constraints' have several sources: self-restraint, social relations, and social spheres.

Field

Field means an area of social action. Bourdieu explains: a field (champ) 'is a network, or configuration, of objective relations between positions. These positions are objectively defined, in their existence and in the determination they impose upon their occupants, agents or institutions, by their present and potential situation (*situs*) in the structure of—species of power (or capital)': P Bourdieu and D Wacquant: *An Invitation to Reflexive Sociology* (Chicago: University of Chicago Press, 1992), p 97. In other words, *field* is a *structured space*. It is also a space of conflict and competition. Field defines 'the broadest possible range of factors that shape behaviour rather than delimit a precise area of activity': Schwartz: *Culture and Power*, p 121. Action results from the interaction of *habitus* and *field*.

Norbert Elias writes in relation to *field*: 'It means first of all to discover the basic structures which give all the individual processes within this field their direction and their specific stamp': *The Civilizing Process*, pp xvii and 411. This way of defining *field* fits well with my account. I take it to mean a field is a distinct area of activity resulting from, and constituted by, an aggregate of social relationships and social spheres. Elias' *processes. Network* is another term often used to convey the idea of an area of activity: an example among many: *Rules and Networks* (eds) RP Appelbaum, WLF Felstiner, and V Gessner (Oxford: Hart, 1995).

Keith Baker captures well the concept of field and its utility. To understand historical events 'we need to reconstitute the field of political discourse in which it occurred, a field in which certain kinds of actions took on meanings', to which he adds: 'that often went far beyond what particular actors intended': *Inventing the French Revolution*, p 20. Chapter 1 offers an enlightening account of that field of political discourse in eighteenth-century France.

Power

A sound starting point is Max Weber: *Economy & Society*, but as shown in my text needs to be expanded. Power winds its way through much of volume I. Pierre Bourdieu's writings are well-summarized by David Schwartz: *Culture & Power* (1987). Michael Mann's monumental treatise is of much interest and insight: *The Sources of Social Power* (Cambridge: Cambridge University Press, 1986, 2012) (four volumes).

Identifying power beyond Weber's model based on direct relationships has attracted a large literature. Stephen Lukes' *Power: A Radical View* (London: Macmillan, 1974) set the course. Once embarked on the exploration of the many diffuse sites of power there is no stopping, as Michel Foucault shows: *Discipline and Punish: The Birth of the Prison* (London: Penguin,

1991) and *The History of Sexuality: The Will to Knowledge* (London: Penguin, 1998). For commentary: J Gaventa: *Power After Lukes: A Review of the Literature* (Brighton: Institute of Development Studies, 2003). The drawback is that once power is so diffused, penetrating subtly so many aspects of daily life, the explanatory value is depleted.

The common good as an exertion of power

The point in the text is that the construction of the common good, which consists of ideas and values, is an exercise of power. It is not power occurring in a direct relationship between two or more persons. It is rather the power ideas and values have over a person or group. Such ideas and values are likely to have a mixed and complex origin, partly material, partly abstract. They tend to form and re-form over time, although sometimes are stated abruptly and plainly, as in a successful revolution of the kind seen in central and eastern Europe in the 1990s. Such ideas and values in the constitutional context have their origins in the social and economic structure of society, and the distribution of power within it, although the path from raw interests to constitutional order is likely to be long and rambling and twisted, subject to other influences, and sometimes losing its way.

Power of this kind is often referred to as *ideological* power. Stephen Lukes' third dimension of power is defined as the ways by which the powerful transform the way the powerless think without coercion of force: *Power: A Radical View*. While the focus on ideology or ideas catches the essence of such power, the link is made too plain and too direct. The better image is of a chain stretching between the two ends with many links in between. HC Kelman's account of the three stages through which power proceeds helps to fill the space between the two ends of the chain: compliance to identification to internalization: 'Compliance, identification, and internalization: Three processes of attitude change' (1958) 1 *Journal of Conflict Resolution* 51–60. Perhaps Thomas Hobbes has the last word: 'in the well-governing of opinions, consisteth the well-governing of Men's Actions': *Leviathan*, Chapter XVIII, p 124.

Self-restraint

Appetite an insatiable wolf: for RN Lebow, as for Ulysses in *Troilus and Cressida*, appetite the insatiable wolf tempts lack of restraint on the part of both the people and the leaders. After discussing the ideas of Thucydides, Plato, and Socrates, Lebow writes: 'All three attributed civil disorder to lack of sell-restraint, especially on the part of high-status actors': *A Cultural Theory of International Relations* (Cambridge: Cambridge University Press, 2008), p 83.

Lance Banning writes of self-restraint as: 'the self-denying spirit to resist immersion in the private life of acquisition and enjoyment': L Banning: 'Some Second Thoughts on Virtue and the Course of Revolutionary Thinking' in *Conceptual Change and the Constitution* (eds) T Ball and JGA Pocock (Lawrence Kansas: University Press of Kansas, 1968), p 203. John Locke expresses a similar idea in the language of 'Ambition and Luxury': *Second Treatise on Government*, p 111. For J Bentham the need for self-restraint follows from the general maxim that 'self-regarding interest is predominant over all other interests put together', according to which a ruler 'would naturally pursue his own sinister interest at the expense of the general interest': quoted in P Schofield: *Utility and Democracy*, p 272.

Influences on self-restraint: Claus Offe gives an account of the *socializing function* of institutions, which include constitution and law. On the positive side they encourage citizens to behave in certain ways, come to 'adopt the cognitive expectations and moral intuitions from which the institutions themselves derive'. On the negative and more important side 'they encourage the self-imposition, on the part of social actors, of behavioural disciplines that curb 'opportunistic' modes of action': 'Institutions in East European Transitions' in *The Theory of Institutional Design* (ed) R Goodin (Cambridge: Cambridge University Press, 1996), p 200. Vital though the power of institutions be in forming the sentiments and dispositions of people and leaders, it is unlikely to be enough to establish the self-restraint needed on the part of both.

Effects of lack of restraint: Describing the lack of self-restraint and the destructive effects on the Roman state, Keith Baker writes: 'The passions, though restrained in a thousand ways, insensibly reassert themselves, engendering the vices and suddenly destroy the state, or feeding the corruption that leads to despotism and the death of a republic. For that reason, collective inculcation of the civic virtues through public education, is essential to the duration of a free state': KM Baker: *Inventing the French Revolution*. Baker describes well the curse of passions and the cure of public education. Education does not remove the wolfish appetite, only helps contain it.

PART II
CONSTITUTIONAL FIELD

V
Constitutional Field

1. Entering the field

The scene is set to enter the constitutional field to describe the layout, see how it looks from the people's point of view, and single out the main issues they confront. On entering earlier with Hume our guide, we found a field sparsely planted, the ancient oaks of acquiescence the only thing to catch our eye. It is as if we were so taken by the sight of the majestic oaks, the symbol of acquiescence, all other life would go unnoticed.[1] On retracing our steps, now equipped with an account of human action and guided by the purpose of human endeavour, the natural law put plainly, the people's striving to secure and advance well-being, we are struck by the abundance of life between and beneath the oaks. Some half-hidden in the shadows, others towering in the sunlight. We see the field in all its lights and shades, the diversity and disorder; the contest for space and light, soil and moisture. At the same time we detect cooperation among the plants and bushes above the surface, which we know goes on more intensely below, to form a whole where all species, grand or humble, seek to grow and flourish, all sharing the need for space and light, soil and moisture. Along the pathways below the canopy, amid the tangle of bushes and vines, an outline of the design can be traced, clear in places, overgrown and eroded in others, but enough to show there once was a plan in laying out the field. The aim now is to move from the forest to the constitutional field, to find within the thicket of disorder and disarray order and purpose, while being attentive to the unruliness.

Just as a forest beyond a few main landmarks is approached and appraised from one point of view or another, the same applies to the constitutional field. The viewpoint here is that of the people, who are guided by purpose, by the interests in civility and humanity at the foundation of human action, normally concealed and unstated but innate and ready to draw on when needed. Secondly, the people realize the benefits the field has to offer but are cautious; all depends on how well it is cultivated and managed, and how much their interests count. Thirdly, with the images earlier encountered in mind, framed at one end by fortress-like rule, at the other holding out freedom, the people see in between a space that invites other images and other ways of governing that seem more promising. Fourthly, the people need to know how the constitutional field is designed, how power is allocated and used, and the scope for their having influence within it, while noting the

[1] The imagery of the oaks is prompted by the ancient oak forest of Blenheim Park.

Keepers of the Common Good. D.J. Galligan, Oxford University Press.
DOI: 10.1093/9780198907398.003.0005

traps and tricks along the way. In the constitutional field, social relationships replace trunks and branches, the primary relationship that between the people and officials. Relationships among the people are in the background, gathered around the boundary neither in nor out but to be reckoned with in surveying the field. The primary relationship seems at first sight to be simply a few ruling and the rest complying. On closer look, it turns out to be part of a fuller plan that gives to the relationship meaning and content. To the study of the plan we now turn, while for the people to enter the field is to begin a journey of discovery, the purpose plain, the destination known, the pathway uncertain, the stops along the way instructive.

2. Structure and landmarks

The constitutional field is designed around several main landmarks: agencies and officials; sites of power; the nature and purpose of power; the interests of the people; the discretionary space. To continue the rustic imagery, officials have the tools of cultivation, the people decide what seeds to sow, and both work towards a good harvest. Translated into constitutional terms, the people decide the interests to be entrusted to the state, which officials have the power to protect and advance, both parties contributing to a successful outcome. The alliance of people and officials in practice is neither as natural nor as neat. Power can be given and used for purposes other than the well-being of the people; the components of well-being itself, beyond a common base, are liable to be contested; the relationship between the people and officials, and the division of labour between them, are subject to opinion and resolved in different ways at different sites. Against this background, the task now is twofold, one to mark the main features, the prominent landmarks, the other to consider how the people perceive and cope with the field.

The constitution lays out the field and provides for a structure of institutions and officials, together with guidelines for cultivation. Within the structure, the processes of governing take place and relations between officials and the people form. The constitution establishes the main sites of power, the *primary agencies*, legislative, executive, and judicial, and defines the powers of each; adding others of special status, and giving guidance on relations among them. The network of secondary agencies, administrative and regulatory—*administrative agencies*—is left normally for the primary agencies to construct, with guidance from history, the constitution, and judicial interpretation.[2] Administrative agencies tend to function in the shadow of the primary agencies and are kept on the edges of the field as if outside constitutional interest. On the contrary, each being a site of power where

[2] The design of agencies is of much interest but beyond present purposes. For a valuable analysis, see *The Theory of Institutional Design* (ed) RE Goodin (Cambridge: Cambridge University Press, 1996) and C Offe: *Modernity and the State: East, West* (Cambridge: Polity Press, 1996).

relations between officials and the people form and function, they are integral to the structure. The constitutional field is composed of and cultivated around the aggregate of such sites of power, the secondary as well as the primary. Several matters call for explanation: the power to govern, the power to set-up agencies, and the structure of power inside the agencies.

Power is the next landmark, the power of officials conferred, the power of the people innate. Power is everywhere, necessary for purpose but unruly in practice, the potential and the risks understood by study of the many sites.[3] An academic seminar reveals much about relations between power and purpose. The purpose is to educate the students in the subject enough to pass the exam, the power of the lecturer to conduct the seminar to achieve that end. Several features stand out. First, the lecturer has plenary power, from the Latin *plenus* meaning full. Full in the sense of power to conduct the seminar and take all measures to achieve the purpose. Plenary power is guided and restrained by conditions, some express others implicit; some set by law, others from social spheres, still others agreed with the students. That power be held subject to conditions is the difference between plenary and absolute power. Secondly, plenary power endures, always available to call on, a reserve to be tapped at any time. Plenary power authorizes the lecturer to conduct the seminar as thought fit; to adopt practices and principles to guide the process. Thirdly, within the bounds of purpose and subject to the conditions, the lecturer has discretion in the use of power. The notion of a *discretionary space* catches the sense of a sphere of activity, bounded but within the bounds left to be filled according to disposition, preference, and judgement. This leads to a last point. To power as described may be added the adjective *authorized—authorized* power—or to use the noun simply authority. Authority means power to achieve purpose, to educate the students, to advance the well-being of the people.[4]

Purpose is foremost in the people's perspective, the reason and justification for the field, the point of all that happens within it. Purpose defines the boundaries of power, guides the use, and sets the limits. The plan of design is easily lost from sight and the boundaries liable to fade with time; trampled by tugging-and -scrambling in the undergrowth, at threat from incompetence and misrule, and the wolfish appetite. The dilemma the people face is that between their expectations of the field and the reality, there is a gap with other purposes intruding, other interests having priority. The constitutional field, from time to time, is redesigned, the boundaries redrawn, the field refenced, perhaps prompted by measured reason and the good of all, or just as likely to favour the interests of a few. How then in this turbulent setting does the people's well-being feature and fare? Well-being as a bundle of interests, dividing roughly into having needs met and being able to improve life, needs

[3] On power, see Chapter IV:6.
[4] Authority is not to be confused with authorship: see Chapter III:7.

and utilities in Vico's words. Just what that means is given content within each group, community, and nation according to its own perceptions, experience, and priorities. Beyond a common core of needs and a shared wish to improve life, well-being is open to opinion, prompted by shared notions of civility and humanity, while at risk of being sullied by others, self-serving and divisive. Well-being consists of that aggregate of interests the people come to value, from the serious to the trivial, the protection of person and property at one end, to table manners at the other end, and many in between.[5]

This leads to the selection of interests for status in the constitution, the next landmark. One issue is the process of selection, another what interests are selected. The constitutional order forms in a setting of social, economic, and political relations, from which some interests are selected for a place. The people have an interest in engaging in the process, although the opportunities in practice are few, their influence variable. The people normally find themselves in a field already laid out, the selection of interests made, dressed in ideals, and presented as being for the good of all. In approaching the field, the people know and take account of the reality. The design is neither fixed nor absolute, the constitution open to being amended, the concepts reinterpreted, the ideas to revision, all allowing room for change without causing alarm. As Hume and Smith observed, the people value whatever is in place, the protection and the stability limited though they be. Change normally is moderate, adjusting what is there better to serve well-being, resorting to overthrow only in the extreme. Some interests selected for constitutional status are fairly standard across nations, security of person and property the bedrock, respect for justice and rule through law in support. Others are local to time and place, the scope of liberty and the range of rights variable.[6] The selection depends on streams of influence from the force of history and the concerns of the time, to competition among persons, groups, and sectors. Some interests serve the needs and utilities of all, others favour a select few. The selection cannot be insulated from the social context, from relationships among the members, from persons, groups, and sectors intent on advancing their own ends. Some interests are agreed or taken for granted, others the outcome of strife and struggle; some dominate but are ever open to adjustment; others over time fall away.

The form of rule, the last landmark, takes shape within relations between the people and officials, while relations among the people in the background exert influence. Of the many potential forms, the course of history and the patterns of opinion in evidence suggest three main models.[7] Rule by one, known here as *princely rule*, is the most common. Power is in the hands of a prince who rules as

[5] In *The Civilising Process*, a masterly study, Norbert Elias shows the importance of the trivial.
[6] See further Chapter I.
[7] See the account of patterns of opinion in Chapter III:7.

he deems fit, surrounds himself with courtiers and counsellors, while keeping the people at a distance and allowing only marginal engagement. The opposite is the *people ruling themselves*, deciding major issues and being in charge of all aspects of the constitutional order. Self-rule holds much appeal, its values inspire, but is rare in practice. *Rule by representatives* falls somewhere in between, combining elements of princely rule and the people ruling themselves. Representative rule has come to be equated with democracy, or to be precise democracy is taken to mean rule by elected representatives, who in some sense represent the interests of all in the constitutional process. Each form in practice allows variations, yet in substance falls within one or other of the three models. The dominance distracts attention from a fourth, touched on before.[8] Tucked into the thicket, half-hidden in the shadows, maturing in sentiments and dispositions, and quietly securing a place in their actions, is another pattern of opinion among the people, a set of sentiments and dispositions towards the constitutional field. The people are both in the field and able to stand apart from it, engaging in cultivation while keeping watch over it. They neither aspire to govern themselves nor to be passive subjects of princes or representatives. The concept of keepers captures the image of the people as keepers of the constitutional field. The verb *to keep*, from old English but of uncertain derivation, means to maintain in proper and specified condition, whether the household, the inn, or the lighthouse. What it is to be keepers of the constitutional field, the means available to them, and the chances of success are themes emerging as the enquiry proceeds to reach a climax in the last chapter. It is enough to note that surveying the field from the point of view of the people as keepers, sifting through the evidence of opinion, unearths aspects of rule and relations unnoticed and unaccounted for in the other forms of rule, yet invaluable in social understanding, as well as suggesting a title for this book.

A feature to add to the constitutional field, one shared with the forest, is the influence of history. Just as the forest dates back to ancient times while reaching forward to the present, adjusting to cope with change, so the constitutional field bears witness to history. Where there is no text or only part, the influence of the past is most apparent, although written constitutions are not exempt. While laying out the field in anticipation of the future, constitutions are composed against the problems of the past, inheriting concepts and ideas earlier formed.[9] The scale and power of the inheritance we shall see as the work progresses. The reader will meet the claim that concepts at the foundation of modern constitutions written or unwritten: the people as an abstraction, sovereignty, representation, and consent; all stem from the past, have outlived their utility, and cloud the present.

[8] Chapter III:7.

[9] On the influence of the past, see A Sajó: *Limiting Government: An Introduction to Constitutionalism* (Budapest: CEU Press, 1999).

3. Plenary power and the discretionary space

Cultivation of the constitutional field relies on the power of agencies, primary and secondary, to take whatever action is needed or beneficial in advancing purpose. The power is plenary in the sense and with the qualities set out in describing the seminar. It means from the people's point of view the power of each agency is given for their well-being and authorizes whatever is needed or useful in advancing that end. The primary agencies settle matters of high policy, make laws, and oversee their application. Secondary agencies abound, some public and prominent, others in the background, each assigned a portion of the field to cultivate according to what is necessary or of utility in advancing stated objectives. Each agency has power to structure the subfield as it thinks best, while keeping open a space for discretion. Once the agencies primary and secondary are in place, it is easy to lose sight of the residue of plenary power, to conclude it is no longer needed except in extreme situations. On the contrary, the plenary power of each agency remains a resource to draw on at all levels and sites of governing, as if a cloak of discretion draped over the field to be put to work at each site of power in achieving purpose.

The discretionary space conveys the idea of an area infused with power to act for purpose. Each agency of government from the high legislative to the low administrative has a place in the space, a portion in which to govern. The joining of purpose and discretion is a sign that each agency has a job to do and judgement about how to do it. Part of the job is to structure the space, while respecting the constitutional design and guided by the parent law. Structure takes various forms, from detailed rules to open standards to soft guidelines. How much of the space to structure depends partly on the character, partly on purpose, and partly on the preferences of the agency. The legislature fills part of the space with laws, the executive by settling matters of policy and in putting the laws into practice, while leaving room for the future. Alone or together, the legislative and executive set up secondary agencies, each with power over a portion of the space and a duty to give it structure. Subject to direction and restrictions from the constitution, the law, and the primary agencies, while respecting surrounding social spheres, each agency has to decide the form and density of structure: how much of the space to cover with standards; the kinds of standards from rules to guidelines; how much to leave open to discretion. The usual pattern is to fill a portion of the space with rules, which shade into more open standards, then into informal guidelines and understandings, while leaving a reserve of discretion. A reserve enables the agency to reach back to the purpose for which it is empowered, on the one hand to guide its actions in setting and interpreting, even departing from standards, on the other hand to settle novel issues as they occur.

Much of governing takes place in the space left unstructured. Decisions are made and actions taken without declared standards or set procedures, sometimes with interested parties present but often not, how to fill space left to the opinions, preferences, and judgements of officials. Structuring part of the space with standards is normal and expected, although how much and what kind are matters of discretion. Interpretation opens another strand of discretion, for even the most dense and detailed standards have to be interpreted and applied, contextual contingencies settled.[10] At one end is the case for settled rules, at the other end the need to be flexible in judgement, nimble in action. The case for rules, or at least clear and certain standards, is strongest when at stake are the interests of individual persons or groups, while leaving an open space more suitable for matters of policy concerning or affecting a wider set of persons and sectors. Whatever the structure, discretion is present permeating the process, most plainly and vigorously at the level of policy-making, more discreetly on the margin of rules, with many points in between. The broader the discretion, the more power to choose among policies, interests, and courses of action. The space for discretion can be narrower or wider, from a thin belt around a well-ploughed plot to a wild and unhedged common where the route from purpose to action has few signposts. Much of governing is done in the space around each site. Part of the space is structured with standards; much is left open to discretion. Part is conducted in public and according to principle; much goes on in secret, well away from the madding crowd and the clamour of interests, hidden from the gaze of the people. The kinds of decisions and actions taken in governing are undefined and practically unlimited, from high policy to routine administration, from matters of security and defence at the top, right down the line to the mundane affairs of an agency charged to control parking. The reasons and standards applied, the opinions considered, and the interests consulted, are often undisclosed. Yet, to condemn would be pointless, for such a space is innate in governing and essential to governing well. There is a dark side. Each agency tends towards autonomy and independence, a property of power we have encountered before. The discretionary space, although necessary, unavoidable, and useful, also opens entry to incompetence and misrule, while the wolf of appetite is ever on the prowl. The space allows alliances of officials and select groups and sectors; hides from the people the affairs of government; conceals the true motives and reasons for action; and puts at risk the people's well-being. Ways of managing the risk and opening the space to engagement, vigilance, and censure, the means available to the people, are later addressed and an approach outlined.[11] But a note of caution in ending. There is no grand solution, no final reconciling the need for a discretionary space around each agency of government in serving purpose, and the resulting risks of poor rule.

[10] On contextual contingencies, see DJ Galligan: *Law in Modern Society*, Chapter 3.3.
[11] The discretionary space is considered further in Chapter XV.

4. Four figures, four forms

Having observed the layout, noted the potential in advancing their welfare, and registered the risks, the next step is to consider the forms of rule the people encounter. The reasons for entering are worth repeating. There are benefits to be reaped, aspects of well-being advanced, the costs of not entering avoided. Mass refusal is possible but unlikely; were it to happen a new field would soon spring up. The people may have heard how the peasants of Gagliano refused to enter then paid the price. The reasonable course of action is to gain the benefits of being inside and influence what happens, while avoiding the consequences of absence. Perhaps Locke's putting one's self under government catches the sense of turning the negative aspect of entry to positive advantage. Once inside, the benefits gained ease or even erase the feeling of compulsion. Let us imagine the people, approaching the gate, meet four figures. One is *Anarchy*, a jolly fellow dressed, almost, as a clown, a Feste of constitutions, licensed to say what no one else dares, here ridiculing the very idea of a fenced-off field, urging the people to seek well-being in informal and spontaneous relationships. The people are amused rather than persuaded. The second figure, standing slightly apart, courteous in manner and courtly in dress, is the *Emissary* for princely rule. In a voice refined in phrasing and elevated in tone, he announces the surpassing benefits of the people's entrusting their well-being to the prince, who will guarantee harmony, security, and unity, adding under his breath unquestioning obedience the price of entry. The people are charmed, briefly, but soon realize that putting oneself under government where the prince governs, behind the ornament and pomp, has an air of menace.

The people turn with relief to the third, the *Evangelist* of self-rule. A serious figure showing no hint of humour, holding high a banner denouncing the evils and perils of a field ruled by self-serving officials and serving select sectors, exhorting the people to design and cultivate their own. Some see the light and are converted. They are keen to enter the field intent on ruling it themselves. The converts, few in number, are destined for the fields of eighteenth-century America, where the ground turns out to be hard clay resistant to self-cultivation, leaving the people frustrated and mocked for their foolishness.[12] The fourth figure, the Representative, steps up to assure the people that between rule by the prince and the people ruling themselves, rule by a *representative* few is untainted by the defects of each. The despotism of the prince and the disarray of self-rule are avoided by vesting power in a select few who know the well-being of all, are measured and moderate in pursuit, while being elected by and answerable to the people. The people show interest; but are cautious for it seems too good to be true. The Representative reminds them of a salesman whose zeal to sell leads to over-praising the product while brushing aside

[12] There is more on the 'upstarts drunk with liberty' in Chapter X on self-rule.

the flaws. The appeal is plain but the people fear a sleight of hand, do not quite see how the defects of princely rule and self-rule could be neatly cured by a form of rule somewhere between the two.

The people proceed to the gate wiser from the encounter, although uncertain in resolution and mixed in sentiments. The attraction undeniable of no constitutional field at all, no government to order them around; or if there has to be a field, at least be in charge of cultivation; or maybe leave it all to the virtue of the paternal prince or the wisdom of the select few. The very statement of each exposes the shortcomings: the need for more than informal social relations in securing well-being; the practical problems of genuine self-rule; the appeal of princely rule offset by the perils of uncensored power; the suspicion that behind the shine of rule by representatives is the hidden subjunctive, the few ruling *as if* they were the people, while doing what they like. Worldly wisdom and prudent scepticism boost resolve not breed despair. The people know to eschew images of perfection and visions of utopia in favour of practical realism. They anticipate a rough and tough terrain of competing interests and uneven influences, of power necessary but restless, outcomes precarious and uncertain. That is the nature of the field, the reality to which there is no practical alternative. The people accept that the best they can do is to have the field cultivated to benefit everyone to a tolerable level, while braced for setback and resigned to some doing better than others. So fortified in resolve and clear in purpose the people pass through the gate.

5. Perceptions of the field

The people find the field laid out, the design plain in places, obscure in others. They or their forebears might have had some say in the design, although it is mainly the legacy of history and ideas inherited from certain persons, groups, and sectors. The striking features are a conception of constitutional order; primary agencies in place and empowered; relations with the people defined in outline while leaving much unsettled; a small selection of interests given special status. Below the primary agencies of legislature, executive, and judiciary, the people see a network of secondary agencies, each occupying a parcel of the field, each with power over a portion of the people's well-being. The question is how to relate to the agencies, engage in their processes, and keep them to purpose. Several matters confront them. One is a reminder of how the agencies contribute to well-being: the protective, the welfare, and the enabling functions protecting interests, conferring benefits, and helping the people in their own efforts at advancing interests.[13] The interest of first priority is to be treated with respect as the bearer of rights. Next are select interests,

[13] Analysed in Chapter I:3.

property, and security, at least, together with others held to be worthy of special status.[14] Above the base, the people notice how agencies from the legislative to the administrative have power to select and protect other interests. They catch a first glimpse of the discretionary space and an inkling of what governing means and how well-being is served. They notice the space is shared with agencies, each with power to provide benefits and services or to restrict action and impose penalties. The scope for positive action is practically unlimited, from building infrastructure to providing civil and criminal justice, education and healthcare, and social welfare in many forms. They observe the power of agencies to insert into social relations among the people ideas of equity and fair treatment, equality, and non-discrimination. Lastly the people see how agencies are able to help them in their own efforts to improve life, one by providing conditions conducive to endeavour and initiative, the other by regulating the tug-and-scramble to give everyone a chance of engaging and competing.

Having seen the power of agencies and the potential benefits, the people turn their attention to *process*, the means by which agencies use power, and how they reach decisions. Several features stand out. They notice one process is the application of settled standards to specific cases. The *adjudicative* mode is most at home in the courts, while a common feature of administrative agencies. Notions of due process and procedural fairness are central to the process and adjusted to suit context. The main relationship is between the agency and the person or group whose case is in issue, where the aim is to reach an outcome based on evidence, proof, and reasoned application of the rules. However, as rules dense and detailed at one end shade into looser standards, other parties are affected and the process adjusted to take account of their interests and grant them a place in the process. This leads on to the next form where the purpose is to decide on the standards to guide action. Some are set by the constitution, the rest left to agencies, legislative, executive, and judicial at the top, down to administrative agencies at all levels and whatever kind. The people have an interest in the process of standard-setting across the many sites of power. Some matters are routine and without dispute. Other agency actions concern interests commonly shared and valued, although there may be disagreement about the form and content of the standards. Beyond the common ground lie many matters open and contested, leaving the agency to decide which interests count, who has leave to enter the process, and the influence of each party in shaping outcomes, all left to the agency's discretion.

The same unevenness of bargaining power in gaining entry to process applies once inside, with some groups and sectors more persuasive than others. The process widens to embrace not only setting standards, but deciding matters of policy

[14] The range of interests given constitutional interest varies from bare to well-provided to overstocked; some consider the constitutions of Brazil and South Africa to be examples of being overstocked. See Chapter VI.

and selecting courses of action, all central to the functions of agencies at all levels. Two main factors shape the outcome, one the sentiments and dispositions of agency officials, the other the influence of parties who take part in the process. The people learn how the selection and weighting of interests is an open process, how it is filled a contest, one in which they need to engage. Most visible at the legislative level in making laws, patent in executive discretion in deciding major matters of governing, obvious in the adjudicative where select interests are at issue, the contest seeps into every site of administrative action. The people are starting to understand the ways their interests are affected by the processes of governing and the need to engage. A logic begins to unfold; an intuition forms that if their interests be affected by agencies, a special relationship is created with responsibilities and entitlements on both sides. The foundation of that intuition and its profound importance in the constitutional order they learn only later.

The next thing the people notice is that each site of agency power divides between one part structured by standards, the other left open to discretion, with many points in between. The people realize that each agency is created by and draws on a deeper source of power; that behind and beyond the power of each is the general power to govern; that governing relies on a reserve of plenary power; that much goes on out of sight, beyond their gaze and out of reach. The higher the agency, the deeper the discretionary space, where decisions of policy form in a cauldron of fact and opinion, prejudice and prediction, scientific knowledge and speculation, discord and disagreement, without formal process but subject to informal influence. Around and between the two poles, applying rules at one end, deciding high policy at the other, scattered among the sites of power, occur processes varying sharply or subtly in innumerable ways. How the people can be confident that across so many sites power be used for their well-being, is for the time being beyond their grasp. They see the limited scope for formal processes and the need for informal ways of influencing the use of power.

To complete the sketch of process from the people's point of view, several matters need to be noted. Purpose is the criterion by which the people judge governing; purpose is reached by process. At each site of power well-being has to be rendered into concrete ends and process designed to suit. That any one purpose may be reached by different processes adds another variable.[15] On one approach, purpose means no more than a tallying of interests. The parties make known their interests to officials, who decide by weighing and balancing, leaving no remainder, nothing more to decide. The image of officials as clerks tallying interests and finding a resolution among them has appeal, provided all interests are counted. But there is more to governing than counting and weighing interests. This prompts

[15] One need only compare the adversarial and inquisitorial approaches to determining guilt or innocence in a criminal trial. Discussed well in M Damaska: *The Faces of Justice and State Authority* (New Haven: Yale University Press, 1986). See Notes on purpose and process.

an opposite image where process is kept to a low base, and officials decide by taking account of whatever factors and interests seem relevant. The appeal to the people is equally low. The prospect of leaving matters to the discretion of officials, who decide according to their own criteria, taking account of whatever interests they think fit, has no merit. Swift and decisive action, with no time to consult parties affected or to deliberate over options, may be justifiable as an exception. The people's expectations of the normal case are different. Somewhere between the two images, tallying interests and open discretion, the people are on the lookout for another, both more balanced and more realistic.

An alternative starts to take shape, first by taking note of the context and then considering the responsibility of officials. The people, spread across groups and sectors, have variable entry to the sites of power and once inside exert unequal influence. Some sites are simply out of bounds, others restricted to select groups and sectors. Even if entitled to engage, persons and groups lack the competence, confidence, or disposition to take part. Those who gain access realize there is more to the process than balancing interests; they see how the space expands to allow in other factors, some made known, some kept quiet. The parties see that in settling policy their interests count, but as part of wider enquiry reaching into the discretionary space around each site of power. From some sites and spaces the people are absent, their interests unheralded and unknown, or if known, dependent on officials to take them into account or not. If the persons and groups do manage to gain admission to a process, they may find the terrain terraced to favour some, whether due to custom and habit, superior forces, the sentiments and dispositions of officials, or all three, encouraging the people to look for other, informal routes to influence.

A modified, more realistic image of governing emerges. Much is left to the discretion of officials without the parties or present in a minor role. The outcome is not necessarily poor government. Agencies may be conscientious in pursuing purpose, taking account of the complex of interests as best they can, and reaching measured and mature outcomes. That after all is the major theme of the great constitutional symphony. Some know what is best for the whole; know the common good; know how to sort through a tangle of factors and reach an outcome. After opening with the select few at the top, the theme spreads to wind its way down through the network of agencies. Whatever the merits, however good the record, the risks remain, the spectres of incompetence, misrule, and appetite await their cue, the people's well-being ever at peril. The constitutional field may be cultivated, the harvest potentially abundant, and yet the people are uneasy. The crops are not necessarily the ones they want, nor guaranteed to serve their well-being. They would prefer it were otherwise. Any hopes they had of finding the right form for governing are dashed. Form spreads its charm, the siren call hard to resist: if only the right form could be found, all would be well, the people could be confident of sound rule. They now know better. John Warr's words of warning engraved on their souls, they know there is no one form, no simple solution. Sound rule is hard to achieve, has to be earned by effort, and depends on many factors, some under their control, others not. To understand the reality is to gain power, the power to influence the processes of governing by deploying the quintet of actions in the most useful way.

The gap between people, process, and outcomes has consequences. Dissatisfaction and disappointment the mildest, inflamed passions more serious, rebellion the ultimate. One strategy is to narrow the gap by the people's gathering together for collective action through guilds and unions, communities and societies. Collective action needs leaders to plan and coordinate action. As leaders emerge power follows, gradually shifting from the members to the leaders, ideas of representation entering to smooth the passage. A subtle shift takes place from being coordinator of collective action to the one who speaks for the actors; one who knows the common purpose and how to achieve it; who comes to present or represent the interests of the whole. The relationship between members and leaders changes, at first barely noticed, the bond between them kept close, the one careful to present the views of the others. Representation however has an inner dynamic, driven by a logic that ends in the representative assuming more and more authority to speak for all, unfolding even to embody them. A gulf opens between the people and the processes of governing, representation the only bridge across. An assessment of representation in serving the people's well-being is left for later.[16] Enough to note for now is that the people see the appeal of representation, how it not just bridges but removes the gap between them and leaders. If leaders stand in and are substitutes for the people, there is no gap to bridge. On a more moderate view, leaders claim to know the interests of the people better than the people themselves. Fortified by such claims and armed against opposition, representation long ago entered the constitutional field, dug itself in, and proved diligent in defining relations between the people and rulers, consent a close companion.[17] The spokesman for rule by representatives we encountered earlier. The reason for his confidence is now plain: rule by representatives has become the standard form, relations between the people and leaders settled, the riddle of the constitution solved. Despite the confidence and the widespread reliance, the people, not so easily beguiled or cowed, cast upon it the eye of an impartial spectator. On the one hand noting the benefits of someone speaking for them at the main sites of governing; on the other hand aware of the traps in entrusting to others custody of their well-being, while keeping them at a distance. A shrewd, practical people know that handing over responsibility to others, while reducing their own burdens in cultivating the field, allows alien plants to seed, unwelcome weeds to encroach, confirming the need to be wary.

[16] Representation and rule by representatives are considered in Chapters VI and XIV.
[17] Consent is discussed in Chapter VIII.

6. Managing the field

Cultivation of the constitutional field and relations between rulers and ruled turn out to be more complex and contentious than expected. How in such conditions can the seedlings of purpose grow and ripen to serve the people's well-being? The method displayed in the university seminar is again instructive. Conducting a seminar and governing have structural similarities, share the same dynamics, and are moderated by the same sentiments and dispositions. Each is designed for a dimension of well-being, the one plain and modest, the path to success well-marked; the other ambitious in purpose and open to opinion, the paths to success several and uncertain. Still, the same tools of management are at hand to be put to use in governing.

Promoting well-being gives content to the quintet of actions: self-restraint and support, engagement, vigilance, and censure. The people's valuing a constitutional order serving well-being gives rise to sentiments of support.[18] *Self-restraint* means at base obedience to law but requires more. It means entering the legal environment around the rules, a zone of openness not only for officials but the people as well, where trimming one's actions according to the spirit of the law is needed to sustain the constitutional order.[19] The environment around law merges into the discretionary space, where actions taken rely on the people's acceptance and tolerance. Restraint leads on to support, meaning 'to hold up, keep from failing or sinking, give strength to, encourage'.[20] Such ends are served by actions of many kinds, some scarcely noticed, others declared and celebrated. Consent would be the high point, the ultimate act of support, below which gather actions from the minor to the major, from oaths of allegiance to the newly crowned monarch to addresses of loyalty, from voting in elections to defending the realm.[21] Support encourages and is strengthened by engagement, the people's having an active part in the processes of governing, just as they are disposed to engage in any relationship affecting their well-being. The levels of engagement and the forms it takes again are variable, higher or lower, many or few. At the high end, engagement means the people's being responsible for major decisions, edging towards governing themselves, the officials serving as clerks. The appeal of such an order and the practical problems to confront are examined later. The low end of engagement is met in princely rule where the people, rigorously ruled, are neither expected to engage nor welcome.

In the middle field between the outliers, at the many sites of cultivation, we have caught a glimpse of how the people might engage and the obstacles. One

[18] Discussed in Chapter IV:7.

[19] For analysis of the legal environment, see DJ Galligan: *Law in Modern Society*, Chapter 16.

[20] *Concise Oxford Dictionary of Current English* (1964).

[21] On consent, see Chapter VIII. Just how much support is needed to sustain a constitutional order and what kinds is uncertain and remains a subject for empirical enquiry.

factor is the kind of process. Each process along the scale, from election at one end, to addressing an administrative agency at the other, has a form and a logic to guide the mode of engagement by persons, groups, and sectors. Applying the rules to a set of facts engages the parties directly affected, although the more open the rules the more discretion enters, and the case builds for wider participation. The setting of standards affects wider interests and attracts more attention. Beyond these two forms, the discretionary space is not so easily evaluated. The kinds of decisions and actions are diverse, some resolution of a single issue, some routine and of no wider interest, others of high policy with serious consequences. Some call for swift action, others lay the ground for the longer term. The scope for engagement, the form it takes, and who qualifies, are bound to be matters of contention, while interested parties being excluded is not uncommon. There is more to engagement than getting one's interest onto the scales. It extends to influencing the process, urging a sound and sensible outcome acceptable to all parties. The interplay between particular interests of persons, groups, and sectors, and the common interest is a critical feature of process. The people know the need for and value of balancing the two. They share an interest in finding a satisfactory, or at least tolerable resolution, reaching an outcome from which all benefit enough to warrant support.

The play of forces and factors within the discretionary space is endlessly interesting and much analysed. Here we have to be content with mention of one or two features rather than a full account. Part of the space is openly on display, cultivated by agencies, standards set and processes designed. Relations among the parties with interests, and between them and the agencies, are defined to create predictability and stability. The trouble is only a portion of the discretionary space is so settled; the larger part left open to allow whatever action may be needed. It is a shifting space, some segments open to view, others murky, confined to backrooms out of sight, secret and undisclosed. What goes on in the space, whose interests are considered, who has influence who wins who loses, are matters kept hidden. The people, unaware, only later realize the consequences. The two faces of the discretionary space are on view, one positive, a necessary tool in governing, another negative, a threat to the proper use of power and the people's well-being. The need and scope for vigilance and censure, the two other tools of management, is now plain. *Vigilance* signifies the people, aware of the risks of power, watching over government, keeping it under their gaze, and alert to and ready to expose deviation from purpose. Just how they do that, how they keep agencies under their gaze and how to have influence are matters for later. *Censure* follows vigilance. Censure means adverse judgement; expression of disapproval leading to reprimand. The forms of censure again are many from adverse comment to condemnation to removal from office. Prudence, justice, and beneficence are on hand to guide and moderate the conduct of censure. Just how they are put to use, how they penetrate the discretionary space, are matters weaving their way through the following chapters. And last but not least, in addition to the processes provided by law, the people have available informal means of engagement, vigilance, and censure.

The need for restraint does not rule out the people's taking action to alter the design of the constitutional field and processes of governing within it. Rarely is either design or process a graceful construction erected in harmony with the single purpose of well-being. Both are instead the clumsy outcome of influence, opinion, and tradition, among which the well-being of the people is present, but masked and muted and of low standing. As long as well-being is served 'with ordinary moderation and tolerable decency', the people have a reason for not just acquiescing but supporting and engaging.[22] That in Bolingbroke's memorable words is 'the measure of our submission', the ground of self-restraint and support. Against that is the competing interest in redesigning the order to serve well-being better. The course of history shows how the people divide their actions and allegiance between the two, the order in place and the vision of another more suited to their needs and utilities. The disposition to conserve what they have, however meagre, allied with caution in putting it at risk, confronts another for change and improvement. The tug of each and the tension between the two mark out much of the history of constitutional authority.

7. Officials, self-restraint, and the route to purpose

The people need self-restraint in the face of power, officials in the use of power. The self-restraint of officials, a condition of effective government, rejection a licence to illicit ends, has its own reason and logic. Power once in place opens up possibilities beyond purpose. Ulysses, addressing the Greek generals as the siege of Troy stalls, states the logic: 'Power into will, will into appetite/And appetite, an universal wolf/So doubly seconded with will and power'.[23] Power tempts the holder to think how it might be used to satisfy *appetite*, the *universal wolf*, the appetite to satisfy interests suppressed but soon aroused and inflamed. Interests valued but banned from the constitutional field, now slip through the fence, incite sentiments and dispositions, and encourage action for which power is on hand. Ulysses had in mind the people, the *plebs*, and how power would fuel their appetites, while blind to the appetite of people like himself the rulers, here a cluster of dim-witted generals. The better, indeed perfect case appears in the next play, *Measure for Measure*, which we imagine Shakespeare planning as he neared the end of Troilus and Cressida. Perhaps he had in mind Angelo the acting duke of Vienna who is under watch by Vincentio, the duke who has taken leave in order to see 'If power change purpose'.[24]

22 Q Skinner: *The Foundations of Modern Political Thought*, Volume 2 (Cambridge: Cambridge University Press, 1988), p 322.

23 W Shakespeare: *Troilus and Cressida* (1603), Act 1: 1: 120.

24 W Shakespeare: *Measure for Measure* (1604), Act 1: 3: 54.

It does, drastically, and his suspicions are confirmed. Angelo uses the power of rule to satiate appetite for Isabella, the sister of the condemned Claudio, for whom she begs clemency. The principle is universal: power needed to govern by nature tempts the holder to change purpose, and arouses the appetite to do so, for which will and power unite.

Appetite in officials, rarely as shameless, greedy, or so easily bared as Angelo's, normally takes more subtle forms. Officials who use the power of office to avoid the rules and cultivate connections to their benefit; who favour friends and relations in posts and contracts; who weaken agencies to exert influence. Just a few cases of the same lack of restraint in governing, usually concealed, sometimes admitted and displayed openly. How to control the appetite of officials is a major theme in the history of constitutions. The measures are several: that rule be conducted within the law; that power be limited by the constitution and divided among agencies; that account be given. The emphasis is on structural constraints, the purpose twofold. One to place limits on power, the other to arouse and sustain sentiments and dispositions of self-restraint.[25] The trouble is much of governing occurs within the discretionary space beyond the reach of the constraints of law and constitution, beyond the gaze of the people. Some actions are open and stated and tied to rules, many are out of sight, unregulated, and undocumented, and yet all are essential to governing well.[26] How the discretionary space can be regulated, opened to scrutiny, and officials made accountable is a central issue in managing the constitutional field.

Restraint by officials is a necessary condition of governing well, but not sufficient. Restraint protects against misuse of power, but does not tell how to govern well, to be effective in achieving purpose. In earlier discourse, the personal qualities of the ruler mattered. Even to rule according to law is hard to achieve. As late as the seventeenth century, Stuart kings resisted the restraint of law and relied on personal qualities. Bringing rulers within constitution and law is a landmark, a trophy of constitutionalism. Yet, the reach of constitution and law leaves untouched what happens within the field to achieve purpose, to cope with the discretionary space, to govern well. The idea across history and peoples is that good rule depends on the qualities of the ruler, and the sentiments and dispositions generated, although exactly which personal qualities was never wholly clear. *Virtue* is the family concept. If the one or the few are to rule well and restrain appetite, they need virtue. *Buon Governo* shows a move from *virtue* or *virtu'* to the virtues, which gather around the site of power to guide and constrain its use.[27] Justice and

[25] Harrington is one of many who argued that institutions, not virtue, are the means to good rule: 'Give us good orders and they will make us good men'. See J Harrington: *The Commonwealth of Oceana and a System of Politics* (1770) (ed) JGA Pocock (Cambridge: Cambridge University Press, 1992), discussed by P Rahe (ed): *Machiavelli's Liberal Republican Legacy* (Cambridge: Cambridge University Press, 2006), pp 22*ff*. Institutions contribute to good rule but plainly are not enough.

[26] The discretionary space is analysed further in Chapter XV.

[27] Discussed in Chapter XII.

prudence, magnanimity and clemency, temperance and fortitude, to which others could be added. Handbooks of instruction, mirrors for princes, set out the qualities, the sentiments, and dispositions needed to foster the self-restraint of rulers and to rule well. The link between such qualities and good government is assumed rather than shown, and just how the qualities are cultivated remains a mystery. As commitment to constitutionalism grew, two ideas replaced the need for personal qualities. One that power be limited, spread among agencies, guided and controlled by legal principles. The other that power be confined to certain persons, men of prudence and a sound sense of the common good who know by nature and instinct how to rule well. The *signori* of twelfth-century Florence an early model, the parliamentarians of eighteenth-century England and the Virginian owners of land and slaves the modern expression. Such persons were presumed to be wise and prudent, to know what is good for all, and to rule accordingly. And, being heirs of Henry Ireton, they know good rule means, foremost, preserving a social order protecting property.[28] Confidence in rule by men of such kind, if ever high, has waned but the legacy of a few knowing best lives on.

Ideas of constitutionalism reached a point almost of perfection in the twentieth century. Relations between the people and government were defined, values stated, and power distributed among institutions designed for purpose. Within the constitutional field so well laid out, principles were laid down and the worst excesses kept under control. Nevertheless, the discretion inherent in and vital to governing remained an uncharted field, the secret of good government still under search. The search is misguided for there is no secret. The route to good government is marked and judged by purpose, the seminar again instructive. The lecturer knows the purpose is to teach the subject to the students, enabling them to learn and pass the exam. That is the lecturer's primary interest, the source of sentiments and dispositions, and actions to match. Purpose is guided by common sense and prudence: not too much material to prepare, not to rush; the need to be clear and precise in exposition; to deal patiently with comments and questions. Justice modestly dressed as fairness has a place in guiding the course of the seminar. The students are to be treated fairly; no favourites; no picking on one or another due to looks or origins or opinions; equal concern given to each piece of written work, each marked consistently and on merit. Beneficence, the disposition to help each student master the subject and succeed in the exam, is built into purpose and guides action. On the cautionary side, the temptation to exploit the seminar or its members for personal gain or satisfaction is ever present, the issue how to contain it. The primary sentiments of prudence, fairness, and beneficence are strengthened by a second order of qualities or virtues, modesty and generosity, patience and tolerance, even good humour. From the people's perspective the seminar, calm, controlled, and centred,

[28] On Henry Ireton, see Chapter VII.

seems a long way from the processes of governing, rough and ruthless; and yet they have in common the pursuit of purpose and the qualities to achieve it. The people come to realize there is no perfect solution; that governing whatever the form is prone to the same risks. Armed with the quintet of actions, they approach the field intent on learning how to reduce the risks enough to secure sound rule.

8. Social relations among the people

The principal relationship in the constitutional field is that between the people and officials. Less prominent are relations among the people. The people come to the field with sentiments and dispositions formed in social relations and guided by social spheres. Relations and spheres form around interests and ideas generally shared; but also are shaped by and slanted towards those of certain sectors. They tend to dominate the broader social field, which they cultivate to their advantage by setting the standards and encouraging modes of thought, fostering a discourse backed by pressures often subtle, sometimes severe. It is as if some sectors were able to entwine the people in a pattern of thought, a perception of social life, from which there is no unwinding, no escape. Some observers attribute to the resulting social order the power to engulf the people, who lose all sense of other interests and ideas, other ways of ordering society. That does not do the people justice. We have seen before that no matter how dominated and repressed, or seemingly backward, the people retain a vision of well-being, and value a foundation of interests and ideas to match, often dormant, awaiting summons to wake and rise. Even if it never comes and no matter how repressive the order, the people retain an innate and indelible capacity to see beyond the boundaries of the field, to imagine another more fertile in fostering their well-being.

Both Quince the carpenter and Caliban the slave live in conditions of subjection, the one less obvious and less severe than the other. Both imagine things could be different, a world where the common man would not be hanged for frightening a lady and slaves would have their freedom; where each would be respected and allowed to flourish.[29] The study of rebellion reveals the same alternative vision of well-being, the same foundation of interests, suppressed but irrepressible, ever alert and ready to rise.[30] The same lesson is learnt from the Levellers. They were not outright rebels and began by appealing to the integrity of the constitutional order, asking only that rights be respected. Scrutiny, once launched, led back to a foundation of well-being and values from which to judge and condemn, not only

[29] *The Tempest* for Caliban, *A Midsummer's Night Dream* for Peter Quince.
[30] See Chapter IX.

particular practices, but the order itself.[31] That foundation is prior to and endures beyond the discourse and the institutions that grow out of, then come adrift from it. The people find there a foothold from which to view and assess the social structure as it is, and to imagine how it could be different. The vision of well-being, the reserve of interests, and the sentiments aroused, may dispose the people to action. Or the vision may be only dimly viewed, the sentiments vague and fleeting, figures in a dream disappearing with the dawn. A dawn of harsh authority leaving no room for competing sentiments. It is one thing to imagine a different social world, another to put it into practice. Safety cautions forbearance and resistance to the inclination to unrest; if a disposition does form, the step to action is still long and hard, bound to be opposed, and often prudently avoided.

How then is change possible; how to account for progress from passive acceptance of a place low in the social order, to one of active engagement and an enriched quality of life? Two variables govern, one the strength of the disposition to action, the other the power of the settled order to prevent action. The people find ways to gain a foothold on the margins and, from there, to edge forward to assert interests and achieve engagement in governing. Pitched against the safe course of passive compliance is the natural law of peoples, an engine of progress urging the people to venture beyond bare needs to improve the quality of their lives. They want to prosper, use their talents and exploit their potential; they want freedom to move about, take initiatives and compete in the tug-and-scramble. They confront a social order framed to keep each sector in its place, but know it could be different, imagine how their lives could be enriched. That everyone values the interest to improve their lives regardless of time or place is after all the starting point of human endeavour and the reason for collective action. How that interest is rendered in practice is contingent on history and circumstance, understandings, and ambition. The sentiment to improve life, nevertheless, is universal. That is the master interest, the incentive enduring and unquenchable, often unnoticed and neglected, but a constant and powerful source of dispositions and actions. The other variable, the power of rulers and select sectors to resist change, runs from weak and unstable to strong and confident. The one open to the rise of popular engagement and the staking of interests, the other closed and resistant, most somewhere in between. Ever in the background is Hume's timely reminder that the most fortress-like order of authority still rests on the people's opinion, the sentiment of support and the disposition to restraint. The last variable to mention in passing is force from outside, from events and occurrences beyond human control, a sobering case of the plague raging through history and, as I write, while the clouds of global conflict gather.

[31] Discussed in DJ Galligan, 'The Levellers, the People, and the Constitution' in *Constitutions and the Classics: Patterns of Constitutional Thought from Fortescue to Bentham* (Oxford: Oxford University Press, 14), pp 122–51.

The question remains whether the quintet of actions is enough to ensure the constitutional order serves well-being. Some streams of discourse insist on more, on sentiments higher and nobler, without which the constitutional order would be unstable, ineffective, and short-lived. Zeal, not acquiescence, is said to be needed to guarantee delivery even of basic goods. As expectations for more benefits rise, the need for active government follows, and the case for stronger sentiments and dispositions of the people rises with it. The idea is expressed in different ways, often as loyalty and patriotism, or love for the city, the republic, the nation. Montesquieu writes of 'love of the laws and of the country'.[32] Others replace love with the more moderate sentiment of respect; for Adam Smith 'reverence and respect',[33] for Baron d'Holbach simply 'respect for law'.[34] Testaments to similar sentiments abound and the need for each to sustain authority affirmed. It is enough here to mention two points.

One separates the practical and the ideal, one based on sentiments generated by interests at the base of well-being, the other sentiments expressing interests elevated and abstract. The constitutional order is valued by one for the tangible benefits, by the other for the refinement of civility and humanity. The portrait by Rafaello is valued not only for the pleasure it gives the viewer but as an object of beauty, for the genius of the artist and his rendering a young woman immortal.[35] That such ideas and entities be abstract does not lessen their value in the scheme of human ambition and endeavour. Once needs are satisfied and certain utilities advanced, the people raise their gaze to the finer signs of civility and humanity, to the abstract and the aesthetic. The constitutional order follows a similar logic, stimulates the same sentiments and dispositions. The order is valued not only for contributing to material well-being but as part of an admired artefact within the course of human action and the eternal task of advancing humanity and civility. Practical benefits could follow; the sentiment of value could strengthen the disposition to defend the order, and the more secure the order the more the benefits. Whether practice follows logic we need not here enquire.

The other point is one of caution, of higher sentiments distracting attention from the practical process of governing, from the need for the quintet of actions, demanding and tedious, but necessary. Noble sentiments of love and loyalty, patriotism and high virtue, while helping to sustain a constitutional order, run the risk of sedating the people, diverting them from the reality of rule and the practical actions assigned to them. A people so distracted courts peril. On the one hand,

[32] Montesquieu: *The Spirit of the Laws*, Book IV: Chapter 5.

[33] A Smith: *The Theory of Moral Sentiments*, p 273.

[34] P-HT Holbach: *Systeme social ou principes naturels de la morale et de la politique* (Paris: 1773), quoted in: J-F Spitz: 'From Civism to Civility: D'Holbach's Critique of Republicanism' in: *Republicanism: A Shared European Heritage*, Volume II (eds) M van Gelden and Q Skinner (Cambridge: Cambridge University Press, 2002), p 121.

[35] Introduced in Chapter IV.

trusting officials to pursue high ideals adds to their power and tempts the straying from purpose. On the other hand, the direct appeal to high ideals and abstract sentiments bypasses the practical processes marking and mediating the route from purpose to action, essential in keeping action to purpose. The consequences are plain, the pages of history stained by the appeal of ideals to neglect of all else. A theme weaving its way through the following chapters is not high ideals but instead the social context in which the people take practical measures, the quintet of actions, to achieve moderate results. More noble sentiments may be added and nurtured, sentiments of respect and trust, even admiration and affection. Yet, the people remain cautious and resist being distracted from the mundane and the practical. They temper lofty sentiments with a touch of scepticism, at times mounting to distrust and occasionally condemnation. Their hope is that when dispositions and actions match the balance of sentiments, a tolerable, even commendable, constitutional order becomes possible.

9. The precarious route to common purposes

In describing the scramble in pursuit of well-being, Adam Smith warns that the destination is known but the journey precarious. Two contrasting images come to mind. One presented in Lorenzetti's *Buon Governo*, where the people join together in concord and peace to attain common ends. The white cord passing through their hands unites citizens in forming social relations and creating institutions for common purposes, all centred on the classic virtues, under the eye of justice.[36] Something is missing. Only a select few, *i signori*, grasp the white cord, so where is *il popolo*, the common people? The tug-and-scramble conjures up a very different image, one more in tune with the other Italian tradition presented by Nicolò Machiavelli, an image of discord rather than concord.[37] Around this image, Giambattista Vico, the third Italian, weaves the theory of human action on which this study so promiscuously draws. Extracting from the foundation of Rome an eternal truth, Vico viewed history as the struggle of the have-nots, the people at the bottom for rights and powers economic, social, legal, including the power to engage in governing. The people being property-less flee for refuge to the property-owners, the first fathers. As refugees, they in time gain status, a rudimentary recognition, and become the *plebs*, the property-owners the patricians. The plebs agitate for *quiritary* rights, rights of ownership of land, which the patricians in time concede. The plebs later press for *connubium*, the right to marry, which is the condition of citizenship, and which again the patricians grant. As citizens they

[36] *Buon Governo* is discussed further in Chapter XII:3.
[37] Put forward in detail in *The Discourses*.

are qualified to enter the constitutional field, share in the cultivation, and take part in making laws apply to all.[38]

The experience of Rome promotes a general pattern, a parable of universal application and appeal. The people's progress from refugees to citizens is one of struggle and conflict, of discord not concord. An active people replaces the passive, all intent on advancing well-being, all engaged in the tugging and scrambling. Status and wealth count for less; select sectors lose special status; the people left free to contest the order of power and control of resources. They reject the idea of a few knowing what is best for all, concord the guiding goddess. Open competition takes their place; interests compete and conflict, and seem irreconcilable; ambition, greed, and lust for power are unleashed. How then out of discord can concord, enough to enable collective action, ever be achieved? Two courses are familiar. The most common is for powerful persons and sectors to form or re-form, restore firm rule, and return the people to the fortress. Stable government is re-established, the people's scope to improve their lives curtailed. The less common and harder is for the people to influence the construction of a constitutional order, so that the aims of governing go beyond property and order to embrace other aspects of well-being. Where governing is left to a few, the people having some say in how they govern; where the people support the few in governing and engage where practicable, while keeping open a watchful eye and a willingness to censure. The outcome they hope for is a social order not just peaceful and prosperous for a few, but one where the well-being of all is met to a reasonable level.

The conditions needed to reach and secure such a society are easy to state and hard to meet. How from discord do the people come together, not to create, but to shape a system of government? The answer has two parts, one the quintet of actions from self-restraint to censure, the other an alliance of prudence, justice, and beneficence. Self-restraint is a founding condition of collective action as Hume made plain; but it is not enough and has to work in harness with support and engagement, vigilance, and censure. On that foundation, prudence, justice, and beneficence moderate by reconciling self-interest and the interests of others. A constitutional order depends on such actions and the influence of each, all working together to establish a threshold of concord. Vico more ambitiously envisaged an equilibrium, a balanced tension among the sectors of society, adjusting from one era to another, as from ancient Israel to republican Rome, from medieval Europe to contemporary nations, the aim of each to attain a level of well-being for all. The people know any form of rule will be imperfect, that some do better than others, and even basic well-being is hard to secure, let alone allow room to improve

[38] *New Science*, p 69.

their lives. The people of Israel thought princely rule the best overall; republican Romans settled for a division of power between plebs and patricians; the freemen of Pennsylvania preferred to rule themselves; while contemporary constitutional orders contain strands of each.

10. The need for justification

A last landmark to chart, another set of sentiments and dispositions to build in, is the need the parties dominating such relationships feel to justify their position. The reasons are not obvious and have to be reconstructed from social relationships. The disposition flows from a sentiment valuing equality: all start as equals in a rudimentary sense from which any rupture has to be justified.[39] At a pre-social stage, all have the same needs and share the same aspirations of securing and advancing well-being. As social relations form, the appeal of natural equality is left behind, overshadowed by stronger sentiments flowing from more forceful interests. Vestiges linger; but as society advances in enterprise and invention, becomes stratified and breeds disparities, the sentiment of equality is lost from sight. A pattern of inequality takes its place, defined by status, wealth, and power. And yet the disposition to justify the inequalities persists and needs to be explained. Two accounts are credible. The nobler of the two appeals to a sentiment of respect of one for another based on equality. According to the Western tradition, the sentiments and dispositions inherited from Rome and still a guide to social understanding, each person is entitled to be treated with respect, each is the bearer of rights.[40] The founders' giving refuge to the homeless multitude signifies respect, recognition of a quality unique to the human person, a quality in which justice originates.[41] A quality denied to the slave to whom no more respect is due than to a chattel, a plank of timber to be turned to the master's will. Social relations in any meaningful sense are founded on mutual respect among the members as bearers of rights. The shared interest in respect, even if barely noticeable, is enough to form a matching sentiment and a disposition to action.

The impartial spectator, Adam Smith's figure of detached common sense, the Virgil of social understanding, offers guidance. The impartial spectator, briefed to give counsel on advancing humanity and civility, advises that among the sentiments shared is the need to justify the advantages of one over another. Disparities and inequalities have to be justified, not condemned or censured, but justified. Justification follows from the human desire for a life that has reason and meaning; a life coherent and rational; a life of which each is able to make sense. Sense is

[39] For the notion of basic equality and what flows from it, see Chapter IX.
[40] This elemental sense of equality is analysed in Chapter IX:4–6.
[41] On justice, see Chapter I:2.

found in interests and reason; interests that transcend position and power, and appeal to all, and from which reasons and actions follow. In the course of living well and prospering, life takes many directions and interests become unanchored from the base, become contingent and selective. The wider the gap, the harder it is to justify. Justification appeals to universality, to a foundation common to all and valued by all, while the purpose is to defend a social structure deeply unequal and an order of authority sustaining it. According to Weber, values are 'invented by man and imposed on the world'. That is too blunt. Values are founded on interests and serve the purpose of justifying interests, rather than being invented. Above the foundation of interests, Weber is a surer guide in singling out 'the human capacity to impose a world of values (ideas, ideals) on the universe of facts'.[42] Values once proclaimed become detached from the foundation of interests. *Authority*, 'an artefact of the will', empowers some to invoke values, as if of universal appeal, divorcing ideas from their foundation to justify a social order of one kind or another. That is part of the function of the upper register, to weave around social relations a set of ideas and values, the other part to present them as universal and for the good of everyone.

The other reason, less noble, for the sentiment of justification is fear. Fear that disparities of property and power, of opportunity and achievement, arouse discontent among the people. Moderate disparities of both are accepted as a normal dimension of social relations. Industry and effort deserve reward, conserving and accumulating assets is commendable, while initiatives enriching the few benefit all.[43] Power is justified on similar lines that the welfare of all is served by vesting power in a few. The impartial spectator urges a balance be found; that disparities of power and resources, even if short of ideal and unfair, be admitted as a condition of prosperity and the well-being of all. The people's self- restraint is critical, but the wider the disparities the more severe the strain. The timelessness of Hume's axiom is apparent, for any equilibrium depends on the opinion, the sentiments, and dispositions of those with the least share. Their inclination to tear down the fortress, gain a fairer deal, and enlarge their portion, has to be curbed to keep the calm, for between the interest in stability and the interest in improving lives is a constant tension. Select sectors encourage the self-restraint of the people by presenting the equilibrium as an appeal to timeless values of harmony and unity, stability and prosperity. Their efforts to reach beyond sectional interests to invoke ideas and images universal and compelling are charted in the following chapters.

Such ideas and images we have noted constitute a register of thought and discourse with which all can identify, and powerful enough to overshadow other

[42] So put by Anthony Kronman in commenting on Weber. See AT Kronman: *Max Weber* (London: Edward Arnold, 1983), p 43.

[43] The moral dimension is discussed in J Rawls: *A Theory of Justice* (Oxford: Clarendon Press, 1972).

options. Appearances are misleading, assumptions unfounded, ambitions thwarted. The people, the less privileged sectors, are not figures of wax to mould at will; they have their own purposes, images, and ideas to match, their own register, immanent in which is a sense of constitution. Ideas and images lead back to interests, which generate sentiments and dispositions, distinctive and powerful, to secure and improve their position. Not only to increase their share of power and material goods, but to have access to resources of other kinds, including education, employment, and culture. The most casual comparison of a European citizen of two hundred years ago with the citizen of today shows how effective such sentiments and dispositions have been in prompting action to improve their lives. My purpose in the following chapters is to enquire into the people's interests; to examine the sentiments and dispositions formed around them; and to bring out the sense of constitution within. At the core of the enquiry are the images and ideas with which the people make sense of their social world, their place within it, and relations among them, and between them and those who rule. This means constructing the register of thought and discourse, a *lower register*, and drawing out the sense of constitution within it, the point of the enquiry sharpened by contrast with the *upper register* of constitutional thought.

Notes

Relativity of interests

A glance at a nation's history soon shows how notions of well-being form and change, how interests once held sacred lose their shine, how others once damned as the work of the devil take their place. While everyone has an interest in well-being, what it means beyond a threshold and how far it reaches are conditioned, even dictated by the social setting, the field of social relations, and social spheres in which people find themselves.

The field of relations among the Nuer is a long way from that of the British anthropologists studying them: E Evans Pritchard: *The Nuer* (Oxford: Oxford University Press, 1940) that of the refined Roman citizen a foreign field to the uncouth hordes pounding down from the north. To the native Australians of Botany Bay, the Europeans landing on their shores were as if spirits from another world. Even within the same nation, the social fields can be wildly different, each alien to the other, as we have seen in the south of Italy, less than a century ago, where the peasants lived in a world 'Christ never reached', a pre-Christian world caught in the twilight between beasts and humans, a world utterly alien to the refined *Piemontesi* and the literary *Torinesi* of the north, as was theirs to the peasants. See Carlo Levi: *Cristo si è fermato a Eboli* (discussed in the Introduction).

Justifying values

While Weber's understanding of the constitutional order is much repeated, Douglas North's view, noted earlier, is worth repeating: 'the rules are created to serve the interests of those with the bargaining power to decide the rules'. See D North: *Institutions, Institutional Change, and Economic Performance*, p 16.

Authority

Authority is a necessary element of social structure, but particular forms of authority have to be explained and justified. It is often said that constitutional authority, unlike other forms, such as within the family, is in a way artificial, creating social relations that are not steeped in family, group, or community. State power is necessary but built on top of social relations rather than emerging within them. This description has to be refined. On the one hand, the need for overall authority is grounded in elementary social relations and required by common purposes; on the other hand, the form it takes is artificial in the sense that it is invented and propagated by the more powerful groups and sectors, who try to combine the well-being of all and advantage to particular sectors.

Design of agencies

The point of process is to steer agencies to outcomes, which leads to questions about the design of agencies. The constitution creates the primary agencies, legislative, executive, and judicial, and states the form, power, and process of each and the division of labour among them. The directions are often sketchy, with much left to be settled within the field according to experience, ideas, and the competition among agencies.

Substance and Procedure

Once the constitution is in place, the people have an interest in influencing the process of governing; the legislative process deciding law and policy, the executive, regulatory, and administrative exercising discretion, the adjudicative settling disputes. The interest here is the people's being empowered to engage and exert influence over each arm of government. The degree and density differ over time and place, but a pattern can be detected. The people are normally confined to a minor role, from which they struggle to escape and to gain influence, mostly gradual, at times dramatic and decisive. Gains are often short-lived, superior sectors prevail, and the people pushed back to the margins. Sometimes, they manage to secure and sustain a position of moderate engagement in the process of governing.

Along this line I later map models of engagement, each designed to show the place of the people in the constitutional order. It is enough for now to note how changeable the place of the people can be and how fluid their engagement in governing. This is the second variable in the social understanding of constitutional authority: the nature and intensity of the people's engagement in, and power over the processes of governing.

The procedural aspect of engagement in selecting interests for protection needs to be explained and refined. Interests are of two kinds, substance and process. One refers to interests valued for contributing directly to well-being, such as security, liberty, and respect for rights. The other refers to the steps to be taken, procedures followed to secure such interests. If the people value an interest, liberty, for instance, they have a companion interest in the procedures for securing liberty. Agencies across the board have to rule on what liberty means and to decide the balance with other interests. The people's interest in process applies to the actions of government, the legislative and the executive, and the administrative. Their general interest gives birth to more specific interests in the process of governing, from settling the constitution to the details of administration.

Processes and procedures are the means by which agencies are kept to purpose in securing substantive interests. They are the means for containing power and guarding against abuse or misuse. To summarize, the people have three kinds of interests in the constitutional field: interests in well-being generally; interests in selecting aspects of well-being for constitutional status; and interests in the processes of governing affecting well-being. For fuller discussion of substance and procedure see DJ Galligan: *Due Process and Fair Procedures.*

Justice and beneficence elements of collective action

Collective action generally, and in the constitutional field in particular, is made possible by, and conducted through social relations, to which sentiments of justice and beneficence are essential. Justice as we have seen combines self-interest, the interest of others, and an abstract interest. The sentiment of beneficence flows from valuing the interests of others, supported perhaps by self-interest in the satisfaction felt and by the potential gains to oneself in cooperating with and helping others. Each sentiment, while serving a principal interest, overlaps and intersects with the others.

VI
The Sovereignty Deficit

1. Situating sovereignty

A study of the people in the constitution starts with the concept of *sovereignty*. The people constitute the sovereign body that launches the constitutional order and authorizes all that happens within it. The aim of this chapter is to enquire further into the concept, assess its place in constitutional discourse, and the function it performs in the constitutional order. But first, a few points of clarification. Sovereignty is associated with the idea of a sovereign people ruling itself, which is in turn associated, loosely, with democracy. What it means to be self-ruling, the social foundations, and the instabilities are analysed later.[1] It is enough to note that the number of nations broadly democratic is just under a half of the total.[2] It is reasonable to assume the people would want the constitutional order to acknowledge and provide for their sovereignty, and so protect self-rule and hence democracy.[3] The issue now is to test that assumption, or more precisely to consider how sovereignty is expressed in contemporary constitutions broadly democratic. We hear a lot about the democratic deficit but nothing about the sovereignty deficit. But why focus attention on sovereignty rather than democracy?

On one approach the two are inseparable, democracy depends on the people's being sovereign, while the point of sovereignty is to enable democracy. There are, however, two reasons for giving sovereignty priority. First, sovereignty is the language of constitutions, while democracy is either not mentioned, or is an aspiration without practical support. The other reason is that while acknowledging the complexity of relations between the two concepts, sovereignty is the foundation of constitutional authority, while democracy is one form of government, not necessarily the only form that a sovereign body might choose. Since constitutions lay the foundations of government and normally are written in the language of sovereignty, a study of sovereignty is the most direct route to understanding the place of the people in the constitutions of nations broadly democratic. The concept of the people has a long history in constitutional thought, touched on in other chapters.

[1] See Chapters X–XI.

[2] This chapter is a modified version of an article published in 2013: DJ Galligan, 'The Sovereignty Deficit of Modern Constitutions' (2013) 33 *Oxford Journal of Legal Studies* 703–32. Some changes have taken place since but the general pattern of constitutions remains constant and serves the purpose of this chapter.

[3] Democracy could be defined in terms other than self-government; here I adopt the standard approach, which is to define democracy in terms of self-government. For a variation, see Chapter XV Notes.

Keepers of the Common Good. D.J. Galligan, Oxford University Press. © D.J. Galligan 2024.
DOI: 10.1093/9780198907398.003.0006

A history we need not enter here beyond noting that, among the different meanings *the people* has borne at different times, three stand out: the people as individual persons; the people coming together as an aggregate of individual persons; the people as an abstract entity distinct from its individual members.[4] Modern constitutions use the concept of the people liberally and loosely, without explanation or definition, so that all three meanings bounce in and out. The abstract or corporate entity of the people has a special place and utility in constitutional discourse.[5] Sovereignty has its own collection of meanings. Of interest here is the meaning within a nation, rather than among nations where it signifies a separate, self-governing entity. Within a nation, sovereignty has three main meanings: legal, constitutional, and political.

2. The language of sovereignty

Sovereignty in a legal sense refers to the ultimate authority within a legal order. Parliaments are often sovereign in this sense. Sovereignty is used in a second wider sense to indicate the entity that makes or authorizes the making of the constitution and the conferring of authority on agencies and officials.[6] The people may be sovereign in this sense, although constitutions sometimes distinguish between the people as the *source* of sovereignty while vesting sovereignty itself in the nation or in the institutions of government. An intriguing idea that serves a useful purpose; it is also a warning sign of how flexible and elusive sovereignty in a constitutional sense can be.[7] The constitutional texts do not always refer to sovereignty at all, but rest on the understanding that behind the constitution the people are in a political sense supreme. The Australian Constitution says nothing about sovereignty, yet in providing for elections and related matters, assumes the people to be in some sense supreme. This idea may conveniently be expressed as political sovereignty. The interplay between the people and sovereignty in the three senses identified becomes apparent as the chapter progresses.

The language of sovereignty and the sovereignty of the people is not reserved for nations claiming to be democratic but occurs across the spectrum of all nations.

[4] Margaret Canovan provides a concise and helpful account of the various meanings and their constitutional setting: M Canovan: *The People* (Cambridge: Polity Press, 2005); also P Ihalainen: *Agents of the People: Democracy and Popular Sovereignty in British and Swedish Parliamentary and Public Debates 1734–1800* (Brill, 2010) and DJ Galligan: 'The People, the Constitution, and the Idea of Representation' in DJ Galligan and M Versteeg (eds), *The Social and Political Foundations of Constitutions* (Cambridge: Cambridge University Press, 2013).

[5] Discussed in Chapter II:3.

[6] In some constitutions, the language is not that of sovereignty but instead supreme or constituent power.

[7] Among a large literature on the subject of authority, Jeffrey Goldsworthy has an admirable introduction to the various senses of sovereignty: J Goldsworthy: *The Sovereignty of Parliament* (Oxford: Clarendon Press, 1999).

Some are classified *anocratic*, a hybrid of democracy and autocracy; others are *autocratic* in the sense of lacking democratic character. Both proclaim the people to be sovereign. According to standards developed by the *Polity Score*, just over half the world's nations are ranked, broadly, as democratic.[8] The analysis here is confined to the constitutions of the most democratic nations, which are, roughly, one-third of the total.[9] Occasional reference will be made to the constitutions of anocratic and autocratic nations, and to state constitutions within nations, but the main issue is the place of the people in the constitutions of nations classified as democratic.

The following analysis discloses much about popular sovereignty and unearths some surprises. Any expectation of constitutions being clear and confident assertions by the people of their sovereignty, whereby they design a constitutional order and authorize a system of government in which they have a role and which is accountable to them, will, on the whole, be disappointed. On the contrary, whether sovereignty vests in the people is not always clear, and even if it does, its meaning and purpose are obscure. Government normally is by a combination of representatives and officials over whom the people have control of varying degrees, often minimal, beyond the election of representatives. After a survey of the constitutions of democratic nations, my conclusion is that despite common resort to the concept, rather than popular sovereignty being triumphant, there is a *sovereignty deficit*.

The sovereignty deficit is a metaphor, a way of expressing the gap between the idea of the people ruling themselves and the constitutional text. It is also a sign to social reality, that social relations between the people and officials do not match those of the people ruling themselves. This suggests the need to uncouple the idea from the reality, to begin with the text, and instead of assuming it to be the expression of popular sovereignty and the social relations of self-government, work backwards, excavating the ideas and the social reality underlying the text. If in the course of the voyage we mark, but sail past, the shoals of popular sovereignty and are deaf to the sirens of self-government, we shall discover a different explanation for the text. One grounded in social relations between rulers and the ruled, one awaiting reconstruction from the legal, social, and political foundations of constitutions. Rule through representatives emerges as the standard case, the people left to play a minor role both in governing and in controlling the governors. Cause will be shown to question, indeed abandon, the view that representative government

[8] The Polity Score is based on a method of evaluation of forms of governance that ranges from fully institutionalized democracies through anocracies (meaning mixed or hybrid regimes) to full autocracies. The scale is based on six factors that measure key qualities of executive government, constraints on executive authority, and political competition. The resulting scale ranges from +10 to -10, that is to say, from democracies (+6 to +10) to anocracies (+5 to -5) and autocracies (-5 to -10). The current rating is set out in MG Marshall and BR Cole: *Global Report 2017: Conflict, Governance, and State Fragility* (Centre for Systematic Peace USA, 2017). The Polity Score considers a nation to be one with a population of at least 500,000.

[9] The nations included here are listed in the Appendix.

is a mere practical adjustment to popular sovereignty and self-government, an adjustment necessary in the interests of efficient government.[10] The grounds will then be laid to question the claim that the principle of representative democracy is that 'the mass of everyday citizens in their collective capacity' decide on 'the laws, norms, and policies' produced by government.[11] These are larger questions to which this chapter is the prologue leaving the plot to unfold in later chapters. The prior purpose is to understand how contemporary constitutions portray the people, what they say about popular sovereignty, and the role of the people in the processes of government.

The point of entry is the study of how the people are presented in the texts of constitutions, focusing on relations between the people and the primary institutions of government (other than the judiciary). The analysis is confined to the constitutions of the most democratic nations, with some reference to state constitutions within nations in discussing popular initiatives. Since the question is how these nations present the people in the constitution, it is reasonable to examine those that come closest to the ideal of self-rule and to ask: (i) where sovereignty lies and how it is expressed; (ii) the role of the people in making constitutions; (iii) how sovereignty is exercised; (iv) the features of representative government, in particular the relations between representatives and the people; and (v) the forms of direct action available to the people.

3. Sovereignty of the people

We the people Sovereignty of the people is provided for in a majority of the democratic nations either expressly or by implication. Fourteen constitutions (14/65) make no reference to the people, while in the rest (51/65) reference is made to the people but in different ways and for different purposes. Within this group, some (17/51) begin with the words 'We the People', or some variant: We the people of Albania, the Philippines, the Czech Republic, Ghana, and Japan being examples. The founders of the United States' Constitution seem to have been the first to use the expression, from where it spread to state constitutions so that all but one begin *We the people*.[12] That the Constitution of Japan should open with those words is understandable, given oversight by occupying American forces during the process of drafting and adoption;[13] less so that the words should appear in the

[10] The critique of rule by representatives is continued in Chapter XIV. For a concise statement on the need to find accommodation between democracy and the practical needs of governing, see R Dahl: *How Democratic is the American Constitution?* (Yale University Press, 2001).

[11] JE Green: *Eyes of the People: Democracy in an Age of Spectatorship* (Oxford: Oxford University Press, 2010), p 176.

[12] Vermont is the exception.

[13] D Law: 'The Myth of Imposed Constitutionalism in Japan' in Galligan and Versteeg: *Social and Political Foundations of Constitutions.*

constitutions of nations as diverse as Albania, India, and South Korea. The words suggest a coming together of the people to declare their sovereignty, which they affirm on each reading from one generation to another. Appearances are misleading, for it emerges that such confident openings do not necessarily imply the sovereignty of the people. In some cases the words are followed by a declaration of sovereignty (7/17); in others (6/17) the people are said to be the source of sovereignty or supremacy, while sovereignty either vests elsewhere or is not mentioned. In a few cases (4/17), including the Constitution of the USA, despite opening with *We the people* there is no declaration of sovereignty in the people or elsewhere.

The people as sovereign A group of just over half the constitutions in the cohort (34/65) replaces the first-person we with an announcement of the *sovereignty of the people*: the Andorran people, the Colombian people, the Indonesian people and many other peoples are declared to be sovereign.[14] The French Constitution is typical in declaring that national sovereignty shall vest in the people,[15] while the German Constitution, in a slight variation, declares that 'the German people, in the exercise of their constituent power, have adopted this basic law'.[16] The distinction between the people as the source of sovereignty, and being sovereign, again appears. The Constitution of Turkey makes a threefold distinction between: the people as the source of sovereignty, sovereignty which vests 'fully and unconditionally' in the nation, and the exercise of sovereignty by the elected assembly.[17] Other constitutions, lacking such awareness and rigour, tend not to distinguish between the people's being the source of sovereignty and being sovereign.[18] The word sovereignty is not always used. The German people are both the constituent power and the source of all state power.[19] In some cases it is said that law emanates from the people;[20] in others that 'all public power' comes from the people,[21] while in another variation the people exercise the legislative power but do so through parliament.[22] In the Indian Constitution, the people 'resolve to create India into a Sovereign republic'.[23] These are just some of the ways constitutions acknowledge the people as the sovereign authority or the source of that authority or both. Whether the form of words matters is not clear, although the political and symbolic significance of recent changes to the Constitution of Hungary, from the detached

[14] Two within the group are slight variations: the German Constitution refers to the people as the constituent power rather than sovereign: Basic Law for the Federal Republic of Germany (1949) preamble. The Constitutions of Montenegro and Serbia vest sovereignty in the citizen rather than the people: Constitution of Montenegro (2007) art 2; Constitution of the Republic of Serbia (2006) art 2.

[15] Constitution of the Fifth Republic (1958, 1962, 2008) art 3.

[16] Basic Law for the Federal Republic of Germany (1949) preamble.

[17] Constitution of the Republic of Turkey (1982) art 6.

[18] Examples are Ghana, Brazil, and Greece.

[19] Basic Law of the Federal Republic of Germany (1949) preamble, art 20.

[20] Federal Constitutional Law of Austria (1920, 1929, 1945) art 1.

[21] Instrument of Government (1810, 1949, 1975, 1991) Chapter I, art 1.

[22] Constitution of the Kingdom of Norway (1814, 2007) art 49.

[23] Constitution of the Republic of India (1950, 1970) preamble.

statement that supreme power is in the people to the possessive and suggestive 'We the members of the Hungarian nation',[24] is striking.

The nation of the people In some constitutions (9/65) sovereignty vests in the nation rather than the people. The Constitution of Turkey, as just noted, vests sovereignty in the nation, although its source is the people. The Constitution of Poland is typical of several cases in providing that 'supreme power in the Republic of Poland shall be vested in the Nation' without making plain its source, although a reference to 'all citizens of the republic' implies it is the people.[25] The position is not always straightforward. The Constitution of Chile refers to the 'nation' within which 'sovereignty rests essentially', without linking it to the people.[26] It then goes on to introduce another distinction between having sovereignty and exercising it, the exercise being shared between the people through 'plebiscites and periodic elections' and 'authorities established by the Constitution'.[27] The idea of sovereignty resting 'essentially in the nation' raises questions about the concept of the nation and its relation to the people.[28]

Normally, 'nation' is used without explanation, assuming earlier ideas, especially those of Emmanuel Sieyès, according to whom a nation emerges when individual persons unite to form a common will, a necessary step in creating society. The people in expressing the common will are the nation, the constituent power, which then delegates authority to representatives, the constituted power, who then conduct government and are the only ones empowered to do so. In the language of sovereignty, which Sieyès does not use, the people as the nation are sovereign.[29] The Turkish Constitution fits this account, while the Constitution of Chile in declaring that the people share in the exercise of sovereignty through forms of direct action, inserts a distinctly un-Sieyèsian idea.[30] A similar reservation of 'the power to propose laws and amendments' to the constitution by the citizens of Colorado is justified as a legitimate exercise of their sovereignty.[31] The Belgian

[24] Fundamental Law of Hungary (2011) preamble.

[25] Constitution of the Republic of Poland (1997) preamble, art 4.

[26] Uruguay has adopted a similar approach of referring to the nation as the sovereign body: Constitution of the Oriental Republic of Uruguay (1830) art 4; see also Constitution of the Republic of Turkey (1982) art 6.

[27] Constitution of the Republic of Chile (1980, 2005) art 5.

[28] The Constitution of Luxembourg also vests sovereignty in the Nation: Constitution of Luxembourg (1868, 1948, 1998, 2009) art 32.

[29] On Sieyès' account the people as the nation remain the constituent (or sovereign) power, government being a constituted or delegated power: 'What is the Third Estate?' in M Sonenscher (ed), *Sieyès: Political Writings* (Hackett Publishing Coy, 2003); by contrast on Hobbes' account the people give up sovereignty to their representative: *Leviathan* (ed) R Tuck (Cambridge: Cambridge University Press, 1991), Chapter XVIII.

[30] Sieyès' case for the people, the constituent power, delegating authority to representatives is based on the pragmatism and prudence of leaving government to representatives, not high principle; see further: DJ Galligan: 'The Paradox of Constitutionalism or the Potential of Constitutional Theory' (2008) 28 *Oxford Journal of Legal Studies* 343.

[31] D Pothill: *Protecting the People's Voice: Identifying the Obstacles to Colorado's Initiative and Referendum Process* (Independence Institute, 2009).

Constitution[32] adds a twist by providing that 'all powers emanate from the nation' without explaining what the nation is or how it comes to have powers.[33]

The parliament of the people A small, final group of constitutions is based on parliament without reference to the people.[34] The UK parliament, notwithstanding its lack of a definitive constitutional text, is the parent whose offspring include Australia, Canada, Malta, and New Zealand. In each one, parliament is expressly or impliedly the sovereign authority, although in England the doctrine emerged from the idea that parliament, that is the Queen-in-Parliament, embodies the people.[35] If the people are embodied in parliament, then in one sense the people are sovereign, the full statement being the people in parliament are sovereign, although that has been forgotten. This view of parliament did not spread beyond the UK to nations such as Australia and Canada, which regard parliament in the exercise of supreme legislative authority as representing the people rather than embodying them.[36] Outside the British Commonwealth, several other nations adopted parliamentary systems. The Constitution of the Netherlands, to take just one case, states simply that 'the Parliament shall represent the entire people of the Netherlands' without mention of sovereignty.[37]

While the sovereignty of parliament is fundamental to the Constitution of the UK, the constitutions of other parliamentary systems focus on legislative power rather than sovereignty, so that whoever has the power to make laws is the supreme constitutional authority. To add sovereignty would be to add nothing. The Constitution of Malta simply states 'there shall be a Parliament', which has authority not only to make laws but also to amend the constitution.[38] In cases of this kind, parliament is elected by the people, although that is not always secured in the constitution, so it is implicitly understood that outside and beyond the legal constitution, at the political level, the people have a key role. Whether this quite

[32] The Belgian Constitution (1994, 2007) art 33.

[33] Other constitutions that vest sovereignty in the nation are Constitution of Luxembourg (1868, 1948, 1998, 2007) art 32; Constitution of the Republic of Poland (1997) art 4; Constitution of the Republic of India (1950, 1970) preamble (although a less clear case); Constitution of the Slovak Republic (1992, 1999, 2001) preamble; Constitution of the Oriental Republic of Uruguay (1830) art 4; Constitution of Costa Rica (1949, 1989) art 2.

[34] The nations in this category are Canada, Denmark, Iceland, Malta, Netherlands, Norway, and Romania.

[35] This curious idea is further explained in DJ Galligan: 'The People, the Constitution, and the Idea of Representation' in DJ Galligan and M Versteeg (eds), *Social and Political Foundations of Constitution* (New York: Cambridge University Press, 2013), pp 134–56. For a detailed study of these ideas in the eighteenth century, see P Ihalainen: *Agents of the People*.

[36] The constitutions of former British colonies, such as Australia and Canada, are usually created by an Act of the UK Parliament. The Commonwealth of Australia Act (1900), which creates the Federal Constitution, recites the agreement of the people of the existing states to 'unite in one indissoluble Federal Commonwealth': preamble. The Constitution itself is made by an Act of the UK parliament, and the agreement of the people is the agreement of their representatives in the states.

[37] Constitution of the Kingdom of the Netherlands (1983) art 50; the Constitution of Romania is similar: Constitution of Romania (1991, 2003) art 58.

[38] Constitution of Malta (1964) art 51.

fits the notion of sovereignty is unclear. In the Australian Constitution there is no mention of sovereignty, although the constitution derives from the people agreeing to unite in 'one indissoluble Federal Commonwealth', implying that the people are the source of constitutional authority if not the bearers of sovereignty.[39] Some constitutions within the parliamentary family, such as that of Norway, in providing that the people exercise the legislative power through parliament, despite not referring to sovereignty, acknowledge the people as the supreme political power.[40]

Conclusions Just over half of the most democratic constitutions vest sovereignty in the people.[41] In the rest, the place of the people is lesser: they are either the source of sovereignty but not sovereign; or referred to without reference to sovereignty; or a political entity vital to the constitution but outside its written provisions.[42] Secondly, of the constitutions beginning *we the people* only a handful declare the people to be sovereign, and so throw into question whether the words mean anything. Thirdly, in a number of constitutions the people are the source of authority but not sovereign, while sovereignty vests in another entity, normally the nation, or in other cases is not mentioned. Being the source of sovereignty but having no sovereign power is not straightforward conceptually, and in practice renders the people constitutionally powerless. Fourthly, in the few cases where sovereignty vests in the nation, the exact relationship between nation and the people is not clear, except in the case of Turkey, which makes plain what other constitutions leave unsaid. Fifthly, where no reference is made to the people in the constitution, or the reference does not relate to sovereignty, which tends to be the case in parliamentary systems, there are indications of the people's being present outside or prior to the constitution, either in appointing representatives to create a constitution or electing parliament as the supreme law-maker. The people are in some sense the ultimate political power, even if legal sovereignty is located elsewhere.[43] Finally, it is striking how much of constitutional importance concerning the people and their relations with government is not covered but occurs outside or prior to the text, and depends on conventions, practices, and understandings. That a self-governing people should not be more diligent, exacting, and purposive in expressing their sovereignty, or at least clarifying their relationship to government, is unexpected.

39 Commonwealth of Australia Constitution Act (1900) preamble.

40 Constitution of the Kingdom of Norway (1814, 2007) art 40.

41 Included are Montenegro and Serbia, which vest sovereignty in citizens, and Germany which invests the people with constituent power: Constitution of Montenegro (2007) art 2; Constitution of the Republic of Serbia (2006) art 2; Basic Law for the Federal Republic of Germany (1949) art 1.

42 The same applies to the three acknowledged to be without a declared written constitution (the UK, Israel, and New Zealand). Whether or not these nations regard parliament as sovereign, they assume the parliament is elected by the people.

43 For further discussion, Canavon: *The People*.

4. Making and ratifying constitutions

A sovereign people would be expected to take a close interest in the process of constitution-making through participation and scrutiny, supervision and ratification.[44] The majority of constitutions in the cohort say nothing about how they were made or by whom, although nine (9/65) declare they are the work of representatives rather than the people. The Constitution of Argentina states: 'We, the representatives of the people of the Argentine Nation— do ordain, decree, and establish this constitution for the Argentine Nation.'[45] The Constitution does not reveal the identity of the representatives or how they were appointed, for these are matters settled outside and prior to the Constitution. Nor does it make clear relations between the representatives and the people. The Constitution of Brazil is similar in declaring it is made by representatives, although it differs in confirming that sovereignty vests in the people, from whom all power emanates and who have used their power to appoint representatives to devise a constitution.[46] The retention of sovereignty in the people is the usual pattern among nations which entrust the making of the constitution to representatives.[47] In the wake of war, the 1946 Constitution of Japan had a troubled birth, at which the people were present only through their representatives in the two houses of parliament. The constitution having been adopted by the two houses, the Constitution Popularization Society set about promoting its spirit to the people, apparently with success. Sovereignty remained throughout with the Japanese people.[48]

Once we look to the origins of the text, it becomes clear that the people's sovereignty does not guarantee their participation in making or ratifying the constitution. Even where the people declare the constitution to be an act of their sovereign or constituent power, as in cases such as Albania, Colombia, and Germany, they have not necessarily had any part in its making. The same applies to most other constitutions beginning *We the people*, including that of the USA, whose constitution was made by a group of representatives who had not been charged with the task and whose text was not submitted to popular referendum. In investigating constitution-making, there are several questions to consider: who makes the constitution? If made by a special assembly, who appoints or elects its members? Are the people involved, and if so, in what ways? Does the text need to be ratified by

[44] For further discussion, see A Arato and Z Miklosi: 'Constitution Making and Transitional Politics in Hungary' in L Miller (ed), *Framing the State in Times of Transition: Case Studies in Constitution Making* (US Institute of Peace Press, 2010), pp 530ff.

[45] Constitution of the Republic of Argentine (1853, 1994) preamble.

[46] Constitution of the Federative Republic of Brazil (1988, 1995, 2006) art 1.

[47] This category includes Costa Rica, Guatemala, Nicaragua, Slovakia, and Ukraine: Constitution of Costa Rica (1949) art 2; Constitution of the Republic of Guatemala (1985, 1993) preamble; Constitution of the Republic of Nicaragua (1987) art 2; Constitution of the Slovak Republic (1992, 1999, 2001) preamble; Constitution of the Ukrainian National Republic (1996) art 5.

[48] Constitution of Japan (1946) preamble.

the people? Since the data necessary to answer these questions is incomplete and patchy, I shall not attempt to answer in full but merely sketch the patterns that seem to be emerging.

People's participation in constitution-making The advocate of popular sovereignty is likely to concede that making a constitution is a task unsuited to mass participation and best left to a select group and their advisers. This usually means either the creation of a special assembly or delegation of the task to the legislative authority, or some variation of the two. The people are sometimes involved in the selection of special assemblies, although a full study of the issue is yet to be carried out. An assembly once established might consider itself representative of the people but is just as likely to assume an independent stance.[49] Once the process is underway, the people might have direct input into the drafting process or be consulted about issues, or they might have more indirect involvement through oversight and ratification.[50] South Africa, Brazil, and more recently Ireland and Iceland, are often commended for involving the people, although public participation brings its own problems and is likely to make agreement harder to reach.[51] The coherence of the resulting text may be jeopardized, leading to 'a hodgepodge of inconsistent and convoluted provisions', as the Constitution of Brazil has been described.[52] Participation in itself does not guarantee that the views expressed are taken into account or that they influence the content of the constitution. It certainly does not result in the people's having a more secure and prominent place in it.[53] A small study conducted for this chapter shows that the people usually have some scope for involvement in the constitution-making process, although there is wide variation in the procedures and the degree of intensity, which ranges from practically nothing to very high.[54] There is some evidence of recognition in recent

[49] One study shows that for constitutions adopted since 1987 worldwide, in 65 per cent of cases the special assembly was elected by the people: J Widner: *Constitution Writing and Conflict Resolution: Data and Summaries* (Princeton University) <www.princeton.edu/power/data/> first posted 2006, accessed 11 September 2012. Lacking figures for the cohort on this point, we may reasonably assume the percentage is higher since we are dealing only with democracies.

[50] These are discussed in T Ginsburg, Z Elkins, and J Blount: 'Does the Process of Constitution-Making Matter?' (2009) 5 *Annual Review of Law and Social Science* 201 and Widner *ibid.* A recent example is Iceland, where extensive measures were taken to create a people's constitution: A Meuwese: 'Constitution-Making in Iceland' in Galligan and Versteeg: *Social and Political Foundations of Constitutions.*

[51] See further Ginsburg, Elkins, and Blount, *ibid*; L Miller: 'Designing Constitution-Making Processes; Lessons from the Past, Questions for the Future' in Miller: *Framing the State in Times of Transition*, pp 629*ff.*

[52] KS Rosenn: 'Conflict Resolution and Constitutionalism: The Making of the Brazilian Constitution' in Miller: *Framing the State in Times of Transition*, p 458.

[53] For discussion see S Voigt: 'The Consequences of Popular Participation in Constitutional Choice—Towards a Comparative Analysis' in A van Aaken (ed), *Deliberation and Decision* (Ashgate, 2003) and J Blount: 'How do Constitutions Matter: Popular Representation in the Drafting Process' (Workshop: How do Constitutions Matter, Foundation for Law Justice and Society, Oxford, 29 June 2012).

[54] The role of the people in making the constitution was examined in the following nine cases: USA, Australia, Japan, Hungary, Iceland, Brazil, South Africa, Spain, and Serbia.

years of the importance of the people's being involved in constitution-making. Yet, both opinion and practice still fall far short of a general commitment to the principle of popular participation in and control over the making of constitutions.[55]

Ratification Although there may be good reasons for leaving the drafting of constitutions to representatives, we should expect ratification to be an essential element of popular sovereignty. Ratification refers to the people voting to accept or reject the draft constitution. Again such expectations are on the whole disappointed. Some member states of the European Union allowed their citizens to vote on the proposed constitution of 2004, which the electors of France and the Netherlands soon rendered a dead letter. Since 1950, the use of the referendum has increased, but still fewer than half the constitutions now in force have been ratified by the people in this way.[56] A referendum was held in just less than half the nations in the cohort.[57]

5. Identity of the people

Who are the people, the 'we' in 'we the people', the people in whom sovereignty is vested or from whom it comes? Considering the complexity of this issue, I do no more here than suggest two lines of approach; one the realist after Thomas Hobbes, the other the corporate after Emmanuel Sieyès. On the realist approach, 'the people' means and can only mean the individual members or citizens of a nation, and the issue is how they come to settle on a constitution. Notions of the collective of the people as somehow distinct from individual persons are considered incoherent.[58] The logic of self-government requires individual persons agreeing to make a constitution and then deciding how to do it. The notion of a contract or covenant among them is often invoked to depict the process, a notion the Levellers took to the limits in urging that all citizens agree in writing to the terms of government.[59] The reality is different: constitutions are made by a few in the name of the many. The most the people can hope for is to exert some influence on content and to vote on its acceptance. Most constitutions fall short even of that, with the people acquiescing in a constitution rather than exerting authority over it. Acquiescence also accounts for continuity after the force of the original act of making or ratifying

[55] Blount: 'How do Constitutions Matter'.

[56] Elkins, Ginsburg, and Blount: 'Does the Process of Constitution-Making Matter?', p 377; it would be worthwhile to know how many constitutions have been rejected by referendum, in addition to that of the European Union.

[57] For further analysis of popular participation in constitution-making, see DJ Galligan and M Versteeg: 'The Social and Political Foundations of Constitutions: an Analysis of the Issues' in Galligan and Versteeg: *Social and Political Foundations of Constitutions*.

[58] Hobbes discusses this issue extensively in Hobbes: *Leviathan*.

[59] On the Levellers, see DJ Galligan: 'The Levellers, Arbitrary Power, Representation, and the Constitution' in DJ Galligan (ed), *Constitutions and the Classics: Patterns of Constitutional Thought from Fortescue to Bentham* (Oxford: Oxford University Press, 2014).

peters out.[60] Origins are not decisive of effectiveness and continuity, and other social forces come into play: the constitution becomes enmeshed in the society, and forms part of its legal, political, and social culture, as the post-war constitutions of Germany and Japan show.[61] The constitution is naturalized, socialized, and internalized, clothed in symbols and adorned with ideals, and embedded in social relations so that its role and its status are reconfirmed by daily practice.[62] This cultivates the belief that the constitution is the people's, an expression of sovereignty and self-government, a source of ownership and pride.

It is just possible on the realist approach to sustain the notion of individual persons' being the source of sovereign authority even that they are themselves sovereign, as a few constitutions state.[63] Some constitutions provide for the direct exercise by the people of sovereignty through referenda and initiatives; but the majority make no such provision, and even in those that do the scope for acts of popular sovereignty is small and their efficacy limited. Subject to that, the realist solution is to accept the need for concerted action by a few, which is achieved by the people's delegating their natural authority (or sovereignty) to representatives, who then govern in the interests of all. The modern realist will accept as legitimate limits on the powers of the representative sovereign, in a manner Hobbes would not allow.[64] The really realistic realists will admit that the individual person plays a minor part in the constitutional process.

The corporate account of the people has a different logic and serves different functions, as the Constitution of Turkey shows. Whether or not the founders were tutored in Sieyesian ideas, the constitution follows his model. The people of Turkey, the source of authority, to constitute a nation create collectively a representative sovereign as a separate entity, the nation or the state, which then establishes the institutions of government to exercise sovereignty. The creation of a collective or corporate entity, separate and distinct from individual persons, is the critical difference between this approach and the realist.[65] Once in place, the corporate entity solves some fundamental problems. With its origins in the universitas of Roman Law, which through Canon Law found its way into secular thought, the corporate

[60] For further discussion of acquiescence, see R Hardin: 'Constitution as Coordination' in Galligan and Versteeg: *Social and Political Foundations of Constitutions*. Recent research shows that while some constitutions have great longevity, many have rather short lives: see Z Elkins, T Ginsburg, and J Melton: *The Lifespan of Written Constitutions* (Cambridge: Cambridge University Press, 2009).

[61] Hume's idea that 'antiquity begets the opinion of right': see Chapter I:4.

[62] Practice is based on the norms of the system; practice, in turn, reconfirms and strengthens the norms. For further discussion of this notion of reflexivity, see A Giddens: *The Constitution of Society* (Cambridge: Polity Press, 1984).

[63] Constitution of the Republic of Serbia (2006) art 2; Constitution of Montenegro (2007) art 2; Constitution of the Republic of Moldova (1994) preamble, arts 2 and 25.

[64] Hobbes: *Leviathan*.

[65] See Chapter II.

entity of the people has many of the features of a modern corporation.[66] It has its own identity separate from the individual persons who are its members, and it speaks and acts only through representatives. Individual persons have a place in the corporation in a way similar to that of the shareholders of a company, with their interests as individual members being absorbed into the good of the whole. They have no right to speak or act for the corporation; whether they are involved in the selection of the corporation's directors (or representatives) varies and historically has not been tied to popular election. The corporate concept accounts for the constitution's being the people's constitution, while at the same time denying the people any role in government. Since a corporation persists over time, it also accounts for the continuity of constitutions. Just as the act of a corporation a century ago is still the act of the corporation today, so the act of the people in making and accepting the constitution a century ago continues to be the act of the people today.[67] It has the added merit that the identity of the people as a corporation does not depend on who happen to be members at any time; people come and go, the corporation goes on indefinitely. A final advantage is that the people as a corporation act through representatives who have plenary powers, including authority to legislate and in some cases to amend the constitution. Representative government and the corporate identity of the people go together: the form being the logical outcome of corporate identity; conversely, where the form is present its foundation is the corporate identity of the people. We now have a new and secure basis for explaining in good part, if not completely, the basis of representative government as it is understood in modern constitutions. *We the people* now makes sense as a declaration of the corporate entity of the people, not the real people.[68]

The corporate concept lies behind expressions such as: 'we the representatives of the people of the Argentine nation—do ordain, decree, and establish this constitution for the Argentine nation' and 'the people neither deliberate nor govern except through their representatives and authorities established by this Constitution'.[69] The language of a 'nation of the people', combined with exclusion of the real people from constitution-making and governing, becomes intelligible if a distinction is drawn between the real people and their corporate embodiment in the nation. In providing that 'the parliament shall represent the whole people', the Constitution of the Netherlands endorses such a reading. The corporate concept makes credible the fantastic idea of the British people all being present in parliament. The real people are not entirely absent, since political power finally depends on them and

[66] See G Post: *Studies in Medieval Legal Thought* (Princeton: Princeton University Press, 1964) and B Tierney: *Religion, Law, and the Growth of Constitutional Thought 1150–1650* (Cambridge: Cambridge University Press, 1982). See also Chapter VIII herein for more on origins.

[67] Generally, on corporations, see J Scott: *Corporations, Classes and Capitalism* (London: Hutchinson, 1979).

[68] Representative is examined more fully in Chapter XIV.

[69] Constitution of Argentina (1994) preamble and art 22.

they may bring the tower tumbling down; unless and until that happens, the legal and political power of the people is transferred to the corporate entity.

6. Exercising sovereignty

The exercise of sovereignty and the role of the people are usually provided for in the constitution. One approach is to proclaim the sovereignty of the people, state that sovereignty is to be used according to the constitution, then define the mode. The German Constitution is a model. After affirming the people as the source of state authority, it provides that authority be exercised 'through elections and other votes and through specific legislative, executive, and judicial bodies'.[70] The constitutions of another group of countries, of which Greece is one, after stating that the powers of the people 'shall be exercised as specified by the Constitution', creates and defines the offices and institutions to do so, and states how they are to be elected or appointed.[71] These examples are by no means standard forms, for in practice the means by which the people exercise sovereignty vary as follows:

i. In some constitutions the people's exercise of sovereignty consists of the election of representatives. The German Constitution, as noted, provides that state authority derives from the people who exercise it through 'elections and other votes'.[72] The Constitution of Brazil states: 'the Sovereignty of the people is exercised by universal suffrage and by direct and secret ballot'.[73] The act of voting is the sole exertion of sovereignty.
ii. More common is a subtle but serious variation where the people, instead of using sovereignty themselves, do so through representatives[74] or through 'the parliament'.[75] The Constitution of India, after stating that we the people have constituted a sovereign state, declares that there shall be a parliament with constituent powers.[76] In France, 'national sovereignty' vests in the people who 'exercise it through their representatives and by means of referendum'.[77] Sweden is similar in providing that democracy is 'realized through a representative and parliamentary form of government' while adding 'and through local self-government'.[78] The Constitution of Finland states simply that the

[70] Basic Law of the Federal Republic of Germany (1949) art 20.
[71] Constitution of Greece (1975, 1986, 2001, 2008) art 1.
[72] Basic Law of the Federal Republic of Germany (1949) art 20.
[73] Constitution of the Federative Republic of Brazil (1988, 1995, 2006) art 14.
[74] Fundamental Law of Hungary (2011) art B(4)2; Constitution of the Fifth Republic (1958, 1962, 2008) art 3.
[75] Constitution of the Kingdom of Norway (1814, 2007) art 49; Constitution of Finland (2000) s 2.
[76] Constitution of the Republic of India (1950, 1970) preamble, arts 79 and 368. A 'constituent power' is presumably different from and more powerful than a 'representative' body.
[77] Constitution of the Fifth Republic (1958, 1962, 2008) art 3.
[78] Instrument of Government (1974) art 1.

people, in whom the 'powers of the State are vested', are 'represented by the Parliament'.[79]

iii. A related idea is that the people exercise sovereignty through the institutions and offices set up by the constitution, which usually means the legislative branch and sometimes includes the executive and judicial. The Czech Constitution states that: 'the people are the source of all power in the state; they exercise it through bodies of legislative, executive, and judiciary powers'.[80] Some such bodies are elected representatives, but others, such as courts, are representative only in a special sense.[81]

iv. In several systems, where parliament is created without mention of the people or sovereignty, the understandings are: first, that parliament is the sovereign body, as in the UK, or has supreme legislative powers, as in Australia and Canada; and secondly, that parliament is elected by the people. The Constitution of Canada in providing that 'every citizen has the right to vote in elections for the houses of parliament', leaves much unsaid.[82] In similar mode, the Constitution of Denmark creates a parliament and states that 'the members of the parliament shall be elected by general and direct ballot'.[83]

v. Provision is sometimes made for the people to exercise sovereignty or part of it directly. The Hungarian Fundamental Law is typical of a group of constitutions in providing the people exercise 'their sovereign rights through its elected representatives or, in exceptional cases, in a direct manner'.[84] The issues allowing direct action include such matters as voting on a constitutional amendment, a new law, or a matter of policy; in some cases the people may abrogate a law or propose a new one.

Several conclusions may be drawn. The first is that in all constitutions in the cohort, sovereignty or supreme authority is vested in or delegated to representatives. Representative government is the common core of the constitutions of democratic nations. Secondly, the act of delegation of authority is in some cases the sovereign act; in other cases representatives exercise sovereignty in the name of the people without the need for delegation; while in many the delegation of authority occurs without mention of sovereignty. In another group of constitutions, the exercise of sovereign authority is delegated to official institutions and agencies other than the legislature, such as the executive and the courts, without making clear whether they are representatives of the people. A third conclusion is that in roughly half the

[79] Constitution of Finland (2000) s 2.
[80] Constitution of the Czech Republic (1992) art 2.1.
[81] I touch on that special sense of courts as representatives in DJ Galligan: 'Ally or Enemy: Friend or Foe' in DJ Galligan (ed), *The Courts and the People: Friend or Foe?* (Oxford: Hart Bloomsbury, 2021), pp 233–6.
[82] Constitution Act (1982) part 1 art 3.
[83] Constitution of Denmark (1949) preamble and art 31.1.
[84] Fundamental Law of Hungary (2011) art B(4)2.

constitutions the people reserve the authority to exercise sovereignty by direct action with respect to a limited range of issues.

7. Representative government

The method common to all sixty-five constitutions is government through representatives. Some make express reference to representatives and representative government. The Constitution of Japan states the representative principle in declaring government to be 'a sacred trust of the people, the authority for which is derived from the people, the powers of which are exercised by representatives of the people, and the benefits of which are enjoyed by the people'.[85] In half the constitutions (32/65), the words representation and representatives do not appear although the idea is implicit, normally by creating a parliament or other legislative body on the understanding that it will be representative, leaving the details to be settled elsewhere.[86] The Constitution of Nigeria provides that the 'legislative powers of the Federal Republic of Nigeria shall be vested in a National Assembly',[87] while in Norway, 'the people exercise the legislative power through the Parliament',[88] the assumption in both cases being that the legislative body represents the people.

In selecting representatives, the expectation is that they will be elected by the people, although not all constitutions make that clear. Some are explicit in providing for election, others in stating the principle of full adult suffrage. The Constitution of Ireland proclaims the people's right 'to designate the rulers of the State',[89] while others, such as those of Australia, Canada, South Africa, South Korea, Sweden, and the People's Republic of China,[90] remove any doubt about the issue by providing for the election of representatives. How the idea is expressed differs. Canada puts it in terms of rights: 'every citizen of Canada has the right to vote in an election of members of the House of Commons'.[91] The Austrian Constitution stipulates election by the people in accordance with the principle of 'proportional representation',[92] while both Houses of the Australian Parliament are 'composed of members directly chosen by the people'.[93] The same notion lies behind the Lithuanian reference to 'democratically elected representatives'.[94] Such expressions are exceptional, while most constitutions make no reference to representatives

[85] Constitution of Japan (1946) preamble and art 43.

[86] The Constitution of Malta provides simply that 'there shall be a Parliament of Malta which shall consist of a President and a House of Representatives': Constitution of Malta (1964) art 51.

[87] Constitution of the Federative Republic of Nigeria (1999) art 4.

[88] Constitution of the Kingdom of Norway (1814, 2007) art 49.

[89] Constitution of Ireland (1937) art 6.

[90] The People's Republic of China is classified as an autocracy on the Polity Score.

[91] Constitution Act (1982) Part 1, art 3.

[92] Federal Constitutional Law of Austria (1920, 1929, 1945) art 26.

[93] Constitution of the Commonwealth of Australia (1900) arts 7 and 24.

[94] Constitution of the Republic of Lithuania (1992) art 4.

being elected, although it is taken for granted they will be. The Constitution of Finland is typical in declaring the representative principle and then saying nothing about selection of representatives: 'National sovereignty is vested in the people, who shall exercise it through their representatives and by means of referendum.'[95]

Between the people and representatives: five models The notion of government through representatives and relations between them and the people can be understood in several ways:

- representatives rule in the name of the people without authorization: the *nominal* model;
- the people authorize representatives to rule: the *authorization* model;
- the people authorize representatives to rule and hold them accountable for how they rule: the *accountability* model;
- the people authorize representatives to rule in accordance with the people's directions and hold them accountable: the *direction* model; and to be complete;
- the people rule themselves: the *self-rule* model.

Relations between the people and representatives could be calibrated from the weakest to the strongest form of representative government as follows: (i) rule in the name of the people with passive acquiescence by the people; (ii) authorization of representatives by the people without additional requirements; (iii) authorization of representatives by the people to rule with the added duty that they account to the people for their actions; (iv) rule by representatives under directions from the people, which (v) is still markedly different from the people ruling themselves directly. To the conventional models, the *keepers* add a subtle but critical variation whereby the people cede power to the elected few, together with agencies and institutions, to rule while developing ways of influencing rule and watching over rule. Signs of this form of rule appear, and evidence and opinion in support gathers in the following chapters, reaching a climax in the last.

Direction from the people Expectations that a constitution dictates what representatives do or how they behave are on the whole unfulfilled. Representatives are sometimes instructed to express the people's will,[96] or to govern for the peace, order and good government of the nation,[97] a general prescription often followed by a list of specific powers such as: taxation, trade and commerce, and defence.[98]

[95] Constitution of Finland (2000) art 3.

[96] Constitution of the Principality of Andorra (1993) art 7; Constitution of the Republic of Bulgaria (1991) preamble.

[97] A set of instructions common in constitutions of former colonies within the British Empire.

[98] See for instance the Constitution of the Commonwealth of Australia (1900) art 51. The enumeration of specific powers is particularly important in federal systems where government is divided between the federal and the states.

Some constitutions state simply that representatives exercise legislative power, to which particular powers are sometimes added, such as approving the budget.[99] The Constitution of Sweden is one of the few to impose duties on representatives as to how they govern. The duties include respecting the equal worth, liberty, and dignity of the individual, and securing the right to employment, housing, and education.[100] Within the scope of representatives' powers, the question arises whether constitutions provide for the people's having a say in how powers are used. Such provisions are rare. The South African Constitution imposes on representatives the duty 'to ensure government *by the people* under the Constitution' (emphasis added), which is curious since the people have just handed over government to representatives. This makes sense only if 'the people' is understood as a corporate entity for then the acts of the representatives are the acts of the people.[101] The only instruction to appear with any frequency is that representatives should represent all the people, the entire nation.[102] To this is sometimes added the injunction, echoing Edmund Burke's speech to the electors of Bristol,[103] that 'representatives shall not be bound by any instructions of the electorate', a sentiment the Constitution of Poland decrees.[104] The Constitution of Germany states that representatives represent the 'whole people, are not bound by orders or instructions, and responsible only to their conscience',[105] the unspoken fear being that representatives might act for sectors, interests, or factions rather than the common good.

The premise that it would be wrong for representatives to do so is not so straightforward. The parliamentary tradition of the United Kingdom is based on a member of parliament representing a constituency and the interests and sectors within it. Representing a constituency falls short of taking instructions, although a case can be made for a self-governing people retaining the power to give directions to representatives as to how authority is to be used. The case is strengthened if government be considered a means for resolving competition among interests, sectors, and communities, and bearing in mind that representatives normally depend for re-election on the support of such bodies. Among written constitutions, Turkey seems to be alone in expressly allowing representatives to take account of the wishes of their constituents, provided it is not to the exclusion of the interests of the nation as a whole.[106] That is the point: a member represents both the local constituency and the whole nation, and tension between the two roles is unavoidable.

[99] An example is the Constitution of the Italian Republic (1947) arts 70 and 81.

[100] Instrument of Government (1974) art 2.

[101] Constitution of the Republic of South Africa (1996) art 42.

[102] Constitution of the Kingdom of the Netherlands (1983) art 50.

[103] E Burke: 'Speech to the Electors of Bristol at the Conclusion of the Poll' (1774) in *The Works of the RH Edmund Burke* (London: HG Bohn, 1854), pp 446–8. In the British context, the idea long preceded Burke; see M Knights: *Representation and Misrepresentation in Later Stuart Britain* (Oxford: Oxford University Press, 2005).

[104] Constitution of the Republic of Poland (1997) art 104.

[105] Basic Law of the Federal Republic of Germany (1949) art 38.

[106] Constitution of the Republic of Turkey (1982) art 80.

Apart from the few that forbid representatives from taking instructions from interests, sectors, or localities and require them to act according to their conscience, most constitutions say nothing about the matter. The assumption is that representatives act as they think best for the whole nation. The idea of the people issuing directions to their representatives apparently has no place in the constitutions of democratic nations.

Accountability of representatives If there are good reasons for allowing representatives to decide what is best in the interest of all, a sovereign people would surely insist on representatives' accounting to them for their actions, and so tempering authorization with accountability.[107] By accountability, representatives explain their actions and justify them according to settled standards. Yet constitutions do not normally contain standards for judging the actions of representatives beyond the general terms of empowerment noted above. Nor do constitutions commonly impose duties of accountability or devise mechanisms designed to achieve it. The Constitution of South Korea stands alone in providing that 'all public officials are servants of the entire people and responsible to the people'.[108] There may be questions as to whom representatives ought to be accountable, whether the people as a whole or those who elect them. Constitutions rarely say anything about either. The threat of removal at the next election is a means of accountability, and in a drastic once-and-for-all sense it is; but that falls far short of a system of regular accountability that judges performance according to settled standards within a continuing relationship.[109] The related mechanism of allowing electors to recall representatives, which a few constitutions allow, is drastic and rarely used.[110]

In practice, forms of accountability of representatives and other officials often emerge outside and independently of the written constitution. Since our interest here is in constitutional texts, the puzzle is why a sovereign people would not wish to set out the terms on which representatives are accountable to them. Some might see here the hand of Hobbes whose sovereign once appointed is representative of each person and has authority to govern for and on behalf of each, as if each were governing himself, so rendering accountability not only unwelcome but incoherent and anyhow unnecessary.[111] It would take a stretch of the imagination to consider this a form of self-government, and it is hard to see why a sovereign people would not insist on more rigorous accountability and processes of enforcement.[112]

[107] For discussion of accountability of representatives: H Pitkin: *The Concept of Representation* (University of California Press, 1967), pp 55*ff*. Accountability is analysed in later chapters.

[108] Constitution of the Republic of Korea (1948) art 7.

[109] Compare Pitkin: *The Concept of Representation*, pp 55*ff* where election is presented as the form of accountability. Why self-governing people would be content with that and not insist on more regular accountability is not clear. This issue is discussed in the previous chapter and recurs at several places in the following chapters. On the function of elections and the influences that follow, see Chapter XV.

[110] See the later section on recall.

[111] Hobbes: *Leviathan*; on representation as authorization, see Pitkin: *The Concept of Representation*, pp 39*ff*.

[112] There is an argument that contemporary emphasis on judicial review as a form of accountability weakens more clearly political forms. See DJ Galligan: 'The Indirect Origins of the Juridical

Some consider constitutional devices such as the separation of powers and judicial review to be enough.

The separation of powers has the capacity to limit the powers of representatives, and for that matter of the other branches of government; but there is a lack of empirical evidence as to whether it does. It is anyhow more a case of representatives limiting themselves than being accountable to the people. Judicial review is now regarded as a necessary and effective means of accountability of political leaders, whether legislative, executive or administrative. The reach however is limited and the rationale is the protection of individual persons or groups, and only in an indirect sense can it be considered a form of accountability to the people as a whole.[113]

The willingness of a sovereign people to delegate government to representatives with neither instructions on governing nor means of accountability, except the final sanction of removal, could be considered the route to effective government, even good and wise government. Our interest here is whether it is self-government, an exertion of sovereignty, government by the people, of the people, for the people. The answer must be it is so only in a weak sense of the concept. If we were to extend the discussion to include the unelected parts of government—the mighty machinery of executive and administration, as well as regulatory bodies, commissions and agents, together with all sorts of semi-governmental organs—the gap between the people and government according to the model of rule by representatives would be further widened.

8. Direct action by the people

Direct engagement of the people in government is gauged according to several variables: (i) the nature of the action; (ii) whether it involves the constitution or relates to non-constitutional issues; (iii) whether the people have the power to take the initiative, or do so only with permission of officials; and (iv) the consequences of an initiative of the people, whether it is binding or advisory.[114]

Nature of direct action Direct actions are of three kinds: (a) referendum or plebiscite, meaning the people's voting on an issue; (b) popular initiatives, meaning the people's being empowered to take the initiative, which in addition to a referendum, means proposing, abrogating, or introducing a law; (c) consultation, which means officials seeking and taking account of the people's opinions. While all are forms of

Constitution' (Law and Society Annual Lecture, University of Oxford, 15 June 2011) and Galligan: *The Courts and the People.*

[113] Weber's views on modern political leadership are also illuminating. See M Weber: 'The Profession and Vocation of Politics' in P Lassman and R Spiers (eds), *Political Writings* (CUP 1994).

[114] For reflection on democracy and direct action, see M Weber: 'Parliament and Government in Germany' in Lassman and Spiers: *Political Writings.*

direct engagement of the people in government, the most direct occurs when the people initiate action that is binding on officials. There is a big difference, for instance, between officials deciding at their discretion to refer a matter to the people by way of referendum, and the people being able to initiate a referendum without the consent of officials.

Referendum on changes to the constitution Among the nations with written constitutions,[115] just over half (32/62) make provision for the people's engagement in amending the constitution. Their role varies a lot: eight constitutions (8/32) require a referendum on all amendments, nine (9/32) with respect to certain fundamental changes only, while the remaining fifteen (15/32) allow a referendum at the discretion of officials. Of the other thirty constitutions (30/62), the pattern is for amendments to be made by a special constituent assembly or by the parliament, usually with special majorities and sometimes subject to the assent of the head of state. The Czech Republic in requiring a three-fifths majority of both houses of parliament is typical. Federal systems normally require, in addition, the approval of a majority of state parliaments, where special majorities are often necessary. In the case of India, constitutional amendments require special majorities in both houses of parliament and ratification by the legislatures of at least half the states.[116] The Constitution of Angola is one of the few positively to prohibit referenda on constitutional issues.[117] Several constitutions protect certain provisions against amendment, including the Constitution of France which does not allow change to the republican form of government. The Constitution of Greece applies a similar prohibition against change to the parliamentary republican model.[118] How such restrictions could be justified to a self-governing people needs explanation.

An initiative to amend the constitution normally comes from officials, either the head of state or a number of legislators.[119] After adopting the initiative, the head of state or the assembly may in certain cases, at their discretion, submit the matter to a referendum. A few constitutions allow the initiative for amendment to come from the people. The people of Switzerland may demand a partial or total revision of the constitution, provided 100,000 citizens support the initiative,[120] as may the people of Colombia, Italy, Lithuania, Slovakia, and several other nations. All are subject to their obtaining the signature of a set number of voters, normally a high number in proportion to the size of the electorate. In a few cases, the proposal must be submitted to referendum, as in the Swiss case, but more often, upon receiving the

115 The notable nations without a written constitution: United Kingdom, New Zealand, and Switzerland.

116 Constitution of the Republic of India (1950, 1970) art 368.

117 Constitution of the Republic of Angola (2010) art 168.

118 Constitution of the Fifth Republic (1958, 1962, 2008) art 89; Constitution of Greece (1975, 1986, 2001, 2008) art 110.

119 It is noteworthy that all states of the USA, except Delaware, require a confirmatory referendum to constitutional amendments.

120 Federal Constitution of the Swiss Confederation (1999) arts 138, 139, 140, 193, 194.

proposal, the parliament decides in its discretion whether or not to proceed with it. Under the Italian constitution, where the chambers have a discretion to refer to the people proposals for constitutional amendments, approved by the chambers, 500,000 voters may force a referendum, subject to a number of exacting conditions being met.[121]

Referendum on non-constitutional matters A few constitutions allow a referendum on non-constitutional matters, which may be initiated either by state officials (normally the parliament) or by the people. The first is the standard approach, with only a few constitutions allowing the people to initiate a referendum on non-constitutional matters (as we shall see below). Where the decision rests with officials, it is a matter of either duty or discretion, discretion being the more usual. Among the constitutions requiring officials to refer a matter to a referendum at the people's initiative, and provided certain conditions are met, are those of Hungary, Italy, Lithuania, Moldova, and Poland. Lithuania raises intriguing questions in providing that 'the most significant issues concerning the life of the state and the people shall be decided by a referendum',[122] the intention being that parliament state in legislation which issues qualify. Or the people choose the issue provided 300,000 of them concur.[123] Moldova goes further in mandating referenda to resolve 'problems of utmost gravity or urgency confronting the Moldovan society or state'.[124] The Italian Constitution allows 50,000 voters to introduce a bill, which the two legislative chambers are required to consider and vote on clause by clause.[125]

More often the decision to refer a matter to referendum is in the discretion of the parliament or the head of state. The Austrian Constitution makes provision for the House of Representatives in its discretion to refer 'every enactment' to a referendum of the people, although in practice it rarely does.[126] Other constitutions have similar provisions but often couched in broader terms, for instance in the Bulgarian Constitution, the parliament may decide by resolution on the holding of a referendum on any issue.[127] The Polish Constitution grants authority to the House of Representatives or the President, acting with the support of the Senate, to order a national referendum on 'matters of particular importance to the state'.[128] The Constitution of Cameroon allows a referendum on proposed laws which 'could have profound repercussions on the future of the nation and national institutions'; who decides is left unstated.[129] South Korea narrows the scope by stating the matters on which the President may, but is not obligated to refer to a referendum.

[121] Constitution of the Italian Republic (1947) art 138.
[122] Constitution of the Republic of Lithuania (1992) art 9.
[123] *Ibid* art 9.3.
[124] Constitution of the Republic of Moldova (1994) art 75.
[125] Constitution of the Italian Republic (1947) art 138.
[126] Federal Constitutional Law of Austria (1920, 1929, 1945) art 43.
[127] Constitution of the Republic of Bulgaria (1991) art 84(5).
[128] Constitution of the Republic of Poland (1997) art 125.
[129] Constitution of the Republic of Cameroon (1972) art 36.

They include 'important policies relating to diplomacy, national defence, unification with North Korea, and other matters relating to the national destiny'.[130] Some constitutions specify the matters on which a referendum may be held, for instance to remove the president or recall a member of parliament, or in Nigeria for the creation of a new state.[131] Several constitutions provide for a consultative referendum on a specific issue, consultative meaning that the views of the people are taken into account but are not binding on parliament. Under the Constitution of Finland, the terms of a consultative referendum, and the choices to be presented to the people, must be set out in an act of parliament.[132] The Constitution of Sweden provides for a consultative referendum on matters to be set out in law.[133]

9. People's Initiatives

While few constitutions allow the people to propose amendment to the constitution, Switzerland notably being one of the few, popular initiatives on non-constitutional matters are more common. As noted, within the cohort twenty-one constitutions provide for some kind of popular initiative, to which should be added the European Union. Initiatives are of six main kinds: (i) abrogating a law; (ii) introducing a bill to parliament; (iii) voting on a law passed by the parliament; (iv) proposing a referendum on an issue of importance; (v) proposing a referendum on a constitutional matter; and (vi) recalling a representative.

The idea of the people's initiative has a long history and appears in several European constitutions, the Constitution of Switzerland being the best known. Initiatives depend on a set number of voters' signatures in support of a proposal. They are common in numerous states of the USA,[134] where they stem from populist movements in the late nineteenth century against the grip of special interests on the legislative process. They were used in addition to open the way for reform of such issues as women's vote, secret ballots, and recall of elected representatives. Following Nebraska's lead in 1897, other states mainly in the west followed suit so that by 1918 the constitutions of twenty-four states made provision for people's initiatives. Support has waxed and waned over the years with the people's attitudes ranging from zeal to apathy and legislators being consistently opposed. California became the benchmark after the adoption of Proposition 13 in 1978, which cut property tax, a measure imitated by other states, some also reducing income tax. Measures of moment have included the length of the working day, abortion and anti-discrimination, campaign financing and assisted suicide; others of lesser rank

[130] Constitution of the Republic of Korea (1948) art 72.
[131] Constitution of the Federal Republic of Nigeria (1999) art 8(1).
[132] Constitution of Finland (2000) s 53.
[133] Instrument of Government (1974) ch 8, art 2(5).
[134] I have drawn on D Schmidt: *Citizen Lawmakers* (Temple University Press, 1989).

to the outside eye include opening on the Sabbath, the use of steel traps in hunting, and the colour of margarine.

Of the 2,051 initiatives since 1904, 840 have been adopted, the majority of them in just six states. Year 1996 was the high-water mark with ninety-three initiatives on state ballots, of which forty-four were adopted. The annual number has since dropped. In order to keep a sense of proportion, we should compare the forty-four successful popular initiatives with the 14,000 laws and resolutions adopted by legislators in the same group of states. That only 26 per cent of all initiatives in California have proceeded to the popular vote, and only 8 per cent are adopted by the people, is another indicator in assessing the value of initiatives.

Abrogation Abrogation means repealing or annulling a law. The Italian Constitution provides for abrogation at the request of 500,000 voters. 'A general referendum may be held to repeal, in whole or in part, a law or a measure having the force of law'.[135] Even then the measure will succeed only if a majority of registered voters vote and a majority of them are in favour. The figures on abrogation are revealing. Since its introduction in 1974, sixteen referenda have been held at the people's initiative, posing sixty-two questions. The quorum of a majority of voters voting was not met in six of the sixteen referenda; of the sixty-two questions, nineteen were approved. The people of Colombia have a similar power to require the holding of a referendum 'for the repeal of a law', provided one-tenth of voters agree,[136] while in Albania it is enough to muster the support of 50,000 citizens, although considering the population of the country that is a tall order.[137] Abrogation by popular initiative is fairly rare with only three countries in the cohort making provision for it.

Introducing a new law The opposite of abrogation is popular action to introduce a new law, although that might involve repealing an existing law. A few constitutions, the Italian again an example, allow the people both to abrogate an existing law and introduce a new one.[138] The power to introduce a new law is more widespread than strict abrogation, but still a small minority within the cohort. The Constitution of Argentina is to the point in stating: 'Citizens shall have the right to introduce bills before the House of Deputies, Congress shall consider them within the term of twelve months'.[139] The Austrian Constitution gives a fuller account of the procedure and the consequences: 100,000 voters, or one-sixth of the voters in three states, may put forward an initiative in the form of a draft law, which is submitted by the electoral board to the House of Representatives.[140] In all cases where

135 Constitution of the Italian Republic (1947) art 75.
136 Constitution of Colombia (1991) art 170.
137 Albanian Constitution (1998) art 150.
138 Constitution of the Italian Republic (1947) arts 71 and 75.
139 Constitution of the Argentine Nation (1853, 1994) art 39.
140 Federal Constitutional Law of Austria (1920, 1929, 1945) art 41.

the people propose a bill, the decision as to whether it becomes law remains with the legislative authority; the people have no power to demand its enactment.[141]

Voting on a law passed by the legislature Some of the early American state constitutions experimented with the idea that all laws passed by the legislature had to be submitted to the voters for their approval, but in the face of criticism and mockery they did not last.[142] The practice continues, however, in a few national constitutions, Switzerland being the leading case where 50,000 voters may force a vote on any statute passed by the Federal Parliament.[143]

Initiating a referendum on non-constitutional issues The opposite of voting down a law passed by parliament is to propose a new one. The position under the Italian Constitution is noted above. The Constitution of Hungary provides for a national referendum to decide a matter, or as an expression of opinion, in some circumstances mandatory, in others at the discretion of parliament. The mandatory provision takes effect if at least 200,000 citizens request it. The result is binding on parliament.[144] A referendum may be ordered by parliament if requested by specified officials or by a body of citizens, in this case 100,000. The parliament is not bound to implement the outcome, although the constitution is not wholly clear on the point. In Honduras, in order to 'strengthen and operate participatory democracy', provision is made for consulting citizens on matters of vital importance in national life.[145] Six per cent of registered voters may request a referendum or plebiscite on an issue, although it is up to the National Congress to decide by special majority whether to proceed.

Initiating a referendum on constitutional issues That several constitutions allow the people to initiate a referendum on constitutional issues is noted above.[146] Switzerland is again the outstanding case: if the people propose a revision of the constitution, and obtain 100,000 voters' signatures in support, then a referendum must be held. Similar provision for popular constitutional initiatives is made in 16 or around 35 per cent of American states.

Recall Some constitutions allow the people to recall a representative or other official, sometimes including judges, which means simply removal from office.[147] While such provisions are fairly rare, where they do exist they are resounding expressions of the people's wishes. In California in 2003, the Governor of California was removed by this method after 1.6 million signatures were obtained. In

[141] Among the state constitutions of the USA, fourteen allow the people to initiate legislation.

[142] The early constitutions are described in G Wood: *Creation of the American Republic* (University of North Carolina Press, 1969). For discussion of the experiments in Pennsylvania, see Chapter XII herein.

[143] Federal Constitution of the Swiss Confederation (1999) art 141.

[144] Fundamental Law of Hungary (2011) art 8(1).

[145] Constitution of the Republic of Honduras (1982) art 5.

[146] Among the state constitutions of the USA, sixteen provide for the people's initiating a referendum on constitutional issues.

[147] For further discussion: V Beramendi and others: *Direct Democracy: The International IDEA Handbook* (International Institute for Democracy and Electoral Assistance, 2008) ch 5.

Venezuela in 2004, 3.4 million signatures were obtained for the recall of President Chaves, although the measure failed after he obtained 59 per cent of the votes in the election that followed.[148]

10. Conclusions

The aim of this chapter is to consider how contemporary constitutions of broadly democratic nations provide for the people. Sovereignty is the critical concept, the idea being that a study of sovereignty will show how constitutions present the people, the role they have, and relations between them and representatives and other officials. Things turn out to be more variable and nuanced than one might have imagined, but the following conclusions are warranted.

(i) A majority of constitutions in the cohort use the language of sovereignty, for which a few substitute the notion of supremacy, although a noticeable number use neither.

(ii) Just under half the constitutions vest sovereignty in the people. Another percentage sees the people as the source of sovereignty, while vesting sovereignty in representatives, the nation, or the parliament. A third group, usually those of a parliamentary character, does not mention sovereignty, leaving relations between the people and the agencies of government to be settled outside or prior to the written constitution, if there is one.

(iii) The people normally have a minor role in constitution-making and only in a minority of cases is popular ratification required. In most cases the constitution may be changed without the approval of the people at referendum.

(iv) Sovereignty or supreme authority is exercised by representatives and other government bodies, in some because they claim to be sovereign, in others by delegation from the people as the sovereign body.

(v) Some constitutions provide for the election of representatives, while others are silent, leaving the matter to be dealt with outside the constitution.

(vi) In relations between the people and representatives, the authorization model dominates, that is, authority to govern is granted to representatives who may be ousted and replaced at the next election.

(vii) Other forms of accountability are not normally provided for in the constitution and representatives are not subject to direction from the people.

(viii) In a minority of constitutions, the people exercise aspects of sovereignty directly through referenda and initiatives, abrogation and consultation, although the scope and efficacy of such measures are severely limited.

[148] *Ibid* p 16.

The conclusion must be that sovereignty of the people is of limited use in interpreting and explaining the constitutions of democratic nations. There is in short a sovereignty deficit. If sovereignty be the concept through which the people express self-government and hence democracy, then constitutions fall far short of being clear and firm affirmations of government of the people, by the people, for the people. Elements of self-government are present, the most important the authority of the people to elect and later reject representatives, although this does not apply to all representatives and only to a few government officials. The value of election is plain, but if that be the crux of the people's power, the result is a very narrow sense of self-government.[149] We the people becomes we the representatives of the people who, in most cases, make the constitution for the people, give ourselves authority to govern as we think best, free of constitutional controls or constraints.

This is a far cry from the image of free citizens confidently governing themselves and cannot be explained away by the need to compromise stronger forms of self-rule in favour of the practical business of government. The practical needs of effective government have to be taken into account, but that is a wholly inadequate basis on which to account for the place of the people in, or rather their absence from constitutions. There remains a chasm between the promise of self-government and the practical reality. This is something of a relief, for once the need to explain constitutions in terms of self-government is cast aside, the way is open to make a fresh start and propose another account. An account buried in the history of constitutional thought and practice, steeped in the social conditions of the times, in which the people do not rule but are ruled. And yet they are able to engage in, be vigilant towards, and exact censure over the processes of rule. All aimed at keeping rulers to the purpose of securing and advancing the well-being of the people. That is the task for the following chapters, culminating in the last, while along the way learning to read constitutions differently.

[149] On the value of elections, see Chapter XV.

VII
Upper Register of Constitutional Discourse

1. A reflective Peter Quince

Peter Quince, the Athenian carpenter and leader of the mechanicals, would seem to be the model subject. He accepts rule and obeys the ruler. Not obedience in the classical sense of the people who, knowing how to rule, obey deliberately and purposefully. That is not for the common people. Theirs is blind obedience born of ignorance and bred on deference. They are to dwell, according to Duke Theseus, 'in the modesty of fearful duty'.[1] They accept being ruled according to the wishes of the prince and in return expect benefits, protection of person and property, certain rights granted. The mechanicals have no role in ruling and minor influence over the duke's actions. There is no calling to account, no recourse for misuse of power, limited redress for wrongs. They are subject to the prince's will which is often capricious and at times oppressive, but on the whole tolerable. That is the system; the system to which they are born, the system of their forebears, the system that appears to be as natural as other social relationships guiding and restraining their actions. They are schooled from birth to accept authority, at first in parental form, later in other forms of which rule of the prince is one. Social pressure to fit into and accept the system is strong, sanctions for disobedience severe. The disposition to obey has a positive side. Why else would the mechanicals, busy at their trades, take the time and trouble to present a play in celebration of the duke's wedding? The reason is elusive, perhaps to show gratitude for the benefits they receive, perhaps an expression of Hume's notion that 'antiquity always begets the opinion of right'.

There is another side to the story. While showing a positive disposition to the Duke's rule, the mechanicals hold back, keep a certain detachment, enough to cast over it a mildly critical eye. In preparing the play for the wedding, they are worried Bottom as lion will roar too loudly and frighten the ladies.

> *Bottom*: 'Let me play the lion too. I will roar that I will do any man's heart good to hear me. I will roar that I will make the Duke say "Let him roar again; let him roar again"'.

> *Quince*: 'And you should do it too terribly you would fright the Duchess and the ladies that they would shriek, and that were enough to hang us all.'

[1] W Shakespeare: *A Midsummer's Night Dream*, Act 5: 1: 101.

Keepers of the Common Good. D.J. Galligan, Oxford University Press. © D.J. Galligan 2024.
DOI: 10.1093/9780198907398.003.0007

The other mechanicals: 'That would hang us, every mother's son.'[2]

Enough to hang them all! Better to avoid the risk by casting someone else as the lion. In these few lines the kindly mask of princely rule is lifted, fleetingly, to expose another side, one of arbitrary power and latent brutality. Behind the curtain of civility, the good-natured nodding of the duke, the position of the people is precarious, their fate dependent on his goodwill, his sense of decency and self-restraint. That a man should be hanged for such a trivial offence, without hint of trial let alone a fair trial, is evidence enough of the arbitrariness and injustice barely below the surface. Well-read enough to write and mount the play *Pyramus and Thisbe*, Peter Quince we might imagine had heard Hamlet's soliloquy on oppression[3] and read Lear's lament for his own abuse of princely authority;[4] maybe knew of the injustice inflicted on Shylock by the merchants of Venice,[5] even Angelo's oppression of Claudio and his sister Isabella.[6] Fanciful it may be, yet the mechanicals, Peter Quince most astutely, have a sense of the true nature of princely rule and its fatal flaw. Beneath the calm acceptance, the resigned obedience, there smoulders a sense of anger, of 'angry obedience' as William Tyndale described it.[7]

It is not only a matter of seeing the truth of the system. Peter Quince has a sense things could be different, that relations between ruler and ruler could be otherwise. No more than a hint but enough to imagine what he might be thinking. He could conceive of a body politic where frightening a lady would not be a capital crime, where laws are not dependent on the wishes and whims of one person, where each citizen is entitled to fair and reasonable treatment whatever their status. How that could be achieved, what reordering of social relations would bring it about were beyond Peter's grasp. That he peered into princely rule and saw the dark hole at the core is perception enough. We know things can be different, that relations between the people and the prince need not be those of the *Midsummer Night's Dream*. We know there is an alternative to arbitrary rule and mute obedience; rule neither due to nor dependent on the personal dispositions of the ruler. A form of rule innate to the people themselves, drawing on a hinterland of ideas and values, casting light on how relations between people and rulers could be structured; a form showing wisdom in conception and moderation in application. There is awaiting Peter Quince and his companions a universe of association very different from the court of Duke Theseus. Relations between rulers and ruled, the foundations of constitutional authority, being part of that hinterland of ideas and language, are now refracted through a new prism.

[2] *Ibid* Act 1: 2: 70*ff.*

[3] W Shakespeare: *Hamlet: Prince of Denmark.*

[4] W Shakespeare: *The Tragedy of King Lear.*

[5] W Shakespeare: *The Merchant of Venice.*

[6] W Shakespeare: *Measure for Measure.*

[7] Quoted in D Rollinson: *A Commonwealth of the People: Popular Politics and England's Long Social Revolution, 1066–1649* (Cambridge: Cambridge University Press, 2010), p 140.

Much has happened constitutionally since Peter Quince reflected on the rule of Duke Theseus, and since Hume asked why the people resign their own sentiments to those of their rulers. The people now have a place in the constitutional order and a balance has been reached between them and those who rule. The gap between the two seems to have been closed and a single register of discourse composed to structure the relationship. Contemporary constitutions contain a language, a set of concepts, and a cluster of ideas resolving the earlier conflicts, removing the corrosions of unity, cementing relations between the rulers and the ruled in a manner acceptable to all. The people come together as a community of which they are in some sense sovereign, the task of governing entrusted to representatives who govern with their consent. The language varies but the content is constant, signalling the end of centuries of struggle, out of which comes a people in charge of their own affairs. Yet the reality is not as presented. The legacy of the past is visible in the discourse, the calm surface concealing contradiction and turbulence. We saw in the previous chapter that while the constitution is proclaimed to be the people's, they are only marginally present. Their sovereignty is in deficit, their constitutional role fairly much limited to election of representatives, who once elected claim autonomy and independence, while the scope for engagement, vigilance, and censure is limited. The narrative of a people emerging to govern themselves is partly authentic and partly fantasy. The people have acquired constitutional status but, as is plain from the texts, it does not match the sovereignty-self-governing narrative. What then is the basis of contemporary constitutional orders, what factors create and sustain the balance among the people and between rulers and the people? If the power to rule is in the hands of a few, how do the people make sure it is used to advance civility and humanity and their well-being? Under what conditions is a balance reached and Leviathan shackled when for most peoples Leviathan roams at large.[8] The analysis of the constitutional texts suggests that the ideas, the concepts, and the language have their origins in the past, in an earlier discourse that influences the present. To the excavation of that discourse I now turn in the expectation it will add to understanding the foundations of constitutional authority.

2. 'Let them obey that knows not how to rule'[9]

The line from Richard Duke of York catches the sentiment of the superior sector of society towards the common people. A few exceptions aside, that was the view held and heralded in England well into the seventeenth century. The people's place in the constitutional order is to obey because they do not know how to rule, and

[8] The image of Leviathan shackled and unshackled comes from D Acemoglu and JA Robinson: *The Secret Corridor* (London: Viking Press, 2019).

[9] W Shakespeare: *First Part of the Contention,* Act 5: 1: 6.

anyhow many of them are not true members of the nation but admitted on sufferance. To make matters worse they are ever on the edge of becoming the mob intent on levelling estates. The duty to obey was clear and absolute, unless the ruler turned into a tyrant and broke bond with the people. The people then were entitled to resist or even rebel, although the definition of tyranny and the action justified were matters of dispute and resistance of any kind was dangerous.[10] Behind the rhetoric of blind obedience lie calmer reasons. Thomas Hobbes states it simply and clearly. Civil society comes into being on 'the basis of a calculation of advantage', the ends being 'security and well-being'. Reason dictates that the people 'trade submission for protection', an idea later shared by Hume and consistent with the present approach to social understanding. Hobbes adds that the constitutional order being 'artificial and fragile' is sustained only if the ruler has absolute power and the ruled an absolute duty to obey.[11] That both are assertions, not conclusions drawn from the premise, did not deter others from repeating the claim as if beyond dispute.

Two related ideas recur, one the status of the people, the other their ability. It is hard to know which comes first, whether lowly status is due to lack of ability or the other way round. Let us begin with lack of ability. Roger Whiteley, a royalist and holder of high office writing in mid-seventeenth century, confided to his diary a venomous position parsimoniously put: 'the judgements of ye people are judgements of folly; and their affections are always indiscreet; they reject ye good for ye bad; what they say is false; what they commend is infamous; what they undertake fury'.[12] Judgements of folly are 'giddy judgements', as Queen Margaret wife of Henry VI was fond of declaring.[13] The Archbishop of York had earlier declared: 'An habitation giddy and unsure/Hath he that buildeth on the common heart'.[14] The people's ignorance is understandable considering they 'were never blessed with a liberal education, never taught to read; men so dull and stupid, that they cannot apprehend, much less remember the strength of an argument'.[15] It must surely follow, or so thought Thomas Scott, that 'drovers, brewers, tipplers, and base mechanics ought not to hold civil office'.[16] This is not a plea to educate

[10] Discussed in AP Monahan: *Consent, Coercion and Limit: The Medieval Origins of Parliamentary Democracy* (Kingston and Montreal: McGill University Press, 1987), pp 159–78.

[11] See Chapter II:4.

[12] R Whitley: *Diary of Roger Whitely* quoted in: M Knights: *Representation and Misrepresentation in Later Stuart Britain* (Oxford: Oxford University Press, 2005), p 90.

[13] W Shakespeare: *Henry IV Part 2*.

[14] *Henry IV Part 2*, Act 1: 3: 99–100: *giddy* has many shades of meaning, including dizzy, incapable of attention, frivolous, and inconstant, the origins in *gidig*, an old English word meaning 'possessed by a god', which is to say insane.

[15] E Gregory: *A Modest Plea for the Due Regulation of the Press* (1698) quoted in Knights: *Representation and Misrepresentation in Later Stuart Britain*, p 203.

[16] T Scott quoted in D Underdown: *Revel, Riot, and Rebellion: Politics and Culture in England 1603–1663* (Oxford: Clarendon Press, 1985), p 46; for further accounts: D Zaret: *Origins of Democratic Culture* (Princeton: Princeton University Press, 2000).

these base fellows. On the contrary, as the Earl of Northampton pronounced, there is 'nothing so hurtful to the commonwealth as the multitude of free schools' which 'gave young men ideas above their station, breeding new opinions', opinions with no place in a settled social order.[17] The common people 'have no voice or authority in our commonwealth, and no account is made of them but only to be ruled'.[18] Letting the people influence government would be a return to the state of nature.[19]

Lack of ability justifies low status. The people on the margins of a society in which they have no stake are denied membership and admitted on sufferance. Membership turns on property.[20] Those without property have no true stake and no right to vote. During the first Putney Debates of 1647, Henry Ireton, Oliver Cromwell's son-in-law and counsellor, is blunt.[21] Replying to Colonel Rainsborough's speech, profound in reason and moving in sentiment, urging the vote be given to the soldiers who had just won the civil war, Ireton explains that constitutions are about property and only property-owners are entitled to vote. We noticed before how Cromwell enriched the discourse by dismissing the rest as 'mere breathers', while full manhood suffrage would lead to anarchy.[22] Since only adult males were eligible to vote and since only 9 per cent met the property qualification, the majority of men and all women had no 'permanent interest' and hence no stake. An opinion shared by the author Daniel Defoe, for whom only freeholders were truly 'the people', the rest 'inhabitants who live upon sufferance'.[23] Mere breathers, offensive enough, is mild compared to other accounts of the people. They are rascal rabble, the dregs and doss of men, 'wretched upstarts' pledged 'to dim the ancient families'. They are told to remember 'the dunghill whence by God they were raised'. The stain of birth survives high office and even Cardinal Wolsey is 'a wretched poor man of greasy genealogy'.[24]

More than contemptible, the people are a threat to the settled order, to harmony, stability, and unity. Always on the edge of becoming the mob, an ugly mindless multitude, evoking the image of a monster, a many-headed monster, 'contumacious, tending to sedition and riot and always keen on new things'.[25] Disorder and

[17] Earl of Northampton quoted in Underdown: *Revel, Riot, and Rebellion*, p 46.

[18] T Smith quoted in C Hill: *Change and Continuity in 17th Century England* (London: Nicholson, 1974), p 186.

[19] C Davenant: *Essays Upon Peace at Home and War Abroad* (1704) quoted in Knights: *Representation and Misrepresentation in Later Stuart Britain*, p 200.

[20] Underdown: *Revel, Riot, and Rebellion*, p 89.

[21] Putney Debates: Second Day.

[22] TC Pease, *The Leveller Movement* (1923) (London: Nabu Press, 2012), p 119. Noted in the *Foreword*.

[23] D Defoe, *Some Remarks on the First Chapter in Dr Davenant's Essays* (1704) quoted in Knights: *Representation and Misrepresentation in Later Stuart Britain*, p 201.

[24] L Humphrey: *The Nobles, or of Nobility* (16th c) quoted in Q Skinner: *The Foundations of Modern Political Thought* (Cambridge: Cambridge University Press, 1987) Volume 1, p 238.

[25] J Micraelius: *Syntagma historiarum ecclesiae omnium* (1644) quoted in *Republicanism: A Shared European Heritage* (eds) M van Gelderin and Q Skinner (Cambridge: Cambridge University Press, 2002) Volume I, p 142.

discord are bad enough but worse the monster is intent on levelling estates and destroying social distinction. 'Look how they gaze, see how the giddy multitude do point', lamented Lady Eleanor as she is paraded through the streets to banishment, as if gazing and pointing were harbingers of what is to come, of what the commons are capable. Jack Cade lives up to promise. 'All the realm shall be in common', he assures his followers, the system of rule, monarchy itself, must come under threat. Jack is plain in intent, vain in ambition: 'my mouth shall be the Parliament of England'.[26] Two centuries later, James I warned of the risk of popular movements which 'give a snatch against monarchy, through their puritanical itching after popularity'.[27] Even moderate puritanism is associated with disorder and rebellion.[28] Charles I his heir, true to a reputation for bluntness, turned his attention to the common people, who 'grow weary of journey-work, and set-up for themselves, call parity and independence liberty, — destroy all rights and liberties, all distinctions of family and merit, — and end in a dark, equal chaos of confusion, and the long line of noble ancestors in a Jack Cade or a Watt Tyler'.[29]

The citations could continue and the invective heighten, but enough has been said to signal a set of ideas and a language with sentiments and dispositions to match. The evidence is abundant from which to form a model of how one sector of society viewed another and how constitutional authority was constructed. The objection could be raised that while such ideas and sentiments dominated medieval and pre-modern England, by the eighteenth century their force had waned and by the nineteenth century was spent. Even in the seventeenth century, the position of the people was changing, the elected chamber gaining in authority in relation to king and peers. A position strengthened in the following centuries as the voice of the people grew louder and their power made visible. However, to consign this register of discourse to historical curiosity would be to neglect the origins of contemporary constitutions. The past as Vico teaches is a foreign country, but to understand the present one has to know the past, an axiom the force of which will be felt in the following chapters.

3. The body politic: 'a horse whereon the governor doth ride'[30]

The attack from the foot soldiers of invective, alone, would not last long. It is after all the attack of a few, which in the face of the power of the people would soon peter out. The people did from time to time exert power by protest, riot, and

[26] W Shakespeare: *Henry VI Part II*, Act 4: 7: 13.
[27] James I quoted in Underdown: *Revel, Riot, and Rebellion*, p 25.
[28] Underdown : *Revel, Riot, and Rebellion*, p 89.
[29] Charles Stuart, King Charles I: *The King's Answer to the Nineteen Propositions* (1642) in *The Stuart Constitution 1603–1688* (ed) JP Kenyon (Cambridge: Cambridge University Press, 1986), p 20.
[30] W Shakespeare: *Measure for Measure*, Act 1: 2: 147.

rebellion, even revolution, yet most of the time they acquiesced, restrained themselves, and accepted a place low in the constitutional order. The aim now is to chart how that happened, to consider the ideas and the images behind the language of the front line, transcending social and material divisions to secure not just obedience but support. Having before touched on the resort to abstractions and fictions in justifying the social order, we now enter the field of official discourse and try to make sense of what we find.[31] That means rising above the swamp of fear and loathing to engage with the ideas, images, and language aimed at smoothing social division, enough to form a unity and make government possible. The nation is cast as a body politic and a register of discourse invented in which concord and harmony, stability, and unity replace discord and division.

The body politic parallels the body natural. Both contain a collection of organs, each with a function, each essential, all contributing to the good health of the whole. The functions are many and diverse, some more noble, some better nourished, some bearing the weight of the body, all dependent on each other. John of Salisbury of the twelfth century memorably assigned to each organ a function, all together constituting the body.[32] The prince is the brain in charge of the body, the arms the militia for defence and security, the tax-collectors the belly, which swells in girth or shrinks according to how much they collect.[33] Parliament is 'the pulse of the people', whose concerns it knows and conveys to the head.[34] The people, the ordinary people, predictably, are the feet far from the head, their function to bear the load of the body, to carry it along whatever course be set from above. When all organs are working well and together the body politic is in good health; when signs of poor health appear a cure must be found. Good health relies on the prince, on his being virtuous, ruling with the counsel of the wise and looking after each of the organs. 'The excellence of the head must always flourish because the health of the whole body depends upon it.'[35] The wise and virtuous head wins the affection of the people. As late as the eighteenth century, John Wilkes could be condemned by the House of Commons for 'alienating the affections of the people'.[36] The prince in turn has a duty to look after the organs, to ensure their well-being, not least the people for whom his duty is that of 'the wise guardian' for his ward. A duty beyond justice, a duty to love and cherish the people. In addition to fatherly affection, wisdom and prudence commend special care for the people, the feet, on which the health of the body depends. If the feet are exposed to injuries 'it is as if the republic

[31] See Chapter II.

[32] John of Salisbury: *Polycraticus* (1200s) (ed) CJ Nederman (Cambridge: Cambridge University Press, 1990).

[33] For a different view of the belly, see Notes.

[34] *Vox Patriae; or, The Resentments & Indignation of the Free-Born Subjects of England* (1681) quoted in M Knights: *Representation and Misrepresentation*, p 78.

[35] *Ibid* p 140.

[36] For an account of this episode: P Ihalainen: *Agents of the People: Democracy and Popular Sovereignty in British and Swedish Parliamentary and Public Debates 1734–1800* (Leiden: Brill, 2010), p 129.

is barefoot; there can be nothing more ignominious'.[37] The fear is not only that the feet stop working but that idle feet are restless and become ambitious, and there is nothing worse than 'a barefoot republic'. In the troubled mid-sixteenth century, William Paget complained to Lord Protector Somerset that 'the foot taketh upon him the part of the head and commyns is become king: a king appointing laws and conditions to the governors'.[38] Words Hamlet might have had in mind in musing on how 'the age is grown so picked that the toe of the peasant comes so near the heel of the courtier he galls his kibe'.[39]

The image of the body politic has a long history. Inspired by ideas from early classical thought, cited as a point of reference in the disorders of seventeenth-century England, while its shadow touches constitutional discourse even today. In the opening years of the seventeenth century, James I likened himself to the head of the body politic, the father of the family.[40] The head must be nourished 'for the body cannot be sustained without the head'. A balance has to be found to avoid 'a danger of receiving all nourishments and causing the other members to fail and the whole man to die'. Authority is depicted as masculine, the body politic as feminine, 'our dear mother the commonwealth', the people prone to 'chaos, disorder, and revolt' likened to a good and obedient wife in need of masculine guidance.[41] The imagery takes a religious turn. God created an ordered universe to be sustained by the responsible use of power and respectful obedience. As the rule of Charles I fell short, images of health and the perils of poor health were invoked. Parliament has to be 'the great physician of the state, possessing a greater power to heal than the king alone'.[42] To preserve the health of the body politic was the premise on which the House of Commons built its case against the king. Serious illness called for drastic treatment.[43] Law as the 'sinews' of the body politic is essential to good health, when faithfully applied and respected, a healthy body politic is assured.[44] Law is being abused by both the judges and the king's counsellors; the judges in the ship-money cases are using the law against the people; Lord Strafford the king's adviser is guilty of 'supplanting the function of law'.[45]

[37] John of Salisbury: *Polycraticus*, p 126.

[38] William Paget: Letter to Somerset (7th July 1549) quoted in A Wood: *The 1549 Rebellions and the Making of Early Modern England* (Cambridge: Cambridge University Press, 2007), p 22.

[39] W Shakespeare: *The Tragedy of Hamlet, Prince of Denmark*, Act 5: 1: 135. *Galls his kibe*: chafes or irritates his ulcerated chilblain. The foot holds much appeal: 'The service of the foot,/Being once gangrened, is not then respected/For what it was before': *The Tragedy of Coriolanus*, Act 3: 2: 398. Earlier in the play, Menenius addresses the First Citizen as 'the great toe of this assembly': Act 1: 1: 153.

[40] D Underdown: *Revel, Riot, and Rebellion*, p 13.

[41] William Hakewell speaking in the House of Commons, quoted in D Underdown, *Revel, Riot, and Rebellion*, p 27.

[42] *Pax Vobis* (1641) quoted in M Judson: *The Crisis of the Constitution: An Essay in Constitutional and Political Thought in England 1603–1645* (New Brunswick: Rutgers University Press, 1949) (Paperback 1988), p 352.

[43] Discussed fully and well by M Judson, *ibid*, pp 353*ff*.

[44] See further Underdown: *Revel, Riot, and Rebellion*, p 125.

[45] Mr St.John's Speech to the Lords concerning Ship-Money (1640) quoted in Judson: *The Crisis of the Constitution*, p 357.

4. Harmony, stability, unity

The body politic strong and healthy, a nation forms ordered by rank and status, whole and harmonious, confident in pursuit of common purposes. The body politic has just the right qualities, while a nation so designed takes its place in a God-given universe equally well-ordered. To be part of that universe, two qualities are essential: 'the proper, responsible exercise of power and the respectful obedience of the people'.[46] Not order in 'the sense of tidiness and command, but order as harmony between the several parts of the body politic, each with reciprocal rights and duties'.[47] Order is fragile, easily fractured, always at risk of being turned upside down.[48] The question is how the qualities of harmony, stability, and unity transcend disparities of power and property to earn respectful obedience. The appeal has several parts. One is the intrinsic worth of such qualities. Who would not find value in a society harmonious, stable, and united? Each quality serves the interests of and is valued by each person, from which follows a sentiment and a disposition of self-restraint on one hand, positive action in support on the other. How strong the sentiment and disposition, and whether they lead to action, depends on other factors. Valued interests compete, some valued more than others. The value Jack Cade and his crew put on changing the system and improving their position led to their suspending the disposition to promote harmony, peace, and stability; to put aside self-restraint in pursuit of other things valued, other interests more pressing. The qualities of harmony, stability, and unity cultivated by the body politic, although somewhat nebulous and sometimes overridden, advance the interests of the people and encourage restraint and support, while being vulnerable to the appeal of competing interests.

In conditions of harmony, stability, and unity, the people are secure in advancing their own well-being. Conditions of strife, instability, and division open opportunities for some, but for most threaten disruption and loss of the means already meagre to improve life. Another reason not to be neglected is that the body politic signals benevolence of the head towards the people, a familial affection for all parts, not just the nobler members but the feet as well. John of Salisbury's urging that the feet be well shod, while a plea for prudence, is infused with benevolence. The lower organs work best in a healthy body, firm rule the best assurance of good health. The final appeal of the body politic is the benefit to all organs, the feet included, of rights being secure and protected, an appeal pulsing through the body politic from head to toe. Beneath the imagery lies Hume's maxim that a people secure in their rights will acquiesce in the system. Since each organ is vital to the

[46] J Winthrop: *History of New England 1630–1649* (ed) JK Hosmer (New York: C Scribner, 1908), p 239.

[47] P Slack: *Poverty and Policy in Tudor and Stuart England* (London: Longman, 1988), pp 144–8.

[48] See generally: C Hill: *The World Turned Upside Down: Radical Ideas During the English Revolution* (London: Penguin, 1972).

health of the whole, and remember John's warning about the feet stopping work, each must be respected. Along the route to respect, justice is a landmark. Not justice as a founding principle on which to build social relations; rather justice for each person within settled social relations.[49] Justice in the narrow sense of rights protected by law and redress when infringed. The rights of the commoners may be few, but those they have are to be respected and protected. In stating rights and decreeing protection, law is the sinews of the body politic, the cement of society, the bonding of persons and sectors, and so has a critical hand in the good health of the body, its abuse a sure sign of illness. Justice within the law and the easy access of the common people to the courts are common features of constitutional orders whatever the social structure.[50] The Leveller movement of the seventeenth was born out of the abuse of law, the arbitrary and oppressive treatment of its leader John Lilburne.[51]

Behind the ideas and the imagery of the body politic is a philosophy of society, among the exponents of which Thomas Aquinas holds first place. Human beings know by reason the need for, and have a natural tendency to associate. Association has to be governed, someone among the group must guide it by rule. The purpose of rule, the only purpose, is the common good, to promote the welfare of the people, preserving 'unity in peace'. To rule is to direct the association to that end. Aquinas goes on to connect good rule and living well to virtue, the virtue of the prince and the people.[52] The common good is the defining concept, the goal of association, government the means to it. Government appears in various forms each with advantages, but princely rule is praised as best at securing the common good.

5. Common good of the upper register

The common good is presented as the unifying goal of social endeavour. The journey has taken us from the battlefield of invective where the people are browbeaten into their rightful place low in the order of things, mere breathers barely tolerated and forced to the fringes. Only then the reality of the people's power dawns, the fragility of the social order is displayed, the prospect of popular unrest looms. The realm of ideas, images, and language unite to form out of rude reality an elegant figure. The body politic promotes concord in place of discord, order and stability overcome disorder, unity is forged from division. Such qualities appeal to

[49] The two senses of justice are explained in Chapter I:2.

[50] For discussion and additional references on the value of individualized justice and the availability of redress in the courts: DJ Galligan: 'Ally or Enemy; Friend or Foe' in *The People and the Courts: Friend or Foe?* (ed) DJ Galligan (Oxford: Bloomsbury Hart, 2021), pp 223–40.

[51] For an account: DJ Galligan: 'The Levellers, the People, and the Constitution' in *Constitutions and the Classics* (ed) DJ Galligan (Oxford: Oxford University Press, 2014), pp 132–51.

[52] Discussed in AP Monahan: *Consent, Coercion and Limit*, pp 159–77.

the people, stimulate sentiments and dispositions to acquiesce, ideally to render active support. Now we reach the final goal, the secret of community: the common good to which the register of ideas, images, and language leads. A coherent concept of community emerges, its protection the purpose of authority. James Stuart prided himself on 'thinking ever the Wealth and Weal of the Commonwealth to be my greatest Weal and worldly Felicity'. Distinguishing himself from the tyrant, he went on to preach that 'the righteous and just king doth acknowledge himself to be ordained for the procuring of the Wealth and Prosperitie of his People'.[53] Weal or *wele* means benefit, so the *commonweal* means to the benefit of all, which came to be rendered the *common good*.[54] Wealth and prosperity shared by all is one way of describing the benefits constituting the common good. Other benefits follow, safety and security endorsed by James Harrington, public quiet and safety praised by Adam Smith. Locke is more exact. People join the political order for 'their comfortable, safe, and peaceful living', to which property, 'the secure enjoyment of their property' is a critical part.[55] Property means 'lives, liberties, and Estates'.[56] Property in this ample sense, being in the state of nature precarious, is to the benefit of each person, an incentive to enter political society and acquiesce in a system of rule.

Counting *liberty* as property adds to the worth of the common good. Liberty is an interest valued both for itself and as a means to other social goods. Liberty allows a space within which one is free to act, where action includes improving well-being, better securing needs, and advancing utilities. It goes beyond protecting what one has to enable addition and improvement, contributing to comfort, safety, and peace, all interests at the core of the common good. We now see why the common good is often said to consist in providing and securing liberty. Liberty like property being vulnerable to invasion, its protection is a primary duty of government. The theories of Locke on property and Machiavelli on liberty come together to suggest a coherent sense of the common good and the need for the power of the state. The common good as the comfort, safety, and peace of the nation and each person, together with the liberty to act to achieve such ends, sits well within the structure of social understanding proposed here. The ideas and language of political theory are given a social foundation. Comfort, safety, and peace are interests the people value and act to achieve, and so come within the common purposes of human endeavour, serving in the tug-and-scramble as a compass.[57]

The realm of the upper register is now complete. The body politic cultivates harmony, stability, and unity, qualities which in turn are essential to preserving the

[53] James Stuart, *Speech to Parliament* (1603) quoted by J Locke: *Two Treatises on Government* (ed) P Laslett (Cambridge: Cambridge University Press, 1960), p 399.

[54] Discussed fully and very helpfully in D Rollinson: *A Commonwealth of the People*, pp 236*ff.*

[55] Locke: *Two Treatises on Government*, pp 95, 331.

[56] *Ibid* pp 123, 350.

[57] See further J Warr: *The Privileges of the People* in *A Spark in the Ashes*, Section III.

comfort, safety, and peace of the people. Social relations are settled, simple, and resistant to change, the law their witness and guardian. The people know and accept their place in the social order and tend their houses and gardens, according to Machiavelli's homely image, secure in their possessions, safe in their persons, their minds at ease. When rights are violated or disputes break out, the courts are on hand to give protection and resolution. The arm of the law reaches beyond the civil sphere to be the custodian of order. The limits of liberty are defined by law, which the courts are diligent in declaring, the machinery of state zealous in upholding. No wonder the law is cast as the sinews binding together the body politic to ensure the good health of the whole and each part. The appeal of the common good conceived in this way is plain. The images of an organic whole and the ideas of harmony, stability, and unity are attractive to all, bring tangible benefits to all, while the settled order of social relations is kept intact. Within the bounds of law the people are free to improve their position, to show enterprise in securing their needs, initiative in enhancing their enjoyment of life.

6. The constitutional order of the body politic

Constitution as a concept enters the discourse only later as the body politic fades away.[58] Implicit in the body politic, between the pleasing imagery and the vulgar invective, are the elements of a constitutional order. The prince rules both as a natural person and as the embodiment of the realm. As a natural person he must acquire virtue in order to rule well. In embodying the realm the prince knows and rules for the interests of all subjects; he is in that sense the representative of all. In order to rule well, the prince takes counsel from a few, prudent and wise, at first the magnates later broadened to embrace lesser orders of nobility. The purpose of rule is the good of the realm, the common good, the good of all.[59] In ruling for the common good, the prince has the consent of the whole realm, normally an implied consent, in some cases express. Consent whether express or implied is conveyed by nobles and knights on behalf of the whole.[60] The people have no active place in the constitution, only the negative duty to accept and obey. That is not to say they are absent; they are present as a constituent part of the realm for the well-being of which the prince rules. Their interests are doubly represented, by the prince in

[58] For an account of the changing meaning of *constitution* G Stourzh: '*Constitution:* Changing Meanings of the Term from the Early Seventeenth to the Late Eighteenth Century' in *Conceptual Change and the Constitution* (eds) T Ball and JGA Pocock (University of Kansas Press, 1988), pp 35–54.

[59] These ideas are well-stated by John Watts whose account of early-modern kingship is most enlightening: J Watts: *Henry VI and the Politics of Kingship* (Cambridge: Cambridge University Press, 1996), especially Chapter 2. For other references, see the Notes.

[60] Marjorie Clarke writes well of consent to taxation: M Clarke: *Medieval Representation and Consent* (New York: Russell & Russell, 1964).

acting for their well-being and by the parliament in making known their needs and utilities.

Here in concise form are the concepts of constitution implicit in traditional conceptions of the body politic: sovereignty and representation, consent and the common good. The very same concepts structure modern constitutions.[61] The body politic has passed away while its ideas, images, and language live on. The social, economic, and political conditions of the twenty-first century compared to the fifteenth, sixteenth, or seventeenth are dramatically different; social relations among the people are transformed. Nevertheless, the concepts of constitution have a family resemblance. The meanings are adjusted and the content responsive to social reality, but the concepts are constant. How a register of constitutional ideas and language is able to transcend social, economic, and political conditions calls for explanation. The common good may seem the exception and to have been interred with the body politic. On the contrary, it lives on in contemporary constitutions with a modified identity to be unveiled later. Constitutional discourse shifts discreetly from outcome to process, from a settled sense of the common good to the process by which outcomes are reached. According to the narrative the people are now in charge and whatever they decide constitutes the common good. There is neither need nor place for a separate and settled sense of common good. If William Paget were looking on he could report to the Lord Keeper that what he dreaded has come to pass. The people have ascended from the feet to the head, from dumbly bearing the weight of the body to directing it.

Such a narrative, pleasing to some and deplored by others, under scrutiny falters. Between the people and where the head used to be stand representatives, the few who rule and whose actions are deemed to be for the good of all. To the spectres of Paget and the Lord Keeper some consolation is afforded, the people have risen but rule remains in the hands of a capable few. No longer king or queen or nobility, now a few who know the good of all. The common good, although not often declared in the texts, is out of sight but present, defining the purpose of constitutional authority and guiding representatives towards it. The constitutional revolutions of the eighteenth century in England, France, and the United States of America followed their own paths to reach the same conclusion that the common good is best reached by the rule of a few representatives. That idea is now widely entrenched in the constitutions of nations where the people are said to be in charge of their own affairs. The result is two contrasting sets of social relations between the people and representatives, one the people in some sense ruling themselves, the other rule by representatives. That takes us to the core of contemporary constitutions and calls for enquiry.[62] But first brief scrutiny of the body politic and its successor the body corporate.

[61] On the social function of concepts, see further comment in the Notes.
[62] Rule by representatives is examined in Chapters VI and XIV.

7. The body politic under scrutiny

Let us step back from the register of images, ideas, and language of the body politic and view it through the frame of social understanding. There are two issues, one the narrow notion of the common good, the other its relation to law. As to the first, the bounds of the common good are narrow and strictly guarded. The language of the upper register is of preservation, keeping in place a settled order of social relations, an order the image of the body politic makes immutable. An order portrayed by William Paget's horror at the very idea of 'the foot taking upon him the part of the head'. The people are destined to stay where they are, where room for change and betterment are confined to the narrow margin of liberty. The notion of the common good is equally narrow. Preserving certain qualities of the body politic is justifiable as being for the good of all, but not enough. The people have an abiding interest in improving their well-being. They need to be free to tug-and-scramble and to have some say in setting the rules for doing so. Social relations within the body politic are already set so there is no scramble to enter, no room to tug. The distinction between preservation and progress is not trivial but discloses an ambiguity in the meaning of the common good. If it be to preserve what is in place, to maintain the existing social order, then room for the people to improve their lives is bound to be narrow. That suits ideas of medieval and early modern society where the social order is fixed and settled, the common good to maintain the order not change it.

A different point of entry is easily imagined. One that eschews the artifice of the body politic and begins with an image of complex social relations reflecting a different reality. A reality where common purposes are sought in divers ways, where cooperation jostles with competition and conflict; where concord and harmony are neither immanent nor imposed but carved out of discord and disharmony. Instead of a people passively resigned to a place in the social order prescribed by others, the theory of social understanding sees a citizenship knowing its needs and utilities, willing to strive for them, ever conscious of the need to balance freedom and restraint. Where compromise and cooperation temper the zeal for self-interest; where government is accepted as an essential partner in the quest for humanity and civility; but is neither a power unto itself nor the instrument of one or other sector, one or other set of interests. Rather government is an agent of the people on whose behalf it contributes to the cause of humanity and civility and to advancing the well-being of all.

8. Law and the common good

The law as the sinews of the body politic, like the white cord winding through the hands of the *signori* of Siena, fastens the bonds of society.[63] The upper register

[63] Discussed in Chapter XI.

relies on law to define and cement social relations among the people, and between the people and rulers. The account is enriched with the concept of liberty, the boundaries of which law draws. Within the boundaries, the people join the tug-and-scramble to improve their position, safe from obstruction by others or the agencies of government. The notion of a margin of liberty is chosen carefully. It is neither absolute nor unrestrained, but a zone of freedom granted by the state and marked out by law and discretion. Law and discretion, liberty and common purposes, relate to each other in the following way. The agencies of government make law by way of legislative and executive action, administration and adjudication, the purpose to protect existing social relations or create new ones. Law forms a framework enabling and facilitating, guiding and restricting the actions of individual persons and their relations with others, leaving oversight to the agencies of government. In more colloquial terms, law and government frame and fence the field of tug-and-scramble. Within the bounds of law, the people are at liberty to pursue whatever ends they choose by whatever means they prefer, either alone or together with others. Law does more than set and patrol the boundaries. Law authorizes the agencies actively to assist the pursuit of purposes in various ways, some protective, others enabling, where that means providing or strengthening the conditions within which the tug-and-scramble take place, the aim to ensure a threshold of fairness and equality. Once outcomes are reached and advances made, the law deems them rights, which the agencies of government then make secure. When disputes occur, the means for doing justice, for fair and ordered resolution, are at hand.

Against the value of law in securing the settled sense of the common good must be set another discourse. If we were to enquire how the boundaries are set, why the people's efforts to improve their lives are confined to the margins, what grounds guide government in making the law, the answers would be several and revealing. Some are legacies from the past enacted for reasons forgotten, others deal with matters as they arise, some of moment, others trivial; some of national interest, others local. If we were to dig deeper, a connection would be discovered between the social order, the sum of settled social relations and spheres on the one hand, and law on the other hand. In early modern England, from which the upper register is drawn, the point of the body politic was to keep the social order as it is, not change it. If good health depends on the union of organs, each functioning as defined, then the purpose of law as the sinews is to preserve the body intact. To allow any organ to stray from its place would put at risk the whole body. The reality behind the allegory is a social order based on settled social relations of status and property, government vested in king, nobles, parliamentary elite, centralized agencies, and trusted officials, all pledged to uphold a constitutional order built partly on property, partly on status. The common good is to preserve the social structure, law the instrument to that end.

The grievances of the Levellers illustrate the point. At one level their appeal is to the upper register to honour its own undertakings by treating Lilburne and others not arbitrarily or abusively, but by the rules and procedures of law. Laws are 'the rules for the Commons of England whereby to walk'.[64] At another level their appeal goes beyond law, indeed throws the law itself into question. Far from being the frontier of freedom, the common law is now a 'badge of slavery imposed on the free people by the Norman Conquest'.[65] *Magna Carta* is at first cited to condemn the actions of king and parliament, until it comes under fire and is exposed as 'a beggarly thing'. Two reasons drive such disdain. One lies in an ideal of pre-Norman Anglo-Saxon society where freemen form social relations as they choose and all take part in the *folkmoot* to make law and to settle disputes. Courts over time acquire independence, yet remain rooted in the community. The king's function is not to make law but to see justice done according to law. There is no need to invent a sense of community other than or abstracted from the aggregate of individual freemen; and since freemen speak for themselves there is no need for representatives. The social order of their own making breeds harmony and stability and a sense of unity, and within the law men are free to secure and improve their lives.[66]

The other reason for the Levellers harking back to earlier English society is the very concept of law being prior to and a standard by which to judge social relations. Somewhere in the past is to be found an order of legal principles manifest in the habits and customs of the freemen of Anglo-Saxon society. This order of fundamental law, despite its origins being obscured by time, once uncovered remains the guide to social relations regardless of time or place. King and parliament as well as the people are subject to the fundamental law. The Levellers condemn the actions of parliament for breach of fundamental law,[67] which continues across time and nation because it is the law of reason, existing 'by virtue of a perceptive power innate in every man'.[68] The bible bears witness to God's 'instituting a perpetual, morall, unchangeable, and everlasting LAW'.[69] Whether the fundamental law of reason has been violated is finally for the people to judge, 'however mean their intellect'. A people prevented from judging the actions of their rulers are no better than slaves.[70] The law of reason gives birth to rights, some of which are listed in Magna Carta but many left out. Magna Carta is not only patchy on rights

[64] J Lilburne, *England's Birthright Justified* (1645) in *The Levellers in the English Revolution* (ed) G Aylmer (London: Thames and Hudson, 1975), p 57.

[65] J Lilburne, *Just Man's Justification* (1646) quoted in Pease: *The Leveller Movement.*

[66] These ideas are well explained in JEA Joliffe, *The Constitutional History of Medieval England* (London: Adam and Charles Black, 1937).

[67] J Lilburne: *England's Birthright Justified* (1645) quoted in Pease: *The Leveller Movement,* p 63.

[68] L Lilburne: *Innocency and Truth Justified* (1645) quoted in Pease: *The Leveller Movement,* p 64.

[69] J Lilburne: *Postscript to London's Liberty* (1646) in *The Levellers in the English Revolution,* p 71.

[70] *England's Lamentable Slavery* author uncertain, possibly William Walwyn, quoted in *The Leveller Tracts 1647–1653* (eds) W Hallett & G Davies (New York: Columbia University Press, 1944), p 301 and Pease: *The Leveller Movement,* p 64.

but is used by parliament for its own ends, as if that 'messe of pottage were their birthright'.[71]

Here we catch a glimpse of another way of viewing relations between the people and rulers, a different register of constitutional thought, starkly different from that of the upper register. It is enough for now to note the competing conceptions of law, one as an instrument at the disposal of rulers, king and parliament, to decree at will, the other a foundation of principles formed by natural reason innate in everyone. Confronted with the king's iniquity towards her son, Lady Costance is blunt: 'he that holds his kingdom holds the law'.[72] He who 'holds the law' rules as he wishes, all to sustain the body politic, the social order as it is; to protect property and status, to keep the people in their place. An alternative view sees law as prior to rule, a set of principles awaiting discovery, then used to gird and guide rule. The Levellers sought law in this sense. They failed in their search, as they were bound to fail because there is no law out there to be found separate from social relationships. That concepts of law be conceived and mature within social relationships and become embedded in social spheres, is a subject to which I return in considering the lower register of constitutional discourse.

9. From body politic to body corporate

As the health of the body politic declined, the body corporate rose to take its place.[73] The old body staggered on to show signs of life, and the date of death is hard to pinpoint. In England by the 1640s a new conception of constitutional authority was gaining ground. The people had shed the shoes of servile feet to take their place at the centre of the constitutional order. The social order was changing and social relations were being reconstructed, among the causes of which two stand out. One, the balance of king, peers, and commons was upended by the personal rule of Charles I; the other, the people were stirring to air grievances and declare aspirations. The House of Commons had used its position as the arm of government elected by the people to gain advantage over king and peers. If the purpose of constitutional authority were the welfare of the people, the *salus populi*, endlessly repeated and no one dared doubt, then the elected chamber could claim special status as their representatives. As people roused themselves for action, the old social order was crumbling to be replaced by one in which they had more liberty to move about and associate, to transfer labour from one place to another, to engage in economic enterprise, and generally to improve lives and well-being.

[71] *England's Lamentable Slavery*: in Pease: *The Leveller Movement*, p. 66.

[72] W Shakespeare: *King John*, Act 3: 1: 112.

[73] See the introductory remarks in Chapter II.3. I have given a fuller account elsewhere so here shall be brief: DJ Galligan: 'The People, the Constitution, and the Idea of Representation' in *Social and Political Foundations of Constitutions*, pp 134–56.

The ideas and images of the body politic were outdated and a new sense of constitutional order was needed to cope with the people.

Here common-cause ends and the path divides. It is one thing for parliament to enlist the people in defeating the king, another to concede their claim to constitutional authority. The discourse of the upper register is at hand, the ideas and language of the body politic to be borrowed and burnished to found the new order. A simple idea served the purpose: the people constitute a corporate entity which acts and only may act through representatives.[74] The corporate body has a legal identity separate and distinct from its members in the same way that a modern corporation relates to shareholders. The concept plays on the double meaning of the people, one referring to the aggregate of individual persons, the other to the people as an abstract whole. The abstract concept of the people has origins in Roman law, migrated to medieval canon law to resolve issues of government in the Church, from where it found its way into secular constitutional discourse. The concept of a corporation could easily be extracted from the imagery of the body politic where the king, the head, acts on behalf of the body, his actions the actions of the body. The focus shifts from the corporate body politic to the corporate people. Once corporate identity is settled, constitutional structure follows. Parliament represents the corporate body of the people, its actions become their actions. The original meaning of representation as *re-presenting* catches the idea: the representative takes the aggregate of individual persons and re-presents them as a corporate whole. When king, peers, and commons come together as the king-in-parliament, they represent the corporation of the people and have exclusive authority to do so. The idea is backed with pleasing sentiments. The people are cited as the source of authority; they consent to the newly crowned king; the king and parliament act with their advice and consent. The image is softened, while the reality of representative's acting for the whole remains intact.

As the commons chamber of parliament broadened its electoral base, fostered relations with the people, and gained in power compared to king and peers, it faced a dilemma. On the one hand its authority, the claim to a reserve of social capital, depended on election by the people; on the other hand its power to act independently had to be protected. The people wanted more say in the affairs of government, while from parliament's perspective old attitudes lingered on. The people are unreliable, even dangerous, and still prone to become the mob. The solution was found in a further refinement of the corporate logic. The precedent was there to be exploited, displayed in the proclamation of James Stuart as King James I of England: 'In this High Court of Parliament, where the whole body of the realm, and every particular member thereof, either in person or by representation—are by the laws of this realm *deemed to be personally present* (italic added)'.[75] The logic

[74] See account in Chapter II.

[75] Quoted in MRLL Kelly: 'King and Crown' (Doctoral Thesis: Macquarie University, Sydney, 1998), p 126.

unfolds. The people are in some sense sovereign but cannot exercise the power of sovereignty; that has to be left to their representatives in parliament. Then comes the master stroke. When parliament assembles in the chamber, it is as if the whole people were there assembled. The members go beyond representing the people to becoming them, being their embodiment.[76] A claim on its face absurd makes sense against the heritage of constitutional discourse distinguishing between the people as the aggregate of persons and as a corporate whole. If parliament becomes the corporate entity of the people, then the real people have no place and are out in the constitutional cold. The doctrine of the sovereignty of parliament is born and still holds, although its origin and proper title as *the sovereignty of the people in parliament* is forgotten. Changes have been made since the eighteenth century. The people have advanced in their influence on parliament and holding it to account. Although the sovereignty doctrine has come under scrutiny, the ideas of ancient origin defining relations between the people and the parliament still hold influence over the structure and the discourse of contemporary constitutions.

10. The people are 'not a stop for fortune's fingers to sound what stop she pleases'[77]

A register of ideas and discourse long ago entered the constitutional field to structure social relations and direct the actions of the people and officials. The register is still present in contemporary texts of nations in which the people are said to be governing themselves. Sovereignty is in deficit, rule is by representatives, elected but over whom the electors have only moderate influence, and to whose actions the people are deemed to consent. The question looming over the analysis is why the people settle for, even actively support the constitutional order that results. The question could be approached from several standpoints and answered in several ways. The aim here is to make sense of the people's sentiments and dispositions of restraint and support. The people have the power to design the constitutional order as they think best to serve their interests; yet they accept the inheritance of an order built to suit a social, economic, and political system markedly different from their own. Adjustments have been made as social conditions have changed, but the ideas and the discourse of the past are embedded and mark out much of the field. The task now is to make sense of the two seemingly contrasting ideas at the centre of contemporary constitutional orders.

[76] Pasi Ihalainen has delivered a full and enlightening account of the reasoning among members of parliament in reaching the conclusion that they embody the people: P Ihalainen: *Agents of the People: Democracy and Popular Sovereignty in British and Swedish Parliamentary Debates 1734–1800* (Leiden: Brill, 2010).

[77] *The Tragedy of Prince Hamlet*, Act 3: 2: 2.

A brief review of the upper register is a suitable prelude. The continuity of ideas as the people rise from the feet to be head is both intriguing and enlightening. The point of the body politic was to keep in place a settled social order. As the people gained ground socially and economically, they could no longer be barred entry to the constitutional field and so the utility of the body politic ended. Its heir the body corporate proved useful in tempering popular action and keeping the power of the state in the hands of a few. Rule by the few is now firmly rooted and able to stand alone, and so the corporate concept of the people has lost its utility. Rule by a few comes under strain from time to time and on some matters of high moment the people insist on having the final say. On the whole that is rare, leaving intact rule by representatives. That leads one to ask what holds the system together, or to be more precise, how the people's interests are served by vesting the power of the state in a few representatives and a complex of agencies. How is a surrender of power to the organs of government in the interest of a people intent on advancing their well-being personally and collectively? The briefest sketch will do for now as a prelude to a fuller answer unfolding in later chapters.

The power of the state is a resource for which sectors compete as a means to advance their interests. The competition does not stop at the gates of the constitutional field but continues in settling the rules of governing within. The same success some sectors have in the tug-and-scramble outside extends into the field to influence the conduct of government and to cement the social and economic ordering. Influence is a variable from weak and marginal at one end to domination and even capture at the other end. Influence is more easily achieved where authority is concentrated in the hands of a few rather than distributed among many. Directing the few, guiding their actions, even replacing them is easier than it would be if the power of government were diffused among the people. The sentiments and dispositions of the people are not so easily explained. The people appear to be content to support, sometimes design, a constitutional order based on ideas and discourse inherited from the past. An order intended to keep them out of the constitutional field and, when eventually admitted, to assign them a modest place. Behind the imagery of self-government is a reality, in which the people concede constitutional authority to a few rather than keep it for themselves, a few who no longer claiming to embody the people, profess to know what is best for them. Why then do the people, capable of being in charge of their affairs, squeeze themselves into an ill-fitting frame designed for a different purpose? Several reasons could be given. One is the appeal of continuity fortified by Hume's observation that 'antiquity begets the opinion of right' and Smith's discovery of a natural respect for authority.[78] The order is valued, arouses sentiments and dispositions because it

[78] Discussed in Chapter I:4.

is in place and provides certain benefits, the ideas and values a secondary matter. Another reason is that that once within the field, moderate adjustments can be made to the layout, the interests of the people better served. This goes some way towards but falls short of explaining the people's support for a constitutional order not designed for their benefit.

There is another reason to account for the people's support to which concepts are the clue. A concept is a shell into which meaning is inserted. Meaning is generated from experience and changes as experience changes. Concepts created with one set of meanings are receptive to other sets. The sequence is: experience is based around interests; interests arouse sentiments; sentiments lead to dispositions; dispositions prompt the interpretation of constitutional concepts to suit their interests. In other words, a concept acquires meaning from context, the ordering of social relations, and adjusts as social relations change. The concepts invented to serve one set of meanings, a certain order of social relations, are now given new meanings to serve a different order. The concepts remain the same while meanings change. Above a base of shared meanings, without which social order would be impossible, concepts are amenable to the perceptions and preferences of persons and sectors, some meanings consensual others contested. The same concept may have different meanings, be understood in different ways. Meanings are traced back to and originate in the interests of persons and sectors, and in the sentiments and dispositions aroused. Drawing on this account of the openness of concepts, we are now able better to understand the people's position in the constitutional field. They know that the concepts of sovereignty and representation, the corporate concept of the people and consent all have their origins in the past, the purpose to keep them on the fringe of the constitutional field, not to occupy the centre. They are aware that those meanings, while modified, still overshadow contemporary texts and discourse. The people are secure at the centre of the social structure and firmly dug into the constitutional field, not to govern themselves in any serious sense, but to be governed for their benefit.

Why then tolerate a set of concepts from the past? Part of the answer is the concepts of constitution are open to be construed to serve their interests, the other part that the concepts do not, in practice, matter much. The subtleties of sovereignty—are the people sovereign or just the source, does sovereignty vest in the government or the nation—while of abiding intellectual interest are of no practical importance. Representation is a more serious matter, although few spend time admiring the nuances or unravelling the alleged paradoxes of Abbé Sieyès, the high priest of representation.[79] It is enough that the people see through representation

[79] Discussed in Chapter XIV.

as inflating the place of officials and diminishing their own. What matters is more mundane: that the governing few act for the people's well-being; how best to describe officials, whether agents or servants, rectors or representatives, a secondary matter. Consent, uprooted from its ancient site at the centre of the field, likened before to Ariel waiting to be summoned to action, is now more a mascot than an active agent. Having brought down to earth relations with officials, the people's purpose is to be governed well. They are inclined to the view that rule by a few and a network of agencies has the potential to govern well, possibly better than the people trying to rule themselves. As long as they are governed well, the people are not too troubled that concepts are leftovers from another age and designed for other purposes. To the extent it matters, concepts are open enough to cope with different sets of social relations and social spheres. That suits the people well because openness and ambiguity allow continuity of concepts while the social structure changes, a quality of value in a constitutional order. That the upper register of discourse live on in texts and conventions is noted then ignored as of no practical concern.

At this point the common good returns to its rightful place in the constitutional order. Gone is the dominance of form, of equating the common good with a fixed structure, such as the body politic, or assuming it to be whatever the representatives decide. While dismissing such understandings or conceptions of the common good, the people retain the concept. They know that, despite the tendency of the few to take ownership and define it to suit their interests, the idea of the common good remains central to social endeavour, to the formation of social relations and the structure of the constitutional order. The common good means simply the well-being of the people within the setting of civility and humanity. That is the substantive outcome for which the constitutional order supplies the process. Well-being as the common good does not come packaged and labelled and ready for use, but has to be worked out in the course of social endeavour. Most noteworthy of all, the people are responsible for the common good, to give it meaning, to be guided by it, and to enlist government as a means to it. Fancy ideas of government and forms of subterfuge are replaced by the simple notion that leaders and officials are there to advance the well-being of the people, one means among many, for which they are equipped with worldly wisdom, power, and a discretionary space within which to work. The people coax them towards that end and keep an eye on them; try to make sure they do the job well; if not, replace them. The people are the guides to governing and the judges of success, the custodians or, to borrow an ancient term rich and suggestive, the *keepers of the common good*. To understand what that means we start with another register of ideas and language, a lower register as opposed to an upper. However, before that, the old warrior *consent* has to be reviewed and demoted, rebooted, and returned to service.

Notes

Government's failure to honour its own legal principles

England's Miserie and Remedie (1645) author unknown, most likely Sexby: D Wootton (ed): *Divine Right and Democracy: An Anthology of Political Writing in Stuart England* (London: Penguin, 1986), p 276, 'who but a madman will yield obedience unto those who are regardless of their laws and liberties, --of their subsistence, livelihood, and safety'.

Fundamental Law

'The laws of England are not laws unless in accord with the axioms of "right and justice, self-evident to any rational man however mean his intellect"': J Lilburne: *London's Liberty in Chains* (1646) in Pease, *The Leveller Movement*, p 75.

Images of the body politic and its health

Images of the body politic were common across Europe. Francesco Guicciardini diagnosed Florence in the sixteenth century as an old as well as diseased body, and old bodies are harder to cure. The sickness set in under the Medici who took all business of state into their own hands, trusted no one, and repressed rivals. Discussed in JGA Pocock: *The Machiavellian Moment* (Princeton: Princeton University Press, 1975), Chapter V, especially p 123.

Speaking on the parliamentary side before the civil war, John Pym adopts the bodily images to describe the common good: 'The form of government is that which doth actuate and dispose every part and member of a state to the common good; and as those parts give strength and ornament to the whole, so they receive from it again strength and protection in their several stations and degrees. If this mutual relation and intercourse be broken, the whole frame will quickly be dissolved and fall in pieces, and instead of the concord and interchange of support --- they [the parts] will miserably consume and devour one another': Speech on Mainwaring's impeachment 4 June 1628 quoted in *The Stuart Constitution 1603–1688* (ed) JP Kenyon (Cambridge: Cambridge University Press, 1986), p 15.

Law

On Richard Sexby's account, writing in support of the Leveller cause, by subjection and submission to law, we achieve the ends of 'a sociable life': *Killing Noe Murder*

(1657) in *Divine Right and Democracy* (ed) D Wootton (London: Penguin Books, 1986), p 371. Laws are 'the nerves and sinews of every society or commonwealth, without which they must necessarily dissolve and fall asunder': p 371. The prince as well as the people must submit to law. In stating a prince's view, James I is eloquent and subtle: *Speech to Parliament* 21 March 1610 in *The Stuart Constitution*, pp 11–13.

The head

The head stands above the rest of the body, a position depicted almost poetically by James I: 'We are content to descend many degrees beneath ourself, first by communicating to all our people the reasons of a resolution of state. – And lastly – opening to them that forbidden ark of our absolute and indisputable prerogative, concerning the call, continuing, and dissolution of Parliament': James I's proclamation on dissolving the parliament of 1621. Quoted in D Zaret: *Origins of Democratic Culture*, p 55. David Zaret recounts at length the sentiments and dispositions of King and Councillors toward the common people. The head must be nourished: 'to take from the body and give to the head is proper, for the body cannot be sustained without the head': quoted in Underdown, p 13.

Breathers

How 'breathers' came to bear the contempt intended by Cromwell is not clear. There is a gentler sense: 'Your monument shall be my gentle verse,/ —/When all the breathers of this world are dead./You still shall live—such virtue hath my pen—/Where breath most breathes, even in the mouths of men': *Sonnet* 81.

The feet

The image of the feet on the head is not uncommon: Richard II resigned himself to: 'be buried in the King's highway/Some way of common trade where subjects' feet/May hourly trample on their sovereign's head': W Shakespeare: *The Tragedy of King Richard II*, Act 3: 3: 154. A new perspective on Hamlet's image of 'the toe of the peasant' touching 'the heel of the courtier': see section 3 above.

The belly

While John of Salisbury assigns the belly to collect taxes, Shakespeare attributes a more elevated function. In *The Tragedy of Coriolanus*, a citizen condemns the belly as 'idle and unactive/Still cupboarding the viand, never bearing/Like labour like the rest'. Menenius, the patrician, answers for the belly: 'I receive the general food at first/Which you do live upon, and fit it is,/Because I am the storehouse and the shop/Of the whole body. But if you remember,/I send it through the rivers of your blood' to nourish all the organs of the body: Act 1: 1: 125*ff*.

Degree the key to social order and harmony

Degree is a concept often invoked to capture the essence of an harmonious social order. Ulysses uses the word seven times in the course of his famous speech recounting the reasons for the weakness of Troy: degree vizarded; observe degree; degree shaked; degrees in schools; degree in authentic place; degree taken away; degree suffocated: *Troilus and Cressida*, Act 1: 3: 74–137.

Faction

As David Zaret writes: 'Prevailing conceptions of the political order abhorred faction. The ideal of organic unity made it difficult for contemporaries to think about political faction in terms other than sedition, treason, or corruption': *Origins of Democratic Culture*, p 93.

Faction destroys unity: 'Amongst the soldiers this is muttered:/That here you maintain several factions,/And whilst a field should be dispatched and fought,/ You are disputing with your general': W Shakespeare: *The First Part of Henry the Sixth*, Act 1: 1: 70. Faction is treason: 'He is a traitor; let him to the Tower/And chop away that factious pate of his': *Richard II*, Act 5: 1: 132.

Parliament as Representatives of the Nation

In the course of conflict with King Charles I, parliament set out its claim to be representatives of the whole nation. Parliament claimed to have been entrusted 'with the responsibility for the general welfare of the commonwealth' and did so with the consent of the people. Marjorie Judson examines with insight and wisdom such claims and the social relations on which they are based: M Judson, *The Crisis of the Constitution: An Essay in Constitutional and Political Thought in England* 1603–1645 (Rutgers University Press, 1949) Chapter VII.

Concepts

On concepts in constitutional and political discourse: J Farr: 'Conceptual Change and Constitutional Innovation' in *Conceptual Change and the Constitution*, p 13. Farr writes: 'Conceptual change—varies from wholesale changes across an entire constellation of words and concepts, to more localized changes in the sense, the reference, or the attitudinal expressiveness of a single concept' p 22.

Ernest Gellner issued a warning: 'it is not true to understand the concepts of a society (in the way its members do) is to understand the society. Concepts are as liable to mask reality as to reveal it, and masking some of it may be part of their function': E Gellner: 'Concepts and Society' in *Sociological Theory and Philosophical Analysis* (eds) D Emmet and A Macintyre (London: Macmillan, 1970). The upper register of concepts confirms the masking function. The concepts of sovereignty, consent, and representation, together with the organic wholeness of the body politic, are detached from the reality of social relations; the image presented different from the reality.

Nevertheless, the function of concepts is more complex and more subtle. First, concepts normally have their origins in social relations from which, over time, they acquire independence. Secondly, concepts once separated project an image of social relations that does not match the reality. Sovereignty illustrates the point. The people are sovereign but, in fact, sovereign power is in the hands of representatives. Thirdly, concepts detached in this way may still enter into the people's sentiments and dispositions and guide their actions. Whether they do and to what extent are variables to be investigated empirically. Fourthly, concepts on their face, inclusive of the people, may, in practice, have the effect of excluding them. The concepts of the upper register have this double function. Fifthly, the people are capable of and, in fact, do see through the subterfuge, as I argue in the text. That is a function of the lower register; it gives the people an alternative set of concepts to draw on in assessing those of the upper register. For further analysis of the relationship between concepts and experience: DJ Galligan: 'Concepts the Currency of Social Explanation' (2013) 33 *Oxford Journal of Legal Studies* 345–68 and 'Legal Theory and Empirical Research' in *Oxford Handbook of Empirical Studies* (eds) P Cane and H Kitzer (Oxford: Oxford University Press, 2010), pp 976–1001.

Edmund Burke wrote at length about sentiments and dispositions, *prejudice*, as he named it. The social order is maintained by the people acting in line with the ideas and concepts prevailing, which they are conditioned to do: discussed by John Plamenatz, *Man and Society* (London: Longman, 1963), Volume I, pp 346*ff*. Such claims have to be treated with a touch of scepticism. They take no account of the people's being able to see beyond the dominating concepts, to view them against a set of more fundamental ideas and concepts.

On openness of concept

Karl Renner has shown how concepts, in this case, legal concepts, may serve different social functions: the concepts constant while the function changes: *The Institutions of Private Law and Their Social Functions* (London: Routledge & Kegan Paul, 1949, 1976).

VIII
Consensus and Consent

1. The ubiquity of consent and the mystery

Enquiry into constitutional discourse soon meets consent. The meaning uncertain and of no fixed abode, this Ariel of the constitution hovers about awaiting the bidding of a Prospero to settle some strife and be gone, never far and ready to be recalled. Adam Smith wrote of consent as 'figurative metaphorical'; Hume saw no need for it unless acquiescence equals consent; Vico makes no mention of it. Consent comes into service in constitutional discourse, although even here it is elusive, summoned by different parties for different purposes. Locke makes consent the foundation of the constitutional order, but when it turns out to consist in 'putting oneself under government', its credentials are uncertain. The idea is ambiguous, meaning at best agreement inferred from action and scarcely an inch from Hume's acquiescence. Hobbes strikes out in the opposite direction, making an act of consent of each person a condition of authority, then shifting from reality to fiction by imagining the people covenanting among themselves to establish government, the *as if* form of argument.[1] How consent can be essential for some, a pillar of the constitutional order, while for others marginal or not needed, calls for explanation. The task here is to consider consent in social understanding, the place it holds in social relations, and how it enters the constitutional field.

Consent enters the constitutional field to solve a problem that presents itself at two levels, one pressing and practical, the other profound and structural. As a practical matter, to be effective and to last, a constitutional order needs the support of the people, something more than the restraint implicit in acquiescence, although precisely what is hard to say. Consent indicates support and so fills the gap. That leads to the more profound matter of consent: what it means and what purpose it serves. Here opinion divides, some contending consent be an essential part of the structure, others finding no need for it. Summoned to justify constitutional authority, consent is critical to the discourse of the upper register in defining the relationship between rulers and ruled. The people consent to rule and, by consenting, accept the actions of rulers to be justified.[2] Consent may carry conditions limiting the actions of rulers, although on one view, a unity of ruler and ruled renders the acts of the one the acts of the other.[3] What consent means and how it is

[1] See Chapter II:4.
[2] On the need for justification see Chapter VII:9.
[3] Thomas Hobbes, an advocate of this approach, states: 'the acts of the prince are the acts of the subject': *Leviathan*, Chapter XVI, p 5.

Keepers of the Common Good. D.J. Galligan, Oxford University Press. © D.J. Galligan 2024.
DOI: 10.1093/9780198907398.003.0008

conveyed is another matter open to opinion. Consent in purest form is an expression of agreement to a proposed course of action; in modified form consent is inferred from actions; while at the far end consent is dependent on the submerged subjunctive, *as if* the people consented. The lower register, by contrast, has neither place nor use for consent. The relationship between officials and people, formed to secure and advance their well-being, is complete without adding an act of consent. Restraint and support on the one hand, engagement, vigilance, and censure on the other hand, seasoned with prudence, justice, and beneficence, are the qualities of the relationship, the signs marking the constitutional field. Consent slips through the fence not to add conditions but to put its brand and bestow its blessing to what is already there.

Practice, however, is neither so neatly confined nor consent so easily banished. Consent sprouts from a seedbed of sentiments to weave its way into social relations of all kinds, guiding the formation and disciplining the practice, more welcome in some than others. A seedbed fertilized by the sentiment that power of one over another has to be justified, a sentiment grounded in the concept of civic equality, which, as we have seen, has origins in the idea that each member of society is a person worthy of respect. Consent justifies actions by one that affect another's interests. It is valued both as a mark of respect mutual among persons and as a practical aid in achieving common purposes. The duty to justify actions is discharged, normally, by the person subject to them having consented. And so consent enters the constitutional field to justify the actions of officials and agencies.[4] The risk is that, once admitted to the constitutional field, consent has no settled place and lends itself to being exploited for purposes unplanned and questionable. How consent as a property of social relations has found a place and purpose in constitutional discourse is the theme of this chapter. The enquiry begins with the meaning and the ambiguities, from which emerges two senses of consent critical to constitutional understanding.

2. Between consensus and consent

The word *consent* comes from the Latin *consentire*, an intransitive verb, composed of *con* (together) and *sentire* (to feel): to feel together, to share feelings. Consensus means shared feelings. The noun *sentiment* also comes from *sentire* and enters the sequence to express feelings, shared sentiments being shared feelings. Just as sentiments vary in intensity, the level of consensus varies and easily dissolves into *dissensus* or divided sentiments. Consensus is passive in tone, suggesting shared feelings *about something*. The verb *consentire* generates another sense of consent,

[4] Discussed in: G Vico: *The New Science*.

positive in tone: the action of agreeing to something.[5] Consent signals a relationship in which one party agrees to the action of another. It is not simply shared feelings, agreement *about a matter*, but agreement *to something*. The power of government to tax shows the difference. In early modern England, there was among the people consensus that their interests were served by a system of taxation, the forms of which were settled. If a new tax were proposed, an added burden would be imposed on the people, for which positive consent was needed.[6] The difference between the two concepts is implicit in the simple case. When action changes or falls outside, threatens, or is an exception to the settled consensus, justification is needed, which positive consent provides. Applied to the constitutional context, there is among the people consensus as to the utility of government in advancing well-being, regardless of who rules provided well-being is served; the people share consensus as to 'the general advantage of government', as Hume put it, and acquiesce. If change be proposed, such as separate states coming together to form a federation, or the constitution be amended to give the indigenous people a voice, or to leave the European Union, each beyond or a disruption of the consensus, then the people's positive consent may be needed. The differences are subtle and rarely noticed, consent so dominating the discourse that consensus has been lost from sight. Consensus or consent may be positively declared, although in practice each is likely to be inferred from other actions. Relations between the two senses and the function of each is either not known or ignored. Consent enters the constitutional field bearing the two meanings, unnoticed, unseparated, and bound to cause confusion.

Consensus is implicit in the ideas and images of the body politic. The organic wholeness creates harmony, stability, and unity. The function of each organ is settled; contributes to and benefits from the whole; and is guided by the head to good health. All organs work together supporting each other and contributing to the whole. As an organic whole, the body politic has no need for consent as a positive act of agreement. As the social order changes and appeal of the body politic wanes, social relations are viewed in a fresh light. The social order turns out to be a rough and tumble arena with the people restless, resourceful, and often resentful, intent on improving their position, yet restricted in action, the resigned acceptance of Peter Quince no longer true to the age. Power replaces fatherly care but power divides as well as unites society in forming and defending social relations. All benefit from firm rule, but some benefit more than others. That is the reality rulers confront. The issue then is how to sustain consensus to the altered order despite the disparities and the limits on initiative.

The stage is reset for a social order in which the people demand a place and from which they want more benefits. The head, no longer the fatherly figure, dons

[5] *Oxford English Dictionary* (Compact Edition, 1964).

[6] Discussed in M Clarke: *Medieval Representation and Consent* (New York: Russell & Russell, 1964).

the cloak of the prince who is expected to rule wisely with the counsel of nobles, while in touch with the people through parliamentary representatives. The people having outgrown the shoes of their feet—become too big for their boots—take a more active role in the constitutional order, although they are still unfit to govern. The prince is, in time, replaced by representatives who know the 'true interests of the real people', rendering too-frequent elections unnecessary and avoiding the 'inconveniences', in Horace Walpole's words, of the people ruling themselves.[7] The wisdom and measured judgement of the few, whether the parliament, the assembly, or the propertied gentry, is decreed to be the foundation of good government. That the people are in some sense sovereign could be conceded, for it had no practical bearing on the constitutional order. The select few know how to govern well in the interests of all, and so consensus is restored.[8] As imagery and reality diverge the claim of the few comes into question. The people feel free to assert broader interests and to nurture new sentiments born of their own power. They want not just to be admitted to the constitutional field but to have some say in how it is cultivated. Ambition breeds discord and dissent, gnawing at the harmonious whole, casting doubt on the wisdom of rule by the few, and nudging consensus to the margins. The question then is how rule by a few is to be justified.

Despite the discord and division, all still have an interest in effective government, an order of rule capable of deciding and taking courses of action. The trouble is that shared interest has to confront and compete with other interests the people value and work to advance. Questions about who governs cannot be kept separate, and so the shared interest in having a system of government is overshadowed, even overlooked, by the people's wanting a form that better serves their interests. Rule by a few is no longer regarded as natural and neutral, but instead a device designed for the benefit of select sectors. Consensus as to the need for government, regardless of who governs, is not strong enough to prevail over other interests and the appeal of other forms of rule. The people turn attention to the structure of the order and who rules within it. The form of rule, whether the prince or the few, is hard to sustain in the face of competing interests; opposition mounts, and instability follows. Consensus is not up to the task, is not able to cope with the people's being intent on advancing their interests, the competition that results; nor is it enough to sustain support for government regardless of who governs. The solution is to avoid the competition by putting support on a different foundation.

Consent as a positive act of agreement comes to the rescue. To consent to the constitutional order is to agree to the form of rule and the actions of government, and to restrain the pursuit of competing interests. Actions agreed are actions authorized and justified. The sentiment of consent as positive agreement occupies a conceptual space different from and more powerful than the sentiment of

[7] P Ihalainen: *Agents of the People*, pp 73–5.
[8] *Ibid*, generally, Chapter 2 especially.

consensus. The logic is sound, the difference between the two concepts critical, although application in practice faces obstacles. Acts of positive consent are rare. The Levellers' case for an agreement between the people and parliament, signed by each person, never came to pass. The freeholders of Pennsylvania and other states came close to a form of positive agreement, but the experiment was short-lived. One solution is to assemble evidence from which to infer positive consent, although here the line between consensus and positive agreement becomes blurred. The evidence and the signs available are likely to be the same as those for consensus, and so the line between the two is hard to find and sustain. Another obstacle is that, in the rough and tumble of practical affairs, conceptual clarity loses its edge and the line between the two concepts smudged, leaving consent a flabby notion of uncertain content. There is another solution, a way of avoiding the problem of finding evidence of consent and keeping the two senses clear. The classic approach, the response of the upper register, is to imagine an act of consent, to recall the submerged subjunctive, and proceed *as if* the people consented to the constitutional order. The function and force of this approach will show as the chapter proceeds.

3. Search for consent

Preaching a sermon at Norwich Cathedral in 1696, as addresses and petitions poured into London, Henry Meriton encouraged the faithful to affirm their support for the new king, for consent is 'the only way to preserve government and keep it steddy without tottering or shaking'.[9] Without the support of the people, government would 'totter and shake' and be at risk of collapse. Appeal is to the need for government, consent critical to its effectiveness, even survival. In a few words, the Reverend captures the reality that the people's support is indispensable to the constitutional order. But does giving support mean the people are expressing consensus; or does it mean more, a positive act of consent? Support is evidence of consensus among the people as to the utility of government; consent in a more positive sense is not needed. That interests valued by the people depend on and be protected by government is enough to arouse sentiments and dispositions of support. The empirical premise behind the Reverend's plea is that government could not function, would not be able to provide social goods without the people's support. There is no sign of the people's taking the extra step of indicating positive consent, or that it was needed. Yet, despite being logically distinct, the two meanings are inclined to drift seamlessly into each other, the risk that positive consent

[9] H Meriton: *A Sermon Preacht at the Cathedral Church in Norwich* (1696) quoted in M Knights: *Representation and Misrepresentation in Later Stuart Britain* (Oxford: Oxford University Press, 2005), p 156.

be assumed where the evidence, accurately assessed, points only to consensus. The ambiguity, the running together of the two senses, and the drawing of unwarranted inferences, are commonly encountered.

Consensus is most evident in small communities. The yeomen and yeowomen of Vacy Plains, the ranchers of Shasta County, and the diamond traders of New York City are a few communities among many whose members work together in reasonable harmony on conditions unstated but understood. Adam Smith found the earliest form of society to be consensual, the coming together of shepherds for mutual benefit and protection of their flocks.[10] Consensus captures the spirit of the community, relations among the members, the purpose, and understandings. Consensus among the farmers and ranchers is high, grounded in and reinforced by social relations and social spheres. Matters occasionally come up where there is no consensus and active agreement is sought. They are exceptions, consensus normally being strong enough to sustain the community. The logic of consensus does not transfer easily from a tight-knit community to the nation. The reasons are worth noting. In securing needs and advancing utility, individual persons, groups, and sectors bring to the political arena an array of interests, some shared, some in conflict. The tug-and-scramble divides rather than unites sentiments and lowers consensus. The risk is that the lowering of consensus spills over to weaken shared sentiment towards the authority of government. The solution is to put the shared interest in government on a different footing. Consent as positive agreement serves the purpose. Acknowledging the need for effective government, the people declare their consent to the form in place. The contest among interests then takes place within the bounds set and without putting government at risk. The drawback is that the citizens of nation-states rarely have the chance to start afresh and design the field as they would wish. The alternative is for the ruling one or few to persuade the people to give positive consent to the order in place; if that fails, the fiction of consent is enlisted.

4. Consent inferred

In the absence of an act of agreement, consent to the form of the constitutional order could be inferred from the evidence. Signs of consent are abundant, sometimes to the order as a whole, sometimes to events and actions. Associations and localities were encouraged, historically, to endorse by addresses and petitions the newly crowned monarch and to swear allegiance.[11] During the coronation ceremony, the people still convey consent to the new monarch through representatives,

[10] A Smith: *Lectures on Jurisprudence*, pp 201*ff.*

[11] Described well by M Knights: *Representation and Misrepresentation*, Chapter 3.

as witnessed in the crowning of Charles III.[12] Mark Knights recounts the many signs of support from which consent can reasonably be inferred. A subtle shift is to infer consent from involuntary acclamation. A Roman citizen nominated for consul needed the people's consent, which they were expected, indeed required, to give by acclaiming the nominee. Their refusal to acclaim Coriolanus due to his arrogance was not well received, and revenge was taken.[13] The British case is less dramatic, but the people's declining to acclaim the newly crowned monarch, so far without precedent, would be a minor revolution. What, then, is the point of such signs of support? They are in some cases expressions of consent, in other cases acts of support from which consent is inferred. The reasoning is rarely revealed, and the ambiguity remains unresolved. Consent may be implicit in the people's words and actions. Locke's notion of putting oneself under government is an example: if I put myself under government, implicitly I consent to government. The argument is to be handled with care. If it means subjecting oneself to government and obeying the rule, that is not consent in a meaningful sense. The hostage with a gun to his head can hardly be said to consent to the power of the captors by obeying their orders and so 'putting himself under' them. The reasoning applies to government. Submission is ambiguous in meaning and may be no more than a measure to avoid the wrath of the state, hardly consent in a worthwhile sense, the motive to obey no nobler than self-preservation. The very idea of choosing to put oneself under government stretches reality, the more accurate description that government puts itself over one. Consent in positive form needs something more.

The accounts of Hume and Smith could be interpreted to include a sense of implied consent, although that was not intended by either. Always alert to reality, they are less intent on locating consent than finding practical reasons to explain the people's complying with and supporting government, restraining their own actions, and deferring to rule. If government secures certain social goods, the people have reasons to comply, leading to a disposition to acquiescence and restrain one's own actions. The leap from compliance to consent is not one the cautious Scotchmen were disposed to make. On their accounts, the people are inclined to suppress their disdain and distaste for the regime as long as it is capable of securing basic social goods, government of whatever kind normally being better than none. Faced with persistent failure to meet moderate expectations, the people may stop acquiescing. When the princes and bishops of medieval Florence lost the capacity to provide essential social goods, the people sought security and protection

[12] The authoritative source is: MRLL Kelly: 'The Coronation Oath' (Doctoral Thesis, Macquarie University, 1982).

[13] At least according to William Shakespeare in *The Tragedy of Coriolanus* (around 1608) in *The Oxford Shakespeare* (eds) S Wells and G Taylor (London: Guild Publishing, 1990). The fate of Coriolanus is examined in Chapter XV.

in other forms of association, from which grew the city republics Lorenzetti celebrated in *Buon Governo*.[14] The discourse is less of consent than practical reasons for accepting the actions of government. If the need be felt to include consent, it would be the minimal sense of acquiescence, one rung down the ladder from Locke's tacit consent.

In the pragmatic approaches of Hume and Smith, as noticed before, the sentiment of support for government and the disposition to self-restraint are strengthened by a matching sentiment of respect for authority, in particular for 'the path, in which their ancestors have trod'.[15] The path need not be straight or the going smooth; that it be the path trodden, well-marked, and passed on is enough to foster consensus and could stretch to a sentiment of consent, guarded and moderate, but enough to sustain support for government even when the benefits are thin, the gains few. Better to stay on the path we know, as rough as it is, than to stray into the bush in search of a better one. Perhaps this played on Peter Quine's mind as he prepared the play for the Duke's wedding. One can be careful not to offend a lady and not be hanged; and there are benefits to ducal rule, peace and stability, even harmony, not lightly to be overlooked. So why not signal one's support by celebrating the wedding? That is the point. As long as there are benefits, the provision of social goods, the meeting of expectations, a sentiment of respect for authority adds to and fortifies the sentiment of support. If the benefits fall below a certain point, consensus is likely to weaken and risk being lost.

The people do not often have say in designing the constitutional field; when they do, the place of consent is elusive. Whether engagement be integral or marginal, intense or casual, from negotiating terms to voting on the draft, conclusions about consent are to be drawn with caution. Even if the people take part in constitution-making, it does not follow they consent to the outcome. Those in favour of the proposed text are reasonably judged to consent, while a minority may be left disappointed, their interests neglected, overridden, or ignored. The assumption that participation in a process amounts to consent to the outcome, although commonly claimed, is logically false and an unwarranted inference. Even the position of those who vote to approve the draft is not straightforward. While agreeing to the proposed constitution overall, some may have misgivings about the terms. The position of the next generation, inheriting rather than making the constitution, is more uncertain. The members might find enough merit to overcome doubts and endorse their inheritance; see enough benefits to merit support; realize the value of continuity and respect for their forbears. Whatever the reasons, consent is inferred rather than expressed. The question is whether the evidence is enough or

[14] On Italian City-Republics, see D Whaley and T Dean: *The Italian City-Republics* (London: Longman, 4th edn 2010). Discussed in Chapter XII.

[15] See the discussion in Chapter I:IV.

the right kind to justify a finding of consent, while looming over all is the question of whether the correct inference is one of consent or simply enough consensus to sustain the constitutional order.

Consent conveyed through representatives is another variation on the theme, one central to constitutional discourse. Rule by representatives, touched on earlier and considered again later, raises issues of consent. Consent conveyed through representatives takes two main forms. In one, the representative acts as agent or delegate appointed to speak on behalf of the people, the principal, and therefore, with their consent. The representative is a conduit, a vehicle to convey, and adds nothing to the brief from the people. In the absence of a brief, the representatives distil guidance from the clues available and present them in their own words. In an alternative role, the representative rises above being agent or delegate to stand in the place of, be their substitutes, even to become the people. A variation on the *as if* style of argument, the representatives merge with, acts as if they were the people represented. The origins are found in the theatre where the actor *represents* and, for the purpose of the play, becomes the character of the script. The difference is that, unlike the actor who keeps to the script, representatives of the people write the script, presenting the words declaimed and the sentiments portrayed *as if* those of the people. Traces of the body politic are in evidence. The prince, as the head, knows what is good for the well-being of the body and naturally speaks for the whole and each organ, including the feet, which could hardly be expected to have a voice or one worth hearing.

5. Re-presenting a seasoned warrior

So far we have two accounts of consent, one consensus as shared sentiments, the other consent as positive agreement, both having a place in constitutional authority. Not the prominent place normally assigned, which leaves two questions. One is to account for the gap between consent in the discourse of the upper register and its place in practice; the other is to consider the place of consent from the stance of the people. Separation of the two meanings is an advance but not enough to mark the full measure of consent. There seems to be another dimension somewhat elusive and in need of explanation. The signs are there in the language, discourse, and sentiments, not only of constitutions of the seventeenth and eighteenth centuries but the twenty-first as well. After allowing for inflation of the concept, and discounting the fanciful forms claimed by representatives, the idea of consent as central to social relations of all kinds stubbornly persists. In the logic of social understanding, consent signifies an interest, shared and valued, creating a matching sentiment and a disposition to embed the concept in social relations and practical action. The task now is to unearth the foundation of the sentiment, searching in two directions, one to clear from the site an abiding concept of constitutional orthodoxy, which has little to offer social understanding; then to uncover an alternative and authentic foundation for consent.

An idea central to constitutional discourse is that the power to rule comes from the people with their consent. Power is renamed authority, which presupposes an author, the people. Henry Parker, an influential voice in the troubled years before the civil war, declared: 'power is originally inherent in the People' who are 'the authors, or the ends of all power' and so 'the final cause of Regall Authorite'.[16] It was left to Thomas Hobbes to explain how, by means of a covenant among the people, power moved from them to the prince, and so set the frame of constitutional authority.[17] The frame, although constructed to justify princely rule, holds for representatives' ruling with the consent of the people. The frame has proved hard to hold together, the passage of power from people to rulers rather obscure, the true place of the people, even in constitutions made in their name, cloaked in ambiguity.[18] The whole idea could be dismissed either as another *as if* style of argument or as an ideal to guide thought and action. Yet, Parker and Hobbes and others present the case not as wishful thinking but grounded in social relations. For that to be the case, the people would have to consider themselves the authors of state power and deem consent to be the basis of their relations with government. On one view of history that is just what happened. No longer content to be subject to the power of others, the people claim the power as theirs, which they delegate to officials, who rule with their consent. The process is gradual but the people emerge victorious, the demos dominates, democracy is born, constitutional history consummated, leaving nothing more to say. This is one way of explaining the advance of the people's constitutional standing between the sixteenth century and the twentieth. Consent, having earned a place in defining relations between the people and rulers, takes its place as the founding concept of the constitutional order.

The account is questionable, the idea of consent as the concept guiding the people's efforts to win constitutional status dubious. There is an alternative narrative. The people's main concern, the driving motive has been to secure and improve their lives, the constitutional order a means to that end. How to align the means to the end is the issue. The main obstacle is that the power of rule, the means to the end, tends to gravitate to a select few and is hard to contain. The people have two paths open to them. One is to take power and rule themselves. The appeal of self-rule, in principle, is offset by the practical drawbacks and is hard to do well for reasons discussed later.[19] The solution is to allow a few to rule as representatives in the name of the people and with their consent. The people think themselves in charge of their affairs while gaining the practical advantage of power being vested

[16] Henry Parker: *Observations upon Some of His Majesty's Late Answers and Expresses* (1642) discussed in Q Skinner: 'Hobbes on Representation' (2005) 13 *European Journal of Philosophy* 155.
[17] T Hobbes: *Leviathan*, Chapters XVI and XVII.
[18] Discussed in Chapter VI.
[19] Chapter XII and XIII herein.

in a few. The trouble is this golden bowl of constitutional order has a crack caused by tension between the idea of self-rule and the reality of conferring power on others. Consent is meant to seal the crack, the glue to unite people and representatives. Consent justifies action and so the actions of representatives are justified. Consent signals something more, a sense of ownership, that actions taken with consent are the actions of the people themselves. It is hard to question one's own actions. Having pushed the idea of consent to its peak, the people would be wise not to look down, for the slope of reality below is steep and the path down slippery. Power, once conferred, acquires its own momentum and is hard to control, regardless of who has it. Consent rather than solving the problem makes it worse, makes it harder for the people to monitor and criticize actions to which they have consented. Such logic and the restraint it demands are the reasons consent is so central to the upper register, not to empower the people but the opposite.

The other path open to the people is to put aside consent and ask how well-being is best advanced. Casting an eye on history, the people notice repeated reference to the common good as the standard to guide and by which to judge rule. They know the common good is malleable and has been used as much to keep them in their place as to benefit them. They see, nevertheless, the wisdom in power of rule being for a purpose, a goal to attain, a standard by which to be assessed. The common good is taken to mean the advance of civility and humanity, central to which is the well-being of the people. Rule has a purpose and the people have a criterion by which to appraise rule. Experience confirms that on the one hand power vested in leaders and agencies contributes to well-being, and on the other hand that power defies instruction, is hard to control, and gravitates to unwanted ends. The people's strategy is to influence the use of power and nudge it along to serve their well-being. Ideas of sovereignty, representation, and consent have no practical place, except to soften the reality and encourage the people in their efforts. This account matches the historical record in which the common good as the well-being of all is the reigning concept. Although open to meaning and at hand to serve select interests, the common good as the well-being of all remains the concept guiding constitutional endeavour. Consent is present as a minor theme, a diverting coda in the symphony of constitutional history, its role supportive but modest in securing the common good. Before expanding on this interpretation, let us return to consent in the upper register.[20]

The prospect of power passing to the multitude is not graciously conceded by sectors with a stake in sustaining social superiority and economic advantage. The opposite is true; history is the record of resistance to the idea of the people as the source of authority, its use being conditional on their consent. As a display of the distaste and the degree of opposition, debates in the House of Commons in the eighteenth

[20] The Levellers are a good case study of the interplay between the common good and consent: see Notes.

century are instructive. Regardless of the record of economic and social change, and in the face of changing ideas as to the place of the people, the majority of parliamentarians were resolute in rejecting the idea of the people being sovereign or even having a share in power. There were exceptions, some members advocating new ideas and supporting change, but not enough to influence the whole. The voice of the people growing in volume and hardening in resolve could not be ignored. To this dilemma, the shrewd instincts of elected members found an answer in the notion of *virtual representation*, of the real people being disembodied to become a *corporate* entity, parliament the embodiment. How to interpret the parliamentary performance is not straightforward. It could mean utter rejection of the people as the source of power, rendering their consent irrelevant. Or it could be a sign of the opposite, admission that power comes from the people and their consent is critical to the constitutional order. The task has been to find a way of conceding the need for consent while making sure it has no practical effect. The notion that parliament represents all the people, from the noblest to the most humble, having served well in the past, is no longer convincing.

There is another way of handling the people. Concede they are sovereign, the source of power, and the authors of authority, then deem parliament to be the people and hence sovereign. The doctrine of the *sovereignty of the people in parliament* serves the purpose.[21] Consent is implicit in the actions of the people as a corporate whole, while power stays where it is. The fledgling sentiment of governing with actual consent of the people is overshadowed by their notional consent as a corporate body assembled in parliament. The shade of the body politic returns, parliament governs as the people, as the corporate entity, power is shared among monarch, nobles, and elected members, and harmony, stability, and unity are restored. Despite the pleasing discourse and the beguiling imagery, there is a risk that the real people outside parliament see through it and so cannot be ignored. Measures are taken quietly to allow their influence to be felt, their interests taken into account, and the liberty to improve their lives expanded, while the constitutional order remains intact. And just as the shade of the body politic falls over the eighteenth century, the influence of its successor, the sovereignty of parliament, is still felt today.[22]

Let us return to that other way of framing relations among the people and between the people and government. A frame founded in social relations and wasting no energy on abstractions, fictions, and loose tales of authorship. A different understanding of constitutional authority and the place of the people unfolds. The people hold in reserve and sometimes invoke the raw power to ignore or overthrow government. That such measures be taken only in the extreme is readily

[21] For discussion of the idea of sovereignty of the people in parliament, see DJ Galligan: *Putney Debates* 2019 (Foundation for Law Justice & Society: *fljs.org*).

[22] See in addition the reference to Charles I in Chapter XV.

explained. Government is among the social institutions the people rely on in the pursuit of common purposes, for which government needs power. The people concede, accept, or acquiesce in, even consent to such power, knowing it be a necessary and useful instrument to their ends. They know power is dangerous, prone to excess and misuse, and so find ways of guiding and containing it. Their main interest is the practical matter of making sure power is effective in advancing their well-being. Who holds power is a secondary matter; the primary aim that it be used efficiently and effectively. Experience suggests that among the means to that end, the power to elect and dismiss the leaders ranks high in utility, but is by no means enough and needs support from other measures. In the daylight of experience, abstract ideas and fictions of constitutional theory pale into the twilight, constitutional paradoxes are assigned for resolution to Abbé Sieyès and his disciples, and sovereignty returned to the field of international affairs from whence it came before creeping into a nest not its own.

6. Consent as a quality of social relations

The task now is to trace consent to its origins in social relationships and then plot its progress into constitutional discourse. Consent acquired juridical status in Roman law and became a founding concept of the later European legal tradition. Simply stated, consent is a constitutive element of relationships between two or more parties; what that means in practice varies with the relationship. A constituent element in several ways. One where the parties freely enter a relationship and set the terms; another where the parties, having no choice but to enter, have some say in the terms; a third where the parties have no choice but to enter a relationship, the terms of which are set. Some relationships, such as that between master and slave, lack any notion of reciprocity and fall outside the scheme. The threshold condition is that the parties have for each other a respect based on the intrinsic worth of each, from which follows mutual recognition as a bearer of rights. Rights in the sense of having interests that merit recognition and respect within any social relationship. The sentiment of respect for each person is the foundation for other interests, those more valued given the status of rights. The bedrock of mutual respect arouses sentiments and dispositions to action that enter into and influence the relationship.

Consent then takes its place not as a stranger from outside, but a quality implicit in the logic of a relationship. In one case the parties consent to enter the relationship and set the terms; in the second they consent to the terms of a relationship they are required to enter; while in the third, despite having no choice but to enter and no say as to terms, once having entered, entitlements accrue which may be lost or lopped only by consent. This last case is revealing, conceptually and historically, in showing how respect for the person is fastened into the architecture of relationships. Dependent neither on choice nor agreement, the interest in mutual respect is embedded, valued, and the source of sentiments, dispositions, and action. From that base other interests flow and merit the same respect, some given legal status as rights. Rights occur within relationships, and we now see how they accrue and why they matter. The worker, the tenant, and the peasant often have no choice in entering relations with employers, landlords, and the manor, and no influence over the terms. Having entered, each acquires rights as interests to be respected. Rights once acquired are the natural companions of justice. Justice in rendering what is due and granting redress where due is not given. Justice, itself a constitutive property of social relations, directs that rights be reduced or negated only with the consent of the right-holder.[23]

7. *Quod omnes tangit*

Respect for the person and the principle of justice combine to secure consent as a juridical concept and the foundation of legal duties. We are indebted for that to Roman law and the wisdom of Roman lawyers. Our indebtedness extends to the late Gaines Post who restored knowledge of the largely forgotten legacy of the Roman law of consent and its influence on constitutional discourse.[24] The maxim *quod omnes tangit* was quoted in early texts and cited by bishops and princes to justify action sacred or secular, despite the Code of Justinian from which the maxim came having been lost from sight. The critical words are *what affects all in like fashion should be approved by all*.[25] Among civilians and canonists of medieval Europe this became the rule that, to quote Post, 'every kind of jus, ie, "right" in the legal sense, was accompanied by the right of consent'.[26] That is to say a primary right to *X* is accompanied by a secondary right that *X* not be compromised without consent. The maxim applies to protect private rights: 'common rights in property or in its use were necessarily accompanied by the common law of consent'.[27]

The writ of the maxim ran through society, entered social relations among the people, and circled around relations between prince and subjects, entering some, abstaining from others. The concept has a dynamic quality, the meaning adjustable according to the case.[28] Meanings ranged from real personal consent, to corporate,

[23] On justice, see Chapter I:2.

[24] G Post: 'A Roman Law Theory of Consent' (1950) *Wisconsin Law Review* 67. For a fuller account: G Post: *Studies in Medieval Political Thought: Public Law and the State, 1100–1322* (Princeton: Princeton University Press, 1964); for further commentary: AP Monahan, *Consent, Coercion and Limit: The Medieval Origins of Parliamentary Democracy* (Kingston and Montreal: McGill-Queen's University Press, 1987), pp 99*ff*.

[25] *Code of Justinian*: 59, 5, 1–3.

[26] Post: *Studies in Medieval Political Thought*, p 69.

[27] *Ibid*, p 70.

[28] For more detailed analysis of meanings, see AP Monahan: *Consent, Coercion and Limit*, pp 102*ff*.

abstract, and notional consent, from an act of positive consent to the right to be heard and to make the case to presumed consent. How consent was conveyed was similarly variable. The maxim's primary application is in the private sphere, in protecting the rights of parties and, in case of breach, justifying redress. The protection of rights, however modest or minimal, is a practical measure within the wider purpose of securing needs and advancing utilities. That is the reason the courts are at the core of constitutional history, why princes were assiduous in making courts accessible to the humble and the poor.[29] The social importance of rights explains why justice in this elemental sense is, as Hume claims, the first virtue of society, why in *Buon Governo* the figure of justice, the dispenser of justice among the people, reigns above other virtues.

The maxim *quot omnes tangit* once at large could not be held to its origins and soon its writ ran wild, beyond the private sphere to the public, to cover relations between the people and the prince. As the power of princes grew and expectations of them rose, ruling impinged on the private sphere, rendering rights vulnerable. The maxim, established in relations between subjects, could be extended to limit the power of the prince.[30] Taxation was ever a cause for concern, disputes common and fiercely fought. In the twelfth and thirteenth centuries, the king was 'invested with three fiscal privileges, each fully sanctioned by law and custom'.[31] By the end of the thirteenth century, kings had surrendered all three, the reason: 'Power pertains to kings, property to individuals'.[32] If property be affected by taxes, it must be with the consent of its owner. Without consent, there would not be cooperation; without cooperation, there could be no rule. Marjorie Clark, in the course of a fine study of fiscal affairs, concludes that the surrender of powers of taxation 'demonstrates the immoveable resistance that the doctrine of consent could offer to royal power'.[33] The prince was entitled to, 'had a superior right' in Post's words, to use prerogative power for the common good, even if rights were affected, although in that case consent was needed and was given,[34] by representatives not by the people, and so the other arm of medieval constitutional understanding enters the field. The people become an abstraction, the *universitas* of Roman law, for which representatives act and give consent where it is required.[35] The asking and the giving are both elements of the procedure legally required for a valid exercise of princely

[29] For further account of the importance of the courts being accessible to all: DJ Galligan: 'Ally or Enemy: Friend or Foe' in *The Courts and the People: Friend or Foe* (ed) DJ Galligan, pp 223–40.
[30] Notions of due process also derive from the maxim. For a study of due process: DJ Galligan: *Due Process and Procedural Fairness*.
[31] M Clark: *Medieval Representation and Consent*, p 268. The three taxes were Danegeld, tallage, and customs duties.
[32] O Gierke: *Medieval Political Theory* (translated by FW Maitland) quoted in Clark, p 276.
[33] M Clark: *Medieval Representations and Consent*, p 276.
[34] Prerogative power is part of the plenary power of rulers: see Chapter V.
[35] Post: *Studies in Medieval Political Thought*, p 76.

prerogative.[36] Consent is part of the procedure of practically all princely actions. Some matters require a positive act of consent; for others consent is inferred from action. Consent is on some matters voluntary, on others required. In all cases it is the consent of representatives, the people kept at one remove.

These are matters of subtle and complex rules founded on the principle that the ruler has to obtain the consent of the people for actions affecting their rights. Such ideas and doctrines trace back to the maxim *quot omnes tangit*, which spread through and came to pervade the private and public spheres. On the one hand the maxim is precise in justifying actions, on the other hand it is open to creative interpretation. Consent as expressed in the maxim takes a seat in the theatre of universal ideas, a point of reference and a taken-for-granted property of social relations. It counts as one of the ideas AN Whitehead describes, ideas that settle on communities and then hover about, somewhat elusive but infiltrating sentiments, jostling dispositions, and ready to be recruited for action.[37] Whitehead makes no reference to the maxim, although slavery the case he considers, fits well as a denial of respect for the person, and violation of civic and juridical equality. Philosophers, popes, and princes knew slavery to be an unjust and unjustifiable practice, yet it persisted across millennia, until finally the principle of respect gained a footing, firm in places, precarious in others. Condemnation of slavery shows the *restraining* power of the maxim of consent. The power to *enable* and *justify* action is less obvious, more subtle, and yet critical to the maxim's place in the constitutional field. As the history of slavery shows, consent once entrenched in social, legal, and political life can be stretched to apply in settings and to justify actions far from its original purpose. Consent as a condition of rule, a legal requirement, the purpose to protect rights, is used to achieve the opposite.

8. The power of consent and the exploitation

That is the crucial point of constitutional interest. Rather than serving as a substantive principle requiring the people's positive act of consent, the maxim is manipulated to turn consent into a formal duty on the part of representatives. It is neither a display of the power of the people nor the seedbed of sentiments of popular sovereignty and self-rule. On the contrary, in the constitutional field, the logic of consent is enlisted to do the opposite, revised to *exclude* the people from active engagement in matters of rule. Once secure in the structure of government, the power of consent is hard to contain. Pushed beyond the original usage, escaping settled boundaries, origins forgotten, consent acquires new meaning and serves novel purposes.

[36] The notion of consent as *procedure* helps in understanding its nature and scope. Due process in legal trials has its origins in the same idea: see Post, *ibid*, p 71.

[37] AN Whitehead: *Adventures of Ideas* (London: Collier-Macmillan, 1933).

The power implicit in consent is used to distance the people from the power of government, rather than secure their place and increase their influence. Consent signifying the central place of the people, and the need for their positive approval to the order of rule, is exploited to justify an order in which the people are at the margins. Taken from its place in social relationships as a restraint on action, consent is represented as if it were the founding principle of constitutional authority. That was not the purpose of consent in Roman law, nor in early constitutional discourse, where consent *moderates* social relations rather than *constitutes the foundation* from which relations arise. The foundation, from the people's perspective, is the practical matter of surviving and prospering, for which they have to cooperate and coordinate their actions, accept power as a useful instrument to their ends, and restrain their own actions. In the course of that process, sets of social relations are formed among the people and between them and the holders of power, their purpose to facilitate the pursuit of common goals. Consent then makes its appearance *within* that framework to moderate relations in the ways just described.

This is another way of presenting the difference between a social understanding of constitution and a discourse abstracted from social relations of the kind displayed by Parker and Hobbes in England and the Abbé Sieyès in France. The issue is how to understand the relationship between the few ruling and the people ruled; how to explain why the people, confronted with a set of institutions holding supreme power, acquiesce. One account centres on consent as a fiction, *as if* the people were to come together to agree on how best to advance their interests. Social understanding is different. It begins with the world we inhabit and tries to make sense of it, tries to understand the sentiments the people hold, their dispositions to action, the actions they take. This kind of knowledge, archaeological rather than metaphysical, is acquired by studying the history of social relations, excavating their sentiments and dispositions, and examining the practical experience of the parties. Consent is entrenched in those sentiments from which dispositions are formed and actions follow. Tracing the sentiments to their origins, tracking their function in practical situations, and mapping the boundaries is the route to knowledge of the people's place and a calming influence on exuberant exploitation of the concept. Consent excavated in this way reveals its origins, its purpose, and how it has been adapted and used for other purposes.

9. Behind the mask

The two images of consent, one the warrior the other a light-footed Ariel, seeming to be in opposition work together, one defending consent as a property of social relations, the other nimble in spreading it to new fields. With such imagery in the background, what conclusions are to be drawn about consent in the constitutional order? There are two perspectives, one from the upper register, one from the lower.

Consent is essential to the upper register, to the set of ideas, sentiments, and dispositions regarding the constitutional order, the nature of rule, the structure of power, and the justification. To restate the problem and the resolution, the people, although deemed unfit to engage in ruling, have to be won over, for without their support government will fail. Escape from social reality to the safety of a body politic high in consensus is no longer viable. The people wanting more than being well-shod, tentatively but with determination, act to improve their lives. The body politic loses its utility, the level of consensus from shared sentiments is lost or much lowered. The raw power of the people unleashed knows no bounds, and the constitutional order, precariously poised on opinion in Hume's term and sentiment in Smith's, is at risk. The solution lies in two courses: one taking measures to improve the well-being of the people, the other making consent the foundation of the constitutional order.

Between the seventeenth century and the twenty-first, the lot of the people much improved materially and constitutionally. Status by rank eased in favour of individualism and liberty, allowing the people to be mobile and take initiatives. The economic order opened to encourage industry and enterprise, while the people's capacity to engage increased as standards of education rose and training spread. Expectations of life and ability to achieve them were on the rise, aided by advances in science and technology. The reshaping of social relations had constitutional consequences. Ways were found, gradual and incremental, for the people's voices to be heard and their interests to be weighed in the political process. The vote was extended, petitions on policy matters more freely accepted, and parliamentarians more attentive to the views of their electors, while complaints and grievances were heard and handled. Positions of power and privilege came under scrutiny, notions of popular sovereignty gained ground, and a vision of the people ruling themselves became a real prospect. If constitutional authority were to stay in the hands of a select few, the discourse had to be adjusted. The appeal to consensus as shared sentiments no longer matched the social order of fragmentation and competition, and the discord that followed. Consent as a positive act of agreement is the solution. It has two parts, the first enlists the power of consent in social relations, the second assigns to representatives the power to consent. Despite the unruliness from opening up social relations and the lowering, even loss of consensus, the people's interest in effective government remains firm. The concept of consent, already embedded in social relations, is put to use to preserve the structure of authority. Consent justifies authority, positive consent more firmly than passive consensus. As the tide of social change rises, a constitutional order founded on positive consent is securely anchored, its ascent from everyday social relations to the crown of constitutional authority testimony to its power.

The ascent to constitutional status is the first stage, the second stage is how consent be conveyed and by whom. Abstraction and fiction enter to work their magic. On the one hand, historically, the *people* meant not individual persons but an abstract concept of the people; on the other hand, consent is conveyed by representatives of the people as an abstraction. The logic, place, and power of consent in the upper register are now plain. The people's consent, even in this diminished manner, is dressed in evocative imagery and used to justify a constitutional order in which power remains with a select few. The people as an abstraction eventually lose its force. Having won the right to vote, the people elect the representatives, whose actions are deemed to have their consent. Consent enthroned in the eighteenth century as the justifying principle of constitutional, shrewdly adjusted, reigns in the twenty-first. The people's capacity to engage in ways besides voting has risen and extends to influencing the terms of the constitution. But the point remains that consent is *deemed* not *actual*, inferred from the act of voting and falls far short of the people positively agreeing to the constitutional order or actions taken within it. Efforts by the Levellers in England were wasted and attempts by the freemen of Pennsylvania to insist on the people's actual consent short-lived.[38] That consent has to be inferred from actions rather than a positive act of agreement has not weakened its virility or its utility in justifying constitutional authority.

It is a shame not to greet with pride the passage of consent from humble origins to a pivotal place in the constitutional field, a tribute to dogged endeavour and the durability of a concept. Yet, scepticism is called for, Hume's finding no need for the concept beyond acquiescence a warning sign, while efforts to equate consent with acquiescence would have been frowned upon. More intriguing is Adam Smith's dismissal of consent as 'only very figurative metaphorical'. If that were the case for taxation where private rights are affected, to which Smith is referring, then how much more figurative and metaphorical consent would be in areas where rights are only marginally affected or not at all. Let us imagine Adam Smith, taking a moment of ease before his morning lecture, reading to calm his nerves a scene from *The Merchant of Venice*, which he happened to have with him. Broaching the subject of consent in the lecture, he had freshly in mind the words of Count Bassanio, the worldly Venetian, who in an aside confides: 'So may the outward signs be least themselves/The world is still deceived with ornament'.[39] For *ornament* read figurative and metaphorical, different words but conveying the same idea, *figurative* meaning emblematic, pictorial; *metaphorical* the application of a name to an object to which it is not literally applicable. The outward signs of acquiescence, compliance, and support are dressed in the ornament of consent by which the people are meant to be deceived. Deception arouses sentiments and dispositions leading them to act *as if* they had consented. Whether the people are deceived is the question now to be answered.

On route from the ornament of Venice to the cool reason of Edinburgh, let us call on the carpenter-playwright of Athens. Who better to consult than Peter Quince

[38] Discussed in Chapter XIII.
[39] *The Merchant of Venice*, Act 3: 2: 73.

the good citizen. As he muses on the idea of being hanged for offending a lady, suppose we were to mention Locke's *Second Treatise on Government*, which as a thoughtful literate man he might have read, leaving aside a small problem of dates. Would he be reassured by our pointing out that, if the penal code seem harsh, it is part of the system under which he has put himself and, thus, to which he consents? After all, Peter and his fellow mechanicals mount a play to celebrate the Duke's wedding, surely a sign of something more than begrudging obedience, 'fearful duty' as the Duke calls it, perhaps even an expression of positive consent to his rule. Peter true to his slightly sceptical nature is more puzzled than ever. He has by obeying in some sense put himself under rule, even shown positive support by putting on the play. He sees the benefits of firm rule, the safety and stability in which to live and work as a carpenter. He cannot agree with the earthy Bottom whose 'chief humour is for a tyrant', a duke who keeps the peace at whatever cost to his subjects.[40] Nor can he accept the opposite that actions of support beyond obedience amount to positive consent. Somewhere between the two, between fearful duty and positive consent, prudence and wisdom combine to guide the actions of the good citizen. Prudence in acquiescing in what is familiar, partly to avoid penalty and partly because the consequences of any alternative are unknown. Wisdom in knowledge, first, that ducal rule imperfect as it is, protects some interests and provides some benefits; secondly, that to sustain such a system fearful obedience must be paired with acts of support. To prudence and wisdom, both critical to the sentiments of Quince, optimism is to be added. Optimism that life can be improved, needs and utilities better secured and advanced, efforts rewarded. Perhaps that finally is the driving sentiment in his staging the play for 'What cannot be eschewed must be embraced'.[41]

10. The people's perspective

The imagined reflections of citizen Quince, the spirit of everyman and the vane of popular opinion, lead back to the people, to their sentiments and dispositions towards consent. The people are cautious. The elusiveness of the concept, the subtly changeable meaning, that it rarely appears without a qualifying adjective, are warning signs. Consent implied or tacit, virtual or deemed, even forced or required, are terms to confuse rather than inspire. Then there is the question of what is being consented to. Is it consent to the constitutional order and all that occurs within it, from high legislation to low level administration, or to the actions of government until the next election, or somewhere in between? While such matters

[40] *A Midsummer Night's Dream*, Act 3: 1.
[41] W Shakespeare: *The Merry Wives of Windsor*, Act 5: 5: 229.

could be cleared-up, the question remains whether consent has a place in the sentiments and dispositions of the people towards constitutional authority. Is the concept so critical to the constitutional order that to leave it out would distort our understanding; or is consent an ornament of marginal influence on the people's sentiments and dispositions? The answer is found in the origins of collective action, the common purpose of advancing civility, humanity, and well-being, and how the power of government contributes. The people's interest is that the power of the state be used to protect them, provide social goods, and help them to improve their lives. In the relationships formed for that purpose consent as active agreement is not needed, its presence even a touch malevolent. The reasons for such a departure from convention must now be given.

According to the *Digest* of Roman Law, as interpreted by Azo and commonly by the Glossators, the people *assign* power to the Emperor, as *rectore*, as a matter of administrative convenience, not in the form of a *donation*.[42] The people assign or cede power to the prince for particular purposes. This account fits well the idea that government, even that of the Roman Emperor, beneath the purple and the pomp, is an instrument to help the people pursue common purposes. The social relationship being an assignment of power from one to another, consent is not mentioned nor need be. Locke's metaphor of putting oneself under government perhaps is best interpreted to convey the same idea. The people's interest is that power assigned to government be used for their well-being. That calls on their part for restraint in league with support and engagement, vigilance and censure. That their well-being be served depends on practical processes by which to keep officials under their gaze, to hold them to account, and when needed to replace them. Consent as a distinct concept has no active role in the relationship. Labelling it as one of consent may be good for marketing, has a ready buyer in the upper register, but leaves unchanged the contents. Labelling may be harmless, a practice common enough for the people to know the difference between the label and the contents.

However, labels can mislead and the user beguiled into believing the contents match the label. Here lies the malevolent side of consent. Consent signifies the transfer of power from the people to officials. It is as if consent were a pipe draining power from one vessel, the people, and pouring it another, the officials. The more positive the consent, the more total the transfer of power, until the people are left with no reserve. Power once transferred is hard to reclaim, and the more total the transfer the harder it is. Consent has its own power to influence the sentiments of the people and dispose them to accept the actions of government, regardless of whether well-being is fostered or fractured.[43] The people understand government

[42] See Quentin Skinner's account: *Visions of Politics: Renaissance Virtues* (Volume II) (Cambridge: Cambridge University Press, 2002), pp 14–15.

[43] On power, see Chapter IV:6 herein.

is imperfect, that acceptance of authority includes actions that disappoint, that a band of toleration is a condition for stable and effective government. The trouble is positive consent both inflates the band and makes dissent difficult. How can one protest at action taken with one's consent, the very argument Hobbes used to justify the power of *Leviathan*. Whether the claim is philosophically sound we need not here enquire. The issue for social understanding is how consent weighs on sentiments and dispositions to weaken, even remove, the people's power to watch over officials. That is the function of consent in the upper register, under cover of the fiction of empowerment to achieve the opposite. A people freed from the restraining power of consent is able to define for itself the space allowed to officials and the breadth of tolerance of imperfection, while keeping in its own hands the power to disapprove, to intervene, and to sanction. Rather than seal the relationship in the concept of consent, the people hold firm to the idea of officials as *rectores* or *rettori* appointed to act only for the purpose of protecting and advancing their well-being. That is the guiding purpose and the measure of their submission. Openness within the relationship, moderated by restraint, strengthened by engagement and support, supervised by vigilance and censure, are the means to government effective in serving the people's interests. To this logic consent is an outsider.

11. Back to consensus

Before retiring consent from the constitutional field we should recall the two senses, consent as a positive act and consensus as shared sentiments. Positive consent may safely be put to pasture on the fringes while consensus has a claim to stay in the centre. This takes us back to the common sense preached by the Reverend Meriton, the idea that without the people's support government will totter and shake. The Reverend goes on to equate support with consent, while leaving open the sense. That it means consent as consensus is now plain. Among the people is a shared sentiment that a system of government serves their interests, from which follows a disposition to take action in support. Support is shown by the people's exercising restraint and by positive acts, some loudly proclaimed, others quietly taken. That government depends on shared sentiments of support was the lesson for the congregation. Shared sentiments as to the purpose and value of government, whatever the form and in whoever's hands; value in serving the people's common interests; value that stands above the divisions among people, groups, and sectors. Fear that the sentiment of support be lost in the tug-and-scramble, in the conflict and competition for advantage, prompted the quest for positive consent. Consensus is enough. Agreement on the value of government is essential and enough to win the support of the people. Within this frame of understanding of shared sentiments and dispositions, the people know the need to balance their expectations of government and the imperfections in delivery. The Reverend Meriton has the last word and consensus returns to take its place in the constitutional field. Now that is settled, the field is open for further enquiry into the sentiments and dispositions of the people, an enquiry into the foundation of interests on which they draw, obscured and overshadowed but real and enduring, all contained in the lower register of constitutional discourse.

Notes

Government depends on assent

Referring to the uprising of 1381, David Rollison writes: 'The populace had done as they were told, but only what they were told, thus illustrating the point that ultimately government only be effective if it had the assent of the people': *A Commonwealth of the People*. For assent may be substituted consensus.

Consent actively conveyed

Mark Knights in his account of later Stuart England cites cases of the people's showing allegiance to the state: 'Seeing the addresses as forms by which subjects repeatedly signified their active consent to the state opens up a more radical dimension.' *Representation and Misrepresentation in Later Stuart Britain*, p 154. *Active consent* is ambiguous. It could mean acts of positive consent or simply an expression of consensus.

Consent: 'a virtue from necessity'

John of Salisbury states the case in this way: 'if everyone pretends to will that which has been directed—making or appearing to make, a virtue of necessity, in so far as necessity is joined to consent—and embraces gratefully that which is impressed on one': *Polycraticus*, p 23; 'People will accept the authority of the prince if they see he subjects himself to law and justice': *Polycraticus*, p 35. John is an early advocate of the *as if* approach.

Resisting the leap to consent, *Cicero* writes of Republican Rome that liberty was granted to the common people 'in such a measure that people were induced by many excellent provisions to yield to the authority of the nobles': *On the Republic of Laws* (Harvard University Press: Loeb Classics, 1943), p 487. The case for the people's support is firm without resort to consent.

Acclamation as consent

In describing elections, Andy Wood writes: 'The selected candidate would have to be presented to the election crowd for their passive acclamation': A Wood: *Riot, Rebellion, and Popular Politics in Early Modern England* (London: Palgrave: 2002), p 124. 'Passive acclamation' looks like consensus.

Consent through representatives

Richard Baxter: 'The first capacity of Parliaments is to Represent the People as a People, to secure their liberties as Trustees.—As All are represented, so All are obliged by the consent of their Representatives': *Holy Commonwealth* (Cambridge: Cambridge University Press, 1994). A striking *non sequitur* of conclusion from premise.

Hobbes on consent

Explaining the creation of the state, how the people 'erect such a common power' enabling 'everyone to own and acknowledge himself to be the author', Hobbes concludes: 'is more than consent, or concord; it is real unity of them all, in one and the same person, made by covenant of every man with every man': *Leviathan*, Chapter XVII, p 13. The only legitimate mechanism through which the sovereign might acquire his 'Rights and Facultyes' is by the 'consent of the People assembled': *Leviathan*, Chapter XVIII, p 6.

A genealogical account of consent

Michel Foucault uses the concept of *genealogy* to excavate relations between the past and the present. Here we encounter two visions of history, one as evolutionary, edging towards an historical climax, and the other contingent, heterogeneous, stumbling along, subject to setbacks, and reverses. The latter is the more accurate. The contingency and instability appears in relations between the upper register of ideas and discourse on the one hand, and the social foundations on the other hand. The social foundations are divisive, tending to favour the interests of select sectors over other sectors. On that foundation is erected a register of ideas and discourse claiming inclusiveness and universality. The tension between the social foundation and the register of ideas is plain.

Consent fits this account. The concept is advanced as inclusive, the consent of all, the purpose to construct a constitutional order that rises above the social and economic disparities. To serve that purpose consent has to be the consent of all. To obtain actual consent would be fraught with the risk of the people refusing consent to a constitutional order based on deep disparities. Yet, consent is needed and has to be invented by the double fiction of the people as an abstraction and consent by representatives. This chapter is not based on but is congruent with, in some ways an application of Foucault's approach. Generally, see M Foucault: *Discipline and Punish* and *The Foucault Reader.*

Benjamin Constant wrote of *the masks of virtue,* the expropriation and misuse of intrinsically admirable ideas and concepts, such as *the people,* to justify a particular order of power and social relations. He exposes the few who 'illicitly usurp the name of the people'. Discussed by Stephen Holmes in: *Benjamin Constant and the Making of Modern Liberalism* (New Haven & London: Yale University Press, 1984).

Examples of *quod omnes*

Magna Carta Clause 12 states: 'the king must obtain the individual consent of prelates, barons and earls, in order to get any extraordinary tax approved': see G Post: 'A Roman Theory of Consent, Quod Omnes Tangit, in *Medieval Representation*', p 6.

In introducing John Fortescue, Shelley Lockwood shows the need for the people's consent for changes to law that affect their rights: *Sir John Fortescue: On the Laws and Governance of England* (ed) S Lockwood (Cambridge: Cambridge University Press, 1997), Introduction p xxviii. The analysis could be placed within the *omnes tangit* discourse.

On the people being present in parliament

An early statement of the idea in a Leicestershire Address: 'the people are present in Parliament—by knights and burgesses—and thereby is presumed to give his consent to all things that pass in Parliament': (1659) quoted in M Knights: *Representation and Misrepresentation*, p 120.

Locke on consent

In the *Second Treatise on Government*, Locke makes the following claims:

1. A political society forms when 'every one of the members hath quitted this natural power, resigned it up into the hands of the community': p 87.

2. Each member authorizes the Legislature 'to make laws for him as the Publick of the society shall require': p 89.
3. 'No one can be put out of his estate, and subjected to the Political Power of another, without his own consent.': p 95.
4. A person can divest himself of natural liberty 'only by agreeing with others to join and unite into a community': p 95.
5. Man when he comes of age 'puts himself under the Government': p 117.
6. 'Every man that hath any possession, or Enjoyment, of any part of the Dominion of any Government, doth thereby give his tacit consent and is then obligated to obey': p 119.

The adaptability of consent, the Ariel-like qualities, on Locke's account are plainly on view.

On parliamentarians as agents or attorneys for the people

Locke states relations between parliament and the people: 'what is done in Parliament—ay be truely sayd to be the consent of the nation, because—done by their representatives who are empowered by the nation': *Critical Notes*, p 168. Notice the ambiguities: *consent of the nation* and representatives *being empowered* to *consent*. *Nation* makes sense only as the corporate concept of the people, which *empowers* representatives. The real people are nowhere to be seen.

Robert Filmer is out of fashion but his scepticism of consent of the people, as a concept critical to constitutional authority, is soundly reasoned: R Filmer: *Patriarcha and Other Writings* (ed) JP Somerville (Cambridge: Cambridge University Press, 1919), pp 140–1. Filmer rejected the idea of popular sovereignty, of power originating in the people, and scorned attempts to show how that power passes to the parliament.

Arguing the opposite, Joseph Trapp ridiculed the idea that the governors were 'a sort of agents or attornies for the people': *The Character and Principles of the Present Set of Whigs* (1711) quoted in M Knights: *Representation and Misrepresentation*, p 102. Culpeper went a step further, speaking as a parliamentarian, economically stating: 'We are not sent to please the people': quoted in D Zaret: *The Origins of Democratic Culture: Printing, Petitions, and the Public Sphere in Early Modern England* (Princeton: Princeton University Press, 2000).

Hobbes on relations between the prince and the people

The view of representation refined by Parliament in the late seventeenth and eighteenth centuries, with a long provenance in historical notions of sovereignty, acquired a firmer foundation under Hobbes's guidance. His account of representation matches the notion of Parliament embodying the people, its acts being the acts of the people. Taking representation on the stage as the central case, Hobbes continues: 'and to personate is to act, or represent, himself or another; and he that acteth another is said to bear his person, or act in his name': *Leviathan,* Chapter XVI, p 5. Notice the words: 'said to bear his person'. But Hobbes does not stop at 'bearing his person', which means, according to Skinner, 'speaking and acting in their name'. Hobbes goes a critical step farther: the acts of the prince *are* the acts of the subject. That is not the same as acting in the name of the subject; indeed, it is no longer representation. If the sovereign *becomes t*he people there is no one left to represent.

Hobbes's account occurs in the course of refuting the view put by the parliamentary writers, the *democratical gentlemen,* that the people could negotiate the terms and conditions of the prince's sovereignty. Such a view Hobbes dismisses as absurd. He defines the relationship in this way: the acts of the sovereign are 'the act both of himself [that is each person] and of all the rest': *Leviathan,* Chapter XVIII, p 4. The sovereign prince cannot commit injustice or injury because 'every subject is author of every act the sovereign doth': XXI, p 7. And: 'whatsoever is commanded by the sovereign power is—justified by the command; for of such command every subject is the author': *Leviathan,* Chapter XXII, p 15. This goes beyond the actor's representation in the theatre. It also goes beyond Cicero's analogy of the lawyer speaking for the client. It is no longer *representation* for one cannot both become and represent. Compare Quentin Skinner's interpretation which conflates the two: Q Skinner: 'Hobbes on Representation' (2005) 13 *European Journal of Philosophy* 155, especially at p 161.

On an instrumental theory of government

According to Jeremy Bentham, democracy is not a method of self-government, but a method of controlling government; holding government to the execution of a programme of public good, which has been settled by the public language of politics. This fits the instrumental model proposed in the text (and developed later as the *keepers' model)* and has no need of consent as an added quality of the relationship. See further: G Postema: *Bentham and the Common Law Tradition* (Oxford: Clarendon Press, 1986).

IX

Lower Register of Constitutional Discourse

1. The lower register in context

The division of power between rulers and ruled is matched by two registers of discourse, one supporting and justifying rule, the other placing rule within the frame of the people's common endeavours. We have seen the trouble taken to construct from on high a discourse of harmony, stability, and unity to which all sectors of society are integral and from which all benefit, presented at first as a body politic, later based on consent. The discourse from below has other origins and rests on another account of the constitutional order. It begins with the people engaged in the common purpose of advancing humanity and civility in all dimensions, starting with the means to secure needs and improve utilities, then embracing other ends, including the cultivation of arts and science, beneficence, justice, and sociability. The shared interest in such ends gives rise to sentiments and dispositions leading under certain conditions to action. The means to common ends are many and diverse. Personal effort, the bedrock, leads to collective action through social relations, some spontaneous and transient, others deliberate and enduring. Some ends are best reached by conceding power to a few, in particular the few yielding the power of the state.[1] The advancement of civility and humanity allows scope for opinion and initiative, competition and conflict, encouraging an unruly tug-and-scramble for which government sets the rules and marks the boundaries. Not all actions or the sentiments and dispositions grounding them are directed at common purposes, for the passions are capricious and tempt along opposing paths. If a community is to survive and prosper, the people's interests served, the passions are to be curbed and temptation resisted, self-restraint practiced and support given. Government earns a place in a dual role, one to set and uphold the bounds, the other to help the people advance their own ends within the bounds.

My purpose now is to draw out the people's ideas of constitutional order and relations among themselves, and with rulers and officials. A *lower register* of constitutional discourse, lower not in status but arising from below, cultivated among the people and expressed in many ways and forms. A register seen in rudimentary form among the peasants of Gagliano, now to be investigated. The view from above is matched by the view from below, an unofficial discourse normally unnoticed and mostly undeclared, yet essential to understanding constitutional authority.

[1] For a fuller account, see Chapter I:2.

Keepers of the Common Good. D.J. Galligan, Oxford University Press. © D.J. Galligan 2024.
DOI: 10.1093/9780198907398.003.0009

The study of rebellion is a good introduction. When pushed to the limits of deprivation or oppression, the people move beyond the prevailing constitutional discourse to frame grievances in another, invoking other ideas and finding the language to express them. The next stage is to draw from rebellion the sentiments and dispositions with which to restructure social relationships; then lastly to assemble an alternative understanding of the constitutional order.

2. 'Peoples precede nations'

Before enquiring into the discourse of rebellion, there are two matters to clarify, sceptical positions to dismiss. One is the people's alleged incapacity to devise a distinct discourse, the other that the people, being so locked into the upper register, form such strong sentiments and dispositions that competitors are locked out. As to incapacity, the charge is that the people, the common people have no constitutional world to inhabit. They are to be ruled and the duty of obedience is ingrained in them. We have seen the passion with which such claims are made, so well put by Duke Theseus for whom the people are to dwell 'in the modesty of fearful duty'.[2] Shakespeare knew better. The supposedly ignorant mechanicals have just written, discussed, and performed *Pyramus and Thisbe*,[3] That Bottom and Quince can debate whether the meter be eight-six or eight-eight shows they are literate,[4] their polished performance that they are no strangers to the theatre. That Tom Snout should warn the audience of gentlewomen that he is not a real lion and will not roar too loudly, shows a concern not to frighten them or offend their sensibilities. Far from being illiterate, unschooled, and uncouth, the mechanicals are moderately educated, respectful yet reflective, and morally astute. The contrast with the audience of the newly-wed duke and his court is striking for the inanity of their remarks, ignorance of the lives of the mechanicals, and the crude prejudice they betray.[5] The mechanicals know the score and play the game, while sensing things could be different. Meanwhile, over in Pentapolis, Prince Pericles is witness to the wisdom of the three rough fisherman, one of whom has just likened society to a whale 'who plays and tumbles, driving the poor fry before him, and at last devours them all at a mouthful'. Pericles marvels at 'How from the finny subjects of the sea/ these fishers tell th'infirmities of men/And from their wat'ry empire recollect/All that may men approve or men detect'.[6]

[2] *A Midsummer Night's Dream*, Act 5: 1: 101.

[3] Its full title as presented: *The Most Lamentable Comedy and Most Cruel Death of Pyramus and Thisbe.*

[4] *A Midsummer Night's Dream*, Act 3: 1: 22*ff.*

[5] See Notes for more on the nature of the lower register.

[6] *Pericles, Prince of Tyre*, Scene 5: 69*ff.* Perhaps John Warr had been reading *Pericles* when he wrote: 'the web of the law entangles the small fries and dismisseth the great': *A Spark in the Ashes*, p 102.

The image of the commons as clay to be moulded by masters, told what sentiments and dispositions to hold, is a false image. Susan Reynolds, in much valued studies of early European society, sums it up in three words: 'peoples precede nations'.[7] The members of a community of whatever rank or station have a sense of law and custom, of rights and liberties, justice and injustice, all born of common sense and experience. The affairs of daily life are conducted within this frame of meanings, social relations formed, the behaviour of leaders and lords assessed. Charters drawn up by local communities seeking special liberties 'are testimonies to the customs and rights which all communities wanted and which many may have enjoyed, at least intermittently, without grants'.[8] Ideas of rights and law are forged from experience, from encounters among the people and with leaders in the parish, the county, and the kingdom. Experience itself is guided by a foundation of ideas and values, and a strong sense of justice, 'however unarticulated and unsystematic'.[9] As peoples precede nations, sentiments and dispositions precede princes. They form in the course of daily life, the struggle to make ends meet, the drive to make life better, the longing to cultivate interests beyond material needs. All a process the powers of leaders help or hinder. The people's understandings and expectations are not static but shift and change, partly indigenous, partly influenced by the need for government, and partly shared with the upper register. When an equilibrium between the two registers is reached, sound and moderate government results and the people are content. Among their understandings is the concept of rule not as domination by a few but a set of institutions and practices to serve common purposes. When government or grandees rupture the equilibrium, act oppressively and unjustly, the people have in reserve a hinterland to return to, and from which to justify their grievances, seek redress, and in dire need mount rebellion.

The other reason for doubting a lower register is that the people are born into a world dominated by a set of ideas over which they have no control, the contours and constraints of which they have no choice but to accept. They come to terms with and naturalize that world, accept it as so normal that anything else is rendered unimaginable. The coarse cloth of fate is magically changed into the mantle of a just and natural order.[10] The people are alienated from their real interests but can do nothing to resist the hegemony of the world they inhabit. If this were true, we would have an answer to the question why the people curb their natural power and acquiesce in the constitutional order. They acquiesce because the order is presented as being in the nature of things and immutable, and comes to be seen as

[7] S Reynolds: *Kingdoms and Communities in Western Europe 900–1300* (Oxford: Clarendon Press, 2nd edn, 1997). See the *Introduction* herein.

[8] *Ibid* p 130.

[9] *Ibid* pp lvii, lxv, 4–5.

[10] For fuller discussion, see JC Scott: *Weapons of the Weak: Everyday Forms of Peasant Resistance* (London & New Haven: Yale University Press, 1985), Chapter 8.

just. Unless truth gains in the retelling we should be sceptical. Alienation and false consciousness exert their force, the power of the upper register is pervasive and not to be ignored.[11] Yet, there is no reason to think the people, even the most modest, incapable of imagining an order different from theirs. The love affair of Bottom the Weaver with the Fairy Queen is all a dream, but if a weaver turned into an ass can mate with a queen, even in a dream, anything is imaginable. Peter Quince the carpenter has no trouble hankering after a world where he would not be hanged for offending a lady. Even the grave-digging clown knows that the equality of the grave is a return to the equality with which all begin: 'There is no ancient gentleman but gardeners, ditchers, and gravemakers'.[12] And remember the wisdom of the fishermen who 'tell th'infirmities of men—all that men approve or men detect'. It is not hard to see how the people are able to view and judge from another stand the power exerted over them, and the social order in support; a stand closer to their needs and daily struggles; a stand respecting the sentiments and dispositions grounded in common purposes. Complying with the prevailing order does not rule out their imagining another and keeping in reserve other sentiments and dispositions, which under certain conditions prompt action.[13]

Evidence abounds of how a people living in conditions of deprivation and oppression, peasants tied to a landowner, serfs ministering to a lord, even slaves at the will of a master, all able to create a discourse within, but wholly different from, that under which they live. James Scott's study of indentured farmers in Indonesia shows the resilience of the human spirit, and the reserve of ideas and concepts with which to form social relations among themselves, even in conditions of utter subjugation. How much more so in conditions more moderate. Even in less oppressive social orders, beneath the seeming harmony, the two registers uncouple. One becomes the official discourse and acquires a life of its own with its own interests and preferences to advance, and invents ideas and concepts to make it seem natural and compelling. The other register, grounded in more elementary social relationships and common purposes, even if unstated and unwritten, obscured and overshadowed, remains a foundation from which to view and judge the upper register. The two discourses share a common base, begin with the same purpose of advancing humanity and civility. The trouble is the power of the state, intended for common purposes, is eyed as a resource, a prize to win and exploit to the benefit of certain interests. Power pushes away from the common base, becomes detached, and is dedicated to creating then sustaining a social order suited to such interests. The people are left poised between the two, their loyalties divided. On the one hand they value the constitutional order for the benefits it brings, while aware of the pretences of the upper register, the gap between the ideas and the reality, the

[11] See the discussion of power in Chapter IV:6.
[12] *The Tragedy of Hamlet, Prince of Denmark*, Act 5: 1: 30.
[13] Ideas well-discussed by Scott in *Weapons of the Weak*.

advantages to some over others. On the other hand the people maintain a distance, a shrewd detachment made possible by the discourse of the lower register, from which to cast a critical eye on the antics of officials.

3. Resistance and rebellion

Resistance and rebellion are signs something has gone wrong to the 'sanity and health' of the body politic,[14] so wrong that acquiescence is suspended. In some cases the source of grievance is dealt with and the ruling order restored; in others resistance and rebellion are launched as the only recourse, occasionally turning into revolution and the overthrow of the old order. Although perhaps over-simplified, this opens enquiry into rebellion loosely defined, while keeping in mind that between quiet resistance and noisy revolution, there are many degrees of dissent, each evidence of relations between the two registers. The appearance when all is quiet of unity, in the face of rebellion dissolves to reveal competing views of social order and a different design of the constitutional field. What is pathology from one point of view, that of the upper register, from another is the restoration of a social order grounded in the purposes of social endeavour and with a stronger claim to legitimacy and authenticity, the concepts of the untutored peasants of Gagliano. The study of rebellion is one route to knowledge of the lower register and how it relates to the upper register.

Rebellion has long caught the interest of historians and social scientists, and a large body of research is available.[15] Here I draw on just three cases: the peasants' revolt 1381, the rebellion of the commons of Kent 1450, and the Levellers' resistance 1644–52. In the logic of rebellion there are two main lines of grievance, one the people suffer material deprivation, the other they are treated badly to a degree that becomes intolerable. When confronted with either one, the people in seeking relief dig down to the foundations of social relations to unearth ideas of community and the values of communal life with which to justify resistance or rebellion. At the first stage, the people disaffected appeal to the principles of the constitutional order, urging they be respected. If pleas go unheeded, the second stage turns attention to the principles themselves, to the doctrines and processes of the settled order, to scrutinize and judge whether they do serve the well-being of the people, the precepts of the lower register on hand to guide the enquiry. A negative verdict leads to the next stage, a call to action, normally moderate, but in the face of

[14] *The Tragedy of Hamlet, Prince of Denmark*, Act 1: 3: 21.

[15] Perez Zagorin's studies are especially useful for covering European rebellions: P Zagorin: *Rebels and Rulers 1500–1660* (2 volumes) (Cambridge: Cambridge University Press, 1982). On England, among many others, see especially A Wood: *Riot, Rebellion, and Popular Politics in Early Modern England* (London: Palgrave, 2002) and *The 1549 Rebellions of Early Modern England* (Cambridge: Cambridge University Press, 2007).

frustration sinking into despair easily escalates into resistance and ends in rebellion. The stages along the way from judgement to action is itself a subject of interest although beyond my present purposes.

4. Peasants' Revolt, 1381

During the years 1377–8, the parliament of peers and commons granted three poll taxes to enable Richard II's government to re-stock an empty treasury. The size of the subsidy, without precedent and payable by all, was accepted by parliament after agitated deliberation as necessary to meet the costs of war with France. Despite the swingeing effects, the subsidy might have been sustained by the common people were it not for the methods of collection. To the people of Essex and Kent, the actions of officials were intolerably oppressive. Henry Knighton, an observer, thought that combined with 'the imposition of new and almost unbearable burdens which seemed endless and without remedy', the methods of collection led the commoners to rebel.[16] The rebellion was not directed against the king or his authority but, according to another contemporary source, 'against the Duke of Lancaster and the other lords of the realm because of the exceptionally severe tenths and fifteenths and other subsidies conceded in parliaments and extortionately levied from the poor'.[17] Resistance spread to become a mass protest marching on London, hunting down royal officials and local agents along the way, their heads summarily removed. The crowd arriving at Blackheath to await a meeting with the king is said to have numbered fifty thousand; it was probably fewer but still a large and menacing mob. Wat Tyler, a Kentish man of uncertain provenance, supported by fierce marshals and counsellors in Jack Straw and John Ball, led the assembly. During a meeting with the king to negotiate a settlement, Tyler was murdered and the movement fell apart. The uprising spelt the death of the poll tax but whether other gains were made is questionable.

In the course of the rebellion other grievances came to light and prompted wider claims. Francis Walsingham, himself nearly a victim and a voluble opponent, blamed the government for allowing the protest to spread and its ambitions to rise. He wrote of the 'nativi', 'bondsmen', and other 'country dwellers' seeking to better themselves, to clamour for liberty, to become the equals of the lords, and no longer to be bound by servitude to a master.[18] Notice the mention of liberty and equality, two concepts commonly invoked in rebellion, symbols of the commoners' purpose

[16] H Knighton: *Chronicon Henrici Knighton* (1380, II, pp 129–30) collected in *The Peasants' Revolt of 1381* (ed) RB Dobson (London: Palgrave, 1983), pp 135–6.

[17] *Anonimalle Chronicle* (1381) in CWC Oman: *The Great Revolt of 1381* (Oxford: Clarendon Press, 1906).

[18] F Walsingham: *Historica Anglicana* (ed) EM Thompson (Rolls Series, 1874), pp 285–8; reprinted in Dobson: *The Peasants' Revolt*, pp 131–4.

to better their lives by reducing inequality, liberty the means to that end. The only taxes to which they could consent, even though they struggled to pay, were those long settled by their fathers and grandfathers, while a new tax added hardship to people already in debt. In preparing for his meeting with the king, Tyler rehearsed the demands to be detailed in a charter. They centre on relations between lord and serf, church and peasant. Lordship was to be abolished except for that of the king, because lordship is the source of oppression of the peasants, many of whom were locked into serfdom. The church itself a mighty lord and landowner was attacked for accumulating land, which Tyler demanded be 'divided among the commons'.[19] In their attack on Walsingham's own monastery at St Albans, the crowd wanted restoration of 'their liberties and rights held by their fathers and ancestors in the days of King Henry'.[20] Grievances were linked to the past, a past less unequal, a past of shared customs and understandings with which to judge and denounce the present. As Parson Ball put it in the *Life and Death of Jack Straw*: 'when Adam delued and Eve span/Who then was a gentleman?'[21]

5. Complaints and requests of the commons of Kent 1450

Sixty-nine years later another group of rebels gathered on Blackheath. Little is known about Jack Cade the leader who must join Wat Tyler in the lower circle of villains. Charles I was not the first to hold up both as masters of demagoguery and to show what happens when the people are incited to become the mob.[22] The reasons for rebellion here set down in writing are better known than in the earlier case. Two 'bills of Articles' were produced by the rebels in reply to Henry VI's request to the assembly to know their cause: one 'the complaint of the commons of Kent and causes of the assembly', the other the 'requests by the Captains of the great assembly in Kent'.[23] The 'common weale', the benefit of all was the foundation stone.[24] Wrongs done in the realm need to be redressed and practices reformed to restore the common weale, which is being destroyed by evil counsellors to the king and by oppression and misgovernment. The king is not to blame for he is the symbol of the common weale. He is prevented from reigning 'like a King royal' by the corruption of those around him. 'Meane persons' have replaced the natural noble counsellors, who run the Privy Council and act behind the king's back.

[19] *Anonimalle Chronicle*, pp 164–5.

[20] Walsingham: *Historia Anglicana*, p 271.

[21] Author unknown: Dobson: *The Peasants Revolt*, p 390. ('Delued' probably means 'delved'.)

[22] Charles Stuart: *Answer to the Nineteen Propositions* (18 June 1642) in Kenyon: *The Stuart Constitution*, p 18.

[23] Contained in J Snow: *Annales* (ed) E Howes (London, 1631) reproduced in Dobson: *The Peasants' Revolt*, pp 336*ff*.

[24] For further analysis, see D Rollison: *A Commonwealth of the People* (Cambridge: Cambridge University Press, 2010).

The common people bear the brunt. They are arrested and imprisoned without trial by law; are daily subjected to extortion and oppression; yet dare not take action to protect title to their lands in the face of seizure by the king's 'meniall servants'. The sheriffs and their men are singled out, tax collectors are oppressive and extort more than is due. Elections of the knights of the shires to represent the commons are corrupt, the great landowners imposing their men in place of those preferred by the people.

Jack Cade's rebellion is well documented and his reputation as a murderous villain, in Shakespeare's hands, well-deserved. Despite the claim that his 'mouth shall be the Parliament of England', Jack would struggle to win our vote.[25] Beneath the bluster and the menace are serious points, familiar grievances. Abuse of rights of person and property; the law nor being properly applied; oppression by officials in collecting tax. To the list is added the corruption of elections, which means the loss of the rights of the commons to have their interests represented in the deliberations of king and counsellors. The several grievances, each compelling in its own right, are now grouped within the structure of the common weale, the idea that all share the realm in common. King and common weale go together, because set apart from the common weale the king has no authority. That the king reigns not rules suggests an impersonal authority, a duty of custody and oversight of the common weale, rather than personally ruling over the people. King and commons together are responsible for the common good, he the fount of goodness and justice, the protector of the people against oppressive lords; they to keep watch to ensure reign be for the common good. When the king reigns with good and wise counsellors, the body politic is in good health, the common good well-served; when counsellors 'labour for their own preferment' it suffers.[26]

A familiar concept now has a new shading, the sign of a revised understanding of constitutional authority. At the core is a renewed sense of common good, one in which the interests of commoners are recognized and better served. The common good has two functions, one restorative, one reformative. The restorative decrees respect for rights within the settled order and practical measures for the purpose. The function less obvious is reformative, the aim to adjust the settled order to provide more scope for the people to improve their lives, equality and liberty the means for doing so. Each is valued on two grounds, one as a quality worth having, the other a means to a better life. That depends on a threshold of equality, on all being able to work for their own benefit and to compete with others on a roughly equal basis. Liberty defines the space within which to work for one's betterment, a space free of obstruction from officials and grandees. The role of government has to be adjusted from conserving the present social order, doing justice within that order, to being in addition an instrument serving the commons in the quest for

[25] *Henry VI: Part II*, Act 4: 7: 13.
[26] *Ibid* Act 1: 1: 179.

more worthwhile lives and a more just social order. From its lofty position as the head of the body politic keeping the body in good order, government—king and counsellors—drops a peg to be an instrument to help the people improve their lives. It has a job to do, tasks to perform mundane as they may be, not to detach itself from its social foundations and be a source of power and privilege of the few. As for the people, it is for them to keep an eye on government, to keep it under their gaze, to see that it serves their share of the common good.[27] This is an interpretation of the words and deeds of the rebels who do not themselves put it so plainly; but beneath the surface the elements are there, an early sign of the people as keepers of the common good. Before developing this revised sense of constitution, let us turn to one more case of rebellion or more accurately resistance, the Levellers.

6. The Levellers 1644–52

The Levellers came to public notice around 1644, were active for a few years after the civil war, until the movement petered out in the early 1650s. Between 1647 and 1649, with the king in captivity and parliament discredited, the constitution suspended if not destroyed, the future was uncertain. The Levellers held some sway with senior officers of the New Model Army, including Cromwell and Ireton, in whose hands the future lay. The debates in St Mary's Church Putney in late 1647, a kind of convention on the constitution, for the fortunes of the Levellers were a defining moment. Their ideas on the constitutional future, set out in the *First Agreement of the People*, were debated, came close to being adopted, then rejected. From being broadly sympathetic at the start, the mood changed as the truth dawned how radically the Levellers were challenging the constitutional order and the foundations of English society. Even in the minds of those who had just destroyed a good part of it and were about to shock the world by killing the king and abolishing the monarchy. It is one thing to tamper with the institutions of government, quite another to threaten the foundations of society by claiming a wider constitutional role for the people. As Cromwell gathered around him the reins of power, his vision was not that of the Levellers, who were soon accusing him of the same abuses condemned in the king, Star Chamber, special commissions, and the Long Parliament. Cromwell struck back, the Levellers were marginalized and then as their attacks mounted, were harassed and arrested, prosecuted and punished, until by the early 1650s the movement and its leader John Lilburne were dead.

The Leveller movement is more a case of resistance than outright rebellion, although some incidents could be so described. The trigger was mistreatment of John

[27] See further the study of gazing in JE Greene: *The Eyes of the People: Democracy in an Age of Spectatorship* (Oxford: Oxford University Press, 2010). Discussed in Chapter XV.

Lilburne, first by the king and Star Chamber, then by the Houses of Parliament, and finally by Cromwell's Council of State.[28] Arbitrary action by the institutions of government, the original cause, became a banner of protest under which the movement spread and its cause grew to call into question the foundations of the constitution. Since arbitrary action is an abuse of law and the proper use of power, the remedy was thought to lie in law. Why does law matter so much? Why should many thousand citizens beg 'you to make a law against all kinds of arbitrary governments as the highest capital offence against the commonwealth?'[29] Arbitrary action is an abuse of law and keeps company with treason, because both destroy the rights and liberties of the people, a mortal threat to the common good of the nation. The remedy is to apply the law and honour the constitution, of which the law is a constituent part. The body politic still casts its shadow: laws are 'the nerves and sinews of every society or commonwealth, without which they must necessarily dissolve and fall asunder'.[30]

So far the Levellers are within the bounds of the constitution, asking only that it be applied properly. Then comes a bold step beyond. Law turns out to be problematical, its capacity to curb arbitrary action questionable. Common law and statute, rather than the solution, are now seen to be part of the problem, the instrument of corrupt judges and oppressive parliamentarians who make and interpret laws for their own ends. John Warr says it well: 'Power is sweet to those who have it and not easily wrested or extorted from them'.[31] Perhaps the Levellers had come across the claim levelled at King John that 'he that holds his kingdom holds the law'.[32] Law must have deeper foundations, prior to and prevailing over kings and courts and parliaments. It must even precede Magna Charta, *The Petition of Right*, and *The Coronation Oath*, long admired as beacons of justice and good order, now seen for that they are, 'a mess of potage, a beggarly thing'.[33] Law must escape the grips of 'Norman bondage' and revive memories of Anglo-Saxon England, all in the cause of restoring the constitution written in 'the hearts of men' and guided by 'the clear light of equity and reason'.[34] Despite talk of restoration, the boundary has been crossed and the Levellers are in new territory where the search for the foundations of law is the search for a new constitutional order. As the search reaches back into the past, the images become blurred, the lines hazy. Law ends up as right reason

[28] For a fuller account, see DJ Galligan: 'The Levellers, the People, and the Constitution' in *Constitutions and the Classics: A Selection of British, French, and American Authors from Fortescue to Bentham* (eds) DJ Galligan (Oxford: Oxford University Press, 2014).

[29] R Overton and W Walwyn: *A Remonstrance of Many Thousand Citizens* (1646).

[30] E Sexby: *Killing Not Murder* (1657) in D Wootton: *Divine Right and Democracy* (London: Penguin, 1986), p 371.

[31] J Warr: *The Dispute Betwixt Equity and Form* (1648–9) *A Spark in the Ashes* (eds) S Sedley and L Kaplan (London: Verso, 1992), p 35.

[32] *King John*, Act 3: 1: 112.

[33] See further DJ Galligan: *Magna Carta: A Mess of Pottage, A Beggarly Thing* (London: Lecture to American Bar Association, 13 June 2015).

[34] J Warr: *The Dispute Betwixt Equity and Form*, p 37.

guided by precepts of God's 'perpetual, morall, unchangeable, and everlasting LAW'.[35] Restoration proves to be an empty vessel launched on a voyage bound to be in vain. Yet, how a constitutional order founded on equity and reason can escape the need for laws and institutions, do away with 'form' in Warr's universe of things, is left unsaid.

The voyage is made more promising with a slight change of course to connect law to other ideas, liberty in particular and its purpose within the constitution. Law, liberty, and rights are close companions; law the means for protecting the others. That certain interests be declared rights and protected by law is at the foundation of a constitutional order. But why is liberty so often invoked in the Levellers' tracts, so central to the discourse? On one account, personal freedom, a certain autonomy of thought and action is an interest we value and wish to protect. The Levellers often contrast the freeman with the slave, one has liberty the other not, so they ask who would choose to be a slave. There is another reason, where the distinction between liberty from and liberty to, rather rough and not too exact, is useful. Liberty as a barrier against being pressed into the navy, forced to labour for a lord, and from bondage of other kinds, is a constant theme, for they are the badges of servitude. Of most concern is liberty from arbitrary power, the power to 'enslave, ruin, and destroy people', of which the House of Commons is accused.[36] Loss of liberty is linked to taxes, the harmful effects a common theme, for they crush a man, 'a plain quiet-minded man—like a harmless sheep in a thicket, which can hardly move or stir but he shall be stretched and lose his wool'.[37] But note the words 'hardly move or stir' that hint at more than the harm of lost liberty. The plain man denied liberty is stuck, not able to act, not only to shore-up what he has but to better his position. This is the positive side of liberty, the freedom to do things, initiate action, pursue purposes. In Edward Sexby's advice to Cromwell the point is made: 'each person has the power of disposing of their own liberty as they as they shall think fit for their own good'.[38] 'For their own good', the betterment of their own situation. Positive liberty marks a space within which one may take initiatives and show enterprise in securing needs and advancing utilities. This other side of liberty I earlier linked to that championed by Machiavelli, not just liberty as a celebration of freedom but liberty as a means to ends. Liberty is valued not only to protect from interference, but to allow scope for adding to and improving one's interests, to be engaged actively in the tug-and-scramble. Monopolies in wool and cloth, printing, even beer and bread, are condemned as evil, and it is now clear

[35] J Lilburne: *Postscript to London's Liberty* (1646) in the *Levellers in the English Revolution* (ed) G Alymer (London: Thames and Hudson, 1975), pp 71*ff.*

[36] *England's Miserie and Remedie* (1645: author uncertain, possibly Richard Sexby) in D Wootton: *Divine Right and Democracy*, p 276.

[37] *Remonstrance*, p 10.

[38] E Sexby: *Killing Not Murder* (1657) in D Wootton: *Divine Right and Democracy*, p 360.

why: in preventing the plain man from competing, they stifle enterprise and suppress initiative, deny him room for betterment.

Talk of liberty lends light to constitutional authority and the purposes of state power. The common good is never far afield. For the Levellers it is the *salus populii*, the safety, the benefit, the good of the people, together constituting their well-being. The well-being of the people is the reason for authority and marks the bounds. The common good is given fresh meaning and purpose, not to sustain the social order as it is, but to act for the good of the people wherever that leads. The idea of the common good in the upper register, correct in concept but distorted in practice, now reverts in the lower register to its true meaning. In Warr's memorable words 'tis the perfection of the shadow to expire into the substance'.[39] The good of the people has two parts, one to preserve the rights and liberties they already have, the other the power to use their rights and the liberty to improve their lives. The common good so re-imagined points the way to the purpose of government and the limits. For what the people do naturally by the labour of each and in cooperation with others, they now enlist the aid of the state. Power is assigned to the state not for the 'ruination and destruction of our lives and liberties' but for 'edification and strengthening of the same'. Invoking imagery similar to Warr's, the author of a daring tract imagines the representatives in parliament as the shadow, the people the substance, and condemns the shadow for presuming to be 'more valuable and considerable than the body they serve'.[40] The social relationship consists of one being 'the servant of the other'. That lofty head of earlier images has tumbled lower, the adornments stripped away, the sole mission now 'to provide for the welfare and freedom' of the people. The purpose of government and the measure of the people's submission is to protect their interests and to enable their betterment. Lilburne takes up the case: the people have by nature the power 'to delegate their natural power of self-preservation to any who will do the work for them', even to the New Model Army.[41] The organs of government have no special status but, like the army, are 'the servants of the people' from whom the people may demand 'an exact account'.[42] As servants of the people, their authority is limited to serving the people.

The English are a free people, 'the sole origin of their own authority', managing their own affairs by 'their own elected Parliaments or Common Councils'. The Levellers disclaim any intention 'to tear up those foundations, to innovate or introduce any new constitution or frame of government'. They wish 'to maintain, defend, and preserve the old',[43] but the old 'freed from encroachments of King,

39 J Warr: *The Dispute Betwixt Equity and Form*, p 36.

40 *England's Miserie and Remedie*, in Wootton: *Divine Right and Democracy*, p 276.

41 J Lilburne quoted in TC Pease: *The Leveller Movement*, p 97.

42 *Ibid* p 2.

43 JW Gough: *Fundamental Law in English Constitutional History* (Oxford: Clarendon Press, 1955), p 123.

Lords, and priest';[44] the old where the House of Commons rules for the people's 'subsistence, livelihood, and safety'.[45] Perhaps the authors of these tracts believed they were within the bounds of the constitution, doing no more than lancing the malignant lump and restoring the pristine form, the good health of the body politic. But the search does not end there. The Levellers probe deeper in quest of the foundation stone, the ultimate principle of the constitutional order. It is no longer a voyage to *recover* foundations that have become unmoored and drifted out of sight; it is now a voyage to *discover* a new constitutional order and to chart its foundations. The centre of constitutional gravity moves to the people, not the corporate image of the people acting through representatives, but the people as individual persons with natural liberty and a birthright of equality. The real people know the utility of government, define its powers, set its limits, and then watch over it, the terms of which are to be rendered into a written document signed by all.[46] Restoration has quietly given way to constitutional revolution.

7. Fragments of constitution

When in the depth of adversity people are driven to defend themselves, they define the interests, sentiments, and dispositions on which to found their actions. The three episodes of rebellion are testimony of that process. Each records a sense of grievance and injustice regarding interests held to be vital and for which direct action is the only recourse. Direct action may be spontaneous and passionate, a desperate attempt to have the wrong righted, motivated by a sense of injustice grave and urgent; or action may be planned and carefully carried out. In the three episodes the rebels are conscientious in justifying their actions. They appeal at first to the constitutional principles in place and urge they be respected. When pleas go unheard and unheeded, the principles come under scrutiny, which once launched is hard to stop, where it leads hard to foresee. In statements explaining and justifying actions, the rebels reveal the fragments of a fresh concept of constitution. They draw on ideas rarely stated yet embedded in their sentiments and dispositions. In the hands of the Levellers the fragments are pieced together to form a notion of constitution, reasonably mature and earnestly promoted. Each episode reveals a distinct understanding of social relations, the expectations of the people, and how they are betrayed. The same pattern appears time and again through the course of history in Europe and elsewhere. The task now is to recover from the discourse of rebellion an understanding of the people's interests, sentiments, and dispositions,

[44] *Ibid* p 123.

[45] *England's Miserie and Remedie*, in Wootton: *Divine Right and Democracy*, p 276.

[46] On the proposals for a written constitution and the history of the *Agreements of the People*: I Gentles 'The Agreements of the People 1647–1649' in *The Putney Debates of 1647* (ed) M Mendles (Cambridge: Cambridge University Press, 2001).

which are then used to develop further that alternative model of constitutional authority outlined earlier. The enquiry is conducted in several stages: the people's conception of the common good, the function of government, the foundation of ideas and concepts, all contributing to a distinct sense of constitution.

In declaring grievances the rebels resort to a bank of interests around which arise sentiments, strong enough to create dispositions, themselves powerful enough to incite the action of rebelling. That one phase lead to the next, despite the barriers around each, and result in actions so dangerous, the consequence so grave, is testimony of the weight the rebels place on the interests under threat. The reason is plain and persuasive because the interests—being secure in what one has and able to improve one's life—are the foundations of social life and human endeavour. Now, having traced back the course of rebellion from action to interests, let us reverse and starting with the same interests plot a passage through sentiments to dispositions to action. To continue John Warr's metaphor, from the shadow of the upper register, the true meaning of the common good emerges in the lower register. Not a holistic notion where the sum is more than the parts; nor an abstraction from reality. Rather the common good is made up of the interests of each person emerging from and constituted by 'each determined to preserve his own'.[47] Liberty is critical to the process of preservation, the liberty to defend, agitate for, and advance interests. Liberty is conserved 'by continued differences and opposition of numbers' rather than by concurrence with government.[48] No wonder rulers of the sixteenth and seventeenth centuries 'abhorred opposition'[49] and dreaded the prospect of *regale* being leavened by *politicum*, the two concepts contrasted by John Fortescue.[50] Interests compete and clash, and the common good means compromising the interests of some in order to protect the interests of others.[51]

Just as the common good of the lower register rests on interests, the common good of the upper register also is grounded on interests, but with a critical difference. The lower register takes for granted everyone has and values the same essential interests, and all share the same disposition to protect and advance them. From that base and with that purpose, social relations form and institutions are created. The upper register comes into being at a later stage when social relations are already formed and a social order already in place. An order racked by division and disparity, where interests are ranked and some acquire priority over others; where social relations form to entrench the disparity and the power conferred to sustain it. Vico recounts the early history of Rome founded on a division between a

[47] A Ferguson: *An Essay on the History of Civil Society* (1767) (ed) F Oz-Salzberger (Cambridge: Cambridge University Press, 1995), pp 124–5.
[48] *Ibid* p 125.
[49] *Ibid* p 125.
[50] J Fortescue: *On the Laws and Governance of England* (around 1545) (ed) S Lockwood (Cambridge: Cambridge University Press, 1997).
[51] The competition and the resolution are well-expressed in the dialogue between Dr Rieux and M Rambert in Albert Camus' account of the plague: A Camus: *La Peste* (London: Methuen, 1959), p 102.

homeless people seeking refuge with a few powerful families. Once granted refuge, the people struggle to be acknowledged as members of the social order. Their efforts are resisted but in time concessions are made; they acquire civic status and become the bearers of rights, although low down in the social order. In order to sustain the disparity, the dominant sectors construct a matching constitutional order, the purpose to preserve the social order while making it seem to be in the interests of all. That is the function of the upper register in appealing to universality, impartiality, and objectivity being for the good of all, while sustaining a social order of disparity and inequality. The reality is softened with a cape of captivating colours and appealing images, embroided in the virtues of harmony, stability, and unity. Within the folds some members are better covered than others, occupy more noble positions, contribute more to the good of the whole, guide the body to good health, and so deserve to benefit more. The people have their interests protected, often just enough to win their compliance. This helps to explain why this ordering of social relations and a constitution to match is, historically, the most common.

Rebellion framed in a different discourse points to another ordering of social relations and another conception of the common good. The discourse starts not with a settled social order but at a prior point, the interest of each person in living a decent life, in having needs secured and space to advance utilities. The rebels, untutored in the wisdom of Vico or Smith or Hume, reach by their own efforts and the lessons of experience the same conclusion. They come to know the irony of human association that the interest common to all in promoting well-being unleashes a tug-and-scramble nasty and brutal, where some win, some cope, many lose. They see no other route to well-being, no alternative course to the good of all. The best they can do is try to structure and control the competition. Rebellion fits the frame, law the instrument at hand. The rebels call on law, on the promise that their interests be protected against sheriffs and landlords, tax collectors and a greedy prince. Their cause starts with the protection of person and property, written into law as rights and liberties. The legal order lets them down, fails to deliver the protection promised. Law is applied selectively and arbitrarily, denying aid to some, repressing others. The freedom to act to improve life, instead of being enlarged and secured by law, is restricted and open to arbitrary intervention. Far from being the sinews of society, a positive force binding together the parts, law and legal institutions turn out to be agents of division and oppression, handy tools in upholding the settled social order and a sturdy staff in the hands of officials.

No wonder the search goes on for a conception of law prior to and more fundamental than a tool at the service of select sectors. Law so conceived is a mere shadow of law in a true sense, prior to rank, property, and power. That the search founders and ends in disappointment is to be expected. It looks in the wrong place for the wrong thing, and must end in failure. There is no law prior to and outside social relations, no concept to invoke as a restraint on social relations, a lesson the Levellers eventually learn. On the contrary, law arises *within* social relations, its purpose to structure and moderate collective action in achieving common purposes.[52] Law is conceived within the course of shared endeavour and reared to moderate the process. Collective action is conducted through social relations, and so the origins of law are internal not drawn from outside. The rebels, disappointed in positive law, realizing it offers no defence against abuse, broaden the field of enquiry. They sense there is more to law than a staff in the hands of a few; but just what it is and where it comes from eludes them. And yet the signs point in the right direction even if the destination is never reached.

An early sign is the focus on liberty, an inkling that tracing liberty back to the beginning will reveal something about the nature of law. Liberty is prominent in the discourse of the rebels, both for its innate worth, as something valued and good to have, and a means to ends, a means by which each and all pursue their purposes. At the same time, degree reigns, some have more liberty than others, dredging a gulf between the plain simple man and the gentleman, fuelling the contempt of courtiers for the mechanicals, keeping the sheep entangled in briars. Denial of liberty inhibits action, bars the plain simple man from acting to improve his position materially, culturally, and socially, even to become a gentleman. That matters because liberty is not a privilege of a few, but a quality at the core of human life and a formative influence on social relations. On probing liberty, we encounter equality and see how the two unite in common cause. Equality most elementary means each person to be worthy of respect. To respect is to acknowledge an interest in living well and acting for that end. The sentiment of respect of one for another has mixed origins, for some an attribute of nature, for others grounded in religion. It is enough for social understanding that equality of respect has a place at the foundation of human relationships. Not in all relationships or in all cultures. Vico's account of the history of Rome and its legacy is ever instructive. The *plebs* once safe in refuge seek the status of citizens because that entails recognition by the *patricians* of each as worthy of respect. To respect each other is to treat each other equally in this sense. From mutual respect follows the concepts of civic and juridical equality and the capacity to have rights. Equality has a dynamic quality parallel to that of liberty. The more equal the people are, the more effective each can be in competing for social goods and improving lives, while the more unequal the less the scope to compete, the more uneven the tug-and-scramble. Equality in competing does not dictate or guarantee equal outcomes; it secures only the right to engage on an equal footing and, in engaging, to have the same liberty as others. The partnership of equality and liberty give practical expression to mutual respect, while law is the means to secure both.

The value of equality is evident in the sentiments of the people, not only the skilled and the accomplished, but the rough fisherman who spend their days

[52] See the discussion of the *Natural Law of Peoples*: Chapter III:6.

casting nets. They know that mutual respect, and the equality and liberty entailed, are at the foundation of social relations, the necessary means to well-being and a standard to measure practice. The fishermen know that mutual respect enables cooperation of one with others in attaining the common good; that governments are valued and empowered to establish and sustain the conditions for cooperation. The dangers are all too plain; that 'men a-land' do what the whale does at sea, 'the great ones eat up the little ones—devours them all at a mouthful',[53] while, they might have added, governments aid and abet or idly stand by. The fishermen would understand the righteous indignation of the boatswain, struggling to keep the ship afloat during a violent storm, abused by the nobles Antonio and Gonzalo, who are asked to stop interfering and get off the deck. The boatswain asks if they 'can command these elements to silence and work peace of the present'; if not, go to your cabin and leave it to the sailors.[54] The abuse aroused bears witness to an absence of respect for the sailors and an ignorance of their skills. The people grasp the idea of mutual respect and its place in human endeavour; they understand its origins in equality and liberty, and show its value in the strength of their sentiments. The very sentiments on which Vico based his account of human action, social cooperation, and the natural law of peoples.

8. An emerging pattern of opinion

Once rid of 'the robes and furred gowns'[55] of the upper register, stripped to the bare weeds of winter, 'the masks of virtue' removed,[56] government appears in a true light. It is a means and nothing more by which officials and agencies are empowered to serve the people, to secure their interests and guard their freedom to improve their lives. The people know government properly conducted is a useful even necessary in adding to and afforcing efforts towards common ends.[57] The means are of two kinds, the more obvious one to protect the people and make secure what they have, the other less-noticed to support them in enriching their lives. The people know that to serve those ends government has to have power; they know power is dangerous, capable of misuse, and the more power the more the danger. Power has to be channelled, confined, and controlled, for which ways and means are to be found. With this image of government in mind, let us now consider further two aspects, one the application of these ideas in practice, the other the

[53] *Pericles, Prince of Tyre*, Scene 5: 69.

[54] *The Tempest*, Act 1: 1: 19*ff.*

[55] King Lear's depiction of authority: *The Tragedy of King Lear*, Act 4: 5: 161.

[56] An evocative image from Benjamin Constant discussed in S Holmes: *Benjamin Constant and the Making of Modern Liberalism* (New Haven & London: Yale University Press, 1984), p 131.

[57] See further A Kronman: *Max Weber* (London: Edward Arnold, 1983) for analysis of Weber's account of the people's accepting the need for authority and their wanting a world that has reason and meaning.

deeper principles that guide practice, civic and juridical equality in particular. The expectation is that from the combination of the practical and the principled will result a constitutional order 'under which the people rejoice and live cheerfully'.[58] The practical conception of government taking shape relies on several ideas, rather common-sense ideas, about the form, conduct, and control of government.

One set of ideas is the people's willingness for rule to be in the hands of a few. Evidence of a deep-seated desire to rule themselves is lacking. Even the Levellers, who made sovereignty of the people the cornerstone of the constitution, did not advocate direct rule by the people. They accepted government's being more likely to be effective if delegated to a few who are responsive to the people's interests. Some of the people would like to be among that few, but for most other pursuits closer to their interests have priority, leaving them content to be governed. A second set of ideas concerns governing well, what is means and how it is achieved. The people expect government to do more than secure their rights and liberties; in addition to create the conditions under which to improve their position. They know competition and collision among interests are unavoidable, that government institutions have to arbitrate and rule on relative weight and importance. The people understand that a matter's being left to be settled by the agencies of government probably means informal institutions have failed or are unable to reach a resolution, although the tendency to underrate civil society and to overload the state we have noted.[59] They expect the agencies to moderate among interests, to curb the power of some to the benefit of others. Not to level as often feared, but to reach a balance based on mutuality and moderation, where some gain more but all gain enough; to remove barriers to the people's pursuit of well-being; and to regulate the arena to allow all to take part on a broadly equal footing.

The people insist, as a third task of government, that their interests be presented, considered, and duly weighed in decision-making. Rebellion echoes the call of the people for a voice, not a voice in the void, but a voice to sound their interests in all their fractured pieces, reflecting the diversity and competition among them. 'Rebellion was a means of opening a dialogue' between the rebels and government, a dialogue directed to their interests being taken seriously.[60] To hear the people, to take account of their interests, and to reach reasoned and defensible outcomes, relies on a network of agencies and processes of the kind familiar in a constitutional order. Being heard means more than being listened to; it means being involved, having avenues of influence and an active role in settling outcomes. Equality again enters the scene, equality in the sense of being able to take part in the process on an equal footing. A fourth set of ideas follows, ideas familiar in calls for rebellion, that resolution among interests be rendered into law as rights and liberties, duties

[58] *England's Miserie and Remedie* quoted in *Divine Right and Democracy*, p 276.
[59] The need for the state and the scope of its powers are discussed in Chapter I:3.
[60] A Wood: *Riot, Rebellion and Popular Politics in Early Modern England* (Basingstoke: Palgrave, 2002).

and responsibilities. The law is invoked in rebellion because it mediates social relationships by declaring rights and liberties, and by imposing duties of respect on officials. Law states what is due and promises to deliver what is due. Where a rush to rights would be unwise or premature, where matters are better left to be settled by discretionary judgements, the people expect processes be in place allowing the parties to engage and be listened to, and a justified outcome delivered. Once rights are settled, substantive or procedural, in private relations or public, the people expect they be upheld. The grievance most often aired in rebellion is just that, the failure to uphold rights, because no matter how sparse they are, to be confident of protection is critical to personal well-being and social relationships.

The last set of ideas emerging from rebellion, by now familiar, draws attention to the dangers of power, whether in governing or advancing private interests. The people know agencies of government are tempted to erect a barrier of autonomy, distance themselves, retreat into secrecy, and resist scrutiny.[61] The people demand the opposite. That agencies be engaged in continuing relations with them, be under their gaze, and held to account. How that can be done, how the agencies of government can be open yet effective, able to make hard decisions even if unpopular, are matters touched on before and taken up in later chapters. The other danger the people face is the tie between state power and sectional interests. The power of the state is a means by which to promote sectional interests. Constitutions according to Ireton are about property, to allow and secure accumulation of property.[62] Madison's asserting the need to moderate the wishes of the people through the wisdom of the few is, in one view, a means to preserve the power and property of the few, of which he was one and for whom slaves were a valuable part.[63] The relationship between property and wealth, and political power, Douglas North states bluntly: 'Institutions are not created to be socially efficient; rather they are created to serve the interests of those with the bargaining power to devise new rules'.[64] Whether such a bold claim stands up to empirical investigation we need not here consider. There are certainly striking cases, such as the enclosure of common land and the loss of commoners' rights, a cause of rebellion across countries and over centuries, of the power of the state being marshalled, blatantly to serve private interests.[65] Alert to the influence of groups and sectors over government, the risk

[61] Max Weber's account of the rise of bureaucratic organizations and their innate tendencies is most valuable: M Weber: *Economy and Society*, pp 956*ff*. See the account of the *discretionary space*: Chapter V:3.

[62] *Putney Debates* (1647).

[63] J Madison: *The Federalist No 10* in A Hamilton, J Madison, and J Jay: *The Federalist* (London: JM Dent, 1971), p 41.

[64] D North: *Institutions, Institutional Change and Economic Performance*, p 16.

[65] Studies of enclosure are abundant. For the cost to the people of resistance and the unspeakable ruthlessness and cruelty of the few, it is enough to read one account set in Sardegna: G Dessì: *Paese d'Ombra* (Milan: Mondadori, 1972).

of outright capture, the people are on guard, on the lookout for ways of curbing the excesses and reaching a tolerable balance among competing interests.

In the eyes of the people a notion of constitutional order takes shape. Government is a practical matter, an instrument indispensable in achieving purposes common to all. Government consists of institutions and agencies of certain qualities and capabilities, a capacity to coordinate action and contribute to common pursuits. Both are easily overstated, some tasks better left to informal action.[66] More empirical research would be useful in drawing a line between the two; more caution needed in allocating tasks to the state. The point is that whatever powers be granted, the purpose from the people's point of view is to protect and further their interests.[67] Once we think of the state in such practical terms, the need to invent fine theories, or to imagine a mystical union with the people disappears. We see why sovereignty, consent, and representation are not needed in constructing relations between the people and government; nor needed to justify the power of officials and agencies. The case for government, the utility and the justification, is plain without such concepts, which are seen as ornaments, at best to cushion, at worst to conceal social reality. The people's hopes for government are moderate, their expectations tempered by realism. They do not want social upheaval or radical levelling of disparities. That has been tried and always fails; gradual adjustment rather than radical reform is normally enough. Nor do the people expect perfection in the processes of government, or deep wisdom in the content. Knowing governing to be a complex matter and success contingent, in the hands of fallible officials, prone to error, corruption, and misuse, the people settle for tolerable levels of competence, proprietary, and protection, enough to meet needs and allow scope to improve their lives. That is enough to earn their support, fortified by common prudence that there is no practical alternative. The people value harmony, stability, and unity, but are aware the opposites, instability, disharmony, and disunity are innate in social relations and can have positive effects. The main concern is to hold a balance among competing interests; a balance hard to attain and hard to maintain. The best to hope for is moderation on the part of government, aided by mutual self-restraint; a generosity of spirit on the part of the people and a margin of tolerance.[68]

For the final fragment of constitution revealed by rebellion, we return to Peter Quince and a sense the world could be different. A world where one does not hang for offending a lady; nor need to cower before the Duke; nor put up with the antics of his feeble-headed courtiers. A world in which each would be respected and measured on grounds other than the fortune or misfortune of birth and status.

[66] For a fuller account, see E Ostrom: *Governing the Commons*; discussed in Chapter I:3.

[67] D Acemoglu and JA Robinson show the risks of not having a powerful state: *The Narrow Corridor: States, Society, and the Fate of Liberty* (London: Viking Penguin, 2019).

[68] That moderation is the guidance concept of government is repeated throughout Hume's essays: D Hume: *Essays Moral, Political, and Literary*, especially pp 27, 45, 53, 94, 575.

In portraying a common wisdom the mechanicals are paradigms of the common people. They know that fictions abound; that harsh reality is prone to be clothed in religion or nature, or dressed as a body politic. They see through them all as images aimed at sustaining a social order, which stripped of such flimsy weeds would be exposed in all its rudeness. With a sense that life is not ordained to be this way, but seeing no other, the mechanicals resign themselves to acceptance. On that note we part company, admiring their shrewd insight into the duke's rule, and Quince's inkling that relations between duke and people could be otherwise; while admitting the benefits gained from ducal rule are real and worthwhile. That however is only half the story, one side of the people's place in relation to rule. The other side is to improve life, to take positive action to advance well-being, for which the rule of dukes, emperors, and princes is unsuitable. Acquiescence has virtue, but if rule were properly to serve the humanity and civility and the blooming of well-being, it would not be enough. Perhaps Hume had in mind the mechanicals when he made acquiescence depend on *opinion*.

9. Civic and juridical equality

Armed with these fragments of opinion and constitution, my purpose now is to enquire further into the concepts of a constitutional order. While the people are normally content that daily affairs be conducted within the form of settled social relations, we are curious to press beyond form to find substance, the firmer ground from which form has sprung. To uncloak form to find substance; to solve in King Lear's phrase 'the mystery of things'.[69] Without substance there is no standard against which to measure form, no foundation on which to draw in correcting and adjusting form. In John Warr's words 'use and custom hath inured the world to bondage, and men are contented herewith as knowing no better'.[70] He found the foundation in equity and reason, which together beget the simple but dynamic principle *do as thou wouldst be done unto*.[71] However, between equity and reason, and practical action, there is a need for form, for structure and meanings, for certainty and predictability. Warr would have known of the courts of equity, where equity, said to be as long as the Chancellor's foot, soon took on settled form as strict as the form of the common law which it was meant to soften. The courts of North Africa used to be cited for doing *khadi justice*, mocked for arbitrary looseness, until Laurence Rosen discovered a pattern of forms not unlike those at home.[72]

[69] Continuing John Warr's evocative imagery of form and substance: *The Dispute Betwixt Equity and Form*.

[70] *Ibid* p 35.

[71] *Ibid* p 32.

[72] L Rosen: *The Anthropology of Justice: Law as Culture in Islamic Society* (Cambridge: Cambridge University Press, 1989).

Law seems to offer another route from substance to form. Said to be the sinews of society, the white cord of unity, the bonds of social relations, law surely has a firm foundation. Beyond the positive rules, the mere expression of will, lie the conventions and traditions grounded in social reality and moral sentiments. Still not enough and the search goes on for a deeper foundation. The Levellers we have seen, having embarked on the voyage, sailed from harbour to harbour in search of the foundation, the Ithaca of law, until they came to realize no such destination exists. Instead of seeking a foundation prior to social relations, one on which social relations then build, the search starts with social relations and asks how they came about and on what concepts they are based. The enquiry is social and historical, the aim to discover the terms on which relations are conducted in practice, the beacon Vico's words that to understand social relations we need to trace them to their origins. The frame of enquiry, the purpose of human endeavour to advance civility and humanity is settled, a purpose to which constitutional authority contributes. Yet, power dressed as authority still poses risks it would be folly for the people to take without precautions. The issue now is how the risks are managed, how authority is used, the concepts guiding sentiments, dispositions, and action.

Rights are a good place to start. The interests most valued, among which security of person and property rank highly, are protected by law and given the status of rights. Other interests lacking the status of substantive rights receive a second-order of protection, a procedural right to be taken into account in decisions affecting them. What then does it mean to have a right whether substantive or procedural? To have a right is to preclude being treated at the will or the whim of another, whether in the private sector or the public. The suspect has a right to be tried according to due process, not summarily punished; property is not lost at the will of another; the party to a contract insists on the terms being honoured. When Thomas More asks 'by what right men may take away from any man against his will, the land that is lawfully his own' he does not mention but implicitly relies on a sense of equality, best described as civic equality.[73] Certain taxes are condemned in statements of grievance because they affect rights and hence destroy civic equality. To see the force of being a right-holder, it is enough to imagine life without rights, to be under the control of another by whom you may be treated however he likes, without restraining principles or means of recourse. The citizens of Rome had rights, enjoyed civic equality, their slaves had neither. The concept of a right is based on a notion of equality, that persons be treated with respect or, to be more exact, a certain equality of respect. On this foundation of equal respect, or concern and respect, Ronald Dworkin in the twentieth century built a theory of rights and law.[74] The expansion of rights in recent years, whether natural, human, or political, is powered by the same idea. Vico long before had shown the centrality of civic

[73] Quoted in JW Gough: *Fundamental Law in English Constitutional History*.

[74] R Dworkin: *Taking Rights Seriously* (London: Duckworth, 1978) especially Chapter 4.

equality to constitutional discourse. Driven by the 'cosmic, purposive tendency' to 'mould institutions and forms of social life' to serve humanity and civility, communities create social institutions, fields of social life governed by rules of which laws are an integral part. Vico discovered in the Roman republic that gradual movement, born of conflict between the classes, towards recognition of each person as entitled to an equality of respect, from which the capacity to bear rights follows.

Civic equality is not natural equality, although a certain sense of all being equal at birth seeps into social relationships, nurtures a rudimentary notion of reciprocity, of mutual respect. The trouble is other forces tend the other way. Luck of birth, native ability, and material chance all cultivate inequality. Civic equality concedes and poses no direct threat to inequality in such contexts, although tension between the two is ever-present. Civic equality, an island in a rough ocean, is under threat of being swamped by the high tides of inequality. Civic equality is won by dogged persistence and defended by eternal vigilance, which Vico charts in the conflict between the plebs and the patricians of Rome, and as the course of rebellion confirms.[75] Civic equality has its own means of counter-espionage, a conscience nagging at substantive inequality, a secret agent needling the settled order, nudging it to explain and justify itself. Several features of civic equality are of constitutional interest. In decreeing that each person count, civic equality is central to constitutional authority in guiding and controlling the use of power. In arguing at Putney against the vote for men without property, Henry Ireton, despite having studied Roman law at Oxford, seemed unaware of civil equality, both in principle and as the practical foundation of English law. Centuries before, in John of Salisbury's organic commonwealth, the people although assigned the lowliest organs had a civil status, were treated with a bare respect, not quite but close to civic equality. Adam Smith describes the forms of government in post-Roman Anglo-Saxon England where all freemen assembled to settle matters of common interest on an equal footing, regardless of social and material status.[76] The idea that each person count, be entitled to be treated with respect similar to that shown to others, is the social foundation of rights.

Civic equality has another outlet less noticed but notable in the legal maxim *quod omnes tangit*. We have seen how the maxim, *what affects all in like fashion should be approved by all* is the basis of consent in constitutional discourse.[77] The maxim's original field of operation is in law, in providing a foundation for legal doctrine. *Quod omnes tangit* is tied to the idea of rights as protected interests, to be removed or modified only with consent. It then spreads to generate doctrines from appointing bishops and princes, accepting a newly crowned monarch, paying new taxes, to due process in criminal proceedings. That does not exhaust its range for

[75] G Vico: *The New Science*.
[76] A Smith: *Lectures on Jurisprudence*, pp 226*ff*.
[77] See Chapter VI:9 herein.

the maxim has the status of a general principle open to novel cases. It is the source of law regulating relations between citizens and the agencies of government, and of rules of procedures, such as knowing the case, being heard, banning bias, and giving reasons. And while some procedural doctrines are tied to, follow from a substantive right, others are based on the more general idea that actions affecting a person's interests are subject to procedural conditions and constraints. Civic equality re-enters the scene as the source of the maxim, and the basis for due process and procedural fairness. Your procedural right to be told of the proposal to route a motorway across fields near your village, although no substantive rights are infringed, to make representations, be given reasons, and to have a chance to appeal, all depend on the notion of civic equality, mediated by the maxim *guod omnes tangit*. Civic equality justifies the claim that a benefit to some, whether supplying a social good or restraining actions of others, applies equally to all. The barons of *Magna Charta* based rebellion not only of the denial of their rights, but the rights of all freemen regardless of wealth and status.[78] Centuries later John Thelwall denounced legislation 'penalizing the poor journeyman who associated together, while rich manufacturers, monopolists, and others, may associate as they please'.[79] Accused of levelling, of wanting to change the economic order, the journeymen in associating to advance their utilities sought no more than civic equality. This element of universality, right conceded to one extending to all, is now relied on in many matters including gender, race and ethnicity, religion and disability. The logic is plain: if the qualification for a benefit is *abc* then anyone who satisfies *abc* is entitled, regardless of gender, race, religion, or any other quality unrelated to the benefit.

This leads to the dynamic nature of civic equality as a basis for new rights, another of Whitehead's principles hovering around eager to enter new fields and render service. Ferdinand Braudel found the issue most recurring from the fifth century to the twentieth to be the struggle over *libertates*, or rights in modern terms. A struggle by one sector to win the right to engage in activities confined to another sector, such matters as commercial enterprise, freely contracting outside one's own sector, owning and transferring property, moving and associating at will.[80] Vico recounts the struggle of the plebs of Rome to gain from the patricians the right to marry and own property, and hence to acquire the status of citizens, sowing in Vico's mind the seed from which grew the notion of civic equality.[81] Monopolies of enterprise and trade were condemned by the Levellers on several grounds, one as a restriction on the people's liberty to engage in economic activities. The claim that the logic of civic equality be applied to permit all persons to advance their interests,

[78] JW Gough: *Fundamental Law in English Constitutional History*, p 29.
[79] J Thelwall quoted in EP Thompson: *Whigs and Hunters* (London: Peregrine Books, 1978), p 174.
[80] F Braudel: *A History of Civilization* (New York: Penguin, 1987), pp 315*ff*; discussed in Galligan: *Law in Modern Society*, pp 271, 291.
[81] G Vico: *The New Science*.

of which economic endeavour is an essential part. In the absence of either a counterclaim from civic equality, or some other compelling reason of common interest, the restriction on open entry and competition cannot be defended. The coalition of civic equality and the pursuit of common purposes becomes apparent, the one a bearer of standards to structure the other, to convert an unruly tug-and-scramble into a justifiable process of shared endeavour.

Civic equality is the basis for juridical equality, the equality of persons before the law. Juridical equality requires, first, that law be expressed in general standards, which, secondly, apply equally to all. Again a touch of caution is called for. Law as general standards is not a quality inherent in the concept of law, nor a concept prior to social relations. Braudel notes that laws historically were commonly particular and selective, directed at one sector or another to its gain or its loss. The concept of law as general standards to be evenly applied is a sign of progress, a product of social relations, stimulated by the sentiment of civic equality. Yet the ambiguity is barely hidden. The seemingly simple and obvious fairness of general standards equally administered skates over the darker depths beneath. A law allowing the vote to males of a certain age and property is general in one sense: any man who qualifies has the right to vote. In another sense it fails by excluding all men without property and all women regardless of age or property. At Putney, Colonel Rainsborough asked what reason can there be for not giving the vote to soldiers who had fought and won the civil war. Ireton's answer in one word *property*, they lack property. The claims are couched in different logics, passing without meeting, each invoking a set of ideas, a distinct discourse. One invokes civic equality to which property and gender are irrelevant; the other draws on that sentiment of distrust and suspicion of the common people, the mere breathers unfit to have a say in public affairs and a threat to the settled social order.[82] A sentiment for which civic equality is no match. As the strength of that sentiment over time waned and that of civic equality waxed, obstacles of gender, ethnicity, and lack of property to universal suffrage have fallen away.[83] Civic equality reveals itself briefly as the undercover agent quietly subverting unfounded inequalities.

10. Justice, law, and juridical equality

'Nothing shall make his people rise, except lack of goods and lack of justice' wrote John Fortescue in the sixteenth century, an opinion borne out in the study of rebellion.[84] Lack of goods leading to rebellion is straightforward, claims of justice less

[82] Discussed in Chapter VII.

[83] The same case from civic equality is made now for lowering the qualifying age.

[84] J Fortescue: *On the Laws and Governance of England* (1468) in *Sir John Fortescue: On the Laws and Governance of England* (ed) S Lockwood (Cambridge: Cambridge University Press, 1997).

so. Why is justice among the most valued interests and forceful sentiments of the people, even the poorest and least tutored? Forceful enough to arouse a disposition to action even when the costs are high and the consequences deadly. Here the two faces of justice reappear, one restorative, the other dynamic, one looking back, the other forward. Justice looking back, a lever to restore the terms of a relationship, is well displayed in the discourse of rebellion. If one party ruptures the relationship to the cost of the other, the claim for redress is to give what is due. Justice as the practical application of civic equality, transfers to the legal order as juridical equality. To respect rights is to give to each party what is due within the relationship. If between two private parties, the authority of the state is called on to intervene; if between a private person and an agency of the state, the state is called on to undo its own mischief.

The other face of justice looks to the future to guide the formation of social relations. Settled social relations come under scrutiny and justice enlisted to order adjustment and revision. Leaving the security of settled relations, justice enters fresh fields to create new sets of social relations, civic equality again the foundation from which to launch the campaign. The tactics are different because the appeal to (re)-construction rather than restoration is harder to turn into practice. The assault on property is a familiar cause. Restorative justice, armed with civic equality, denies the landowner's power to destroy the livelihood of others by enclosing the commons on which they depend. The cause of dynamic or constructive justice is the iniquity of the landowner having so much property in the first place when the commoners have almost none. How can it be just that he live in comfort and plenty when his neighbours and civic equals have to scratch a living? Yet, civic equality for all its persuasive power, its wit and guile, is not enough to topple the reign of property, so deeply embedded in social relations and the foundation of the constitutional order. Even the hint of harm to property rights, Putney the proof, is enough to marshal stout defence. Lesser ambitions have more chance of success, smaller gains more feasible, moderate adjustments more tolerable than radical revision. Action proceeds on many fronts: the liberty of workers to be mobile, form associations, and negotiate the terms of work; the liberty to engage freely in economic enterprise, to modify monopolies and other restrictions; to have access to essential welfare, to education and the professions; or have a say in administrative processes affecting one's interests. These are among the sub-fields most open to claims of justice based on civic equality. Each has space for innovation, to extend the range of interests that count, within which to build on the settled relations by drawing out the logic to justify change. The ship of civic equality is ever afloat, the captain g*uod omnes tangit* always on duty and alert to new fields of adventure, and over time capable of chipping away at even the best fortified social relationships.

The gains made by civic equality, once encased in justice are entrusted to the custody of law, to the standards, procedures, and agencies of law. Writing of events in the lead up to *Magna Charta*, Holt explains the relationship: 'Nothing is so striking in the legal records of John's reign as the subjective assumption of a right of justice, to a reasonable application of the legal process to his own case'.[85] The place of the legal process may now be defined. First, the law, the legal order of standards and the institutions is a means to justice, justice in practice, and in doing justice to preserve civic equality. We see why the search for a foundation of law outside and prior to social relations is misguided, why the image of law as the sinews of society, the bonds of social cohesion, while beguiling is only half true. In the same way the notion of law as simple and settled and somehow neutral, a mechanism rather than a social process, is both wrong and risky. Secondly, law serves justice and civic equality by setting standards before which all are treated in the same way. This is a necessary function but of narrow virtue. All being subject to the same standards applied evenly and accurately, together with a degree of certainty and predictability, are qualities of value in social relationships. The demand most common among rebels is that the law be applied fairly and properly, that whatever its promises, however few or small, they be honoured. The justice of being treated according to the standards of law has to be qualified. General standards strictly applied breed their own injustice. A band of discretion, whether by reference to purpose or in response to the oddities of the case or the compelling need for exception, is a necessary adjunct to the justice of general standards.[86]

The last feature to notice is the justice in applying standards, the justice of form, says nothing about substance, the justice of the standards themselves. That form and substance are separated is the point of Warr's lament. But it is not one or the other; both are necessary to justice, the relationship between them subtle and shifting. On the one hand the worth of form, of certainty and predictability lowers as substantive injustice rises. Substantive injustice is slightly softened if form be upheld, although experience suggests the more unjust the substance, the less likely regard for form. As Henry VII's reign sank into despotism, disregard for the form of law followed.[87] On the other hand, even for moderate laws there is the irony as Adam Ferguson noticed, that laws serve the weak by protecting person and property, while at the same time promoting inequality and enabling sectors to accumulate wealth and power.[88] If the natural alliance between economic and political power be added, irony gives way to the resigned fatalism of Peter Quince. Adam Ferguson proposes a remedy, one now familiar, that if a nation is to prosper laws are needed, not to level, but at least modify inequalities of wealth and power by admitting 'every order of the people' by representatives or otherwise to a share in legislating.[89] Inequalities in the social and economic order are reduced by political action, not by appeal to a quality innate in law. Law is a means to ends and purposes;

[85] JC Holt: *Magna Charta* (Cambridge: Cambridge University Press, 3rd edn 2014), p 92.
[86] On relations between general rules and discretion: DJ Galligan: *Discretionary Powers* generally.
[87] Discussed in Chapter II.
[88] A Ferguson: *An Essay on the History of Civil Society*, p 152.
[89] *Ibid* p 159.

who decides the ends and purposes depends on who controls the law-making process, which in turn depends on the contest among groups and sectors. The outcomes vary according to the contest, with some laws genuinely in the common interests of the people, others advancing the interests of groups and sectors. Laws once settled have to be applied by the agencies at a multitude of sites where the contest duly modified continues. Form has a place at each site but is never enough and matters of substance remain, narrowed to interpretation at one end, broadened to open discretion at the other. The contest between form and substance is between two different logics, two modes of rationality, one the logic of rules, the other the logic of substance. Each exerts its power, one sometimes gaining dominance over the other, but normally a median is reached, although the contest is never over, the skirmishes at each site never ended.[90]

To law as protective must be added law as enabling.[91] The one signifies a process to single out certain interests for protection, the other to help the people in their own efforts to advance well-being. Civic equality, ever the guide, entitles each person to engage in the competition among interests and aims, and to do so on a roughly equal footing. Law guides the process; marks out and fences a sub-field of liberty and equality; which law then enters to remove obstacles to liberty and to open avenues of positive action. The obstacles we have noted include barriers to movement, association, and enterprise. Select interests erect other obstacles by taking control of an area of activity and barring entry to others, or where entry is open the power to bargain is uneven. Enabling measures include infrastructure, a contemporary example among many is access to the internet and all it offers. Even more elementary are opportunities to education, a familiar route to advancing interests; another is access to callings and professions, traditionally the privilege of a few to the exclusion of the many. The list could be longer but enough has been said to show how civic equality, charismatic in character and fertile in function, sits at the base of society, guiding the formation of social relations and how they work in practice, and diligently assisting the design and daily functioning of the legal order.

11. The constitution of the people

The discourse of rebellion displays a sense of constitutional authority from the people's perspective. The critical elements are threefold: the purpose of power; relations among the people and between the people and rulers; and the conditions on use of power. Around these constitutive elements lesser others are added. The

[90] The contesting rationalities are discussed at length by M Weber: *Economy & Society*, Volume I.

[91] HLA Hart distinguishes between duty-imposing and power-conferring rules, a distinction useful here: HLA Hart: *The Concept of Law* (Oxford: Clarendon Press, 1961).

constitution is usually written although historically consisted of fragments spread across several sources, some written, others conventions innate in surrounding social spheres. The text and the conventions are only ever part of the constitution, the upper signs and circles of a structure that reaches down to a lower circle of ideas, language, and images, then deeper to relations between people and rulers, which rest in turn on social relations among the people. A discourse develops, a register forms to simplify complexity and to invent a language to match. That is the official constitution and its companion register. There is as well an unofficial constitution and a matching register founded on another discourse of ideas, language, and images, which constitute another way of expressing the three elements of constitution. This constitution, rarely written or stated in a text, or found in settled conventions, is drawn from the sentiments and dispositions of the people, to offer another version of the body politic and the meaning of good health. Between the two registers, there is some common ground, but on certain critical issues and for the reasons earlier given, they are miles apart. To the plea that however interesting the people's ideas, they do not amount to a concept of constitution, the answer is plain. Rebellion forces to the fore a clarity of thought as to the purposes of constitutional authority and the guiding principles, and the sentiments and dispositions they arouse. The ideas and language that emerge, rightly, are held to be a conception of constitutional authority. The word *constitution* may be missing, the concept unmentioned, but the substance is present.[92]

The people's conception of constitution has several features. First, they share sentiments as to the worth of government and dispositions of restraint and support on one side, engagement, vigilance, and censure on the other. At the same time, they stand back, maintain a certain reserve, retain a certain independence in judging what rule is and why it matters.[93] On the one hand, the people enter a constitutional field already laid out, a network of agencies and officials to confront, support and keep to purpose, while on the lookout for openings and diligent in making adjustments. Confronted because it is there and appears impregnable; supported because it supplies benefits valued by all and not supplied by other means; kept to purpose in the face of appetite, incompetence, and misrule. The institutions of state are embedded in daily life and affect the people in multiple ways, in the same way that family and school, workplace and profession, together with countless other relationships are to be made sense of and supported. On the other hand, the people stand their ground, have that hinterland of interests, sentiments and dispositions on which to draw and with which to cast a critical eye on

[92] The word *constitution* in referring to the rules of government and relations with the people is itself of fairly recent origin: see: J Stourz: '*Constitution:* Changing Meanings of the Term from the Early Seventeenth to the Late Eighteenth Century' in *Conceptual Change and the Constitution* (eds) T Ball and JGA Pocock (Kansas: University Press of Kansas, 1988).

[93] Much of the fame of the impartial spectator is due to A Smith: *Theory of Moral Sentiments.*

the affairs of government. The private person, wrote Benjamin Constant, is able 'to maintain a rational scepticism and flexibility'.[94] Between support and engagement on one side, detachment displayed in vigilance and censure on the other, lies a tension that tactfully handled is conducive to sound government, while ever at risk of collapsing into ineptitude or oppression or both. This leads to purpose, to protect and further their interests, to secure and improve their lives in all dimensions, materially and culturally. The institutions of government support and strengthen the people's own efforts, single and in association, ranging from the casual and the fleeting to the formal and the permanent, some at the choice of the people, others forced on them. Whether by choice or compulsion, each set of relations is expected to contribute in some way to the quality of their lives. The people approach the state with that expectation, enlist its services, support its efforts, and measure its performance. They know the actions of officials and agencies are capable of contributing in many ways, some unique to the state, others in partnership with the people. In the hope these conditions will be met, the people have good reasons for forbearing, restraining their own action; not just complying with but positively supporting constituted authority.

That leads onto the irony of power being positive but dangerous, the more power the more the potential benefits and the more the danger. In confronting the state, the people come armed with sentiments and dispositions well-grounded, fed on ideas and values, formed and refined within social relationships occupied from the earliest age about how power, any power, is to be used, the principles guiding it, and the restraints on it. The same ideas and values are brought to bear on the power of the state to tame and entwine it in a web of constraints, to turn power into acceptable authority. And because officials and agencies need high power in order to govern well, the risk of misuse matches. The risk of power lurching out of control, being used to mistreat and oppress, put to personal ends, and being unduly influenced by select groups and sectors. The people know they must find ways of resolving the dilemma of power being necessary but dangerous; they know the stakes are high and resolution difficult. Measures to guide and limit power to its constitutional purpose are available; institutions designed to mark the boundaries and settle principles within. Officials can be trained to keep to purpose, taught to resist temptation and avoid deviation. The people know, nonetheless, despite the layers of constraint on power, the final burden falls on them; that they ultimately are the custodians of the common good, the keepers of the lighthouse to guide to ship of state. Just how they rise from origins as modest as carpenters and bellows-menders, tinkers and tailors, furriers and fishers to mount the lighthouse has still to be explained.

[94] Quoted in S Holmes: *Benjamin Constant*, p 251.

12. From experience to competing conceptions to social understanding

The last matter to consider is how to integrate the two registers into a social understanding of constitutions. Each register contains a concept of constitutional authority. The upper gives the official version contained in texts, advocated in principle, affirmed in the courts, commended in commentaries. The lower offers an alternative that goes unnoticed because it has no place in the constitution, just as the people, the real people as opposed to an abstraction, historically had no place. Despite exclusion, the lower register appears to be the more authentic, the more fastened to experience, the more grounded in social relations, and in the interests, sentiments, and dispositions of the people universally shared. It has for these reasons a claim to be the true guide to constitutional authority. The trouble is the upper register makes the same claim, attaches itself to the welfare of the people, and asserts authenticity. Were the parliamentarians of the seventeenth and eighteenth centuries in claiming to embody the people, or Henry Ireton in asserting property as the foundation, supposing a constitutional order less authentic, less grounded in social relations than that implicit in the grievances of Jack Cade's rebels, or in the Levellers' search for a foundation more solid? The answer is no choice has to be made between them, the fracture is false. To see why, we return to the social theory of constitutions and the place and problem of power.

The theory is founded on the purpose common to human endeavour of advancing civility and humanity, into which power has to be inserted, the two faces on view, one a necessary means to purpose, the other a threat to well-being. Power once acquired is a valued resource for two reasons, one as a quality of worth, the other as an instrument to ends. As to the first, to have power is have a sphere of control over situations or persons, itself a source of satisfaction.[95] Enough to explain Macbeth's 'vaulting ambition' to be king, to possess the power of kingship, to let nothing even murder stand in the way.[96] Power is valued for another reason, as an instrument to exert control over social relations and to shape them to one's will. Consequences follow. The holder of power is able to favour some interests over others and to fashion social relations, conserving or creating some, repressing others. The power of rule becomes a commodity, an asset that serves the interests of persons and sectors in the quest for well-being, the intensity of the contest witness to the worth of the prize. The contest far from being orderly and genteel,

[95] To understand the sense of satisfaction power stimulates, we would need to enter into the depths of psychology, a venture beyond my purposes. The research is extensive; for instance D Keltner and DH Gruenfeld: 'Power, approach, and inhibition' (2003) 110 *Psychological Review* 265–84 is useful in identifying the effects on the psychology of the holder of power.

[96] W Shakespeare: *The Tragedy of Macbeth*, Act 1: 7: 27.

conducted calmly and according to settled rules, is fierce and ruthlessly fought, better represented in Machiavelli's image of discord than Lorenzetti's of concord. A constitutional order depends on a level of adjustment of each register to enable communal life to be conducted. Or more realistically for the plebs and the patricians to find a point of compromise, tolerable to each but uneasy and unstable, ever at risk of collapse, an excuse for the prince to assert authority, the Caesars to seize control. Somewhere between the two, between discord among the sectors, and collapse into the hands of the prince, concord can be fostered, strong enough to encourage talk of balance, moderation, and equilibrium, words suggesting more than is warranted.

The balance is unavoidably unstable, a fragile equilibrium, easily upset and easily broken. The contest is never over, the settled order of one era open to adjustment in the next, normally marginal and piecemeal, sometimes substantial, occasionally upheaval. The result of the contest, however it turns out, settles the structure of the social order by defining social relations and ranking interests. The structure once settled has to be justified to those who gain least, whose interests are lower down the order, all the way down to the feet, by appeal to concepts transcending social relations. The path to safety is to transcend the reality of power and the uneven distribution of benefits, to project an image of social wholeness, and to present the order as benefiting all. The people with least have to be persuaded to raise their gaze from the their own struggle to secure needs, their own limited capacity to improve the quality of life, the imbalance and unfairness in the pursuit of common purposes, and the resulting disparities of power, wealth, and status. They have to see the social order as it is structured, and accept it for the benefits it does provides. The power of the state to uphold the social order is at hand but not enough. The upper register enters the scene as an ally, to justify and secure the social order that comes out of the contest. The prince's power of enforcement contributes, but is not enough and needs in support the power of discourse. The two together have a long record of success. The upper register presents the social order in a manner aimed at cultivating suitable popular sentiments and dispositions.

The upper register is forced by its own logic to detach itself from the sentiments and dispositions constituting the lower register, and to promote amongst the people an alternative set of ideas, language and values. Where more gentle means of persuasion fail, the power of enforcement is at hand. The two modes of discourse share some common ground, but then take different directions, each proposing its own construction of shared purposes and how to attain them, each based on its own account of constitutional authority. In the struggle to structure social relations, the official discourse dominates, but is ever under pressure from the popular discourse to defend its position. Concessions have to be made to the people, ground conceded, social relations modified, enough to encourage restraint and to maintain a balance, a rough equilibrium between the rulers and supporting sectors, and the people, the ruled. Sometimes the established order becomes so detached from the people, so incapable of serving their needs and utilities, it is overturned and the great wheel of fortune begins to turn again on the same old axis.

Notes

People's sense of law, rights, and justice

Among the revelations from Susan Reynolds's study of English society in the tenth and eleventh centuries, several are especially noteworthy. The idea of parliament as a court rather than, or as much as, a law-making institution. No clear distinction was made between judging and legislating, since king and parliament were there to apply the law, the customs, and the conventions already settled. Courts themselves were assemblies convened to judge a matter according to law, custom, and convention. The practical application of law in this way fostered collective action, which in turn promoted norms, understandings, and expectations. A concern for both justice and consensus is 'plainly present in law suits': S Reynolds: *Kingdoms and Communities.*

Parallel ideas are examined by David Rollison in relation to deposing a king. The decision to depose is the result of an informed assessment based on standards embedded in the community: D Rollison: *A Commonwealth of the People.* John Watts depicts rule as sustaining the existing understandings and expectation: *Henry VI and Politics of Kingship.* The king rules and may rule only if sustained by the 'communal power of his satisfied subjects'. He writes: 'the king was the vehicle for a communal enterprise for the realization of communal interests': p 29. Kingship as a vehicle captures well the relationship between ruler and ruled. The ruler has no standing, no function other than as a *vehicle* to benefit the people, to act for their good. Communities harked back to Anglo-Saxon England where collective action, including kingship, was to sustain the existing order of social relations among freemen, not to impose on or alter it.

A subtle distinction appears between rule as ruling over, and rule as an order of social relations guiding its members towards the common good. Watts goes on to show how this notion of kingship came to be replaced by another, in which the king became an active ruler and went on the offensive against rebellious barons. Obedience to an active ruler replaces the old common weal. Montesquieu writes of a similar notion of a relationship prior to ruling. The king is delegated certain tasks by the people, the aim being to sustain the settled order of social relations: Baron Montesquieu: *The Spirit of the Laws.* See also: EP Thompson: 'The Moral Economy of the Crowd'—Evidence of the people's ideas of law, rights, and justice is gathered and analysed with deep insight by Mark Knights in a study of petitions and addresses in the sixteenth and seventeenth centuries. Both were a vehicle for the expression of popular opinion, from which emerges 'a common sense of the body of the people': p 79. Petitioning itself was defended from attack as 'the hereditary freedom of all subjects': M Knights: *Representation and Misrepresentation*, p 239.

While the people shared much common ground with the upper sectors of society, they had their own 'way of looking at politics', according to David Underdown. They often talked of the 'world-turned-upside-down' in reference to abuse of their rights, or the actions of state officials and greedy landlords: *Revel, Riot, and Rebellion* pp 50, 62. On the people's quest for constitutional ideas prior to the order in which they find themselves: pp 109–10. The people in local communities in opposing enclosure of common law often invoked a sense of fundamental law: described in: C Hill: *The World Turned Upside Down* (London: Penguin Books, 1972), p 55.

Accounts of rebellion

From a vast literature on rebellion, the following studies have proved to be especially useful:

A Wood:*Riot, Rebellion and Popular Politics in Early Modern England* (London: Palgrave, 2002) and *The 1549 Rebellions and the Making of Early Modern England* (Cambridge: Cambridge University Press, 2007).

P Zagorin:*Rebels and Rulers 1500–1660* (2 volumes) (Cambridge: Cambridge University Press, 1982).

D MacCulloch:'Kett's Rebellion in Context' (1979) 84 *Past & Present* 36.

Grievances within the settled order

The three cases cited in the text show how rebellion tends to begin by appealing to the constitutional order in place and pleading for rights and liberties to be respected, that the law be applied. Sometimes the matter ends with the restoration of rights and the correction of wrongs. Rebellions in France during the seventeenth century arose, incited by new taxes: 'Most of all did peasants felt the royal state's assault in its expanding financial requirements. *Tailles*, the ensemble of direct taxes, were the peasant impost par excellence, and indirect taxes of many kinds also depressed peasant livelihood': P Zagorin: *Rebels & Rulers 500–1660*, p 215.

The imposition of taxes and the methods of collection are among the common causes of rebellion. The burden of tax and the effects on the people, the middling sort and the poor, is exposed time and again. John Wildman, a Leveller, wrote: 'that unmerciful taxation of EXCISE . . . eateth the flesh and sucketh the blood of the poor and middling sort': *A call to all the soldiers of the Army* in Haller and Davies (eds) *Leveller Tracts*, p 159.

The running battle over enclosure of common land

'That constant concern of Tudor popular politics, the belief that the rich intended to starve the poor through a combination of the enclosure and high food prices': A Wood, *Riot Rebellion and Popular Politics in Early Modern England*, p 158.

Civic Equality

According to Keith Baker: 'Civic equality is the essence of every true political body'. However, the note of caution he then sounds does not seem to have been borne out in practice: '[civic equality] could not long survive the existence of great disparities of wealth and fortune among citizens': *Inventing the French Revolution*, p 134. On the contrary, civic equality continues as a foundation of constitutional orders, a foundation from which to judge rule. Wendy Brown finds an 'inherent sense of equality in constitutions': W Brown: *Undoing the Demos: Neoliberalism's Stealth Revolution* (New York: Zone Books, 2015), p 206. The distinction between *civic equality* and *substantive equality* is critical to understanding.

Evidence of the lower register

Andy Wood: 'In open confrontations with authority, plebeians were sometimes emboldened to imagine a different ordering to society': *Riot, Rebellion and Popular Politics in Early Modern England*, p 3. The lower register catches the sense and contains the elements of that different ordering.

David Rollison has contributed much to the understanding of what I designate the lower register: 'Concepts and capacities of the vulgar sort: the social history of English as language of politics' (2005) 2 *Cultural History* 141–64; more generally: *A Commonwealth of the People*. JC Scott's account of 'dominant ideologies' and 'the people's sense of justice' matches my distinction between an upper and a lower register: *Weapons of the Weak*.

Opinion: sentiments and dispositions

From a large literature on the opinion of the people across nations, the following are of much interest and add a comparative element:

A Gupta:'Blurred Boundaries: The Discourse of Corruption, the Culture of Politics, and the Imagined State' (1995) 22 *American Ethnologist* 375–402.

TE Kellogg:'Constitutionalism with Chinese Characteristics? Constitutional Development and Civil Litigation in China' (2009) 7 *International Journal of Constitutional Law* 215–46.

L Wedeen:*Peripheral Visions: Politics, Power, and Performance in Yemen* (Chicago and London: University of Chicago Press, 2008).

S Schielke:*Egypt in the Future Tense: Hope, Frustration, and Ambivalence Before and After 2011* (Bloomington: Indiana University Press, 2015).

On liberty

On meanings of liberty: F Braudel: *A History of Civilization*, p 291 and M Weber: *Law & Economy*, Volume I.

People use the law

Writing of the sixteenth century, Michael Braddick describes how the people made use of the law to air grievances and protect rights: 'the law as a whole was not the preserve of a particular social group . . . Legal authority was useful in all kinds of contexts': MJ Braddick: *State Formation in Early Modern England c.1550–1700* (Cambridge: Cambridge University Press, 2000), pp 155*ff*. Law is a resource and a tool 'that could be manipulated, even for those of fairly humble status': p 164.

On moderation

David Hume appeals to such notions as: the spirit of moderation; promotion of moderation rather than zeal; learn the lessons of moderation; modern education and customs instil more humanity and moderation: *Essays Moral Political and Literary*.

PART III
CONSTITUTIONAL FORMS

X

Princely Rule: I

1. Model of princely rule

The people enter a field designed for rule by the prince.[1] Some see the image of the fortress looming and prefer not to enter. A few, convinced of the merits, hold a favourable opinion and are ready to submit to the rigours of the regime. Most have in mind a constitutional field to cultivate, yet are willing to see what princely rule has to offer, and if nothing more, learn what to avoid. Several features arouse their curiosity. Wherever you look, rule by one seems to be the case, the normal form across history and nations. The title *princely*, taken from centuries of monarchy, fits the republic of Cromwell in England, the rule of the Medici in Florence, and many past and present rulers. The people notice a pattern of other forms of rule emerging, full of promise, but soon sinking back to the protection of a prince. The early Italian city-states, after replacing princely rule with a form of self-rule, flourished briefly, before returning to their origins, just one case in a common course of history. The pattern of opinion supporting princely rule, and the persistence, are enough to arouse interest, to see the merits and the defects.

My purpose now is to analyse princely rule as a form of constitutional authority. From among the plenitude of princes prominent in early modern Europe, Henry VII the first of the Tudors is an exemplary case. Falling between the saintly but weak Henry VI and the ruthless but decisive Henry VIII, Henry Tudor VII displays in classic form the qualities of the prince and the appeal of princely rule, the tensions within it, and the instabilities at the core. The analysis begins with a model and then looks more closely at the main features, using the rule of Henry VII as a case study. Then follows enquiry into the social foundations to find the conditions conducive to and sustaining princely rule, and to show the instabilities. The model of princely rule has the following features.

First The prince has plenary power to rule, to coordinate the social, political, and economic orders.

Second The purpose of rule is to protect and advance the common good as judged by the prince.

[1] I refer to princely rule as the rule of one person but it could be the rule of several. A small group ruling in concert matches the model of princely rule, although even there, one tends to dominate.

Keepers of the Common Good. D.J. Galligan, Oxford University Press. © D.J. Galligan 2024.
DOI: 10.1093/9780198907398.003.0010

Third Investing plenary power in one person is justified for providing firm and effective rule. Other supporting reasons are likely to be added, ranging from the will of god to the order of nature.

Fourth The prince is not a tyrant, his rule strong but bridled, his power plenary but bounded.

Fifth The relationship between prince and people is structured by the rights and duties of each party, by law and convention, by understandings and expectations.

Sixth In order to rule well, to use power for purpose, the prince has to acquire virtue and cultivate personal qualities.

Seventh Power is channelled and constrained through settled processes: taking counsel, obtaining consent, respecting the law.

Eighth Rule is conducted with the aid of a core of officials whose first loyalty is to the prince and first duty to do his will, around which other agencies perform the administrative and judicial functions of governing.

Ninth The prince relies on the support of the select sectors of society whose interests are best served by his rule.[2]

Tenth The people are expected to obey the dictates of the prince and the decisions of officials; their engagement in the processes of governing is marginal, a fuller role not needed because the prince knows the common good and strives to achieve it for the benefit of all. The lower local levels of administration offer some scope for the people's being involved.[3]

Eleventh The people are encouraged to have positive sentiments and dispositions towards princely rule; to accept it as founded on good reasons and sound values, and worthy of their support, not just acquiescence and obedience.

Twelfth The prince promotes rule by wrapping power in appealing ideas, language, and concepts. Partly from practical necessity, partly to cultivate positive sentiments and dispositions in the people, the prince projects the image of a caring parent, the father or mother of the nation, firm but affectionate.

Thirteenth The prince is diligent in enabling the people to make complaints and air grievances through the courts and other institutions.

Fourteenth The prince expects in return displays of loyalty, declarations of affection, and boundless gratitude, while forbearing from voicing criticism. The people know little about the workings of government, have few avenues of scrutiny, and practically no means of censure.

[2] For a study of what happens when the sector that benefits most from princely rule becomes dissatisfied; a case study of the against and downfall of Charles I: JSA Adamson: *The Noble Revolt: The Overthrow of Charles* I (London: Orion, 2007).

[3] The very idea of the people as *subjects* rather than *citizens* signals the nature of the relationship.

The model of princely rule, while coherent and to some convincing, in practice confronts obstacles and easily falls short. The level of effectiveness rises and falls; the instabilities take a toll. The concentration of power and weak constraints are a temptation, not only to appetite but to incompetence and misrule. Surrounded with loyal counsellors, the prince can be isolated from a broader base of advice and opinion. The routine affairs of governing are left to agencies, which incline towards autonomy and independence. The people's disposition of support varies from a peak of enthusiasm to a base of passive obedience. Rarely content to be mere inmates of the fortress, they strive to improve their position and to have some influence on princely action; to open avenues of vigilance, even dare to hint at censure. Instability is inherent, founded on stresses and strains that over time tend to grow and to weaken even destroy princely rule. With this sketch in mind, let us examine the main features, drawing on the reign of Henry VII as princely rule in practice, then uncover the social foundations and expose the instabilities.

2. The common good of princely rule

The purpose of princely power is to preserve the common good. The two go together; princely power is needed for the common good, the securing of which justifies princely rule.[4] The logic is plain: the common good is for the benefit of all its members; to secure which strong rule is needed; the prince knows the common good and has the power to secure it. Since all benefit, all have an interest in supporting the prince's rule, because in the words of Polonius 'on his choice depends/ The sanity and health of the whole state'.[5] In constitutional orders of princely rule, whether ancient, medieval, or modern, the common good acquires meaning, settled enough to be a unifying goal, open enough to allow the prince discretion as to what counts and how to achieve it. That is a defining feature of princely rule: the authority of the prince is limited to acting for the common good; yet it is the prince who decides the common good and the means to reach it. In the early-modern monarchies of Europe the common good, or *common weal* or *wele*,[6] meant defending the realm from outside interference, maintaining order and security within, and protecting the rights of subjects as settled by law and custom.[7]

[4] Note the discussion in Chapter VI herein. For an account of the contemporary common good: A Etzioni: *The Common Good* (Cambridge: Polity Press, 2004). For the classical approach: Cicero: *De Officiis* discussed in Q Skinner: *Visions of Politics* II (Cambridge: Cambridge University Press, 2002), p 25.

[5] W Shakespeare: *The Tragedy of Hamlet*, Act I: 3: 19.

[6] *Commonweal*, later *Commonwealth*, comes from common profit; *commons* or *commonalty* means those who work and are not included in the governing ranks. See further: D Rollison: *A Commonwealth of the People: Popular Politics and England's Long Social Revolution, 1066–1649* (Cambridge: Cambridge University Press, 2010).

[7] See further: JH Strayer: *On the Medieval Origins of the Modern State* (Princeton: Princeton University Press, 1970), especially pp 32 *ff.*

The prince is bound and guided by the common good at the two levels of ruling, one in matters of high policy and making law, the other in applying law, adjudicating disputes, and administering policies. The second is easily undervalued, although in the administration and adjudication of rights and duties, subjects encounter and rely most directly on princely authority. The doing of justice in applying the law, and thereby respecting rights, is an essential part of the common good. Justice here is restorative, being given what is due according to the laws, policies, and conventions. In *Buon Governo,* where the figure of justice oversees the ruling of Siena, restorative justice is depicted as the cement of society.[8] Complaints and grievances, discontent and disaffection, or worse, result from neglect of the common good by unjust or oppressive treatment of subjects, not respecting their rights and liberties, not providing remedies to protect them. The wise prince attends diligently to the administration of justice.

Princely rule has two more qualities of note. One is belief in the objectivity of the common good in sustaining a social order, in which the status of each person, the rights and duties of all are settled. No need for a political arena to work out the common good for it is known and taken for granted. A simple notion around which a cloak of ideas and images is woven to make it appealing to all. The concept of the body politic fits well, each sector an organ, each organ fixed in its place and assigned a function, all working together for the good health of the body. That the people should have a place in ruling is as unthinkable as the feet becoming or directing the head. Remember Hamlet's being appalled at the very idea of 'the toe of the peasant' coming near even 'the heel of the courtier'.[9] This leads to the other feature, how the cloak is woven and an image created; how the social order in all its forms is constructed and presented. The upper register enters the scene to render the social order an organic whole, a body born of consensus and sustained by 'satisfied subjects'.[10] Harmony is the sovereign virtue, the sign of good health, disharmony the vice vilified and to be avoided. Harmony breeds stability and unity. The prince as the head guides each organ, each sector of society, to form a whole. The discourse and the imagery are critical to princely rule. The head is the most vital organ yet stands aloof ready to act for the good of the whole.[11] Constitutional authority is integral to, a necessary feature of, the well-functioning body. Authority is not external to the body politic or imposed upon it, for between people and prince there is no division or separation; conceptually they are united in the whole, relations between them defined. John of Salisbury in the twelfth century wrote of the 'corporate community of the realm', a concept further illuminated by Susan

[8] Discussed by Quentin Skinner in *Visions of Politics* II, pp 24 ff.

[9] *The Tragedy of Hamlet*: Act 5: 1: 136.

[10] J Watts: *Henry VI and the Politics of Kingship* (Cambridge: Cambridge University Press: 1996), p29. On communities in medieval England: S Reynolds: *Kingdoms and Communities*.

[11] For further discussion of the relationship between prince and people, see J Watts: *Henry VI and the Politics of Kingship*, Chapter 2.

Reynolds in the twentieth.[12] Where there is a body, issues of health arise. The good health of the body depends on the head, the qualities and judgement, the virtue of the prince.[13] When the body politic suffers ill-health, as Florence under the Medici[14] or England under Charles I, the head knows how to restore good health. If disease strikes the head itself, it must be removed and replaced by another.[15]

Rule acquires a special meaning, less imposed power, more the rule of a guild or a religious order, any coming together for a common purpose.[16] All know the *rule* which is more than a bundle of rules; includes aims and aspirations, expectations and understandings among the members and between them and the prince. All are committed to the rule in regulating daily life, the prince on duty to see it respected. Authority is implicit, constituting and expressing relations between prince and people, between the head and the rest of the body. That 'the king was the vehicle for a communal enterprise for the realization of communal interests' puts the point precisely. John Watts, in his supreme account of kingship, goes on: 'The royal dignity and majesty were primarily sustained—by the communal power of his satisfied subjects'.[17] The prince must enforce rule, but is more than an enforcer and embodies the whole: the order, the rule, the realm. Such sublimation verging on the mystical is the foundation of princely authority, not only historically but in modern versions. The prince's actions are the actions of the realm and beyond reproach. *Representation* here has its origins. In embodying the realm, the prince represents the body politic, has authority to speak on its behalf, an authority only he has and to the use of which there can be no challenge.[18]

Princely rule encased in the community of the realm, the well-formed body politic, appealing to ideas of harmony and wholeness, order and peace spontaneously occurring, is hard to contest, the imagery of such appeal one strains not to conclude that princely rule is the perfect form of rule. The ends of government are achieved, the people are satisfied subjects who, under the eye of the prince, in peace and security attend to their lives. The prince for his part takes pride in the fruits of his virtue. To such a radiant image there is a dark side. One sign is the

[12] John of Salisbury: *Polycraticus* (ed) CJ Nederman (Cambridge: Cambridge University Press, 1990). On the community of the realm and princely rule, see S Reynolds: *Kingdoms and Communities*, Chapter 8.

[13] James I went beyond being head of the body politic by likening himself to a god 'for that they [kings] exercise a manner or resemblance of divine power upon earth': *Speech to Parliament*, 21 March 1610 in JP Kenyon (ed): *The Stuart Constitution*, p 10. See further J Fortescue: *On the Laws and Governance of England* (ed) S Lockwood (Cambridge: Cambridge University Press, 1997), pp 86 *ff.*

[14] Florence by the fifteenth century was said to be an old body and so harder to cure: F Guicciadini: *Discorso di Logrogno* (cited in JGA Pocock: *The Machiavellian Moment* (London and Princeton: Princeton University Press, 1975), pp 121 *ff.*

[15] The body politic is described more fully in Chapter VII.

[16] Anglo-Saxon, pre-Norman England, catches the sense of rule within it. See O Hulme: *An Historical Essay on the English Constitution* (London: Edward & Charles Dilly in the Poultry, 1771).

[17] J Watts: *Henry VI and the Politics of Kingship*, p 29.

[18] On representation, see DJ Galligan: 'The People, the Constitution, and the Idea of Representation' in *Social and Political Foundations of Constitutions* (eds) DJ Galligan & M Versteeg, p 134.

coercive nature of princely rule, a harsh regime of enforcement, the reality behind the kindly mask of Duke Theseus.[19] Rule must be upheld at any cost. But why in a society of satisfied subjects is fear so high and sanctions so severe? The answer is found by descending from abstraction to practice, from an ideal of social relations to the reality. A social order divided by inequality of status, well-being, and power; where discord festers; where interests compete in the tug-and scramble, and oppression is rife; where justice is unevenly administered, obedience demanded and dissent forbidden. A social order in which the prince and loyal supporters impose a select concept of the common good; where power is used to sustain a system geared to the power, glory, and enriching of a few.

3. Rule strong but limited

To sustain the social order and so ensure the common good, strong rule is needed, which the prince is capable of supplying. Without strong rule, the realm is unable to defend itself from outside threats, while internally society becomes divided over interests, riven by faction, and riddled with conflict. Even worse, the absence of strong rule opens the way to 'levelling',[20] the rise of the lower orders against their superiors and the seizure of estates. Levelling is destructive because property is, as Henry Ireton declared at Putney, the foundation of the constitutional order, the symbol of the common good. Strong rule means effective rule, partly due to the prince's freedom to act, partly because constraints from the agencies of government are weak, while agreement of the people is not needed.[21] The prince is spared the burden of having to satisfy arduous processes before acting. Compared to other forms of authority, self-rule and representative rule in particular, the prince has enviable freedom of action.[22] It comes at a price, for the very freedom from constraints places a heavy burden on the prince's judgement and raises the risk of instabilities.

Strong rule is not absolute or unlimited rule. A contrast is made between the just and virtuous prince, and the unjust and wicked tyrant.[23] Occasional acts of

[19] See Chapter VII.1.

[20] 'Levelling' came into usage in the seventeenth century, at first referring to the levelling of hedges enclosing what had been common land, later used more generally to refer to the threat from movements urging more say for the common people. See further: *Homily on Obedience* quoted in DE Underdown: *Revel, Riot, and Rebellion*, p 13.

[21] There may be some exceptions especially in matters of taxation; see M Clark: *Medieval Representation and Consent.* Discussed in Chapter VIII.

[22] Cardinal Richelieu argued for princely rule on the ground that it avoids 'the bristles and thorns of corporate bodies which create difficulties on every matter'. See Montesquieu: *The Spirit of the Laws*, quoted in MM Mosher: 'Monarchy's Paradox' in *Montesquieu's Science of Politics*, p 178.

[23] John of Salisbury's distinction between prince and tyrant is to the point: 'As the philosophers have portrayed him, the tyrant is, therefore, one who oppresses the people by violent domination, just as the prince is one who rules by the laws': *Polycraticus*, p 190.

injustice and oppression are unavoidable in any system of government, even that of the just prince. The difference is the just prince makes provision for remedies and redress, while for the despot it is a matter of indifference. The line clear in theory in practice is easily crossed, the good prince ever at risk of drifting across to despotism. The prince who lacks self-restraint, who loses the will to resist appetite, breaks the bonds of authority and may be deposed.[24] The common good falls from sight, replaced by the prince's ambition, greed, or lust for power, or under duress from the sectors on whose support he relies. [25] Despotism suggests unlimited and unrestrained power, the negation of constitutional authority, which is by nature limited, the limits set by the duty to act for the common good. The distinction between prince and despot, while sound in principle, is not easily kept in practice.[26] Princely rule occurs in a setting of understandings and expectations, principles and conventions, all helping to structure the discretionary space and mediate relations with the people.[27] How much influence in practice such standards have over the prince is a different issue, a practical matter that varies from one princely order to another. In the very concept there is ambiguity. It may describe a form of rule distinct from despotism; or it may mean that within the model the prince has room to use power in a despotic manner. Princely authority is limited in purpose and scope; yet the freedom essential to princely rule restricts the means for enforcing the limits. The agencies of government are to serve the prince not restrain him, the duty of the people to obey the prince not question him. The breach between limits on power, and the lack of means to enforce them, is one of the fault lines and an instability of princely rule.[28]

4. Qualities of princely rule

To rule for the common good, the prince needs power of a discretionary kind and plenty of it, enough to be able to act as he deems necessary. The question then is how the people can be confident power is used for the common good. One risk is that the prince simply be incapable of ruling well; another that power be used for purposes other than the common good; a third that it be used to oppress the people. The more power in the prince, the more effective he can be, while raising

[24] Discussed in AP Monahan: *Consent, Coercion and Limit.*

[25] Thomas Aquinas identified the conditions under which the people are justified in deposing the prince: T Aquinas: *De Regimine Principum* in *Politica Opuscula* (ed) J Mathias (Turin: Marietti, 1948); for commentary, see AP Monahan: *Consent, Coercion, and Limit*, pp 159*ff.*

[26] Machiavelli for broadly similar reasons found no real difference between the prince and the tyrant. Note the account of E Benner: *Machiavelli's Prince: A New Reading* (Oxford: Oxford University Press, 2013).

[27] A distinction needs to be kept in mind between the absence of limits on princely rule, and whether processes are in place to enforce them. A critical feature of princely rule is that it has the first but lacks the second.

[28] James I understood the distinction and thought it a critical feature of princely rule: see *Notes.*

the risk of misuse. Add the tendency of power to expand and increase, the tension between the dynamic of power and the restraint of purpose becomes acute. Attempts at constraint are resented as an unwanted fetter on power and an obstacle to achieving purpose. The solution in other forms of rule takes two main forms, one to encircle the ruler with institutions and processes guiding and constraining power, the other enabling the people to engage in the processes, be vigilant, and have means of censure. The princely model frowns on, even forbids both, relying instead on the prince restraining himself, for which history offered help, that the prince acquire virtue, take counsel, obtain consent, and rule through law.[29]

If virtue be needed to rule well, the issue then is what it means and how it is acquired. Handbooks offered guidance, although much was left unclear, in particular how it contributes to ruling.[30] The classic virtues portrayed in *Buon Governo* include prudence and temperance, clemency, fortitude, and magnanimity, and above all justice. In order to rule well, the virtues somehow have to unite with steely resolve.[31] Henry VI apparently had the virtues in abundance, but so lacked firmness and decisiveness, the queen suggested his being more suited to the throne of St Peter than to be King of England and much of France.[32] According to Richard of York, biding his time, Henry VI's 'bookish rule hath pulled fair England down'.[33] Once the crown was his, Richard displayed the opposite: iron resolve and lethal action, but for the pursuit of his own ends not the common good. Somewhere between saintliness and tyranny lies the true path of princely rule, a path poorly marked.[34] It is enough to be reminded that there is no secret to uncover, no alchemy of virtues for ruling well. Indeed the very use of *virtue* is out of place in relation to rule. Virtue has its origins in the life of the soul: if one leads a life of virtue, one will attain salvation. The same logic has crept into constitutional discourse: if the prince has certain qualities, sound rule results. The sequence is flawed, form has replaced substance. Sound rule is not the logical outcome of certain qualities. It is instead a rough and imperfect process aimed at meeting the needs and utilities of a people, diverse and divided, enough to earn their support. A commitment to purpose, seasoned by prudence, justice, and beneficence is a sound foundation for

[29] On the purpose of such constraints, see S Holmes: *Benjamin Constant and the Making of Modern Liberalism* (London and Yale: Yale University Press, 1984), pp 188–9.

[30] For Montesquieu, virtue in ruling amounts to 'love of the laws and of the country' from which good government follows: *Spirit of the Laws*, Book IV, Chapter 5.

[31] On kingship and virtue, see J Watts: *Henry VI and the Politics of Kingship*, Chapter 2. In *Macbeth* the conversation between Malcolm and Macduff is instructive. After describing vividly the vices of kingship, Malcolm lists numerous virtues: *The Tragedy of Macbeth*, Act 4: 3: see *Notes*.

[32] As imagined by Shakespeare: *The Second Part of the Contention, Henry VI Part I*. Queen Margaret or Shakespeare, or both, had a rosy view of the throne of St Peter, whose occupants were secular rulers as well as religious, and as ruthless.

[33] *Ibid*, Act 1: 1: 258.

[34] See further: IF Spitz: 'From Civism to Civility: D'Holbach's Critique of Republican Virtue' in *Republicanism: A Shared European Heritage* (eds) M von Gelderin and Q Skinner (Cambridge: Cambridge University Press, 2002), pp 19, 107–22.

rule of any kind. On that foundation, the capacity to accommodate, compromise, and conciliate, to be flexible and pragmatic, sometimes ruthless, may count for more than being virtuous.

To rule with counsel is both an aid and a hindrance, a source of information as to opinion and a constraint on action. When Henry VI was a child, 'this land was famously enriched/With politic, grave counsel', remarks a citizen.[35] The English barons, the chief men of the realm whose power and wealth would match the king's, were not to be ignored. The circle of counsel spread from barons to lesser nobility, prominent among them the knights who could speak for the shires.[36] Although the upper register scorned the idea of the common people having an opinion, let alone one worth listening to, the shrewd prince knew better, had seen how the commons aroused can be 'like an angry hive of bees,/That want their leader, scatter up and down/And care not who they sting'.[37] Without knowing and taking account of opinion, not only of the grandees but the commoners, princely rule is precarious. The effects of taking counsel are easily overstated. Whose opinion the prince hears, whose advice he listens to, and how much notice to take are matters in his discretion. Having taken counsel, the prince decides on action. The prince in practice under pressure narrows the range of both counsel and opinion, insulates himself from the outside world, and relies on a few select advisers, opening a ground of instability in the process. Counsel leads on to consent, another element of princely rule. On some matters, taxation especially, taking counsel evolved into obtaining consent. The consent of the people, not directly but through those who spoke on their behalf, who in a rudimentary sense represented them.[38] Counsel and consent became a standard feature of princely rule, the foundation of the idea of the king ruling through parliament, and eventually the shift of power from king and peers to the Commons, from princely rule to representative rule. Taking counsel is not the same as ruling with counsel, as if taking counsel were a form of collective rule, an early form of parliamentary rule. The same caution extends to consent, whose 'figurative metaphorical' and flighty Ariel-like nature we have seen.[39] Two factors cancel the power of consent. First, consent normally is given not by the people but by representatives; and secondly, consent may be required as a formality and given as a matter of duty. Consent stands high in the discourse of princely rule but low in practical effect.

[35] W Shakespeare: *The Tragedy of King Richard III*, Act 2: 3: 19.

[36] On the formation of parliament, see JR Maddicott: *The Origins of the English Parliament 924–1327* (Oxford: Oxford University Press, 2010).

[37] *The Tragedy of King Richard III*, Act 3: 2: 125.

[38] On consent in medieval England, see MV Clarke: *Medieval Representation and Consent*.

[39] See Chapter VI. For an account of pre-modern princely order, the administration and the executive as 'the creation and instrument of the monarchy', see SB Chrimes: *An Introduction to the Administrative History of Medieval England* (Oxford: Basil Blackwell, 1959).

5. Princely rule and the agencies of administration

The prince in order to rule needs the support not only of the people but of officials.[40] In a society of simple social relations, a tight band of officials is enough for the prince to rule well. As societies grow and social relations become more complex, the need for a system of agencies and processes is hard to contain. The risk for the prince is that power shift into the hands of those who have practical experience and acquire specialized knowledge.[41] Bureaucratic institutions have their own logic and structure, an internal dynamic driven by a rationality based on rules, routine, and regimented management,[42] all encouraging autonomy and independence.[43] Several factors contribute: reliance on settled rules, the allocation of defined tasks, the system of hierarchy, and the acquisition of expert knowledge. The more developed these factors, the more effective the agencies are in their functions, while the more detached they become, the harder they are for the prince to control. The added risk is that administrative and judicial institutions become confident enough to view the ruling order with detachment, even to be a source of criticism. Decisions of high policy may be questioned, the wisdom of executive action doubted. Oversight by the courts, the upholding of limits on princely authority, is bound to be contentious no matter how strong the case or clear the law. In other forms of rule, the diffusion of power, the mutual influence among agencies, and insistence that rule be according to law, are thought to contribute to good government. In princely rule they have a minor place, the strategy instead being to retard their expansion, while reminding the judges of their duty to support the prince, not oppose or question him.

A subservient system of administration and courts has consequences. First, tension mounts between professional administration and satisfying the wishes of the prince. Secondly, the guidance administrative agencies could give the prince, drawing on knowledge and experience, is denied or compromised. Thirdly, being subservient to the prince precludes scrutiny and potential censure of his actions. Finally, the people experience rule most directly in the processes of administrative and judicial agencies. They may take an interest in the large issues, but the pressing interest is how they are treated when rights and liberties are at stake. This we have seen to be an empirical truth of seemingly universal application. However few the people's rights and liberties, that they be respected ranks high in their sentiments and dispositions. A truth not lost on despots and tyrants as well as wise princes.

[40] For further analysis, see M Weber, *The Profession and Vocation of Politics* in *Political Writings* (eds) P Laslett and R Spiers.

[41] For a most useful study, see SB Chrimes: *An Introduction to the Administrative History of Medieval England.*

[42] Max Weber dealt with the issue at length: M Weber: *Economy and Society*, Chapter 11.

[43] An issue examined in DJ Galligan: 'Authoritarianism in Government and Administration' [2001] *Current Legal Problems* 86–105.

In sixteenth-century England, courts were plentiful, much of their time spent hearing suits from the common people.[44] Star Chamber, although controversial, was 'a popular resource' with just under half all plaintiffs, not gentlemen, but yeomen and women, husbandmen and labourers. The Court of Requests was established to provide justice for the poor.[45] Mention of courts leads to Henry VII for whom courts, abudnant and accessible, were central to the constitutional order.

6. Princely rule of Henry VII

Henry VII reigned from 1485 to 1509. His son Henry VIII and granddaughter Elizabeth I are better known, while James VII of Scotland, who succeeded Elizabeth to the English throne as James I, prided himself on being the paragon of the prince. Nevertheless, the reign of Henry VII presents princely rule in classic form.[46] Unsure of his claim to the throne, unschooled in the art of governing, encircled by rivals and enemies, he ruled effectively, tried to maintain the dignity of office and the institutions guiding and moderating his rule, although he finally succumbed to a version of personal rule more common in France than in England.[47] On the positive side, Henry ended a long civil war, restored peace to England, and imposed order. Rule consisted in exerting his will on the nation and its people, and deploying the agencies of state to enforce it. Princely power was presented as justified authority, showing respect for institutional constraints and customary understandings. Henry secured the common good by defending the nation from without and maintaining order within. He saw himself as the wise and just prince governing through law and respecting the rights of his subjects, taking counsel, and on some matters seeking the consent of parliament.

The dark side is just as plain. Limits on authority were overlooked or forgotten, the barriers to absolute power broken, the potential to enrich king and courtiers all too tempting. Rivals were removed, critics silenced. The king ruled with a circle of officials charged with giving effect to his will, whose loyalty and

[44] For further analysis, see S Hindle: *The State and Social Change in Early Modern England, 1550–1640* (Basingstoke: Palgrave, 2002), Chapter 3.

[45] On the Court of Requests, see JEA Joliffe: *The Constitutional History of Medieval England from the English Settlement to 1485* (London: Adam and Chares Black, 1961). For further discussion, see DJ Galligan: 'Ally or Enemy: Friend or Foe' in *The Courts and the People: Friend or Foe?* (ed) DJ Galligan (Oxford: Hart Bloomsbury, 2021), pp 233–40.

[46] In Shakespeare's hands, Queen Katherine remembers her late father-in-law, King Henry VII: 'was reputed for/A prince most prudent, of an excellent/And unmatch'd wit and judgement': in W Shakespeare: *All Is True (Henry VIII)*, Act II: IV: 43. This would have been a minority view.

[47] A distinction made by John Fortescue, the one *regale*, the other *regale e politicum*: the first the French form of princely rule, the second the English: J Fortescue: *On the Laws and Governance of England*. For analysis, see MRLL Kelly: *Sir John Fortescue* in *Constitutions and the Classics: Patterns of Constitutional Thought from Fortescue to Bentham* (ed) DJ Galligan (Oxford: Oxford University Press, 2014). There is a suggestion that Henry himself privately identified more with the French version than the English.

obedience were absolute, the slightest lapse earning dismissal and ruin. The institutional constraints proved to be weak and incapable of restraining the prince's power. Parliament was compliant, the courts were the king's courts, the judges his counsellors. And finally relations between the king and his subjects, based on trust and confidence in the king as protector, mediated by law and custom, were eroded by mistrust and tainted by fear. As the reign progressed, the king and his officials were corrupted, power used for personal enrichment, critics punished on flimsy grounds. The common good as the justification of authority became a hollow shell, its content replaced by the personal ends and ambitions of king and officials. The machinery of administration became a tool of repression, a screen to hide abuse of subjects and misuse of power. The mutual restraint between prince and people, once allowed by the prince to lapse, weakened the reason for popular restraint. Justified authority was replaced by raw power; justice according to law gave way to 'extraordinary justice' where discretion was absolute.[48] All neatly captured in the king's own claim that his authority was designed to allow him to keep his subjects 'in danger at his pleasure'.[49]

7. Constitutional order of Henry VII

The rule of Henry VII reveals both the appeal and the precarious nature of princely rule. Let us now consider how the social and political order was given a constitutional foundation. The Coronation Oath, sworn by the king in 1485,[50] serves to confirm the appointment and to confer authority. The king holds the crown 'by the whole assent of all the Lords both Spiritual and Temporal, and of all the Commons of this Land'. Being 'elect, chosen, and required', the king swears he 'will grant and keep to the people of England the laws and customs to them as old rightful and devout kings granted, and the same ratified, and confirmed by you'. The laws and customs empower the king and define relations with the people. Parliament confirmed the kingship of 'our now sovereign Lord King Henry VII' and stated that the king governs for 'the wealth, prosperity, and surety of this realm of England, to the singular comfort of all the king's subjects'.[51]

The body politic is 'compact and compounded of many and almost infinite several and yet well agreeing members'. The king its head 'is instituted and furnished

[48] 'Extraordinary justice' so described by Edmund Dudley, one of the two officials closest to the king and responsible for implementing extraordinary justice: Edmund Dudley: *Tree of Commonwealth* (1509), quoted in T Penn: *Winter King: Henry VII and the Dawn of Tudor England* (London: Simon and Shuster, 2013), p 170.

[49] T Penn: *Winter King*, p 146.

[50] The Coronation Oath is not itself regarded as the constitution, but rather as stating principles established as constitutional.

[51] An Act for the Confirmation of Henry VII (1485) reprinted in GR Elton: *The Tudor Constitution: Documents and Commentary* (Cambridge: Cambridge University Press, 1960).

with plenary and entire power, prerogative and jurisdiction to render justice and right to every part and member of this body'. Authority expressed as 'plenary and entire' barely falls short of, sits perilously close to being absolute. There are meant to be limits. The essence of kingship is to render justice, which he does through the mouth of the judges who apply the 'laws of England'. The contours of authority are cast: the king has plenary power to be used for the common good, according to and subject to the law. Ruling according to law defines the limits of princely rule. It also defines the relationship between king and people, for their rights derive from and depend on the law, enforcement on the king. The king who rules within the law expects in return not bare acquiescence but positive support.

Restraints on the king by other institutions of government were limited in form and weak in practice. Statutes were enacted by the king and the two houses of parliament, lords, and commons. The consent of both to legislation was needed, presumed, and given. Parliament sat when summoned by the king, which Henry VII did seven times during twenty-four years of reign, sittings occupying just twenty-five weeks, averaging one week a year.[52] Most of parliament's business was initiated by the king, many of its members were his counsellors. Debate could be informed and constructive, provided the king's proposals were commended and supported. The mildest criticism was frowned upon, anything robust a ticket to the Tower. Statutes were accepted by the common law courts as the highest form of law, prevailing over the common law. The idea that statutes were subject to more fundamental principles, whether deriving from common law or natural law, lingered in the minds of judges and lawyers into the next century, before finally giving way to the ascending notion of the sovereignty of the king-in-parliament.

The jurisdiction of the courts to curb executive action and hold it to legal principles, a power later to become critical to a constitutional order, had not yet emerged. The common law courts not only dispensed justice in the name of the king, they were his courts in practice as well as name. The judges were appointed by the king and dismissed at his pleasure. Some served in his Council, some occupied high offices of state. Whatever independence of judgement they were able to assert in disputes between subjects did not apply where the will or interest of the king was in issue. Other courts, created or revived by Henry VII, were a central feature of princely rule, especially the Star Chamber, but also the Court of Requests, the conciliar courts in Wales and northern England, even the ecclesiastical courts. In principle bound by common and statutory law, the courts bowed to the king's wishes stated in proclamations or otherwise. The courts in general, the conciliar courts in particular, tended to combine law, equity, and the king's will. The rule of law had not yet gained either the meaning or status it came to have in later constitutional discourse. The purpose of courts and court-like bodies in Henry

[52] The details are supplied in Elton: *The Tudor Constitution*, p 228.

VII's time had two parts, one to do the king's will, the other to provide justice, including justice for the common people. The king's will consisted in more than strictly applying the law; it meant combining law, equity, and his expressly stated or implicitly understood wishes. In the same way the people's sense of justice was not limited to application of the common law or statute, but occurred within a deeper set of ideas, values, and understandings, the signs of a lower register of discourse. Complaints and grievances were likely to be couched in legal doctrine, not as an end but an entry to a sphere of deeper expectations and understandings, the meeting and honouring of which was the measure of justice. The king's judges and counsellors in administering justice tried to combine the two, the law as stated and the deeper sphere, while always respecting and applying the wishes of the king.

8. Power of the prerogative

The constitutional foundations of Henry VII's kingship are common to other cases of princely rule. Beneath the calm and simple surface hide a multitude of legal and practical issues. One was the scope of the king's plenary power, the prerogative power as it came to be known, the power to fill the discretionary space. The prerogative empowered the king to decide such matters as war, foreign affairs, and the coin of the realm. It entitled him to quell civil disorder, to dispense with the law on grounds of equity, in certain cases to punish for actions deemed contrary to the good of the realm even in the absence of law. The administration of justice, central to the prerogative, included the appointment and dismissal of judges and higher officials, the creation of new courts and court-like bodies, the setting and imposing of penalties.[53] Some powers were clear and certain, others vague and unsettled. The residual sense of prerogative, defying precise definition or limitation, was justified on the ground that such power, being the ultimate instrument of government, must be fit for the task. Too fixed or exact a definition would obstruct good government and restrict the king's ability to deal with matters unforeseen and unexpected. The prince as head of the body politic was responsible for the whole and all its parts, for which firm and decisive rule was the means, free from doubting voices and distracting procedures. To discharge such responsibility, prerogative power was the means.

This leads to the constitutional status of the prerogative, the power of the prince to take whatever measures contribute, in his judgement, to good government. How does such plenary power satisfy the principle that the king rules within the law? To unravel the subtleties of English law of the period, intriguing though it be, would take us beyond present purposes, for which it is enough to note a few points of

[53] Thomas Smith: *On the King's Prerogatives*, quoted in Elton: *The Tudor Constitution*, p 19.

interest for princely rule. The main idea is that prerogative power is authorized by law, normally by common law but sometimes by statute. A sixteenth-century commentator wrote of the prerogative: the king 'had his by the order of the common law'.[54] A distinction is made between the legal basis of prerogative power, and how it is used. A prerogative power to be legitimate had to be traceable to some common law principle or statutory provision. The common law origins of some prerogatives are well-founded, others are less known, buried in antiquity, perhaps forgotten but never forfeit. Henry VII, ever alert to ways of boosting his revenues, searched the records to recover ancient prerogatives long forgotten, from which his coffers would benefit and he be rewarded. [55] Once the legal basis be settled, use of the prerogative is at the king's discretion, although restricted in two main ways. The common law rights of subjects were immune from interference, and the prerogative was subordinate to statute. The Act of Proclamations later confirmed the common law doctrine of immunity for a list of rights, liberties, and privileges. The reality was more complex. Some prerogatives by their very nature require restriction or removal of the rights of subjects, as in declaring war, quelling civil disorder, or taking preventive action against serious crime.[56] This was not an end of the matter. Relations between prerogative power and the private rights continued to incite controversy.

Laws made by the king and the two houses of parliament could not be changed by prerogative, and in case of conflict, statute prevailed. This was less a restriction on princely power than appearance suggests. We are now accustomed to an abundance of statutory law on a wide range of subjects; but things were different in the fifteenth and sixteenth centuries. On the one hand law meant principally the common law, occasionally added to or modified by statute; on the other hand there was less law. The contrast with contemporary societies where few social relations escape legal attention, is striking. The scope of law was narrower, social relations less regulated, and parliament was the king's parliament. The king decided when to call it, when to dissolve it, what business to put before it. Debate in the chambers was moderate in tone, criticism of the Crown rarely voiced, the mildest lapses punished or recorded for later retribution.

The prerogative is now thought of as discretionary power to take action to deal with certain situations: declare war, deal with an emergency, detain a troublemaker. Executive discretion is one part, the other, more critical part is authority to legislate, to enact general laws, the power of proclamation. It meant the king's authority to legislate without calling parliament or needing its consent. The king would

[54] William Stanford: *An Exposition of the King's Prerogative* (London, 1548) cited in Elton: *The Tudor Constitution*, p 19. The Act of Proclamations (1539) clarifies the king's authority to rule by proclamation, that is, by executive order. The authority to do so does not require reference to Parliament or its consent.

[55] Detailed in T Penn: *The Winter King.*

[56] Act of Proclamations (1539: 31 Henry VIII, c. 8).

normally consult the Council and heed its advice, although it was not unusual to confine consultation to one or a few of the inner circle, and anyhow membership of the Council was in the gift of the king. The power to legislate by proclamation was authorized by common law as part of the king's prerogative. The Act of Proclamations, while acknowledging the king's authority at common law, added statutory authority. The king was encouraged to 'make and set forth proclamations for the good and politic order and governance of this his realm'. The purpose: 'for the defence of his regal dignity and the advancement of his commonwealth and good quiet of his people, as the cases of necessity shall require'. Power covered imposing 'such penalties and pains and of such sort as to his Highness—shall see necessary and requisite'. In the later reign of Henry VIII, Thomas Cromwell, his Chancellor, recounted to the Duke of Norfolk a conversation with the Chief Justice and other legal officials. Having told of the king's concern that 'money should be conveyed out of the realm', Cromwell asked what action the king lawfully could take, if there were no statutory law on the matter. The Chief Justice advised as follows. First, the king had authority to make proclamations 'and use all other policies at his pleasure' for 'avoiding of any such dangers'. Secondly, 'proclamations and policies so devised by the king and his Council for any such purpose should be of as good effect as any law made by Parliament or otherwise'. Such advice Cromwell assured the Duke he was 'very glad to have'.[57]

9. Relations between prince and people

Henry VII took the crown with 'whole assent of—all the Commons of this Land', according to the Coronation Oath. 'Commons' may mean either the House of Commons or the common people; here the House of Commons as representatives of the people. When the Commons spoke, it spoke not just on behalf of but as the people. 'The consent of Parliament is taken to be the every man's consent' wrote Thomas Smith later in the sixteenth century.[58] Between the king and his realm, an organic unity is sealed.[59] Having consented, the people are expected to obey. The king is presented as the gift of God, as part of 'a most excellent and perfect order'.[60] As head of the body politic, his sacred duty is to sustain the unity and to rule for the good of all its members, to advance the 'whole common weal'.[61] The king is

[57] Thomas Cromwell to the Duke of Norfolk (15 July 1535), reprinted in Elton: *The Tudor Constitution*, p 20.

[58] Thomas Smith: *De Republica Anglorum* (1565), p 48.

[59] Edmund Dudley, one of Henry's most loyal and unscrupulous officials, on the eve of his execution under Henry VIII, wrote of the 'organic unity of king and realm': *Tree of Commonwealth* (1509) cited in Elton: *The Tudor Constitution*, p 230.

[60] *A Homily on Obedience* (1547) in Elton: *The Tudor Constitution*, p 15.

[61] Act for provision to be made for the surety of the Queen's most royal person (1585: 27 Elizabeth I, c. 1).

'instituted and furnished with plenary and entire power to render justice and right to every part and member of this body'.[62]

If such an image of excellence and perfection were not wholly convincing to the people, the darker side of princely rule would be on hand to add persuasion. Disobedience was punished severely and often publicly. Social relations at all levels were infested with agents, informers, and spies, listening, recording, and reporting not just signs of outright rebellion but hints of disaffection or discontent. The Crown and its agents had to maintain at all cost the image of a body politic at ease with itself, all its parts working in harmony to constitute the whole. A statute of 1487, two years into Henry's reign, granted to the Court of Star Chamber power to enquire into and punish for a range of actions, by which 'the policy and good rule of this realm is almost subdued'.[63] Subdued by offences such as sheriffs making untrue returns, the bribing of juries, riots and unlawful assemblies. Noting that the limitations of common law processes to enquire into various matters was leading to 'an increase of murders, robberies, perjuries, and unsureties of all men living and losses of their lands and goods', the jurisdiction of Star Chamber was extended to remedy the omissions and to punish the offenders. This is one example among many of the readiness of the king to act with design and determination in preserving the integrity of the body politic. As the reign lengthened, the list of special courts, commissions, and enquiries grew; the rules of due process were compromised; the penalties made ever more discretionary, all allegedly to protect the realm and advance the common good.[64] Rebellion feared and condemned as 'the most detestable vice', was defined to include actions only remotely connected.[65] While instilling dread and fear, measures were taken to impress the people, to display the splendour and omnipotence of the Crown, through ceremonies, pageants, and festivals.[66] By an alliance of awe and fear, Henry VII strove to keep the people in submission while hoping to win their affection. The image cultivated was that of a stern but benevolent father, devoted to the well-being of his family, expecting its members to respect the conventions of family life, while intolerant of violation.

That was the formal constitutional order, together with the ideas and values supporting it, the constitution seen from above. Let us now consider how it looked from below, from the people's perspective. They had no constitutional role in deciding who was to be king other than notionally through representatives. They saw that the king ruled with the counsel and support of officials, selected and appointed

62 *Cawdrey's Case* (Coke: *Fifth Report*), pp 344–5.

63 An Act to give the Court of Star Chamber authority to punish divers misdemeanours (1487: 3 Henry VII, c. 1).

64 Well described in T Penn: *The Winter King* as: 'twisting and distorting of law and the exploitation of legal technicalities, the indiscriminate suspension of due process and, above all, the imposition of financial penalties in all shapes and sizes: bonds, recognizances, obligations': p 169.

65 *A Homily on Obedience* (1547) cited in Elton: *The Tudor Constitution*, p 15.

66 The efforts of Henry VII and his court to impress in this way are well-described in: T Penn: *The Winter King*.

by him. While the majesty of crown and court was ever on display, the process of governing was distant and secretive. In local government, in the shires, boroughs, and parishes, local residents filled some of the offices, including bailiff and chamberlain, aldermen, constables and church wardens, even that of the ale-taster.[67] The people expected the king to defend the realm, keep order within, and protect their rights and liberties. The last meant both refraining from intrusion on the subject's rights and liberties, and instituting a system of justice accessible to them. The people knew that in ruling according to these three precepts, the king's power was practically unlimited, his discretion unfettered. They had to trust in his having the qualities to use power wisely and justly, their sentiments shaped by how they were treated when touched by the king's authority or seeking redress in his courts. They witnessed the appeal to law and justice as the foundations of the constitution. At a deeper level they saw behind the image of the kindly father, the just and caring head of the body politic, and knew rule to be at his pleasure. Unless matched by the benefits, the social goods the prince is expected to supply and respect for justice, such images soon wore thin.

[67] Recounted by S Greenblat: *Will in the World* (WW Norton & Co: New York, 2004), p 59. John Shakespeare, William's father, held several of these offices in Stratford-on-Avon including ale-taster.

XI
Princely Rule: II

1. In search of social foundations

King Lear's depiction of authority as 'a dog's obeyed in office' may be too cynical but catches the sense of authority as a cloak of justification thrown over power.[1] As proof some would cite princely rule. [2] Being prominent in the history of peoples, the form of rule most common suggests qualities of more substance. Some peoples moved to rule by representatives; a few have tried ruling themselves; others are destined to be ruled by despots. Representative rule, the main rival, has its own instabilities and is ever at risk of lapsing back to princely rule. Notions of the common good and the identity of the prince vary. The common good may be *conservative*, the purpose to sustain the settled social order. Or *restorative* when the nation is in peril, threatened from without or falling apart within, and in need of a strong leader to save it. The Caesars Julius and Augustus seized power to save Rome, Henry VII to save England,[3] the generals to save Pakistan. Princes ancient and modern justify imposing their rule to save the nation from ruin due to incompetence, misrule, or corruption, or all three. The good even noble intentions soon fade as power and privilege cast their spell. The *visionary* form is the most threatening. The prince is now the charismatic leader intent on pursuing a belief, an ideal, or a vision of utopia to which all else gives way.[4] Each of the forms is distinctive, each open to shifts and subtleties, while common to all is the idea that the prince has unique insight into the good to be achieved and the power to achieve it.

Whether conservation, restoration, or utopia, each is presented as the common good, the good of the whole and the good of each member. The prince who serves the common good, whatever it be, the people have reason to support. The boundaries between princely rule as limited authority, and despotism without limits, remain in place but the boundaries are blurred and readily breached. The conservative and restorative forms serve well as a suitable point of reference in analysing princely rule. Princely rule invoked to deal with a threat to the nation's defence,

[1] W Shakespeare: *The Tragedy of King Lear*, Act 4: 5: 160.

[2] An Act for the Confirmation of Henry VII (1485) reprinted in GR Elton: *The Tudor Constitution: Documents and Commentary*, p 4. The actual text of the Coronation Oath of Henry VII is not known. What is preserved is a text prepared for the ceremony by the College of Arms. It is assumed here that, although the text used might have differed in some of the wording, the two foundational principles were as stated above. See further MRLL Kelly: 'The Coronation Oath' (Doctoral Thesis, Macquarie University, 1989).

[3] Discussed in R Syme: *The Roman Revolution* (Oxford: Clarendon Press, 1939).

[4] This idea of a visionary or charismatic leader is considered in Chapter XV.

Keepers of the Common Good. D.J. Galligan, Oxford University Press. © D.J. Galligan 2024.
DOI: 10.1093/9780198907398.003.0011

order, and security may in certain conditions be justified in the opinion of the people. As in Henry VII's case, power is vested in or seized by one person and normal constraints relaxed or removed until the danger passes. Harder to explain and justify is princely rule in normal times; yet, throughout European history and elsewhere it has been the standard form of rule. This prompts enquiry into the social conditions enabling and sustaining the prince's capacity to coordinate social relations, advance the well-being of the people, and gain their support. The issues are several. One is the claim of strong rule; another the conditions conducive to princely rule; a third relations between the people and the prince; a fourth the instabilities.

2. Strong and effective rule

The *Book of Samuel* recounts how the people of Israel displeased both the Lord and Samuel by asking for a king to rule them.[5] The Lord granted their request reluctantly, assuring Samuel that, if the people were to follow divine guidance, they would be secure against enemies and have no need of an earthly ruler. The elders insisted that, like other peoples, they wanted to be ruled by a king who would lead them into battle, provide for their security, and sustain their unity, for which strong rule was needed. Samuel acceded, while at the Lord's request warning the people of the 'wickedness of kings' and the dangers. A king may win in battle but would do much evil in ruling, enslaving his people, imposing taxes, and seizing their property. What then is the point of the biblical story? On one view it shows the tension within princely protection between the need for power practically unlimited, and the risk of its being used to oppress the people. No form of rule is perfect or without risk and so, in the judgement of the elders, princely rule is preferred to other forms, particularly that of the people ruling themselves even with the Lord's guidance. The people's insistence is open to another reading, to their knowledge of society and the reason for authority. With enemies all around and survival threatened, the main concerns were protection, security, and basic needs. Pursuit of the more refined aspects of civility and humanity, while not forgotten, was put aside until the essentials were secure. We have seen how rule, whatever the form, is socialized; how it enters daily life to influence opinion and guide action. If princely rule be regarded as reliable in providing the basic benefits without which life would be wretched, it becomes secure in the sentiments and dispositions of the people.[6]

[5] *Book of Samuel: The Jewish Study Bible* (Tanakh Translation: Oxford University Press, 2004), 810: 574.

[6] Unable to provide basic social goods, the late Soviet Union soon lost its place in the sentiments and dispositions of the people, who turned to other forms of coordination. For studies of the post-communist experience, see *Law and Informal Practices* (eds) DJ Galligan and M Kurkchiyan (Oxford: Oxford University Press, 2003).

The wisdom of the elders and the success of Henry VII deserve praise in dealing with dangerous times; but that does not exhaust the appeal of princely rule. It is said, simply, to be the best form of rule. Thomas Hobbes in championing this approach claims the rule of one to be superior to the rule of an assembly of persons, not only in crisis but at all times. Princely rule has the 'Aptitude to produce the Peace, and the Security of the people; for which end they were instituted'.[7] Rule by one is the most effective in saving the people from the state of nature, providing basic goods, and preventing relapse.[8] A constitutional order and the social conditions supporting it, no matter how stable they seem, perch precariously between order and chaos, between the security of strong rule and the insecurity of the state of nature. To avoid sinking back to the dreaded state, caution is needed, while prudence prompts a society to err in favour of order, which princely rule is best able to supply. Hobbes writes of the 'Inconstancy' that occurs in assemblies where resolutions taken one day by one group are undone the next day by another group. As the wrangling goes on, the time for action passes.

Another advantage is the prince's freedom to act unhindered by process, or by the need to bring groups and factions to agreement, or having to deal with obstruction from other agencies of government. Nor does he have to cope with the clamour of civil society or the babble of the people. The prince is free to take 'counsel of whom, when, and where he pleaseth'.[9] The common good is presented as plain, objective, and to the benefit to all, while the state of nature is kept at bay. A simplified and consensual notion of the common good makes ruling less complex and the process less onerous. The prince relies on and cultivates support of the sectors of society with most to gain from his rule, while confident of the support of the people as a whole, whose expectations are not high. Being saved from the state of nature and having their needs met is said to be enough, while efforts are made by the prince and his counsellors to keep expectations low. Harsh reality is softened and made bearable by fiction, by pretending the prince is really each person, his actions the actions of each.[10] By contrast, to try to construct out of diversity, division, and discord, a concept of common good, more complex processes would be needed and outcomes would be unreliable.

The benefits of princely rule are simple and made to look compelling. The question is whether they are enough to render princely rule the normal form of rule. Is effectiveness in delivering the 'peace and security of the people' enough to be the cement of social foundations? The answer has a theoretical and empirical part. As to theory, there is cause for doubt. In the first place, while firm and decisive rule is needed in time of crisis, it is not obvious that the prince is the only one capable of it.

[7] T Hobbes: *Leviathan* (ed) R Tuck (Cambridge: Cambridge University Press, 1996), p 131.

[8] For Hobbes' reasons for princely rule being the most effective form of rule, see Notes.

[9] T Hobbes: *Leviathan*, Chapter 19, p 131. Hobbes advances several other reasons: see Notes.

[10] See further Chapter II:4.

Other forms of rule have proved capable, while the risk is that action taken without consulting opinion beyond a few loyal counsellors, will fail in its purpose. Another reason for questioning the superiority of princely rule is the failure to distinguish between crisis and normality, between exceptional measures and routine government. Hobbes saw no distinction because society is always on the brink of collapsing back to the state of nature, due either to the enemy at the door or the enemy inside. Dissatisfaction and unrest are the enemy within, leading if left unchecked to disorder, resistance, and rebellion, even civil war, for which the strong and ruthless arm of princely rule is needed. That is to lament the outcome rather than address the cause. Had Hobbes enquired into the causes of collapse into the state of nature, he would have found poor government the main cause, not only at the level of high policy but in failing to provide sound administration and adjudication. The common causes of unrest leading to rebellion, as we have seen in earlier chapters, are neglect and abuse of the people's rights and liberties, the failure to treat the people with respect and justly. Here lies the pathway to the state of nature, less plain and direct than the enemy at the door, but the destination as deadly. If neglect and abuse lead to resistance and rebellion, the strong ruler is ready and equipped. The more serious risk is more subtle, that disaffection and unrest weaken the allegiance to the prince, for once the bond is loosened the people start to doubt the claims of princely rule and to ask how social relations could be different, the constitutional field redesigned to serve better their well-being. Unlike Peter Quince who had doubts but saw no other way, the more astute have in reserve the discourse of the lower register, a foundation to guide them in imagining forms of rule other than princely.

The structure of rule is another problem for even the wise prince. Governing well in all the mundane and routine forms sits awkwardly with power vested in one person. Being decisive and single-minded in crisis is a long way from keeping in working order a network of agencies charged to administer and adjudicate daily affairs among the people, and between the people and officials. The qualities to handle crisis are not the qualities for orderly and routine government. Henry VII was admirable in crisis but lamentable in calm. Other forms of rule are more open to opinion, to knowing the needs and aspirations of the people. Instead of being dismissed as an irritant, keeping open the channels to the voice of the people is an aid to sound and stable government. The same applies to administration and adjudication from the high levels of policy to the low levels of deciding the specific case. Princely rule needs well-working agencies, but cannot risk power flowing away from the prince, while to be effective the agencies need and tend towards autonomy and independence. The tighter the control of the prince, the less effective the agencies are in dealing with matters of law and policy, and resolving disputes.

The same dilemma applies in the prince's confronting civil society. A civil society, thriving and vibrant, is satisfying to the people and a source of guidance for the prince, who needs to be informed but cannot countenance sites of competing power. The prince denied informed guidance is at risk of being isolated from the concerns of those for whose good he governs. Henry Tudor must have missed the story of his kinsman Richard of York, poised to seize the throne, frantic to know the opinion of the people;[11] nor known the price Coriolanus paid for treating with contempt the opinions of the plebs. Henry might have heard but did not heed the lament of the fisherman that 'a fish hangs in the net like a poor man's rights in law; 'twill hardly come out'.[12] Nor did it dawn on him how lament soon mounts to unrest; how the people denied protection of rights and liberties are driven to desperate measures. Even the more moderate route, the people's agitating for a place in the processes of governing, is for the prince a source of dread and danger.

The people have their own concerns about princely rule. They know life in the state of nature without security and order would be miserable and even basic needs not met. The people aspire to more than survival, more than essential needs. The thirst to improve their lives, advance humanity and civility in all their forms, is shared by all and unquenchable. The more the people strive for such ends, the less suited is princely rule to support their efforts. Instead, between the two a crack appears and tends to deepen, causing conflict and rendering precarious the rule of the prince. The prince has to confront, and struggles to overcome, the structural limits in coping with the aspirations of the people. He is most at home when the common good is clear and settled. James I, in declaring his dedication to the common *wele*, had in mind a settled social order of status and property, which he claimed to understood better than anyone, and of which he was the best guardian. The crack in the golden bowl of princely rule, seen by the Tudor and Stuart kings of England, was not so easy to seal, nor the abyss beneath to avoid.

Having grasped the logic and the limits, successive monarchs set out to preserve princely rule. Henry Tudor VII saw the danger parliament posed and allowed it to meet for just a week each year. James Stuart, more gifted than the average, conceded limits on princely power, limits to be respected by the prince in his wisdom, but not to be enforced by the people nor mediated through parliament. Charles Stuart, his father's son in spirit if not intellect, saw the crack and where it led; admitted the elected chamber had a role in protecting *liberty*, in the sense of well-being.[13] But, lacking the nous to fend off parliament and protect himself, he fell into the abyss headlong and headless. Charles 'ingenuously confess[ed] that frequent parliaments is the best means to preserve the right understanding betwixt me and my subjects', which he 'most heartily desired'.[14] A year later, the 'right understanding' was clarified. 'The House of Commons, the representative of the people was never intended for any share in government.' The king alone is able to prevent 'a total

[11] W Shakespeare: *The Tragedy of King Richard the Third* (1592–93), Act 3: 7.
[12] W Shakespeare: *Pericles Prince of Tyre* (1608), Scene 5: 158.
[13] Discussed in Chapter XV.
[14] Speech by Charles I, 25 January 1641: *The Stuart Constitution 1603–1688* (ed) JP Kenyon (Cambridge: Cambridge University Press, 1986), pp 17–18.

subversion of the fundamental laws, and that excellent constitution' for which England is famous. Fine words mask the true intent. If the House of Commons, the elected house, were to have more say in governing, the common people would 'grow weary of journey-work, and set up themselves—destroy all rights and properties, all distinctions of family and merit, and—end in a dark, equal chaos of confusion, and a long list of our many noble ancestors in a Jack Cade or Wat Tyler'.[15] Or more simply, not only would the common good based on property and status be destroyed, it would be replaced by the chaos of groups tugging and scrambling in an unruly pit of competing opinion. Such a prospect must be condemned for it would sound, as indeed it did, the end of princely rule. The only way to avoid such disaster is to seal the union of a settled social order and princely rule.

Behind these issues an empirical dimension awaits investigation. The lack of systematic study of periods of princely rule, the duration, effectiveness, and demise, leaves much to surmise. There is nevertheless ample evidence to show Hobbes' claim for the superiority of princely rule to be unfounded. Other forms of rule have proved able to hold the line against the state of nature, to harness the unruly forces at large in society, not only to protect basic rights and ensure order and security, but to raise the level of social goods and provide conditions for the people to improve their lives. A form of rule where the agencies of government acquire a degree of independence enabling them to contribute to good government, while remaining limited and accountable. Other forms of rule manage to rule competently, to lock out the lord-of-misrule and hold at bay the wolf of appetite, without the ugly side of princely rule.

3. Expanding the social foundations

The attempt to found princely rule on superiority in ruling fails, and with it crumbles the social foundation; yet princely rule is common and often lasts. Instead of placing all the weight on one pillar, an alternative is to identify several, each less sturdy or stable but together capable of propping up princely rule. The route to discovery lies in the sentiments and dispositions of the people. A people discontented asserts itself and agitates for more benefits, demands status in the constitutional order and a place in the processes of governing. Princely rule comes under strain, is modified, and the field opened to other forms of rule. The question then is under what conditions the people are content to be the feet, restrain themselves, and endorse princely rule. The supporting pillars are several: low expectations; respect for justice; reasons justifying action; support of select sectors; repressive measures.

[15] *The Stuart Constitution*, pp 19–20.

The five pillars securely in place are a firm base for princely rule, weakened by a pillar missing or by instability built in.

The first two pillars go together. Princely authority is most common and most secure when the expectations of the people are low. The shrewd prince knows to keep them low. Order and security are the first priority, basic rights and liberties close behind, but not much more. The prince knows the value of justice, how much it means to the people, and takes measures to protect their rights and liberties. Law sets the standards of justice, of what is due, around which ideas of equity and fairness gather. Justice in the limited sense sits at the centre of social relations, while a people is well-disposed towards rule that delivers what is due. The prudent prince takes measures to make sure they are in this sense satisfied citizens. Henry VII would have known of John Fortescue's claim that nothing makes the people rise more than lack of bread and lack of justice. Lack of bread speaks for itself. Lack of justice, less obvious but just as fatal, is denial of respect, central to social relations and the basis of juridical equality; for the people a source of strong sentiments and dispositions. The common complaint, the most pleaded grievance is the failure of justice and fair treatment.[16] Where the content of justice comes under scrutiny and risk of unrest is aroused, the prince is able to act rapidly and resolutely, to make adjustments enough to reassure the people and quell unease.[17] Justice as due is a condition of princely rule, but not enough to sustain it. The people have to accept that maintaining the settled social order has priority over other interests in improving their lives and cultivating humanity and civility.

The third pillar takes the weight, shoulders the burden of justifying the social order by appeal to a register of ideas and values: the body politic, the values it symbolizes, and the benefits to all parts. The purpose is to keep the people, the lower organs, convinced that the good health of the body prevails over other interests and depends on their willing support. Every effort is made to show the value of the order, the fine principles on which it rests, and the worth of a well-working body politic. The danger is the people let their gaze drop from high ideals to social reality, see through the thin veil of the organic whole to view their lowly place within, and wonder why a few do well while most barely manage. The fragility of princely rule is exposed, for a people once aroused want more, know to get more would mean stepping out from below and influencing, even engaging in the processes of governing. That would set princely rule on a path to ruin. Charles I saw the sequence and the consequences; 'the dark, equal chaos of confusion', the destruction of the social order.

[16] Discussed in Chapter IX.

[17] That rights being respected is a condition of the people's support for the prince does not mean a lack of interest in other aspects of rule. The people take a keen interest in ruling at all levels, in matters of high policy and low.

If princely rule is to survive, the sequence has to be prevented before it starts, a task assigned to the last two pillars, the repressive and the supportive. The benevolent side of princely rule is balanced by the repressive. Expectations have to be kept low.[18] Free and open discussion has no place in the order of princely rule; ideas for change are unwelcome, while even mild criticism is forbidden. The fear that open assembly and loose speech pose a threat to the settled order leads to a criminal code long on offences and harsh on penalties. The processes of government are conducted in secret with few exceptions; information about government is strictly controlled. A people kept in the dark finds it hard to question the process. The last pillar, the support of the sectors of society with the highest stake, bears its share of the weight. Whether an aristocracy or landed gentry, entrepreneurs or faithful followers, the prince relies on select sectors, which in return are expected and disposed to give loyalty and support.[19] The five pillars together make princely rule possible and explain why sometimes it lasts.

Relations between the prince and the people merit a further note. The need to shape and sustain the people's sentiments and dispositions, out of cunning if not wisdom, has a modifying effect on the prince's actions. Ceremony and ritual, images and symbols, celebrations and festivals, do much to win the good opinion of the people. The prince knows that unless practical action matches the imagery, the people will not long be deceived. He does not credit them with a sense of constitution, but knows they can tell the difference between good government and bad, between policies for the common good and those not, whether due to incompetence, self-interest, or duress from select sectors. The people, even the most common among them, witness and judge the deeds of princes from the highest level to the lowest. While Richard of York sets out 'to perceive the commons' minds,/How they affect the house and claim of York', [20] Suffolk is told by a commoner about to murder him, he 'will dam this yawning mouth/For swallowing the treasure of the realm'.[21] When the Duke of Gloucester, the Protector, is wrongly accused of violating the common weal, 'The commons, like an angry hive of bees,/That want their leader, scatter up and down/And care not who they sting in their revenge.'[22] The citations could continue but the point is plain, the people have an interest in and knowledge of matters of 'high concernment', an interest that the prince ignores at his peril. Let King John have the last word: 'What you would have reformed that is not well/And well shall you perceive how willingly/I will both hear and grant

[18] The people's voices could be heard through several channels, nationally and locally, including petitions and addresses and representatives. Mark Knights has documented thoroughly the channels and processes in the seventeenth and eighteenth centuries: *Representation and Misrepresentation in Later Stuart England.*

[19] This does not of course rule out conflict within the loyal sector or between parts of it and the prince. Conflicts at this level are often a serious threat to princely rule.

[20] *The First Part of the Contention: Henry VI, Part I,* Act 3: 1: 3.

[21] *Ibid* Act 4: 1: 75.

[22] *Ibid* Act 3: 2: 125.

your requests.'[23] Whether such fine words would have been matched by action is another matter. As long as expectations be met, justice done, and ruling take a tolerable course, the people have reasons to support princely rule. The force of the reasons and the intensity of support vary according to the factors considered.

4. Strengthening the foundations of princely rule

When the five pillars are in place, princely rule has a foundation firm enough to account for its being the standard form of rule. Do other qualities enter the foundations to strengthen the sentiments and dispositions of the people? Could that explain why both Samuel and the Lord accede to the elders' request for a king? Several reasons are suggestive in polishing the image of princely rule. One is its status as the reserve, the reassuring form to fall back on when others fail. It is always there backstage, poised to make an entry when other forms come under strain, weaken, and fall apart. Like the patient parent awaiting the return of the prodigal child, princely rule is ready to rescue the people from their own folly. Another reason is that princely rule, stripped bare, delivers tangible outcomes, at least to meet essential needs and utilities. Two other factors dispose the people towards princely rule. One is the tendency within social relationships of whatever kind for leaders to emerge. Jack Cade, first seen rallying the rebels as one of their number, is soon declaring himself to be in charge, the very 'mouth of parliament'. Although Jack is not an ideal model, the Cade effect is ingrained in the dynamics of collective action.

One part is the tendency for a leader to emerge, the other the advantage of one person coordinating the actions of the group.[24] Linked to that is the natural place of princely rule in a culture where the strong leader is held to be essential to social life. The family and the household, the school and the workplace, the football team and the ship's crew, all take for granted the need for a strong head with power to act swiftly and firmly. Around this feature of social relations, Max Weber develops the concept of *patrimonial authority*.[25] The social foundations are, first, the master of the household who has almost unlimited power over its members, and secondly, the way such power becomes normalized, embedded in experience and tradition, and secured in sentiments and dispositions. This feature of social life enters into and shapes relations between leaders and the people; it also shapes the people's understanding of constitutional authority. The political leader has the role of the patriarch, the whole society his household. The patriarch's power is at first without

[23] W Shakespeare: *The Life and Death of King John*, Act 4: 2: 43.
[24] See Chapter V:2.
[25] M Weber: *Economy and Society*, Volume ii, pp 1106*ff*. Note the link to Adam Smith's account of respect for authority: Chapter I:4.

limits, the members of his household dependent on his will. Over time, the members, whether family or servants, retainers or slaves, begin to claim an element of reciprocity, recognition that in return for obedience, the master must accept them as more than commodities, as having a claim to respect, from which a relationship of mutuality is built. And while natural affection adds force to some relationships, the decisive factor is that the master retains power only with support of the household, and in the face of rebellion is impotent. The members are disposed to give support in order to keep the household intact and to guarantee the benefits it provides. That relationship according to Vico was the social foundation of Rome and of modern constitutional authority.[26]

We now have two lines of explanation for the appeal of princely rule. One concerns the material side of the relationship. Although the benefits are basic, room for betterment marginal, the prince can be relied on to supply them. In a world unstable and dangerous, enemies within and without, the state of nature at the gate, the people value rule that secures peace, order, and essential needs. The ambition to improve lives and enjoy higher benefits is ever present but the means are uncertain. Princely rule would have to be replaced by other kinds of rule less clear in form and unreliable in outcome. Prudence prevails and the people trade aspiration for certainty. That is the argument, whether in practice well-founded a matter for further enquiry. The other line of support stems from the prominence of powerful leaders, at first in the household but spreading to other social relationships, from which grows a sense of normality, of habituation on the part of the people. Princely rule, far from being exceptional, fits the pattern. Yet, as the account of princely rule unfolds, the instabilities mount, and to that we now turn.

5. Princely power a source of instability

In place of King Lear's dog in office, we here call on another familiar figure, the wolf in sheep's clothing, suggesting power once unleashed knows no bounds or natural constraints, has a propensity to expand and be misused, and is hard to control.[27] That is neither a matter of design nor ill-will, but the product of the union of human nature and power. The wolf of appetite, power's constant companion, incites the holder to do things normally prohibited and arouses a primitive instinct that dulls the wits. That power 'continually seeks to augment itself' is one of the working rules of social enquiry.[28] The more power, the bigger the appetite

[26] G Vico: *La Scienza Nuova*. Weber knew Vico's writings and seems to have been influenced by them. His account of patrimonial authority fits well with Vico's earlier ideas.

[27] On power, see Chapter IV:6.

[28] Words from Sharon Krause's essay 'Despotism' in *Montesquieu's Science of Politics: Essays on the Spirit of Laws* (eds) DW Carrithers, MA Mosher, and PA Rahe (New York: Rowan & Littlefield, 2001), p 246. Montesquieu wrote at length on the forms of government, one of which was despotism, which

and the harder to control, so that even the noble prince struggles to keep power within bounds, to curb its native delinquency. What Lear knew from experience, Montesquieu, reflecting 'with a kind of sadness the ills of human nature', concluded that 'despotic tendencies are fundamental to human nature' from which it follows that 'anyone who has power 'is led to abuse it'.[29] Samuel the prophet saw the dilemma of princely rule, the tension at its core, the instability it breeds. In order to provide firm rule, defending the people and making them secure, the prince needs power, but power brings danger, an arrogance of manner and the temptation to succumb to the seduction of riches, the siren call of ambition, the satisfaction of personal gain and glory. The tension appears in princely rule. To rule firmly the prince must have power to act free of constraints; yet the union of strong power and weak constraints increases the propensity to exceed the bounds and be misused. William Blackstone captures the risk in writing that the prince who holds 'all the sinews of government' is most powerful, but 'there is imminent danger of his employing that strength to improvident or oppressive purposes'.[30]

Appetite leads to another propensity and source of instability, the intolerance of constraints. When Charles I tired of his rule being questioned and curbed by parliamentarians and dissenters, he dissolved parliament and embarked on twelve years of personal rule. The circle of counsellors shrank to a few loyal ministers, while the voices of dissent were suppressed or unheard. As constraints on power fell away, rule became more repressive, retaliation more punitive, until resolution was sought in war, setting in motion the decline and fall of princely rule. The king's actions, while condemned, were a normal feature of power. Investing power in one person is to signal trust in his judgement, in his ability to achieve a given goal. To then subject that judgement to the guidance or direction of others, who are bound to be seen as less capable and less knowledgeable, is easily construed as not just an irritation but a risk to, a distortion of the integrity of judgement. To be able to accept and absorb advice and guidance from others demands the qualities essential to princely rule, although beyond the capacity of most princes. King Charles I, rather than being an exception, could claim the crown as the Everyman of Princes.

is well-analysed by Krause. One further quotation: 'In the end, what makes Montesquieu's concept of despotism so powerful is that he shows how common the despotic tendency is in human societies and in human beings as individuals. He shows that the tendency to abuse power is universal and cannot be written off as the vice of particular persons or regimes': p 259.

[29] Krause, *ibid*, p 257.

[30] W Blackstone: *Commentaries* i.49.50 quoted in: W Prest: 'William Blackstone and the Free Constitution of Britain' in *Constitutions and the Classics: Patterns of Constitutional Thought from Fortescue to Bentham* (ed) DJ Galligan (Oxford: Oxford University Press, 2014), p 216.

6. Structural instabilities

Demands on the prince However parcelled and presented, princely rule depends on delivering the social goods for a nation to survive and the people to have a threshold of security, order, and needs. Above the threshold, a nation designs its social structure according to history, carved from fine marble or base stone as the case may be, adorns it with ideals and expectations, tempers it with fears and dangers. Around that social structure is erected a constitutional order suited to the architecture, of which princely rule is one style among several, a style celebrating simplicity, the prince ruling for the good of all.[31] Behind the screen matters are not so straightforward. The constitutional structure of princely rule relies on the firmness of the five pillars, despite each pillar being defective and the union unstable. To the dangers of power must be added two other instabilities, one the personal nature of princely rule, the other the sentiments and dispositions of the people. Structural instabilities begin with the personal qualities needed to rule well. Some are positive, such as fortitude and knowledge, judgement and decisiveness, a sense of justice; others negative, in particular forbearance and self-restraint. Education, training, and the example of others may help in acquiring the qualities to rule, although finally the causes are a mystery. Rule imposes a burden most princes, however thorough their preparation and good their intentions, are not capable of bearing. Expectations set too high open the way for disappointment and disaffection. Another condition of ruling well is knowing the courses of action open, the merits of each, and the likely effects. The prince takes advice and relies on counsel, but mainly from a sector of society whose members have their own interests to advance, and who hesitate at bearing bad news or giving unwelcome counsel. The plurality of opinion from other sectors of society is kept in the background or not heard; the moderating influence of civic associations is likely to be marginal; the voice of the people muted. The lust for firm action, fuelled by simplicity, conviction, and certainty, renders complexity and plurality, disagreement and doubt, corrosive.

Agencies of government Relations between the prince and the agencies of government reveal another instability. The agencies serve two functions, contribute to good government in two ways, one a source of expert knowledge, the other applying laws and policies. The prince faces a dilemma. To serve the two ends, the agencies need a degree of autonomy and independence, which competes with the prince's interest in keeping them under guard.[32] Effective administration depends on and naturally inclines towards a bureaucratic structure and an

[31] On the metaphor of law as architecture, see DJ Galligan: *Law in Modern Society,* Chapter 15.

[32] See M Weber on bureaucracy: *Economy & Society*, section XI; DJ Galligan: 'Authoritarianism in Government and Administration: The Promise of Administrative Justice' [2001] *Current Legal Problems* 86–105.

allocation of tasks, acquiring expertise and uniform rules. Only to a limited degree can the prince tolerate such a system. The more the agencies free themselves from the shadow of the prince, each to become a site of power pursuing its own purposes and following its own processes, the more likely they are to scrutinize his actions and become his critic. The prince relies on the agencies to deliver the social goods on which his rule depends, to have laws and policies applied efficiently and fairly, for here his subjects are most directly affected, their essential interests at stake, their sentiments and dispositions most open to influence. The conscientious prince, knowing sound administration to be part of good rule, has to find a path between the competing forces, allowing effective implementation of law and policy, while keeping the agencies under control. The dilemma and the defect of princely rule are displayed by contrasting constitutional orders that value a network of agencies for serving two purposes. One to supply information and analysis to the leaders as an aid to governing well. The other to conduct administration through settled and open processes, explaining and justifying action to those most affected, whether the criminal suspect or the claimant of welfare. The need to reconcile the two roles of administration, one specialized and reasonably independent of the prince, the other subservient, creates an inner tension and is a source of instability.

Courts The same applies to the courts. A system of justice for the hearing of complaints and grievances, for the resolution of disputes, and the general protection of the rights of subjects, as we have seen, is critical to effective rule. The prince as the source and symbol of justice appoints the judges, expects them to serve his wishes, and removes them at pleasure. The notion of courts being separate from and independent of the prince does not fit the logic of princely rule. Viewed from the heyday of princely rule in England, judicial review of executive action lies far in the future, of legislative action even farther, while neither sits well with princely rule. The courts, viewed from the palace, are there to contribute to effective rule as defined by the prince. Instability is unavoidable. Judicial review of executive and administrative agencies, now held to be part of good government, has no place in princely rule. At the lower levels involving disputes between private parties or administration by agencies, courts may be permitted a degree of independence, allowed to build a legal order of settled rules and suitable processes. In creating and encouraging alternatives to the common law courts, Henry VII knew the need for a system of justice held by the people to be fair and effective. Perhaps he had heard the fisherman's lament for a poor man's rights; knew the value men and women put on justice and how badly they fared in the common law courts. He knew there was more to their sense of justice than applying formal rules; that their ideas of equity and fairness have a foundation that cannot be cramped into rules. The Court of Requests was created and the practices of others, Star Chamber notable, adjusted to take account of the deeper sense of justice. Justice needs both the certainty settled rules bring to rights, leavened by the openness of equity and fairness. Between justice according to settled rules and justice according to conscience, there is tension, another source of instability in princely rule.[33]

The absence or weakness of agencies and processes designed to guide and constrain the prince's actions warrants two further comments. First, the gap tends to be filled by a narrow sector with most at stake, whose counsel is sifted to suit their own interests, 'sinister interests' Bentham called them, and to influence the prince's sentiments and dispositions.[34] The English tradition shows the relationship. The band of counsellors grew from being at first the magnates of the realm to include lesser nobility and the knights of the shire, from which the two houses of parliament emerged. Its members with few exceptions belonged to the small class of landed gentry.[35] Both houses were expected to advise not criticize let alone obstruct, as Thomas More learnt on delivering in parliament the mildest rebuke to Henry VII. This leads on to a second comment, that the prince took counsel but decided the action. The relationships were fraught with tension, a scene of envy and rivalry among the supporting sectors, and between them and the prince, seen in high relief in relations between English kings and the landed elite. The central tension, however, is between the excessive demands of the supporting sector for favour and the prince's need to rule for the good of all.[36] As late as the 1640s, in the dying days of his reign, Charles I could still assert against the tide that while the two houses are of value for their advice, it is for the king alone to govern. The last defiant assertion in England of princely rule before relations were altered, with parliament in the ascendant, the king's authority on the wane, and the course set for princely rule to give way to rule by representatives elected by the people.

7. Contesting the common good

The people are now able to assess the merits of princely rule and decide whether it is the constitutional field they wish to cultivate. A few find all they hoped for and are ready to pledge allegiance to a prince. The majority, having entered with misgivings, now see more clearly the reasons. One is the common good, the other being able to keep rule to purpose. The common good is presented as settled, objective, and immutable, all in their right place, the people low down. They find this hard to reconcile with the purpose of rule being their well-being, their capacity to flourish and prosper. Princely rule may aspire to keep the state of nature at bay and

[33] For further analysis of the courts and the people, see S Hindle: *The State and Social Change in Early Modern England, 1550–1640* (Basingstoke: Palgrave, 2002), Chapter 3; T Stretton: 'The People and the Law' in *A Social History of England 1500–1750* (ed) K Wrightson (Cambridge: Cambridge University Press, 2017).

[34] Discussed in G Postema: *Bentham and the Common Law Tradition* (Oxford: Clarendon Press,1989).

[35] For further discussion, see J Maddicott: *The Origins of the English Parliament 924–1327.*

[36] On solidarity and unity between the prince and supporting elite, see Notes.

meet basic needs, even ensure justice for the people. Practice does not always live up to promise and the cry of the rough fisherman rings in their ears.[37] The call of Cade's butcher to kill all the lawyers, while grotesque, shows the sense of exclusion the people are liable to suffer under princely rule and the resentment they feel.[38] Even if the promise of princely rule be met, the people want more, they want to advance their utilities and improve their lives, cultivate humanity and civility in all forms. The common good defined by princely rule is an obstacle to their aspirations and comes under scrutiny.

The people realize the common good is not a concept awaiting discovery but an idea of how society is to be organized. They soon see the idea arises from and is tied to a social, political, and economic order, in the case of princely rule an order grounded in inequality and disparity of material welfare, social status, and opportunity for betterment.[39] The link between the two, the constitutional and the social, need not be direct or unswerving. It is likely to be complex, half-hidden, subject to diversion, to some degree qualified and modified by other ideas and interests, all of which is manifest in the study of princely rule. A second feature plain to the people is that the common good once settled is dressed up, made to look attractive to all sectors. They see how images are created and a matching discourse invented, both aimed at transcending social divisions. The people see through the imagery and note how the discourse of the constitutional order reflects and reinforces the social structure on which it arises. Finally, they marvel at how the common good of princely rule is presented as ordained, beyond question or alteration, ruling out other conceptions of the common good based on other sets of social relations. And just as the fisherman's words haunt memory, contempt mounts for Charles I's claim that to admit the common people to any place in governing would destroy the social order, license levelling, and incite all sorts of companion evils. A few cling to princely rule, satisfied enough with the threshold of benefits and wary of the risks of other kinds of rule. Others imagine things could be different, although like Peter Quince are unsure what they would be or how to bring them about.

Most judge the defects to outweigh the merits and begin to plan a new design for the constitutional order. The common good is contested and debated, interests declared, competition faced, and shared ground marked. When the arena is opened in this way, the social, economic, and political dimensions, the very structure of social relations, become central to the contest. Resolution and accommodation are not always feasible, nor does effective government always follow. If a balance be reached, it might become embedded in social relations and be the foundation of

[37] W Shakespeare: *Henry VI, The First Part of the Contention*, Act 4: 2: 78.

[38] Discussed in DJ Galligan: 'Ally or Enemy: Friend or Foe' in *The Courts and the People: Friend or Foe?* (Oxford: Hart Bloomsbury, 2021).

[39] Benjamin Constant is one among many who describe the common good as a cover for private interest; discussed in S Holmes: *Benjamin Constant and the Making of Modern Liberalism* (New Haven: Yale University Press, 1984).

a stable government serving the people well. It is just as likely to be fragile, unstable, and short-lived, prone to collapse and open to sabotage by one sector of society or another. Whether or not it produces an effective system of government is contingent on circumstances, ideas, and sectors, and not least on the dispositions and actions the people. They realize that even for the process towards good rule to begin, conditions have to be in place. At one level are freedoms of expression, association, and movement, and a vibrant civil society. At another level, restraint by all parties, officials loyal to purpose and guided by prudence, justice, and beneficence. On the next level, space to engage in the processes of governing, scope for vigilance and censure. The curse laid on dissent and discord, diversity and division, the four dreaded dangers, is lifted and each valued in the quest for a fresh sense of the common good. That is the last level of constitutional endeavour, one not always or even often reached, more a never-ending journey than a defined destination. The common good is not given but crafted, adjusted from port to port, age to age, people to people. Although there is no final port, there is a compass to guide the journey, a compass set to purpose, to the well-being of the people. The passage is open, the routes variable, the ship let sail wherever blow the fair winds of well-being, civility, and humanity. And just as the good sailor knows the difference between fair wind and foul, knows how to avoid the rocks and shoals, so the people know how to cultivate the constitutional field, avoid the traps and snares, and reap harvests for all.

The people now understand the repressive nature of princely rule, why it brings to mind the image of a fortress. The power of the prince is premised on sustaining the social order, on keeping settled social relations in place, while resisting the dynamics for change driven by the power of the people. In defending the settled order, repressing criticism and dissent, silencing opinion, the prince has to be diligent and fierce. Success is invariably partial and never permanent, because repression is never enough to quash the human spirit or to stamp out disquiet. Never enough to cement one conception of the common good in the sentiments and dispositions of the people; never enough to quell their doubts about the justifying reasons. In short, never enough to remove the instability of the common good under princely rule. To the people two fault lines are plain, one a sense of common good that keeps expectations low, the other a constitutional order that denies them the means to improve their place and advance well-being, both adding to the instability of princely rule.

8. The means to advance well-being

Machiavelli urged the prince to win the affection of the people, for dislike soon turns to hatred and plots against him.[40] That is not to say the good prince, the

[40] Discussed by E Benner: *Machiavelli's Prince: A New Reading* (Oxford: Oxford University Press, 2013), p 230.

prince held in high regard even affection is safe, for princely rule is by nature at risk from the people. The design defects are plain: one the people's benefits are restricted, the other they have no direct part in deciding the distribution of social goods, and only weak influence over the process. The parties who have no say in the direction of a social relationship are at risk of their interests being neglected. That is John of Salisbury's point in cautioning the prince to look after the feet for they are easily forgotten. But even well-shod feet know their benefits will never rise above bare necessities. The lack of means to rise in the order of princely rule, to improve their lives, heightens concern. The people accept the tendency for some sectors to rise above the rest, do better in the tug-and-scramble than others. The trouble is princely rule does not encourage tugging and scrambling, instead regards it as a threat to the settled order, to be kept under tight control. Confronted with princely rule, the people grasp more firmly the point and the potential of engagement, vigilance, and censure.

Another principle of social organization enters the constitutional field. The parties to any set of relations strive to improve their lot, try to achieve purpose and advance well-being. The more barren and poor their place, the more vigorous their efforts to improve it. The agencies of government have power to allocate benefits and the people find ways of bringing influence to bear. Two points emerge. First, collective action is the most likely means, the formation of associations, trade unions, guilds, and the like. Such entities acquire power to exert influence on government, best done by having a place in government, but even without, have ways of promoting their cause. The usual tactic is to press at the boundaries, seek incremental gain, adjustments to social relations, a bigger share in social goods and a more equitable distribution.[41] With the rise of ideas of liberty, a licence for social mobility, and an increase in economic diversity, the people have more scope for collective action to improve their position. Secondly, although the pressure to conform is high and the deterrents strong, those who gain least from the system are alert to avenues of change and, despite the risks, work for change. Between the dignified resignation of the mechanicals, the dogged endurance of the Levellers, the defiant rebellion of the Cades and the Ketts, there is scope for action, arenas open for contest, and modest gains to be won. The people invoke two ideas in advancing their cause, one respect as a right-holder, the other the dynamic nature of juridical equality, its capacity to generate and justify new entitlements. The history of protest, resistance, and rebellion shows how powerful juridical equality can be in revising social relations.[42] The resulting instability is plain. Between the princely duty to preserve the existing social order, and the people's interest in rising from the feet to a higher, more noble organ, in having a larger stake in society, conflict is unavoidable.

[41] This is not to suggest that a society of complete equality is the goal; for some that is the case, but for most it is a matter of reducing the inequalities.

[42] Discussed in Chapter VIII.

The dilemma for princely rule is plain. The prince ignores at peril the call of the people for a bigger share of social goods: better living and working conditions, security, welfare, and protection against lords and landowners. The case for concessions is hard to ignore, the demand for a place in governing hard to resist, the people persistent in efforts to improve their lives. The prince is inclined to react along two lines, one to grant concessions, the other resist, while the fewer the concessions, the more the need for repression in sustaining the social order. Repression is of limited efficacy. The people are alienated, the disposition of support weakened, and the bonds of society loosened. The despot knows no bounds, acknowledges no bonds; but princely rule depends on both, on a balance between raw power and concern for subjects. The wiser prince who makes concessions is spared the need for repression, and might succeed in satisfying the people for longer, might survive for generations; but is destined for the same fate. The more concessions allowed, the more the people demand, not only for more social goods but for more say in governing. Either way, princely rule is on the path to ruin, although the fate of one who chooses repression will be less dignified than that of the other who makes concessions, loses power, and quietly fades from view.

There is another dimension to add, another ground of instability to count. Apart from seeking a share in government as a means for bettering well-being, some of the people value a place in governing as a good in itself, as a separate strand of well-being. The two dispositions, although tending to merge, are different, one a means to an end, the other an end in itself. A feature of social institutions is that the members value being in charge of their own affairs. In the constitutional field some consider having a share in governing to be a goal worth campaigning for, even if the risk is high and the cost heavy. The goal for some is to rule themselves, although between that and no place, more moderate positions are open. The people know they can entrust governing to others while keeping it under watch, for which they have at hand the five forms of action. Beyond restraining their own actions and giving support, the people know the power of engagement, vigilance, and censure in keeping rule to purpose. Armed with the quintet of actions, the people are able to begin the process of moderating princely rule and moulding it to their well-being. Consequences follow for princely rule. The very concept is premised on the prince ruling without obstruction from the people, without their being entitled to a place in governing. The prince cannot escape the gaze of the people, but in wielding power is spared having to deal with them. Ignoring or denying their demand for a share breeds discontent merging into disaffection. The wise prince manages to maintain strong rule while allowing the people some place in the processes of governing. An equilibrium may be achieved and princely rule secured. The problem for the prince is that once concessions are granted, once the people engage in governing, even at the margins, momentum for a fuller role builds and is hard to stop. The more concessions made, the more demanded, until a point is reached where people are so entrenched that princely rule is weakened and at risk of destruction.

That is the logic of princely rule; what happens in practice is subject to variable factors. On one sequence, princely rule gives way to the people's engagement, gradual at first but leading finally to the demise of the prince, and the rise of rule through representatives. The new order might become embedded, survive and prosper; or soon collapse and the prince return to restore order. English history shows the sequence: Henry VII ruled mainly without obstruction from the people; his son Henry VIII found good reasons for involving them through parliament without loss to his princely power. His daughter Elizabeth I continued in that manner, perhaps conceding more scope to parliament while ruling much as she wished. James I, her successor, proudly insisted on the same, but came under pressure to accept more engagement by parliament. His son Charles I, forced to confront the tension directly, reacted by restoring vigorous princely rule. Only when war loomed did he admit a popular or democratic element in the constitution, although without conceding to the Commons a share in government.[43] The loss of the war marked a turning point. The people had succeeded in engaging, being vigilant, and imposing censure enough to deprive successive princes, slowly but inexorably, of power. A rare case, the more common course the opposite.

Notes: Chapters XI and XII

Taking counsel

Concerning the prince's being able to take advice, Hobbes writes of the advantage the prince has in being able to receive 'counsel of whom, when, and where he pleaseth'. Weber's view seems to be more accurate. He notes how the prince stands outside or above political discussion. He writes: 'a member of parliament can learn to weigh *the power of words* in party *conflict*, whereas the monarch is required to remain *outside* this struggle;—parliament is in a position to acquire the relevant facts on a subject (by cross-examining experts and witnesses under oath) and thus to control the actions of officials. How is this to be effected by a monarch?': M Weber: *Suffrage and Democracy in Germany* in *Political Writings* (ed) P Lassman and R Spiers (Cambridge: Cambridge University Press, 1994), p 127.

People's disposition towards the prince

William Stubbs writing in the late nineteenth century of the fifteenth century, detected 'a growing feeling of attachment to the king, which may be supposed to form

[43] C Stuart, King Charles I: 'The King's Answer to the Nineteen Propositions (1642)' in *The Stuart Constitution: Documents and Commentary* (ed) JP Kenyon (Cambridge: Cambridge University Press, 1986), p 18.

an essential characteristic of the virtue of loyalty'. He goes on: 'Loyalty is a virtuous habit or sentiment of a very composite character; a habit of strong and faithful attachment to a person, not so much by reason of his personal character as of his official position.—Such loyalty gives far more than it receives; the root of the good is in the loyal people not in the sovereign, who may or may not deserve it; there too is a feeling of proprietorship: 'he is no great hero but he is our king'. W Stubbs: *The Constitutional History of England in Its Origin and Development*, Volume 3 (1878) (Republished by Forgotten Books, London), pp 508–9.

The prince rules according to law

James I describes princely power with precision: 'it is sedition in subjects to dispute what a king may do in the height of his power, but just kings will ever be willing to declare what they will do. I will not be content that my power be disputed upon, but I shall ever be willing to make the reason appear of all my doings and rule my actions according to my laws': *Speech to Parliament* 21 March 1610 in *The Stuart Constitution*, p 13.

Vices and virtues of princely rule

In the *Tragedy of Macbeth*, Malcolm lamenting how 'our country sinks beneath the yoke/It weeps, it bleeds and each new day a gash/Is added to her wounds', lists the vices of King Macbeth: 'I grant him bloody,/Luxurious, avaricious, false, deceitful/ Sudden, malicious, smacking of every sin/That has a name': Act 4: 3: 40*ff*.

By contrast are the 'king-becoming graces'. They are many: 'justice, verity, temp'rance, stableness/Bounty, perseverance, mercy, lowliness,/Devotion, patience, courage, fortitude': Act 4: 3: 91*ff*. Malcolm adds he 'has no relish of them', the king-becoming graces. If he were king he would: 'Pour the sweet milk of concord into hell,/Uproar the universal peace, confound/All unity on earth': 99–100. After Macduff's protestation, Malcolm admits: 'Macduff, this noble passion/Child of integrity, hath from my soul/Wiped the black scruples, reconciled my thoughts/ To thy good truth and honour': 115–17.

Montesquieu's spirit of princely rule

Montesquieu is one of the few to have written about the social foundations of princely rule, the conditions that make and sustain it as a common form of rule.

His *The Spirit of the Laws*,[44] is often described as a work of social science, rather than philosophy. Montesquieu divides the forms of government into three: republican, monarchical, and despotic. Monarchy on his account fits within my concept of princely rule. Having identified the forms or models of government, he makes a distinction between 'the nature of each government' and 'its principle'. In explaining the notion of *principle*, he writes: 'There is this difference between the nature and principles of government that the former is that by which it is constituted, the latter that by which it is made to act. One is its particular structure, and the other the human passions which set it in motion'.[45]

Each form of government is sustained by different passions: a republic by virtue; a despotism by fear; monarchy by *honour*. By passions, Montesquieu means the sentiments and dispositions of members of the people towards government. The principle of monarchy is *honour*: 'the prejudice of every person and rank'.[46] It replaces virtue as the animating spirit of monarchy. Honour is 'capable of inspiring the most glorious actions, and, joined with the force of laws, may lead us to the end of government as well as virtue itself'. Despite scattered comments suggesting they might also have honour, the people have no place in the social understanding of monarchy, other than to obey, an approach squarely within the contours of the upper register of constitutional thought.

Common good

James I of England, VI of Scotland thought of himself as the perfect prince. His speech to Parliament shortly after his accession to the English throne is elegant and exact: 'I will ever prefer the Weal of the Publick, and of the whole Commonwealth to any particular or private Ends of mine. Thinking ever the Wealth and Weal of the Commonwealth to be my greatest Weal, and worldly Felicity, a point wherein a lawful king doth directly differ from a tyrant.... The righteous and just King doth by the contrary acknowledge himself to be ordained for the procuring of the Wealth and Prosperitie of his People.' (Quoted by John Locke: *Second Treatise of Government*, p 399) James I's words are considered again in Chapter XV.

[44] Baron de Montesquieu: *The Spirit of the Laws* (published in 1748, published in English in several editions) (New York: Hafner Publishing, 1949): translated by Thomas Nugent, Introduction by Franz Neumann.

[45] *Ibid*, p 19.

[46] *Ibid*, p 24.

Body politic a harmonious whole

John of Salisbury portrays the body politic and the inherent harmony in this way. 'Then how much more care should be taken by princes to be moderate – at one time by the vigour of mercy, at another by the forgiveness of mercy—so that subjects are made to be of a single mind as in a household and the works of peace and charity create one perfect and great harmony out of disputes that appear discordant': *Polycraticus*, p 51.

On the good health of the body politic, John writes at length. One passage speaks plainly: 'The health of the whole republic will only be secure and splendid if the superior members devote themselves to the inferiors and if the inferiors respond likewise to the legal rights of their superiors, so that each individual may be likened to a part of the others reciprocally and each believes what is to his own advantage to be determined by that which he recognizes to be most useful for others': *Polycraticus*, p 126.

In assessing the consequences of transgressions by inferiors or superiors, John turns to the Book of Isaiah, where it is stated: 'The entire head languishes and the entire heart laments; from the soles of the feet straight up to top of the head there is no health in the body.' *Polycraticus*, p 142.

Effective and ineffective rule

Ineffective rule tells much about effective rule. The reign of Henry IV serves the purpose. William Stubbs describes it in this way: 'The Crown was impoverished, and with impoverishment came inefficiency. The treasury was always low, the peace was never well kept, the law was never well executed; individual life and property were insecure; whole districts were in a permanent alarm of robbery and riot; the local administration was either paralysed by party faction or lodged in the hand of some great lord or some clique of courtiers. The evil of local faction struck upwards and placed the elections to the parliament at the command of the leaders.'[47]

Commenting on the general failure of the Lancastrian kings, Stubbs further illustrates 'lack of governance': 'the court was led by favourites, justice was perverted, strength was pitted against weakness, riots, robberies, forcible entries were prevalent as before.'[48]

[47] W Stubbs: *The Constitutional History of England in its Origin and Development*, p 270.
[48] *Ibid*, p 273.

Prince and administration

In a study of administration during the era of princely rule in England, SB Chrimes writes of the early Tudor system: 'the medieval administrative system was the creation and instrument of the monarchy, designed and fashioned to give expression to the principle of personal government by the king, in whom alone supreme executive authority was vested': (1943–45) *Bulletin of the Institute of Historical Research* 243.

He continues: 'In the period under review—the period from 1399 to 1526—the vicissitudes in administrative history seem due primarily to vicissitudes in the degree to which executive authority was asserted by the kings themselves—': p 243. Chrimes then quotes approvingly from McFarlane: 'The truth is England was a monarchy, which is to say that it depended for its healthy functioning upon the exercise of the kingship': p 179.

Regarding the Tudor monarchs, Chrimes writes: 'The Tudor Monarchy was essentially a rejuvenated personal monarchy, able to instil vigour into the old administrative agencies and to create new ones out of the old; and by maintaining its mastery over the whole, it was able to carry the power of the executive to a level scarcely dreamt of, certainly never attained, in the past': p 262.

XII
The People Ruling Themselves: I

1. Model of self-rule

The people enter a constitutional field where they rule themselves. Having noted the merits of princely rule but deterred by the defects, they are keen to learn what self-rule has to offer. They value being in charge of their affairs and are drawn to the prospect of a constitutional order where being in charge applies to the affairs of government. They are curious to know what ruling themselves would mean in practice, in what sense they would be in charge, and how that would fit with the processes of governing. The people are used to government being distant, engagement kept low, their well-being in the gift of agencies and officials. They learn early on that, while segments of life are lived alone, critical aspects of well-being are best served by forming social relationships for collective action. The fields of everyday life to be well-cultivated need more than the solitary tiller of the soil, and rely on people working together to reap a good harvest. The same reasoning applies to governing, a form of collective action, from which all benefit by conceding power to agencies and officials. Ruling themselves would be different. The people would decide the policies best to serve their well-being and instruct the agencies and officials accordingly. That is the strength and the stumbling block. How the people can be in charge of governing; how they can set the course and decide the main matters; and at the same time have an effective legislative and executive, administrative and judicial system. Even being in charge of major decisions is not straightforward. What does it mean, and how are disagreements to be resolved without some winning some losing? When the machinery of government is added the problem is more acute. The people are unsure how to match the need for agencies and officials with self-rule. The task now is to address these issues by proposing a model of self-rule, showing the appeal, and confronting the drawbacks and the instabilities.

That plenary power to rule vest in the people is the main idea. People refers to the aggregate of persons and is not to be confused with the corporate entity, which has no place in self-rule.[1] To have plenary power means that the people, collectively, are responsible for the course and conduct of government. Some matters they decide themselves, others they delegate to agencies and officials, over whom they keep watch and who answer to them. Certain features follow.

[1] On the people as a corporate entity, see Chapter II:3.

Keepers of the Common Good. D.J. Galligan, Oxford University Press. © D.J. Galligan 2024.
DOI: 10.1093/9780198907398.003.0012

First The people decide the main issues of governing. Just how that is achieved, the processes needed, and how to handle division have to be worked out.

Second Within bounds set by the people, some of the functions of government are delegated to officials and agencies.

Third Provision is made at all levels of government for the people to engage in whatever ways are practicable, while avenues of vigilance are open and easily accessed.

Fourth Agencies and officials are under exacting duties to account for their actions to the people, who have available ample means of censure.

Fifth Each process of governing is designed to balance the need for effective and timely action, and the people's interest in guiding, influencing, and monitoring the process.

Sixth The concept of representation has no place, the people either settle a matter directly or delegate it to persons or agencies.

The model of self-rule is likely to be met with scepticism, scorned as not credible, the form of government not practicable. Perhaps it could work in a small community, among the yeomen and yeowomen of Vacy Plains and the diamond traders of New York, in the financial world of the City of London, even in small states, although the record is not encouraging. The early Italian city-states, after freeing themselves from outside rule, proclaimed self-rule, which came to mean rule by a few, while in many states the princes were soon back in the palaces, the 'upstarts' of self-rule back in their places.[2] In a sizeable nation the model seems implausible and unsuited to reality. Some American states, Pennsylvania principally, cultivated a constitutional field of real self-rule, but were mocked and vilified, accused of being run by 'upstarts drunk on liberty', the crop bound to fail, which in the face of such hostility it did. Let us reserve judgement on upstarts in Siena, Pennsylvania, or wherever who dare to try to rule themselves until we have a better understanding of what that means.

2. Value of self-rule

Liberty is the interest at the foundation of self-rule. Liberty in the sense of 'the right or power to do as one pleases',[3] being free to live as one wishes. Being free, a

[2] The 'upstarts' according to William Bowsky were the new city nobility who tried to replace the old nobility: WM Bowsky: 'Ferdinand Schevill and the History of Medieval Siena: A Critical Essay', introduction to F Schevill: *Siena: The History of a Medieval Commune* (first published 1909) (New York & London: Harper & Row, 1964).

[3] *Concise Oxford English Dictionary*, p 698.

quality of well-being highly valued, gives rise to a sentiment from which follows a disposition to take action. The sentiment and the disposition, while strong, meet opposition from competing interests, over which being free at times prevails but by which it is often defeated. Liberty remains, despite all, a longing deeply embedded in sentiment, 'a spark in the ashes' ever ready to be fanned into flame. Liberty is valued for two reasons, one *intrinsic*, another *instrumental*. Being free is a quality of being a person. Not just one interest among many, being free is constitutive of personhood from which other interests follow. The slave under the will of another, even if well-treated, yearns to be free. Being free is the means to secure other valued interests. In addition to the satisfaction of being free, the free person is able to decide the course of life, select and rank aspects of well-being, form matching sentiments and dispositions, and take action. The instrumental value of liberty lies in a person being able to plan life and put the plan into practice. Some interests are served by personal endeavour, others by collective action. The hermit in the wild is free to live as he wishes, while the urban iconoclast tries to avoid social relationships. They are exceptions. Most people share their lives with others, form relationships, and have the benefits not only of companionship, but collective action in advancing well-being. How free persons come together to produce outcomes compatible with being free is a question central to self-rule.

Collective action means acting together, forming social relations for common ends. Liberty is involved in two ways, one the liberty to enter or not, the other the effect of entry on liberty. Some social relations are enforced rather than freely entered, the liberty to enter or not overridden by other interests, whether education of the child, care for the patient, or protection from the outlaw. Let us put these aside and concentrate on social relations entered freely: family (at least for some members) and friendship, work and leisure, business and enterprise, and many others. The image of a field of action again proves useful, daily life consisting of many sub-fields, each to advance interests and contribute to well-being. One enters freely but having entered accepts that, within the field, freedom has to be curbed in order to gain the benefits of collective action. Curbed in both the process of reaching an outcome and the content of the outcome. The logic of collective action applies to governing, where liberty features in several ways, sometimes gaining, sometimes losing. One is agreeing to submit to rule, to acquiesce in Hume's terms, putting themselves under government in Locke's. Each person is at liberty not to submit but the cost is high. As long as enough benefits are gained, the case for entering the field and restricting liberty is compelling. Submission is easier in the case of self-rule because each is engaged in the process of ruling, each has some say in how power is used, a sharp contrast with princely rule. Although how much say varies, being free to take part is a defining feature, the outcome settled among the people, not a gift of the prince. The next feature of ruling as collective action is the capacity of government to deliver social goods that other forms of collective action cannot, or not as effectively. That after all is the case for the power of the state, as noted back in Chapter I.[4]

The advantage of self-rule is that the people decide how that power is to be used, which interests to advance, which aspects of well-being to foster. The contrast with princely rule is again stark. Instead of the prince deciding which interests count and how much, a process in which the people have at most a minor part, now they are in charge of both. A third feature is that liberty may be one of the social goods advanced directly or indirectly by rule. Directly where rule increases liberty in matters such as association and movement, expression and enterprise. The indirect benefit is less obvious but valued. The people in ruling are able to expand the range of protected interests; to broaden and improve security and welfare, mark out the space in which each person is free to act, a space for initiative and endeavour. These three main functions of government, now under the control of the people, have the potential to improve the quality of life in many ways, including adding to liberty. But liberty has to enter the field and compete with other interests, some enhancing others curtailing, some directly others indirectly. Directly by providing security or defending the nation, handling an emergency or conserving nature; indirectly by removing barriers and opening opportunities for each person to improve life.

The worth of the people's ruling themselves is now plain. First, it serves the interest each person has in being free. Secondly, self-rule enables the people to rank, settle, and secure other interests contributing to well-being, including enabling one to do things and so adding to liberty. Liberty is the foundation of self-rule; but in order to advance other interests, may be restricted and reduced, even removed. That all such matters be under the charge of the people is the defining feature. The case for self-rule will seem to some implausible and impractical, proof on its face that unless the people accept the authority of one or a few, government is bound to fail, with consequences for liberty and well-being. Hobbes insisted that only a ruler with plenary power could provide sound rule. He went on to salvage liberty with the fiction that Leviathan's actions are really the actions of each person. More moderate accounts insist that effective rule depends on power being in the hands of one or a few, who then decide the balance between liberty and other interests; but do so under the watch of the people. Charles I conceded that to be the duty of the elected chamber; not to govern but to keep government under watch to ensure respect for liberty. Just how it fitted with firm rule was left unsaid. Princely rule in time gave way to rule by an elected few, itself a form of government founded on liberty. A balance still had to be found between liberty and other social goods, between the wishes of the people and the good of the nation. Just what the balance or equilibrium is between power and liberty, and how to attain it varies across and

[4] Chapter I:3.

within constitutional orders. The people ruling themselves try to find a balance between the two, firm rule on the one hand, nurturing liberty on the other. How likely that is, whether the scepticism is justified, are best left until the structure of self-rule is fully in place.

3. Self-rule in the Italian city-states

The people's ruling themselves holds such appeal, appears so superior in advancing well-being, one wonders why it is not the common form of rule, when in practice a rarity. To help in grasping the gap between the ideal and the reality, a journey back to the city-states of Italy in the twelfth to fifteenth centuries is instructive. Venice, Florence, Siena, and others were freeing themselves from rule by emperors and popes, princes and bishops, to claim freedom and independence. Fresh ideas emerged of social relations among the people and between the people and government, a conception of constitutional order in part new, in part a revival of ideas reaching back to the Roman republic.[5] Self-rule was the *motif*, the idea that a city-state could be free only if it were ruling itself. The concept proved to be ambiguous in meaning and uncertain in practice, and before long fell out of use, replaced either by the return of the prince or the rise of the representative few. The end may have been foretold but the journey is worthwhile, the turbulence instructive, and how the ground was laid for rule by representatives of interest. The city-state of Siena during the thirteenth and fourteenth centuries is a telling case study.

In the 1320s, the commune of Siena commissioned Ambrogio Lorenzetti to paint a series of frescoes in the *Palazzo Pubblico*, to adorn the meeting room of the ruling council, the *Nove*. The series of three, finished in 1328, is now known as the *Allegoria di Buon Governo*. Having freed itself from outside control, Siena adopted a series of constitutions, *costitui*, the latest in 1262. The Latin text later was translated into Italian, *la lingua volgare* and in large letters to make it readable by the people.[6] The painting displays the effects of good government on the right, bad government on the left. One presents the people of a well-governed city going about their business, the streets bustling and the shops busily trading; the countryside well-tended, farms flourishing, and the youths dancing in the street as they do to this day.[7] The fresco opposite depicts the effects of bad government, the spoil and ruin, a scene of degradation, empty streets and farms untended. Above all the figure of *Justice*, the measure of good government, wrapped in a shroud lies in the gutter.

[5] A tradition of constitutional discourse with its origins in Roman law is analysed in Q Skinner: *Liberty Before Liberalism* (Cambridge: Cambridge University Press, 1998).

[6] An original manuscript is on display in the *Archivio di Stato* of Siena.

[7] Whether the dancers are male or female is debated. There is reason to doubt young women would have been allowed dance in the streets of fourteenth-century Siena.

The central fresco depicts the constitutional order of Siena as a free state. No emperor or pope to be seen, the bishops back in their churches, the *Duomo* tucked into the top corner; the city free from overlords and mercenaries. All absent although never far away, Siena for the time a city-state ruling itself. Around the central figure the constitutional order is assembled. Justice and concord combine to guide the course of governing. A red and white cord from the hand of *Justice* passes to *Concord*, then courses through the hands of twenty-four citizens to end in government. A city-state that acts justly and fosters concord is well-governed. Other qualities, including prudence and fortitude, temperance and magnanimity, cluster around to contribute to good government. The figure of peace, slightly apart, fixes her gaze on the central figure as if to confirm her own place at the core of a well-governed city-state.[8] Liberty is not listed as a guide to or quality of good government, indeed is not mentioned. An inscription at the bottom sums up good government: the 'holy virtue of Justice' induces unity among citizens who exercise through 'their rulers, *per lor signor*, a common good' for themselves.[9] Between justice and concord there is ambiguity. If justice 'induces unity among citizens', concord or consensus is implicit and not needed as a separate concept. Despite the inscription, in listing concord as well as justice, Lorenzetti seems to be warning that justice while essential to good government is not enough; there must be a level of agreement or consensus, a point to return to shortly.

The two sides of *self-rule* are on view, one of Siena as a city-state free from *outside* rule, a field fenced off from intruders; the other the form of rule *inside* the field. Being free from outside control tells nothing about rule within, a matter the people now have to settle. Having rid themselves of princes, sacred or secular, the people adopt rule based on justice and concord. Rule is entrusted to a council, drawn from the superior classes, represented by the twenty-four citizens through whose hands the white cord passes.[10] The placing of rule in the hands of a few raises several points of interest. The people, the ordinary citizens, are absent from the central fresco and have no place in Lorenzetti's order of government. If 'rulers and magistrates' have power delegated 'to them by the sovereign body of the people', as commentators including Bartolus and Marsiglio argued,[11] we should expect the relationship between the people and the council to be centre-stage, not absent. Self-rule still could be saved, for the strongest version allows delegation of authority to officials, although how much is compatible with genuine self-rule is left open. The

[8] A second figure of justice, *Giustizia,* appears to the left of *Buon Governo,* among the qualities guiding good government. The point of the second figure is not clear other than to reinforce the role of justice in good government.

[9] I draw on the translation by Quentin Skinner: *Visions of Politics* (Volume II) (Cambridge: Cambridge University Press, 2002), p 99.

[10] The identity of the twenty-four is examined in G Piccini: *Operazione Buon Governo* (Torino: Einaudi, 2022).

[11] Q Skinner: *The Foundations of Modern Political Thought: The Renaissance* (Cambridge: Cambridge University Press: 1997), Volume 1, p 62.

council of twenty-four had plenary power, full authority to take all measures considered necessary or desirable. Its successor, the council of the *Nove*, was 'granted licence and unrestrained power and authority', leaving no room for popular engagement, or so we might conclude.[12] The process of appointment and the terms of delegation, the painting leaves unexplained. The ruling council is in place and empowered, while how members got there and whether they are accountable is left out, not mentioned. The narrative of self-rule starts to founder. The common people of Siena are not in charge of governing; most are not engaged in any way; nor do they decide who serves on the governing council. The people might be sovereign in an abstract, fictitious sense, but between them and the ruling council there is no direct social relationship, no role in appointing the council, limiting its authority, or holding it to account. Rule inside the constitutional field depicted by Lorenzetti is a long way from the people genuinely ruling themselves.[13]

There is just a hint the people are not wholly absent from good government. By 1328, the governing council of twenty-four, the *Council of the Bell*, had been abolished, and replaced by a smaller council of nine, the *Nove*. Members of the larger council were drawn half from the nobility, half from other sectors of Sienese society. In 1277, the *grandi* were barred from office, the council of twenty-four disbanded and plenary power passed to the *Nove*. The nine members came from a select sector of the people, *i popolani*, a people's party with origins in local military units, which in time came under the influence of a rising merchant class grouped in guilds. Members of the *Nove* served for two months, then nominated their successors from among mainly merchants to the exclusion of other groups and sectors, whether lawyers or notaries, shopkeepers or farm-hands.[14] This is a curiosity rather than a criticism, *Boun Governo* being an allegory and a work of art, not a treatise on history. Yet, Lorenzetti would have known the council of twenty-four had long been replaced by the nine, a ruling council of a more select few rather than the larger council drawn from a range of groups and sectors. Perhaps he was harking back to a notion of government more broadly based, where the consuls were elected, the network of committees more open and responsive to the people, who themselves met in the *Piazza del Campo* as a *parlamentum* and had some say in governing. Lorenzetti could be suggesting that while the *Nove* deserve praise for ruling well, good government generally is more secure if the people have a place, have some influence on the course it takes and some scope for censure.[15] Not governing themselves but at least being engaged and having influence.

[12] *Ibid* pp 40*ff.*

[13] On fictions, see Chapter II:4.

[14] For an assessment of the rule of the *Nove*, see F Schevill: *Siena: The History of a Medieval Commune* (New York: Harper and Row, 1909). In the introduction to the 1964 edition, William Bowsky suggests some corrections; but overall Schevill's account is accurate. See also W Bowsky: *Un comune italiano nel Medioevo: Siena sotto il regime dei Nove (1287–1355)* (Milano: Il Mulino, 1986).

[15] Mauro Ascheri writes with commanding authority of Siena and the city-states generally: *Storia Politica e Sociale della Repubblica di Siena* (Siena: Betti, 2000); *Le Città-Stato* (Bologna: Il Mulino, 2006); M Ascheri and C Papi: *Il Costituto' del Comune di Siena in volgare* (1309–1310) (Siena: ASKA, 2009).

4. Constitutional order of self-rule

The rule of the *Nove* is praised as good rule and to see why we need to enquire into the constitutional order. The critical qualities of *Buon Governo* are justice and concord, liberty at best limping along in the shadows, a result of good government rather than a defining quality. Let us consider justice and concord, then ask about liberty. Protective justice means being entitled to what is due *within* the law, to be treated according to the standards set by law.[16] Justice in this sense is procedural, the means by which to uphold the law. One part is retributive in punishing for breach of the criminal law, the other restitutive in restoring what according to civil law is due within a social relationship. Both are administered by the angels of justice, one on the right of *Giustizia*, the other on the left. Nothing is said about the *justice of the law*, the justice of what is due, the ends to which law is directed, the interests protected, the interests of well-being to advance.[17] Such matters are entrusted to the *Nove* not the people; they have some influence, varying according to status, but the *Nove* decide. A marked contrast with an order in which the people decide what constitutes justice in a substantive sense, settle the terms of social relationships, and render their decisions into law.

Concord has both appeal and drawbacks. Concord means harmony across social relationships, while discord its opposite signals division into factions and strife among them. In societies riddled with both, as Siena and other city-states were, concord among the people was prized, for without concord there can be no peace; and without peace other goals of governing, even justice, would be out of reach. The benefits of concord and the peace it brings during the rule of the *Nove*, Lorenzetti makes plain. The people live in safety in a setting of fine buildings, squares and gardens, curving streets and passages, all grouped around the central piazza, *Il Campo*, the pride of the city and the centre of social life. The arts flourish, education and scholarship are valued, all contributing to the cultivation of civility and humanity. Beyond the city walls, the *contado* is another source of satisfaction for the beauty and fertility, the rhythm of life and abundant harvests. Above all, the people, going about their business in safety and security, appear to be free and content in their lives. Concord, however, comes with a history, a set of meanings settled in medieval discourse of the body politic.[18] Concord consists in all organs being in their right place, each functioning as nature dictates. The head oversees the whole and keeps the lower organs in order. *Buon Governo* fits the imagery of the body politic, the *signore*, the grandee mounted on a fine horse, the groom following on foot, the swineherd bowing as they pass. The people labour at their jobs

[16] For discussion of the two senses, see Chapter I:2.

[17] Lorenzetti marks one as distributive justice, the other commutative. Yet, the one marked distributive portrays the angel administering punishment, while the one marked commutative shows the resolution of a dispute between two persons.

[18] For discussion of the body politic, see Chapter VII:3–6.

and dress according to their place, from the finery of the councillors to the coarse cloth of the shepherd and the simple tunics of the farm-hands. A scene of harmony and peace, the law on duty as guardian.

Is there a hint, however, that concord has a dark side, cementing a social order in which benefits bestowed and openings for improvement are uneven, where a few do well, most cope, many barely manage? The mounted grandee is a long way from the workmen hauling loads of stone and brick to the rooftops in the blazing sun. Whether they rejoice in concord and sing praise in the taverns, or harbour ideas of how things could be otherwise, how they could be free to better themselves, we can only guess. Like Peter Quince they may have a sense things could be different, how labouring men and women, shepherds and swineherds, together with other callings and sectors could have more scope to better their lives, even have a place in governing, some say in the interests to advance, the ends to pursue. On one view, the concord of *Buon Governo* has origins in a discourse the opposite of the people ruling themselves. A discourse that presents social relations in imagery designed to preserve the social structure with no room for change; no space for one organ to leave its ordained place, let alone usurp the place of another. The lower orders, the feet, are to stay where they are, their destiny to add to the health of the whole, which does not include rising in the social order or taking part in ruling. The aim is to smooth over social divisions and the conflicts mounting, to project harmony, stability, and unity as the supreme values, and to cast governing as the care of a loving father for his family. John of Salisbury, the master artist of the body politic, had he lived to visit Siena in 1328, would have admired the allegory of good government and felt at home

A people ruling itself has no use for the body politic, neither the imagery nor the outcome. Beyond such imagery the terrain is uneven, the social order in flux, where concord has to be earned not assumed. Concord means agreement among the people, but agreement as to what? Not agreement across all social relationships, for disagreement is normal and healthy. Concord is valued but so is discord, jarring though it be, in allowing all interests to surface and be counted, and in that way contribute to good government.[19] Some level of agreement is necessary in forming and sustaining social relations, and in turn a constitutional order; how much is hard to say. Here the concept of *consensus* as shared sentiment of support for government proves useful.[20] Support is earned by government's providing for the well-being of all, the level of support dependent on the degree of well-being. Lorenzetti presents Siena as a city-state where the level of support for government is high, despite the people's chances to engage being low. This image suggests another way of explaining how concord as consensus is necessary to good government. Siena was at risk of being torn apart by conflict and feuding among families

[19] Machiavelli will soon be on the scene to advocate the benefits of discord.
[20] Discussed in Chapter VIII.

and factions, groups and sectors. If allowed to continue the well-being of all would suffer, justice would be in the gutter, and the city-state weakened in defence. The people, regardless of their place in the social order, agree on the need to support a form of rule that secures peace, for without peace government is weak and unable to protect well-being.

Several lessons follow. First, strong rule is needed to maintain peace, of which the *Nove* were capable. That was preferable to the return of the prince, the usual solution. The need for firm rule leaves no room for the people's being engaged on more than the margins. The more involved the weaker the rule, while the idea of their being in charge was dismissed out of hand. The price of peace within the city-state is the people's acquiescing, not trying to govern. Secondly, a city-state at peace is able to advance other aspects of well-being, cultivate humanity and civility in the manner of the Sienese; not only within the bounds set by the need for peace, but beyond. Slight adjustments to the social order may be tolerable, anything more serious a threat to peace. Civility and humanity are to be sought, the well-being of the people nurtured within a field designed to secure concord and peace. The body politic has been buried but the ghost stays on to haunt its successors. Settled social relations are to be preserved, the squire and the swineherd, the shepherd and the stonemason all in their proper places. Finally, if concord and peace take root in social relations, reducing reliance on iron rule, the scope for the people to be engaged in governing widens and the interests that count increase. Even discord, natural to any social order but smothered and kept out of sight, suffocated in sustaining concord and peace, could be allowed a modest place in the constitutional field.

5. A modest reappraisal

Buon Governo is open to another interpretation, subtle but persuasive. The constitutional order framing good government is the well-being of the people, of which justice is an essential quality. Each having what is due is a sign of respect for each citizen as a bearer of rights. In leaving the state of nature to enter civil society, the people give up trying to get what they want in exchange for what is due, as Vico wisely observed and Hume would agree. Justice is the measure and the guardian of what is due, and for that reason has a place at the core of a constitutional order. From justice the base, well-being branches out in all directions, some shared, many diverse and competing. To govern well is to provide the conditions in which all interests count, conflicts are resolved, rights and duties defined, the conditions created for all to flourish. The master stroke follows: justice, peace, and concord are best realized by entrusting rule to a few. Not just any few but a few drawn from the superior sectors of society, because they know what is best for the whole. The identity of the citizens through whose hands the white cord passes is now plain. Members of the superior sectors, they know the common good and entrust rule to a few of their number, who in turn represent the society as a whole. The few, like the prince before them, know and act for the common good and the structure of social relations on which it rests. The foundations of rule by representatives are laid. Within the bounds set by the few representatives, the people are encouraged to cultivate well-being, civility, and humanity. The signs of a distinct discourse, an upper register of ideas and language, appear and give meaning and justification to the constitutional structure.

That brings us to liberty, the interest most valued by the people ruling themselves. Liberty is best achieved by the people deciding the course of government and being free to engage in the processes of governing. The two qualities of liberty we have seen, one valued as a good in itself, the other a means to other social goods, which may include liberty. The first, the foundation of self-rule, is absent from *Buon Governo*. During the fifty years of government by the *Nove*, a tiny fraction of the population served on the council of the *Nove*, most from the more prosperous mercantile sectors, at best a few from the lower orders. Some scope was left for others to be engaged in administrative matters, a few at the higher levels, most low down. The core value of self-rule, that the people be in control of government, decide the ranking of interests, settle policies, and make laws—*liberty to make law*—is missing. Liberty in a secondary sense results from government—*liberty under law*. Liberty in this sense occurs within the spaces defined and protected by law. The bankers' liberty to do business within the city and across borders, and the shopkeepers' to trade; the farmers' to cultivate the fields as they judge best, and not least the *signore*'s to strut the streets on his spirited steed. The groom trudging behind, the workers threshing the wheat, and the swineherd taking his pig for a walk, all have some space to do as they please. How much space and, thus, how much liberty varies in scope and quality, defined by law and guarded by justice. Defining the scope and the quality of liberty is a function of government regardless of who governs, whether the prince, the few, or the people. Respect for liberty is shown by marking the protected space, stating what may be done within it, and defining the authority of officials or other persons to interfere. When violated, justice is on duty with remedies accessible to all. Liberty, in brief, is to act as one pleases without interference within a space defined as to scope and quality, the one how broad or narrow the space, the other what may be done within it. Liberty is linked to rights, the scope and quality of liberty determined by the companion right. Rights arise on the foundation of juridical equality to define relations between the people and government.[21] To have a right is to have an interest around which is a band of freedom to act, a space in which the right-holders are free to do what they like. The scope and value of a right depends on several factors: the defining rules; the degree of discretionary intrusion; and the availability of remedies for breach.

[21] On juridical equality, see Chapter IX:9, 10, 11.

Against this background, there are two last points to note. One that rights and liberties are common currency in any constitutional order framed by juridical equality. Social relations between rulers and ruled are conducted within the frame, regardless of who rules. The other point is the people ruling themselves, all persons and sectors engaged, are likely to select for protection as rights a range of interests broadly based and responsive to the needs and utilities of all. Here who rules does matter. The prince, knowing the people value the security of rights, provides protection and recourse for breach, knowledge the *Nine* plainly shared. The difference is not that the prince or the *Nine* fail to make laws protecting rights and hence liberties. Certain rights are likely to be protected no matter *who* rules, while above the threshold the selection depends on who rules. The more engaged the people are in governing, the wider the range of interests chosen for protection is likely to be, and as a result liberty expanded. Promoting the interests of certain groups and sectors weighs on the prince and the few, while the people in selecting and ranking interests are expected to have more regard for the interests of all, among which liberty counts. Whether that would be the case in practice, and what the outcome would be, is a matter for later comment.

The conclusions to be drawn concerning the allegory of good government as imagined in fourteenth-century Siena are several. Good government within the city-state does not mean the people ruling themselves judged by the model of self-rule. Good government is guided by justice and concord, where concord promotes peace, a condition of being able to govern well. Concord means consensus among the people that keeping the peace is the first priority of government, a priority best entrusted to the prudent few. Within the bounds of peace, other interests are advanced. The people accept rule by a few as a reliable means to peace, which leads them to restrain their liberty to engage in governing. As peace comes to prevail, the rigidity of rule eases to allow the people room to engage, although the level and the quality remain narrow. Liberty is valued not as the only or even main purpose of social endeavour, but as one good among others, in Siena concord and peace especially. If social relations become more stable, it may be safe to open up the processes of governing to allow the people more say. Finally, liberty as a function of rights is valued as an outcome of rule, but again in comparison with other social goods, the balancing among them dependent on a mix of practical factors and the judgement of the prince, the few, or the people.

6. Ideas of self-rule and their fate

Siena of the fourteenth century covers just one corner of a canvas of constitutional ideas abroad at the time. Beyond Siena and the allegory of good government, similar ideas of rule were circulating among the city-states of Italy and elsewhere across Europe. Being free from outside control is one thing, how to design the constitution inside quite another, and a subject of interest among scholars and commentators of medieval and renaissance Italy. Liberty is their starting point, the interest said to be most valued in serving the well-being of all. The question then is what kind of constitutional order best preserves liberty. Princes are unreliable and cannot be trusted, and so the mantle of rule is best worn by the people. The path so far well-marked now darkens and divides, throwing into doubt what it means for the people to rule themselves. The more elevated and ambitious imagine 'the whole body of the people' constitute government. Ambition tempered by practicality drops a notch to the more ambiguous idea of each person's having 'an equal opportunity of involving himself in the business of governing'.[22] Then comes the slide from active involvement of all citizens, in practice inconvenient, to delegation of authority to a few. Republican Rome in the background and much admired, dealt with the inconvenience by shifting authority from the people to the magistrates and the nobility.[23] In the hands of the Venetians inconvenience ascends to be high principle, from which to infer the form of rule best serving liberty. The republic of Venice, a city-state saluted as a model of rule grounded in liberty, governed itself through three institutions, the *Consiglio Grande*, the *Senate*, and the *Doge*. Authority shared among institutions, one princely, one noble, one elected, came to be seen as the form of rule best to preserve liberty. A few rule while the rest have at best a foothold on the edges, not a base at the centre.[24] Relations between the people, ruling, and liberty are revised, the idea abandoned that liberty means the people being engaged in governing. Liberty, now focusing on outcome rather than process, is deemed to be safer in the hands of a few than the multitude. The people's having 'equal opportunity' of involving themselves in governing loses its appeal and slips out of sight. Some found rule in Venice not firmly enough in the hands of the few and deplored the elective base of the *Consiglio Grande*. The wisdom displayed in the Sienese allegory of good government, that rule is best left to a council of the few, spread to become received opinion among counsellors, commentators, and of course the few.

The idea took root that some are better qualified to govern than others, know the meaning and value of liberty and how to protect it.[25] Florence was criticized for having a *Consiglio Grande* that 'dangerously overbalanced the constitution in the direction of democracy'.[26] Biding time and ready to re-enter the constitutional field were familiar ideas. One, crisply stated by Francesco Guicciardini, that the people are 'not capable of deciding matters of great importance'.[27] In defending the people

[22] Q Skinner: *Foundations* I, pp 61 and 151.

[23] *Ibid* p 151.

[24] Described in B Manin: *The Principles of Representative Government* (Cambridge: Cambridge University Pres, 2007), pp 63–7.

[25] The force of that idea is shown in Chapter VII.

[26] Words of Quentin Skinner: *Foundations* I, p 172.

[27] F Guicciardini: *Considerations of the 'Discourse' of Machiavelli* quoted in Skinner: *Foundations*, p 161.

against the charge of being 'variable, fickle, and ungrateful', the common view, Machiavelli praised them when 'well-ordered' as 'stable, prudent, and grateful'.[28] His purpose was to show that government by the people is better than by princes. The people, fired by 'a deep desire to be free', best protect freedom, and so rule by the people is better than rule by princes. What rule by the people means is left unclear but seems to be no more than the people's having a 'share' in governing, at least electing officials and keeping a check on them.[29] Machiavelli was not an advocate for rule by the people in a more radical sense. Other commentators urged outright that rule be restricted to the nobility, the small group of grandees who could be trusted to rule for the common good, of which liberty was part.[30] On another view the people delegate power to officials as 'a matter of administrative convenience', a way of getting done the job of governing, a delegation of the people's power to officials not a surrender, although what is left with the people is not clear. That view shades into another: *the people* as an abstract concept may be sovereign, but can act only through real persons appointed for the purpose. It is then a short step to deem those appointed to represent the whole, which as we have seen mutates into their becoming the whole. The short step was later taken and representation moved from the wings to centre-stage. To conclude, the form of government of the Italian city-states was rule by the people as opposed to rule by outsiders; but self-rule only in the modified metaphorical form described. If liberty be the guiding goal, neither princely rule nor rule by the people is to be trusted, the obvious alternative and one of surpassing merit, was considered to be rule by a select few kept under the eye of the many.

Not everyone resigned themselves to the iron bond between liberty and rule by a few. Some clung to a vision of the people's genuinely ruling themselves being liberty's best guardian. That meant the people's not just being engaged in but having charge of governing, deciding which interests to foster, which to fetter. Liberty in that sense is denied by allowing the few to decide. A second reason for standing by real self-rule relates to the outcome of rule, how well the government by a few serves liberty. The risk is that a ruling few in designing the constitutional field affirm or deny liberty according to their own interests rather than the interests of all. The best safeguard is rule by the people, who aim to increase the rights and liberties of all. Much of governing has to be delegated to officials, leaving the people to find a practical balance between being in charge and the need to delegate. Active citizens replace passive subjects and engage in the affairs of the state in a multitude of ways, direct and indirect. Active citizens are vigilant, alert to the actions of officials and insist on reasons, backed by the power to censure. The level

[28] N Machiavelli: *The Discourses* (London: Penguin Books, 1970), p 157.

[29] *Ibid* pp 156–8. This matches the form of government later described by James Madison as *republican: The Federalist* No XXXIX, *Federalist Papers*, pp 190–1.

[30] F Patrizi: *The Founding of a Republic*, quoted in Skinner: *Foundations* I, p 161.

and intensity of their engagement in, and influence on government, together with the scope for scrutiny, are variables from one city-state to another and from one epoch to another. In the Italian city-states such voices and visions were on the margins, the voices drowned out by the noisy clamour for alliance of liberty and rule by a few, the visions dismissed as dangerous delusions.

7. Destiny of the discourse of self-rule

The Italian city-states did not last and the princes were soon back in their palaces. Some lived longer, Venice most notably, while the legacy of ideas and the influence on constitutional discourse survived and flourished. The main elements are worth restating. First, the organic image of society and the body politic where each has an allotted place gives way to personal autonomy and independence. All persons individually and in concert with others are capable of shaping life as they wish and to act for their well-being, for which they need a sphere of liberty. With liberty at the centre, the discourse of pre-modern Italy, inspired by images of republican Rome, imagined a framework of social relations and a constitutional discourse founded on personal freedom, valued for itself and as the means to other valued goods. Secondly, however, the discourse offered scant guidance in designing the constitutional field, the practical matter of governing, and the form most conducive to liberty. At one level a disappointment, at another understandable, even wise. Securing and advancing liberty depends on conditions no one form of government is sure to meet. Some forms are less likely than others, with liberty on the edges rather than the centre. Others, guided by moderation and restraint, can cope with the twists and turns, fend off pirates menacing the passage, steer clear of the cliffs, and end in effective rule with liberty at the core. At one pole princely rule totters on the edge of tyranny, although in moderate form can be conducive to liberty; at the other pole the people ruling themselves is liberty's natural but flawed companion. The openness to discord and the lack of discipline render self-rule prone to factions and feuds, while easing the rise of demagogues and the dominance of select interests. The promise of self-rule is precarious and at risk of ending in the same lack of liberty with which it began. That is why ideas of self-rule gave way to a discourse of rule by representatives, why people ruling themselves is a minor theme in the symphony of constitutional discourse. The link between liberty and self-rule, no matter how compelling conceptually, is tempered by experience, the instabilities inherent, and the hostility of select sectors. Such reasons explain why the form of rule favoured in the discourse of the Italian city-states was not the people ruling themselves; it was instead a discourse based on the coming together of princes, elites, and the people, where different formations are possible, each with a distinct identity, the success of any one in securing and advancing liberty unpredictable and variable.

The monarchy of Charles I of England, the rule of the Doge of Venice and his council, the *Nove* of Siena, all are a kind of mixed rule. And yet the disciples of mixed rule are the princes and elites rather than the common people. Charles' conversion came on the eve of war after twelve years of personal rule. The king ruled with the counsel and support of the superior sectors, while the common people, the 'democratic' element as he called it, was needed to make sure liberty was respected; but not to have a share in ruling.[31] To concede to the people a place, however ambiguous and marginal, was a turning point, the first sign of a crack in the golden bowl of princely rule, once admitted bound to spread. Some see the concession as the start of the descent from 'princely charity'[32] downwards to the point where the people claim the right to rule themselves. The descent encounters and passes through mixed government of many shades, some allowing the people a fuller place, but stopping short of final descent to the people ruling themselves. A few make the full descent, allow the feet to usurp the head, then after a turbulent trial, re-ascend to find safety on a higher plateau, the head restored to its rightful place, although now under the eye of the many. The freemen of Philadelphia made the descent, in their opinion ascent, to self-rule; their fate we shall witness soon.

The destiny of the discourse and the directions it took are worth recording. One as the hymn of revolution in the seventeenth and eighteenth centuries in Europe and beyond; another in the wake of civil war in England; another still at the base of the American republic. The founders of the new constitutional orders fashioned rule partly on the discourse of liberty and partly on ideas of self-rule. The two came together to mean rule by representatives as the major key, with aspects of self-rule a minor. The word democracy, meaning rule by the *demos*, only recently had entered the discourse as a respectable term. Until introduced into constitutional discourse by Charles I, as a last-ditch effort to avoid war, *democracy* had been an expression of contempt and a harbinger of levelling. Having rebelled on the grounds of loss of liberty on the one hand, and in the name of the people on the other hand, the founders of the American nation had to find room for both. Democracy by then secure in the discourse raised alarm. Under the guidance of James Madison, an architect of the new order, the discourse took a new turn. The enemy of good government is faction, a number of citizens who unite for some purpose 'adverse to the rights of other citizens or to the permanent and aggregate interests of the community'.[33] The majority of the people turns out to be a faction, the most dangerous of all, and so 'the great object' must be to protect the public against the majority *and* at the same time 'preserve the spirit and the form of popular government'.[34] Rule by elected representatives is the answer. A trace of self-rule remains by electing

[31] See further Chapter XV.
[32] W Shakespeare: *Two Gentlemen of Verona.*
[33] J Madison: *The Federalist, No 10* in *The Federalist*, p 41. The people as *factions* has replaced the people as *levellers.*
[34] *Ibid* p 44.

representatives, while liberty is secured by leaving government to a few, a better cut of persons who stand above the unruly passions of workmen, shopkeepers, and hillbillies.[35] The few know the true value of liberty and are trusted guardians. They rule but render some account to the people through elections for the way they rule. A portion of the people as electors have a degree of liberty in choosing among candidates placed before them, and may have other avenues of engagement. That falls far short of governing themselves, or 'popular democracy' as it was known, the very name edged with fear and hostility, the concept scarred by glaring defects. Self-rule or popular democracy, although grounded in republican discourse and a genuine alternative form of rule, was discredited and discarded. The wisdom of rule by a few confirmed by the lamentable spectacle of states whose citizens dared to rule themselves.

The English path took its own course, although in settling on rule by the few ended in the same place. An undercurrent of self-rule had long dogged constitutional discourse, although rarely raised in respectable circles and fraught with danger if advocated by commoners. The discourse of self-rule, latent in the lower register of constitutional ideas, flourished briefly in the 1640s as the country drifted towards civil war and opinions normally seditious could be safely aired. The Levellers' design of the field, radical though they were, stopped just short of self-rule.[36] Government would be vested in a single chamber and engage an active people in deciding and consenting to the lay-out of the field, the notable features being election of legislators, keeping close watch on them, and holding them to account. The Leveller movement was soon crushed under Cromwell's heel, the ideas sown left to roam in search of fertile soil, feeding slowly but surely the people's demands for a share in government, until by the mid-eighteenth century a resolution had to be found, the place of the people had to be settled. How the House of Commons, determined to preserve the social order while under pressure to hear the voice of the people, rose to the occasion with vigour and flair, was noted earlier but is worth repeating. The concept of sovereignty, latent in the upper register, was summoned into service and polished to appeal to the modern mind. The House of Commons, elected by (a fraction of) the people was quietly securing its place as the main branch of the three constituting the king or queen-in-parliament. The members were not agents or delegates of the people, rather men of superior quality able to judge the interests of all and to act for the good of the nation. Not content to rest the case on such practical reason, parliamentarians sought conceptual victory. The submerged subjunctive at hand, parliament assembled became the people assembled. Parliament represented the people not just as spokesmen for, but *as if* it were the people, their very embodiment. Whether Madison was following the debates in the Commons or members were studying the musings of Madison, we

[35] Just why the elected few would necessarily be superior persons is not explained.
[36] See further Chapters IX and XV.

do not know; but behind the language local to each, the sentiments, dispositions, and destinations are the same. Whether factions or levellers, the people are unreliable and dangerous; but, no longer the feet content to be well-shod, they cannot be ignored. They have interests and their interests count in designing and cultivating the constitutional field, interests the few wise and prudent know and are best at advancing. The same few know the common good and the place within it of diverse interests. Self-rule as rule by the people themselves quietly slipped away, but not before a brief and brazen appearance in several states.

Republican discourse went west to frame the constitutional debate in post-British American states in the 1770s. A federal constitutional field was being designed, while the states now free from outside control, like the Italian city-states before them, had to redesign their own fields. The goal was to protect and promote the safety and happiness of the people, liberty the means to it. How best to preserve 'the blessings of liberty', liberty of person and property, was the critical issue. The freemen took for granted a form of mixed government to be most effective in preserving liberty. Not the British form unsuited to a society without king or aristocracy; nor a form that included slaves, the native population, or women. Within the bounds and self-images of colonial society, each state had to settle the form of government, what it should be a matter of contention. The right of freemen to vote could not be denied but their ability to govern was doubted. Legislative authority was best divided between two chambers, one elected by freemen, no matter how modest in person or means, the other composed of men of sound ability and substantial property. The old discourse had to adjust to democratic ideas; the solution a revision combining an element of democracy by electing representatives, who by 'a refinement of opinion' would temper wilder ideas and govern for the common interest, rather than 'cater to the interests of the commons'.[37] Republicanism, redefined in America as representative democracy, resembles in substance, if not in name, the form of government emerging from the House of Commons to settle relations between the people and parliament.[38] That representatives once elected act not under the direction of electors but act for the common good, as Edmund Burke explained, became the touchstone of both.[39] The relationship between people and rulers was sealed for the future. From the union of princely rule and the people ruling themselves, representative rule was born.[40]

[37] RL Hanson: 'Democratic Republicanism as the New American Hybrid' in *Conceptual Change and the Constitution* (eds) T Ball and JGA Pocock (Kansas: Kansas University Press, 1988), p 184.

[38] De Tocqueville's acute observations on the American approach are well-analysed in S Wolin: *Tocqueville Between Two Worlds* (Princeton: Princeton University Press, 2001).

[39] E Burke: 'Speech at Mr Burke's Arrival in Bristol' in *The Portable Edmund Burke* (ed) I Kramnick (London: Penguin Books, 1999), p 155.

[40] Madison: *The Federalist,* No 10. For an account of the discussions and debates, see Russell L Hanson: 'Democratic Republicanism as the New American Hybrid' in *Conceptual Change and the Constitution*

8. Upstarts drunk with liberty: Pennsylvania 1776

The republican legacy could be interpreted to mean the people ruling themselves in a real and literal sense. That idea lay at the foundation of the Constitution of Pennsylvania 1776. Several other states took a similar path but none more resolute in self-rule than Pennsylvania. The Preamble records that the citizens of Pennsylvania no longer have the protection of the king of Great Britain, and deplores 'the despotic domination of the British parliament and many other acts of tyranny'. It affirms the need for the colonies 'to be free and independent states' founded 'on the authority of the people only'. The freeman, through their representatives in convention, meet 'deliberately to form for themselves such just rules as they shall think best, for governing their future society'. A form of government 'to promote the general happiness of the people of the state and their prosperity', and 'provide for future improvements', the constitution of which is set out in the *Declaration of Rights and Frame of Government*. The elements of self-rule are several and striking. First, the people have the 'sole, exclusive and inherent right of governing': Article III. Secondly, 'all power [is] originally inherent in, and subsequently derived from, the people'. It follows that 'all officers of government, whether legislative or executive, are their trustees and servants and at all times accountable to them': Article IV. Which means the people have 'an indubitable, unalienable and indefeasible right to reform, alter, or abolish government' and to remove members of the legislative and executive: Articles V and VI. The *Plan or Frame of Government* follows. Government is to be by an assembly of 'representatives of the freemen'. The assembly has 'supreme legislative power' and a president and council with 'supreme executive power': sections 2 and 3. The elected are to 'be noted for wisdom and virtue' and may be elected for no more than four years in ten. Elections are to be held annually. Each member once elected is to swear an oath not to propose or assent to any 'bill, vote, or resolution' injurious to the people or with 'any bill, vote or resolution injurious to the people or with a tendency to lessen or abridge their rights and privileges': section 10.

The bond between people and government is tightened. The doors of the house of representatives 'shall be and remain open for the admission of all persons who behave decently, except only when the welfare of the state may require the doors be shut': section 13. Each week the 'votes and proceedings' are to be printed with details of how members voted, while each member has the right to insert the reasons for his vote: section 14. Self-rule requires that laws enacted 'be more maturely considered' by the people. To ensure against 'the inconveniences of hasty determinations', bills are to be printed 'for the consideration of the people before they are read in general assembly for the last time for debate'. And for the 'more perfect satisfaction of the public, the reasons and motives for making such laws shall be fully and clearly expressed in the preamble': section 15. Members of the executive council are elected by representatives of the people, who are themselves chosen by the people. The mode and duration of service is designed to ensure 'more men will be trained to public business'. That leads to consistency in governing and avoids 'the danger of establishing an inconvenient aristocracy': section 19. Provision is made for the appointment of judges by the executive council, while justices of the peace, sheriffs, and coroners are elected locally: sections 20 to 31. Government at all levels is to be open and accessible to the people. Free speech is guaranteed and 'the printing presses shall be free to every person who undertakes to examine the proceedings of the legislature or any part of government': section 35. In order that 'the freedom of the commonwealth may be preserved inviolate forever' provision is made for a Council of Censors. The members, elected by the cities and counties, are 'to enquire whether the constitution has been observed inviolate in every part, and whether the legislative and executive branches have performed their duty as guardians of the people'. The powers of the Council of Censors are unique and awesome. It may 'send for person, papers, and records'; it may 'pass public censures, order impeachments, and recommend to the legislature the repeal of such laws as appear to have been enacted contrary to the principles of the constitution'. And, finally, the Council of Censors has the power to call a constitutional convention 'if there appear to them an absolute necessity of emending any article of the constitution which may be defective' or adding any article 'necessary for the preservation of the rights and happiness of the people': section 47.

The constitutional order was founded on several simple ideas, the consequences profound. The people means first and foremost the freemen, social relations among them grounded on each having an equal interest in securing and advancing well-being, to which liberty is the gateway and the first principle of the constitutional order. The freemen know being free is essential to well-being, what being free means, and how to protect it. They view government as one instrument among many contributing to well-being; they know good government relies on the freemen being actively engaged. They accept there are practical reasons for delegating functions to officials and conferring power for the purpose. Social relations between people and officials are firmly defined. Officials, whether elected or appointed, are the agents and delegates of the people, by whom they are empowered to act and to whom they are accountable. Liberty is the cardinal quality of well-being and the gateway to other qualities. Power is dangerous and creates risks against which the people know they must take measures. These ideas defined the constitutional field and guided the writing of the Constitution of Pennsylvania 1776. The constitutional order was based on the people, its sole purpose to contribute to their liberty, from which well-being and happiness follow. Where power is delegated to officials, the people have the practical means to keep them to purpose by engagement and vigilance, backed by the power of censure. The risks of power are known and mitigated by several means. Among them limited terms of office for elected legislators, and that office at all levels of government from state to local be elective. Annual elections are to be held for members of the legislative chamber and limits imposed on the term of office. Proposed legislation is to be open to the people's scrutiny and comment. All crowned by regular review of the constitution itself. Citizens are drawn out of their 'political stupor', a state to which they had been reduced by previous orders and to which they had grown accustomed and encouraged to accept. Now the freemen, as the citizen-body, may claim with reason and pride to be in charge of their affairs and governing themselves, while to the observer the constitutional order appears to be the logical and justified working out of what it means to be free within the republic and how freedom is best protected.

The constitution unleashed a pack of angry critics who howled and growled, snarled and sneered at every turn. While the tone and content are now read with bemused detachment, the vaulting ambition of the freemen admired, for the people of Pennsylvania the attack was deadly and the constitutional order damned as 'a political monster deserving only mercifully to be put to death', 'the ridicule of all America, but ourselves who blush too much to laugh'. It is 'a motley mixture of limited monarchy and execrable democracy – a beast without a head'. As if that were not bad enough 'it will shake the very being of this once flourishing country'. To think that 'men of excellent character had been turned out by upstarts who are totally unacquainted with the principles of government'.[41] The framers of the constitution must have been 'drunk with liberty'. And so the invective flows in a spirit and a language faithful to, but even more monstrous than, the scorn and ridicule poured on the common people by the upper register of English constitutional discourse. Behind the language lay several familiar claims. One that mixed government, with a division of powers among the social orders, is the best protection of liberty. A government of single chamber is bound to end in tyranny, the majority oppressing minorities, while a second chamber of different composition moderates the excesses of the other. A supporting refrain is added. Government is too serious a matter to be left to the common people, the upstarts, but can safely be entrusted only to men of education, social standing, and substantial property. Finally, if less candidly, a government of the common people is rule by faction and bound to have a levelling effect in promoting equality at the cost of status and property.

[41] Gordon Wood catalogues the invective at length: *The Creation of the American Republic 1776–1782* (University of North Carolina Press, 1969), pp 233*ff*.

XIII
The People Ruling Themselves: II

1. Social foundations of self-rule

The social foundations of self-rule are several. One satisfies the interest in citizens' having charge of their own affairs; another responds to doubts about being ruled by someone else; a third considers the people ruling themselves to be more likely than other forms of rule to be for the well-being of all. The concept of liberty links the three. Liberty is both of intrinsic value and a means to other valued interests, being secure in person and property, having needs met, and being able to improve the quality of life, one effect of which is to increase liberty. Around these ideas a pattern of opinion emerges. The task now is to enter the constitutional field and show how liberty is served by self-rule. The scene is set by placing liberty in a social setting, reflecting on the function is serves, and the reasons it is valued.

Liberty occurs within social relationships; varies in quantity and quality; is removed or restricted in ways and degrees. At the milder end are relationships such as teacher and pupil, tutor and students; worker and boss in the middle; officer and soldiers more severe; master and slave the ultimate. The terms of the relationship define the nature and extent of the liberty of the parties. The student is free to ask questions of the tutor but not to chatter with other students; the soldier is free to decide how best to conduct the patrol within the bounds set by the officer; even the slave has some freedom in doing tasks dictated by the master. The offender sent to jail loses overall liberty but retains traits, some trivial others critical to well-being.[1] Across the span of social relationships liberty is of many kinds and degrees, some set by the parties and influenced by social spheres, others defined by law. The liberty to say what you like, drive on the roads, and cultivate your garden is restricted by understandings, conventions, and laws of many kinds and in many ways. Liberty on this approach is variable as to quality and quantity. Persons considered free are in practice free and unfree in ways and degrees depending on the terms of the social relationships among themselves and with figures of authority. And just as prisoners, slaves, and servants, although 'the helpless victims of a dominating influence',[2] have pockets of freedom, so persons considered free are in practice free and unfree in ways and degrees depending on the relationships they enter or in which they find themselves.

[1] Not all prisoners would share Ferdinand's view: 'All corners else o'th' earth/Let liberty make use of; space enough/Have I in such a prison': *The Tempest*, Act 1: 2: 402.

[2] The definition of a slave according to the *Concise Oxford Dictionary*, p 1199.

Keepers of the Common Good. D.J. Galligan, Oxford University Press. © D.J. Galligan 2024.
DOI: 10.1093/9780198907398.003.0013

Liberty as a quality of intrinsic value leads down to the foundations of social life and action. Let us begin with a parable, the relationship between Caliban the slave and Prospero his master. Caliban, viewed as a slave, a repulsive monster, comes to think of himself in that way. Yet, he retains a sense of freedom. 'Freedom, high-day! Freedom high-day!' he sings at the prospect of having a more kindly master. He yearns for more. The island once was his before taken from him by Prospero. He dreams the clouds would 'open and show riches, ready to drop upon me, and when I waked I cried to dream again'.[3] And though he dare not say it, cried to be his own master. He was once 'mine own king', until made subject to Prospero. He knows that without his books Prospero would be 'a sot as I am' with 'not one spirit to command'. Despite the toll of servitude, the degradation and abuse, there is still in the ashes that spark of liberty.[4] A smouldering sense of the worth of freedom and how he, Caliban, could be living in freedom as lives Prospero of the island and the Prosperos of Virginia and elsewhere, their own Calibans locked out of sight and mind. The spark of liberty is alive within, awaiting the breeze to fan it into life. Whether the breeze ever blows and how fiercely the flame burns are subject to accident as much as intention, contingent on the flame's durability and the fabric of social relations. Caliban laments the lack of liberty in both senses, being free of Prospero's domination and being free to be 'mine own king', to live life as he wishes, to let the clouds 'open and show riches'.

The value of being free, not under the will of another, is best gauged by contrast with not being free, not being able to act as one wishes, not being in charge of one's self in a meaningful way. Being free is of such value it survives and flickers despite the worst oppression. The innate sense of liberty when allowed to flame lights up other interests: to cultivate one's abilities, to design a way of life and follow where it leads, to seek out satisfactions, all interests awaiting the warmth of freedom's flame. Caliban grasps the logic, the need first to be free from the master before being able to plan his life. It is not that one sense is negative the other positive; rather liberty is valued both as a quality of personhood and as a gateway to a life each is free to cultivate, a life of contentment and fulfilment. The two dimensions of liberty are tied together, conceptually and socially, the one the source of and reason for the other. Being free as a valued interest generates sentiments and dispositions of proportionate intensity. When Caliban wakes to find freedom a dream and 'cries to dream again' his anguish is inconsolable, the sense of loss beyond measure. From the sentiment of freedom flows a disposition to take action to secure and improve life. What actions are open, what measures are available, depends partly on how powerful the supporting sentiments and dispositions are, and partly on the spaces left for liberty. You cannot but feel the depth of Caliban's sentiments, the raw vigour of his dispositions, yet being unfree they come to nothing.

[3] *The Tempest*, Act 1: 2: 94.

[4] To borrow John Warr's evocative image.

Mention of the slave under the will of a master casts in high relief the difference between being free and unfree, the one defined by contrast with the other. The contrast is striking but runs together two separate dimensions of freedom, the *juridical*, and the *practical*. The Code of Justinian defines slavery as 'an institution of the *jus gentium* by which someone is, contrary to nature, subject to the dominion of someone else'.[5] *Dominion* is itself a legal concept, derived from *dominus* the one who has 'lordship, sovereignty, control' over a *domain*, a subject, territory, or person. The person under the dominion of another does not qualify for juridical equality and so has no rights. Roman law distinguishes between the bearer of rights and the slave who is without rights. Lacking juridical equality, and so denied rights, a slave is no more than a chattel. By contrast, to have juridical equality is to be entitled to respect as a person and be a bearer of rights. Rights mark out fields of liberty. Liberty as a property of rights is now a legal concept, the quality and the quantity determined by the rights one has by law. The sharp juridical distinction between freedom and slavery gives way to the practical question of how much freedom one has across the spectrum of social life. That is measured by the rights one has and the field of freedom within each. Fragments of freedom may in practice be conceded to the servant, the prisoner, and the slave, although ever at risk from the will of the master.[6] Our interest here is in persons who have juridical equality, value liberty, and want to design a constitutional order based on their ruling themselves as the best route to liberty.[7]

2. Liberty and self-rule

Self-rule draws strength from experience of being ruled by others. The promise of the prince or the few to be good at ruling is often unfulfilled, breeding in the people disquiet and distrust. The claim to know and respect the people's interests, to be capable of acting for the good of all in practice proves hollow. The feeling of being treated with contempt is inflamed by the few giving preference to their own interests or those of their supporters. No need to be versed in history to know select sectors influence government, occasionally crowned by outright capture. The people see through claims of the common good, how the upper register disguises and dresses in respectability a social order in which they rank lowly, their interests insecure, room for betterment marginal. The people know that, unless they enter the field to champion their own cause, their well-being will be neglected. After persistent effort on their part, the constitutional fortress is transformed into a field, although already laid-out. The terrain is rough, the reception hostile; but the

[5] Quoted in: Q Skinner: *Visions of Politics II* (Cambridge: Cambridge University Press, 2002), p 269.
[6] On the etymology of *slave*, see Notes.
[7] Discussed in Notes.

sentiment of liberty runs deep and the people persist in their efforts at cultivation. It is not that they at once take up the cause of self-rule and under the banner march for victory. The cause is more likely to begin with the actions of groups driven by desperation, as the record of resistance shows: peasants in revolt, workers rising, slaves rebelling, while higher social groups like the Levellers, aggrieved at the misuse of power by officials, sometimes lead the way. However scattered the groups, all share the sentiment of liberty, whether Caliban or Ariel, the peasants of Gagliano, or anyone else enslaved or oppressed. The disposition forms, steeped in the pain of experience and carved in memory, that the only reliable route to liberty is being in charge of one's own affairs, of which ruling oneself is a vital part. Such ambition is realized only rarely and as in Pennsylvania likely to be short-lived. Yet, self-rule, even if mostly silent and suppressed, remains an idea hovering around as the best means to freedom and the benefits of freedom.[8] The idea is valued but the reality hard to achieve. The alternative is to lower the aim, search for ways for the people to engage, be vigilant, and exact censure; to accept there are many stages between exclusion and self-rule. The potential of this approach is considered more fully in the final chapter. For now it is enough to record that the people from time to time do manage to attain a place in governing, usually on the lower rungs of *self-rule*. The term self-rule has been replaced by *democracy*, an open concept, but now settled to mean rule by representatives elected by the people and in some ways answerable to them. The genealogy of rule by representatives and the practice are the subject of the next chapter.

The logic of self-rule is clear and the social foundations laid. The interest of having charge of one's own affairs forms opinion, that is, enters the sequence of action, creates sentiments and dispositions, and leads towards self-rule. Other interests enter the sequence and point to other opinions and courses of action, some supporting self-rule, others inclining to other forms. In fourteenth-century Siena, peace among citizens had priority over self-rule. To be secure against disorder and upheaval called for the firm rule of a few, stifling interest in the people's being more involved. The rule of the prince or the few trades on the need for peace and security, and exploits the opinion, the sentiments, and dispositions aroused. Much else is sacrificed, other aspects of well-being denied; the people encouraged to welcome the benefits and be content to live within the constraints. The satisfactions and social encounters of daily life are enough for some, the agitator for self-rule suspect, a misguided optimist, not a leader to follow. Some sectors find their interests best served by cultivating the prince and his court or winning the favour of the few. Self-rule for them holds no appeal, indeed signals danger and the risk of losing favour in the face of popular government. The squire at ease in rolling acres and the founder of the hedge-fund high in a gleaming tower have nothing to gain

[8] An example of Whitehead's grand ideas: AE Whitehead: *Adventures of Ideas* (London: Collier-Macmillan, 1933).

from a form of rule with levelling tendencies. The range of interests valued by the people or sectors or persons is wide and need not now be charted, except to note that the interest in self-rule has to enter the lists of interests and compete. Where the sentiment and disposition of self-rule rank, and how they fare, depends on the competing strength of other sentiments and dispositions. Even the strongest commitment to self-rule has to confront competing sentiments and dispositions of equal strength, all aimed at the well-being of persons, groups, and sectors.

3. Practical process of self-rule

If self-rule is to gain a footing practical issues of governing have to be faced. Two stand out: how the people are themselves to decide some matters; how to be in charge of matters delegated to officials. The people decide which issues are for them, which to delegate. Between deciding high policy and making law at one end, and applying law and policy at the other, the people have to decide where to draw the line, itself a matter of potential disagreement. Once the division is settled, the people have to work out a process by which to decide the matters reserved for them. All are entitled to take part, to advocate their own interests, and argue for one outcome rather than another. Above a shared threshold, interests are likely to compete and choices among them have to be made, some having preference over others. All want to be free to stake their claims, have their interests taken seriously and measured in the balance. Gone is the white cord signalling an harmonious whole, instead is a loose knot of persons pushing interests, peddling opinions, and applying pressure wherever an opening appears. In a field designed for self-rule, diversity and discord are cultivated and openly displayed, adding to the burden of reaching outcomes and deciding courses of action. Processes enter to bear a heavy load. Where there is no agreed outcome, the focus shifts to process, the question how to design process of such quality that the outcome, whatever it be, is justified. That all interests are taken seriously and all parties have some say, hard enough to achieve, are not enough. No matter how good the process, the outcome to some may be unacceptable. How to avoid the shift from substance to form, how to justify outcome by process, critical issues for self-rule, needs a treatise of its own while here we have to be content with a few brief points.[9]

On one approach, if the process meets certain conditions of fairness, the outcome is justified. This may in some cases be true; but fair process does not necessarily lead to justified outcomes. Outcomes, no matter how reached, need certain qualities to be justified. More exacting process might contribute to outcomes being acceptable. The search then is for common ground by scrutiny of reasons and

[9] My *Due Process and Fair Procedures*, Chapters 1 and 2 could be seen as a first chapter.

attention to evidence, exposing false premises and flawed arguments. Embedded sentiments could turn out to lack a foundation in interests, while strong opinions under the gaze of reason may wither. By deliberative processes of exchange, reasoning, and scrutiny, the parties try to reach an outcome acceptable to all. That is not guaranteed and, in case of failure, the focus shifts to voting as a last resort. Several forms are open. A simple majority might be enough for some issues, while for others self-rule requires procedures more subtle and complex, the variations numerous. Assigning extra weight to certain groups or sectors, requiring special majorities, or guarding certain interests, are all familiar in the design of process.[10] While such measures of deliberation help, success is likely to be uneven and often absent, unable to cope with the diversity of interests and competition among them, unable to contain the imbalance of power among sectors. Enough has been said to show how a people, resolute on ruling themselves, confront complexity, contingency, and a high bar to success. Among those determined to make self-rule work there is a dimension to add. The mutual respect of each for the other as the bearer of rights and juridical equality, is inherent in self-rule, framing and leavening the process. Beneficence and prudence, together with justice, add more by stimulating sentiments of cooperation, mutual support, and self-restraint as the conditions of collective action. All contained in the concept of *sociability*, patient in the shadows of the constitutional field awaiting the people's notice.

4. Sociability and its value

In earlier constitutional discourse, the life and spirit of rule reside in personal qualities of rulers and ruled, without which the constitutional field is a vacant space. Virtue is the quality enabling the prince to be a true monarch and cultivate the good of all; virtue prompts the few joined by the white cord to prefer the good of the republic over their own. The people themselves must have virtue, for unless they share a sense of a common good beyond their own ends, the constitutional order will fail. The classical qualities, the virtues esteemed in early republics, require a nobility of character, a devotion to the republic, a selflessness, and a disinterested concern for the common good. Such qualities appear in art and literature, are depicted in *Buon Governo*, and often cited as the route to good government. To imagine such lofty ideals being at large in mundane societies is out of step with reality, an illusion, allowing virtue to drop out of later constitutional discourse to return to the catechism from whence it came. There is another way

[10] The approach, often referred to as *deliberative democracy*, is much written about; a fine example: C Sunstein: *Designing Democracy: What Constitutions Do* (Oxford: Oxford University Press, 2001).

of understanding the qualities needed for effective government, inherent in and critical to the social understanding of constitutional authority, and critical to self-rule. All wish to advance well-being, partly by self-endeavour and partly by collective action. Collective action requires mutuality, recognition that to advance your interests you need the support and cooperation of others, as others do of you. Mutuality means each has regard for the interests, sentiments, and dispositions of others. That is the basis of cooperation and purposeful action. Cooperation means sharing one's labour with others while accepting the need for an outcome acceptable to all, for which self-restraint, the cooling of passion, and the bridling of ambition, are critical. Practical action succeeds only if such conditions are met.

If comfort be found in virtue, then virtue consists of being sociable. Baron d'Holbach puts it well: 'To be virtuous is to be sociable and to contribute to the happiness of those with whom we are linked by fate in order to make them eager in their turn to contribute to our felicity'.[11] Sociability moulds our sentiments and dispositions, and guides our actions in relations with others.[12] The sentiment of sociability, he might have added, is learnt and practiced in the multitude of social relations through which we daily pass. Sociability requires that each extend to others equality of respect, equality in the sense that their interests as well as one's own count, and weigh evenly in planning and executing a course of action. Sociability is the animating spirit of social relations, and so the foundation of society and a condition of collective action to advance civility, humanity, and well-being. Where self-rule is the means to such ends, sociability has to be infused in the soil of the field, its absence fatal. But there are obstacles to confront. One that sociability among the people is not intense enough to overcome differences. Another is the structure of social relations. In a setting of rank and status and material inequality, the sentiment of sociability struggles to reach the level needed to prevail over competing sentiments. The clash of interests and the gap between them renders a common course hard to find. That there be no one or few finally to decide is another obstacle. Whether mutuality and self-restraint, a willingness to compromise, and consensus as to the priority of self-rule, in conditions of social disparity and economic inequality, are strong enough to secure acceptable outcomes, is a major variable. The risk is that conflict remain unresolved and instability rife, unleashing sentiment for the return of firm rule. The prince and his court, the few and their followers, are ready for recall, awaiting the cue to oust self-rule and to reimpose order and stability. The appeal of self-rule contains the seeds of its demise.

[11] P-H Thiry, Baron d'Holbach: *La Politique naturelle ou discours sur les vrais principes du gouvernement* (1773) quoted in J-F Spitz: 'From Civism to Civility: D'Holbach's Critique of Republican Virtue' in (eds) M Van Gelderen and Q Skinner: *Republicanism: A Shared European Heritage* (Cambridge: Cambridge University Press, 2002), p 116.

[12] *Sociability* may be linked to *interests*, see the account in Chapter IV.

5. People passive or active

The appeal of self-rule and a condition of success is the people's engaging in governing, deciding matters of high policy, and overseeing the agencies. Such active citizenship, the foundation of self-rule and applauded by some, is to others a fantasy, the premise mistaken, the image of the people false for two reasons. One doubts the people's being willing to commit the time and effort, the other whether they would be capable of discharging the duties of governing. The image of the people as passive subjects rather than active citizens is common to the discourse. Machiavelli's view of the people content to tend their houses and gardens, combines a grain of truth with a tinge of cynicism. Most, according to WB Yeats, would be content tucked away in 'a small cabin of clay and wattles made, nine bean-rows, and a hive for the honey bee'.[13] Several reasons support the view of the people as passive recipients rather than active instigators, for resigning to be governed rather than grappling to govern. All are accustomed to being under a figure of authority, whether parent, teacher, or superior, who would be affronted by signs of independence and resent advice on conduct of the relationship. The disposition of deference reaches back to the origins of social relations, to the model of a strong few giving protection to the many weak in return for obedience. A disposition found in early social formations, Rome included, where rootless families sought refuge with settled landowners to whom they submitted passively.[14] A disposition proclaimed in the upper register of constitutional discourse and mirrored in the people's being the feet of the body politic, content to bear the weight of the body, provided they are well-shod. John Fortescue's view that the people stir only for lack of bread and lack of justice we noted earlier.[15] A view often endorsed: 'political fermentation occurs only when rights are violated' wrote William Wyndham in the seventeenth century.[16] Adam Smith found that even despotic rulers, whether emperors of Rome or the Protector of England, were attentive to doing justice.[17] A people secure in their goods and property however rudimentary, assured of justice when needed, on this view is a contented people and asks of government no more. If appeal were made to the good of being engaged in governing, few would be stirred into action.

The people's being naturally passive is to be questioned. Basic needs being met and justice dispensed may be good reasons for not rebelling; but it does not follow they are 'satisfied citizens', their well-being limited to bread and justice, their aspirations to a life of civility and humanity met. Other models are imaginable and different experiences are recorded. The citizens of Pennsylvania looked back with

[13] WB Yeats: *The Lake Isle of Innisfree* (1890). Most would be content with two or three bean-rows!
[14] G Vico: *The New Science.*
[15] J Fortescue: *On the Laws and Governance of England* (1463) (ed) Shelley Lockwood (Cambridge Texts in the History of Political Thought, Cambridge University Press, 1997), p 110.
[16] W Wyndham: debates in HC (1734) in P Ihalainen: *Agents of the People*, p 71.
[17] *Ibid* p 238.

admiration to Anglo-Saxon society where the freemen constituted the *folk*, which gave them 'an equal place in public assemblies' and imposed on them 'the common burden of the folk, service in war and suit and judgement in the courts'.[18] The *folk* signified a community of freemen constituting the *folkmoot*. Within the folkmoot, social relations were settled, the power of the community entrusted to the freemen, who 'are the inheritors and judges of their law', as well as the makers.[19] The king enforced the law but did not make it and officials were confined to enforcement. The community acted through the *witan*, the community assembled, and in this way 'maintained the popularism of public life'.[20] Over time, the power of the people passed out of their hands to a centralized state leaving them to 'fall into a political stupor' from which they never recovered.[21] Among the reasons for such stupor is the rise of leaders as the champions of progress, prizing their position and priding themselves on their superior gifts, their ambition to join the ranks of rulers irresistible. Jack Cade we have seen displays the sequence from being one of the people, a rebel among rebels, to becoming the leader, then a short step to being the master. In charting Cade's progress, Shakespeare exposes a truth, seemingly universal, of passive submission being the rule, positive exertion the exception, out of which rulers are born.[22]

Resignation as the common position of the people, rather than proving native passivity, could be a sign of their intelligence and insight. The people soon learn, as the ranchers of Shasta County and the yeomen and yeowomen of Vacy Plains learnt, that much of well-being is made up of humble and homely qualities within their reach. Qualities they come to know are best realized by acting alone and in social relations with others, while expectations of government are low. Once the threshold is met of order, security, and basic welfare, the people know the quality of life depends on them. Some have a bleaker image picturing government as an alien force threatening their well-being, a force to be suspected and as far as possible kept at bay. Even the more public-spirited have to calculate how much time and effort to devote to governing, mindful of the obstacles to effective action, the frustrations, and the meagre returns, while other avenues appear more rewarding to well-being. The conclusion, however unwelcome, is that for most people and in most cases the benefits of engaging in governing seem small compared to goals more personal, pressing, and within reach.

That the people be passive subjects rather than active citizens is neither a truth about society nor a fixture of the constitutional field. The pattern of relations

[18] JEA Joliffe: *The Constitutional History of Medieval England* (London: Adam and Charles Black, 1937), p 5.

[19] *Ibid* p 23.

[20] *Ibid* p 24.

[21] GS Wood: *The Creation of the American Republic*, p 228 quoting Demophilus, *Genuine Principles of the Ancient Saxon, or English Constitution* (Philadelphia, 1776).

[22] W Shakespeare: *The Second Part of the Contention: Henry VI Part II.*

between people and rulers shown in earlier chapters is one of the few dominating the many. The gentleman cavilling at schools to educate the sons of the common people speaks volumes.[23] The vigour and tenacity shown in repressing the people's stirring are displayed in constitutional experience, none more resolutely than in unseating the upstarts of Pennsylvania. The habit of subjection breeds sentiments and dispositions to match. The people come to think there is no alternative but to accept a lowly place in the constitutional order, fall into line, and work for well-being within the bounds. Through the thicket of history there is another pathway, one set by sentiments and dispositions tapping a deeper sense of interests, a sense blunted by experience but not buried. A sense that in place of being cramped and crushed by government, as the peasants of Gagliano felt, the people's interests could be cultivated, allowed to flourish and prosper in ways and directions only dimly seen. We know the people have in reserve a register of discourse from which to draw the confidence and courage to rebel. A register in which social relations among the people, and between them and government, are torn apart then restitched with civility and humanity to guide common endeavour for common purposes, sociability a supporting sentiment. Rule itself is reconceived and constitutional authority transformed. Government is seen not as the creation of the people but a means to serve their well-being, officials more their agents than their rulers. And, most notably, in place of an image of passive organs doomed to the lower regions, the people are now citizens attentive to all that affects their well-being, governing included. They need not be warriors in the political process, nor imagine that state power replace private endeavour. It means only that being interested in governing, taking part even moderately, and watching over those in authority are now seen as integral to the pursuit of well-being. And just as the people influence the terms and monitor the course of any social relationship into which they enter or are thrust, the same applies to relations with the agencies of government.

This image of social endeavour, the people acting alone, together, and with government, renders obsolete a rigid line between the passive subject and the active citizen. What follows then for self-rule? That the people are inclined to be passive is a set-back but not fatal. That prompts enquiry as to how the people learn to be active, and why being engaged is the best way to protect and advance their interests. The answer draws us back to how the people see their place in the social order, perceive government and construct relations with officials, form sentiments of value and dispositions to action. The people are used to ideas asserting their inferiority and lack of capacity, being no more than a mob and a threat to the social order. But the hegemony of ideas from the upper register, although powerful and penetrating, is never triumphant. Even in the slime of slavery the spark is kept alive

[23] See Chapter VI:2.

by Caliban, Ariel, and all enslaved and oppressed peoples. At times and in places the lower register gains ground, expectations are raised, concessions are won, and place of the people improved. Just occasionally the lower register is victorious and the people rule themselves. That is the exception and generally short-lived, the common people no match for the wiles of the upper register. Between defeat and victory there are many stages shaped by many factors, foremost among them the people's engagement, their vigilance, and their censure. The contempt of the old upper register has been mainly silenced, and the people are able to be involved in the processes of governing at many ways and levels. Their low expectations of the constitutional order, the seeming futility of engagement, and the retreat to passive acquiescence, have been revised. Sustained over centuries by tradition, convention, and practice, policed by force, and fed on the discourse of the upper register, the social order seemed immutable, in the nature of things. When in truth the seed-bed of interests on which the social order is sown remains constant, while the sentiments and dispositions nurtured in the people rise and fall, as if in step with the seasons.[24]

6. Instabilities of self-rule

If a form of self-rule were in place the instabilities would soon show. One is the hazard of finding a balance among interests, another the risk of the people's seeking strength in groups and guilds and sectors, and the shift from sociable competition to ruthless rivalry. The fear of faction returns, the need for sociability and balance gives way to self-interest and a grab for power. The Jack Cades are back to take the lead and the power of the agencies of government swells. The bright image of the people coming together in concord to settle action soon darkens. Beyond protection of basic interests, the waters are murky, discord is rife, and concord hard to reach; above a threshold of common ground, perceptions of interest splinter and the paths of sentiment divide. Divergence on such practical matters are signs of competing visions among groups and sectors of the social order and relations within it. The more uneven the economic order and the more stratified the social, the more ideas of good government are tied to the interests of persons, groups, and sectors. Failing agreement on such matters among a self-ruling people, ambition is lowered from consensus to balance among interests and the focus again shifts from outcomes to process, substance to form. The aim now in this last section is to chart and comment on the main sources of instability of the people ruling themselves.

Balance of interests By enabling the people to engage in the political process and to have their interests considered, the process-approach, as noted earlier, is a way

[24] On passive people in 'a political stupor', see G Wood: *The Creation of the American Republic* (University of North Carolina Press 1969), p 228.

of reaching justified outcomes. Just what kinds of process create an arena for all parties to enter and engage equitably is a complex matter on which opinions differ. Process suitable to the task and broadly acceptable do tend to emerge, partly by design and partly from practice. The process-approach is common, seems reasonable, and the outcomes held to be justified. The move from outcomes back to process harbours a hint of trouble. Some contend the outcome matters no matter how fair and reasonable the process. Fair process is small consolation to consistent losers, the risk that divisions are reinforced rather than resolved. The referendum on the United Kingdom's membership of the European Union left the losers discontented and disdainful of an outcome to them odious. While procedures can be adept and nuanced in ironing out differences and finding common ground, on some matters there is nothing to iron out, no common ground to find. A choice then has to be made between opposing positions. The more divided, unequal, and stratified the society, the wider the gaps and gulfs, the further apart the parties, the less room there is for a balance acceptable to all. Sociability as the guide to social relations has its limits, leaving some issues beyond the boundaries, while sentiments of justice, prudence, and beneficence critical to social coordination, struggle to bridge the divide. The desire for mutual regard, compromise, and moderation is a condition of sound government and normally enough. But on some matters opinions are so divided, perceptions of interests so varied, sentiments and dispositions so opposed, the choice is either to rule out any action, or to force a decision applauded by some deplored by others.

The ideal of citizens coming together to harness their interests and opinions to common ends, a noble ideal, faces the reality of some divisions being unfit for the harness. The reach of the harness depends on the structure of the social order, the power of groups and sectors, and relations among them. The more inclusive the harness, the more scope there is for common cause and the more effective the government; the more narrow its reach, the less chance of common cause and the risk of one group or sector prevailing over others. Several grounds of instability follow. If a group or sector loses in the political process and has to live with outcomes contrary to its interests, the appeal of self-rule fades; and the more often that happens the further it fades. The people know that collective action requires self-restraint and adjusting positions in the cause of common endeavour; they know that despite all efforts on some matters common ground cannot be found. The advocate of self-rule knows the same applies in settling policy in the political process. Loyalty and restraint have their limits and the promise of self-rule is unfulfilled; discontent follows and attention turns to other forms of rule.

Effective rule The instability created by diversity has consequences for the effectiveness of self-rule. Decisive action is not the appeal; princely rule and related forms are more decisive. The appeal of self-rule is a form of government in which the people engage and where the outcomes, if not consensual, are at least responsive to all interests. How to deal with the virus pandemic, the plague, is a useful example. Some governments, backed by scientific opinion, acted swiftly to restrict mixing and moving, heedless of objections and voices of protest. Others hesitated and heard opinions, some supporting severe measures, some doubting the science, some sceptical of the gravity of the threat. Some groups pleaded a natural liberty not to wear a mask, a human right to drink in the pub and attend the match. The more serious were troubled by the need to trade loss of life against the social and financial hardship to households and ruin of the economy. The division of opinion infected the agencies of government and encouraged dither and delay in search of compromise. Which we may ask is the better approach to governing. If effectiveness means being decisive, then agencies' acting swiftly and sternly is better; if it means taking account of opinion, calibrating costs and benefits, aiming at consensus through moderation and compromise, then the regimes' dithering and delaying score high on process, but are less effective. Between the two are many stages, at one end decisive action, driven by one main goal, at the other end a concern to respond to the subtleties of the issue and the diversity of sentiment.

The risk of instability is real but not to be overstated. On another view, the risk rather than condemning self-rule opens the gateway to good government. An active citizenry, aware of the risk, might view competition, conflict, and discord as positive factors fostering deliberation and debate, leading to careful analysis and moderate judgement. Dither and delay, compromise and accommodation, may turn out to be fair price to pay for an outcome grounded in social relations, enough to be broadly acceptable to all sectors. Swift and decisive action is sometimes needed and delay disastrous, the unforeseen and unwanted consequences then borne as the cost of coping with a deadly threat. But for decisive action during those four fateful days in June 1940 that moved the nation from appeasement to war, we should be living in servitude not freedom. That is not the normal case, nor time of the essence, nor a compelling outcome to reach. The normal case is to settle a policy for the long-term, forged from deliberation and discourse, of which discord and disagreement are natural elements. Regardless of the merits, governing in this way is vulnerable, open to being seen as weak and ineffective, lacking the strength and decisiveness of power in the hands of one or a few. The discord and disagreement, celebrated as the route to sound outcomes, is easily recast as dangerous disorder, a sign the nation is sliding into chaos and the need for intervention plain. It falls to the charismatic leader or the sector with much to lose or the military junta to rescue the nation. A self-ruling people is weak in resistance. Power diffused among the institutions of rule rather than concentrated in one or a few, is no match for the wild-eyed demagogue and a band of jackboots, nor for the powerful interest group, nor as a last resort for the force of the generals.[25] The

[25] I was able to witness first-hand the aftermath of military coup in Pakistan early this century, the reasons the generals gave to justify their actions, and the slow road back to rule by elected representatives.

means can be drastic, the collapse of self-rule either instant or eroded over time, until the garments are threadbare and replaced by the dress of the despot, the guild of the few, or the arms of the generals. That was the fate of Pennsylvania, the war of words waged against self-rule soon won.

Ruin by faction Faction is defined as a self-interested, turbulent, or unscrupulous party.[26] More moderately, faction means a group or sector advancing its own interests. Harm sets in when the bounds of sociability are breached and the restraint of cooperative action thrown aside. Turbulence follows and threatens the social order. Fear of faction dominated fourteenth-century Siena, while Charles Stuart in 1642 warned that the reforms for which parliament pressed would 'beget eternal factions and dissentions (as destructive of public happiness as war)'.[27] Just as there is no place in the body natural for a malignant tumour, there is no place in the body politic for factions. A parallel made by Theophilus Parsons: 'every division in any degree, is in a Political, what we call a disease in a Natural Body, which as it weakens its strength, so it tends to its destruction'.[28] As the imagery of the body politic faded from republican discourse, society came to be seen as composed of groups and sectors with disparate interests and the diverse social relations they generate. The risk was that some groups or sectors, so ambitious to expand their interests and dominate others, moved beyond being an interest group among many to being a threat to all. James Madison captures the move: 'the common impulse of passion, or of interest' is now 'adverse to the rights of other citizens, or to the permanent and aggregate interests of the community'.[29]

From interest groups and sectors factions are born. Their actions sabotage settled social relations among groups and sectors, and disrupt the orderly competition and coordination on which self-rule rests. Factions break the boundaries of restraint inherent in sociability and ignore the sentiments moderating and guiding social action. The rise of factions is made easier if power is diffused among the people rather than held in the hands of a few. Once ambition to expand interests takes hold, the power of the state is eyed as a resource, a means to ends, the union of interest and power then a formidable force. An order of self-rule based on diversity of interests and the sentiment of sociability is weak in resisting the determined efforts of a faction. Efforts well-rewarded, as Douglas North noted: 'the returns on opportunism, cheating, and shirking' are rising. The only solution is 'a coercive third party', without it 'political anarchy'.[30] An order of self-rule has coercive third

[26] *Concise Oxford Dictionary.*
[27] *His Majesty's Answers* in Wootton: *Divine Right and Democracy*, p 172.
[28] T Parsons: *Essay Upon Government* referred to in G Wood: *The Creation of the American Republic*, p 59.
[29] J Madison: *Federalist No 10*, p 42
[30] D North: *Institutions, Institutional Change and Economic Performance*, p 35.

parties, officials and agencies with power, but they might not be strong enough to stem the swelling of interest groups or to avoid their own capture.[31]

The Cade-effect The appeal of self-rule in spreading power among persons and groups is at the same time a point of weakness. To the threat of factions others are added. One is the Cade-effect touched on before. The rise of a leader and the shift of power from the people to one or a few is a familiar feature of social relations. Joseph Schumpeter explains: 'collectives act almost exclusively by accepting leadership – this is the dominant mechanism of practically any collective action'.[32] The reasons are not hard to find. Among the supporters of a cause, sentiments range from burning hot to warm to cold indifference, most roughly in the middle. A few stand out for their passion and zeal, for being well-informed and a depth of commitment, their energy admired, a sense of superiority fostered. Add a touch of charisma, a selfless dedication, a visionary eye, and the conditions for leadership are met. Power drifts from the many to the one, and power once tasted unlocks appetite for more, to which the constraints are too weak to be a barrier. Progress from dedicated member to leader to ruler is well-charted and hard to stop. Max Weber defines the Cade-effect, or Caesarism as he prefers, as the 'principle of the small number' gathering power into their hands, a principle that 'always rules political action'.[33] Parliamentary systems are especially prone to Caesarism because elected members 'function only as a following for the leader'. The leader in turn relates and is responsible to the people in a way the 'many-headed governing assembly' cannot. This is especially 'evident in true democracy'.

Self-rule as a model of 'true democracy' is prey to the Cade-effect. The diffusion of power among officials and agencies, while aimed at preventing concentration, has the opposite effect. The more diffused powers are, the less the capacity of officials and agencies to resist the joint force of a natural tendency and the determined efforts of a few, efforts aided by two other principles of social relations. One is the unevenness of resources across persons, groups, and sectors; the other the disposition of persons, alone or in groups and sectors, to expand and increase what they have. The closer a constitutional order is to self-rule, the weaker the defence against Caesarism. The spread of power among officials and agencies makes it easier for one or a few to worm their way into positions of power. Counter measures are available. Select agencies can be strengthened to remain independent and resist undue influence. The courts stand out with judges trained to be strong and detached from the tug-and-scramble, resistant to the offers or threats of powerful

[31] The solution, the defence against the ambition of factions, is to move power from the people to representatives, who are a step removed and who know the common good. And so save the old and withered body politic from oblivion.

[32] J Schumpeter: *Capitalism, Socialism, and Democracy* (London: Allen & Unwin, 5th edn 1976), pp 270, 284–5.

[33] M Weber: *Political Writings* (eds) P Lassman and R Speirs (Cambridge: Cambridge University Press, 2010), p 174. Further discussed in Chapter XV.

persons, and confident to pass judgement according to law.[34] How well they succeed varies across time and place. Administrative law doctrines and processes have developed in recent years to strengthen agencies and arm them against interference, how effectively again variable. Civil society has a part to play, the institutions fortified to make each a site of power capable of engaging with and monitoring the agencies of government, being vigilant in detecting undue influence from officials within government or persons outside, and imposing censure. How to protect the machinery of government against the forces of Caesarism, the drift of power to one or a few, and how to strengthen the institutions of civil society, are subjects for further analysis and of pressing importance.

Keeping agencies to purpose How to protect the agencies of government from the Cades and the Caesars is one issue for a self-ruling people, staying in charge of them another. The agencies—legislative and executive, administrative and judicial—are needed for sound self-rule but each is a risk.[35] The legislative and executive rank just below the people in deciding high policy, and are kept under close watch. The administrative and judicial are less in the sights of the people as a whole, and further from oversight and supervision. Let us consider first the administrative and then a word on the judicial. Administrative agencies tend towards autonomy and independence from the political process, aided and augmented by a mentality and a method, one of specialist knowledge and expertise, the other of consistency in application. This *bureaucratic rationality* has in Weber's words a *levelling* tendency in treating as equals all who enter the sphere of authority, an end to which settled rules are the most suitable means.[36] Social relations between agencies and the people are ordered according to the logic of bureaucracy, social action is rendered as 'rationally organized'.[37] The passion and discord, the flux and flair of the political arena are replaced by the calculus of cool reason within bounds set by clear rules. The two models of action in practice are blurred, each overlapping with and borrowing from the other, but at core very different.

The rise of administrative agencies and the drift of power towards them, a feature of any form of rule, is said to be most pronounced under self-rule. According to Weber, whose account of bureaucracy remains the anchor of analysis: 'Bureaucracy inevitably accompanies modern mass democracy' and the two grow 'in parallel'.[38] Although *mass democracy* is used loosely, the idea fits the model of self-rule. Guided by the purpose of advancing the well-being of all, government

[34] For recent studies of judicial independence, the purpose, and the practice: *Courts and the People: Friend or Foe?* (ed) DJ Galligan.

[35] See the account in Chapter I:3.

[36] M Weber: *Economy & Society* (eds) G Roth and C Wittich (Berkeley, London: University of California Press, 1978), pp 973*ff*. For further analysis, see: DJ Galligan: 'Authoritarianism in Government and Administration: The Promise of Administrative Justice' (2001) 54 *Current Legal Problems* 79–102.

[37] *Ibid* p 984.

[38] *Ibid* pp 226 and 983.

by the people expands to cover more interests and reaches far into social relationships to fortify, curb, or foster them. The people's reliance on administrative agencies adds to the number and types, allows their powers to grow, and fuels the tendency to independence. Weber goes on to doubt the ability of the people to control 'the content and the direction of administrative activities'. *Democracy* in his sense 'does not necessarily mean an increasingly active share of the subject in government'.[39] Here we differ. Self-rule on my model assumes active citizens engaging in and exerting influence over administrative agencies. The logic is that, as the powers of agencies increase, the people are more active in their efforts to keep them under control. The means at their disposal, within the bounds of restraint and support, are the now familiar trio of engagement, vigilance, and censure. How effective they are in practice awaits further research. Here we rejoin Weber for his account of bureaucratic rationality, 'its technical superiority over any other form of organization' and the effect it has on administration. Agencies become more closed and self-contained, and harder for the amateur outsider to penetrate and understand, let alone control.[40] The two sources of instability, powerful agencies insulated from outside scrutiny, and the heavy demands on active citizens, come together to present a high hurdle for a self-ruling people to overcome.

Setting and applying standards The risks of agencies to self-rule are made clear by dividing power at each site according to the three actions of setting standards, applying them, and governing within the discretionary space. In setting standards, the procedures are designed to allow persons with an interest to take part. The aim is to identify at each site of agency power the interests likely to be affected, the range at some narrowly defined, at others wide and uncertain, merging into a vague notion of public interest. Decisions have to be made and lines drawn, a process perhaps best entrusted to boards separate from the agencies, the members selected from among the people, the task to devise procedures suited to the subject and the type of agency, the aim to identify the interests with a stake.[41] The complex and lengthy processes likely to result, while a drawback, are justified by producing standards responsive to all relevant interests. At the next stage, the process moves from the disorderly clash of competing interests to the orderly application of the standards to particular cases, the process confined to the parties whose interests are at issue under the standards. The mode edges towards the adjudicative: gathering evidence, hearing the parties, and reaching a reasoned outcome according to the standards. The function of administrative agencies applying standards approaches that of judicial agencies, where the adjudicative process is most complete and refined. The adjudicative function of agencies at first sight presents no particular problem for a self-governing people.[42]

39 *Ibid* p 985.
40 *Ibid* pp 973–80.
41 For additional analysis, see Chapter V.
42 These issues are considered further in Chapter XV.

Closer scrutiny reveals two potential hazards in applying standards, one the ubiquity of discretion, the other the effect of 'Warr's law'. The process of applying standards, while normally one of logic and reason, on occasions may be more open and complex. Interpretation then involves discretion, the reaching back into the social context to settle meaning and to draw lines among competing factors. Besides the interests directly in issue, others may be uncovered and affected enough to have a claim on the process.[43] The tendency towards bureaucratic rationality, where action is based on precise rules applied logically, is said to render the social setting irrelevant. An idea repeated in jurisdictions where judges declare themselves the mere mouthpieces of the law, as if applying the law were pure logic.[44] According to Warres' law, reliance on form alone, separate from content, is a kind of bondage, from which the only escape is equity and reason.[45] The idea at one level reinforces the need to look beyond the rules to the social context. Invoking *equity* suggests a deeper level, points not only to the social setting but to the principles within the setting, chief among them justice. And justice as we have seen guides entry to social relations, gives birth to juridical equality and demands each have what is due. What is due *within the rules* cannot be wholly distinct from *justice of the rules*, which like a good parent is on hand to urge its offspring towards justice in a deeper sense. While protective justice confines judgement to a narrow slice of social life, the parent has a deeper vision of justice as substance not just form. It is never easy to keep the two apart, even harder for a self-ruling people whose instincts are for justice in the fuller sense, prompted by ideas of equality.

How justice and equality relate, their respective roles at any site of decision-making is hard to pin down and depends on the context. Consider the distribution of welfare benefits. On one approach equality of entitlement is the substantive principle, clear and exact rules the form. An alternative principle just as compelling would be to meet the needs of each person, for which discretion is a necessary means.[46] The rule-based approach simplifies welfare into clear and certain categories, according to which all claimants are treated equally. The substantive approach assumes welfare needs are to some degree particular to the claimant, dependent on circumstances, and not open to rigid rules. The one advances a sense of justice as equal treatment, the other justice as outcomes. If two such contrasting models of authority are implicit in providing welfare, they are bound to appear in the other activities of agencies. Both senses of justice, one ruled-based and procedural, the other content-based and substantive, have a place in social relations. A self-ruling people knows the value of both, but finds Warre's law, the equity of the case, the priority of content over form, has special appeal. Just how that applies

[43] The 'contextual contingencies' of rules are explained in DJ Galligan: *Law in Modern Society*, Chapter 3:4.

[44] Analysed in DJ Galligan and M Matczak: *Strategies of Judicial Review* (Warsaw, 2005).

[45] The ideas of John Warre are considered in Chapter IX:9.

[46] Discussed further in DJ Galligan: *Discretionary Powers.*

to the agencies, how it relates to justice within the standards, is a matter on which opinions differ and a source of instability of self-rule.[47] Much could be learnt from attempts by the courts, confronted with the same dilemma, to find ways of doing justice in both senses, applying rules leavened by equity.[48]

Unfit to rule A familiar refrain in objection to self-rule, and the reason for failure, is that the people do not know how to rule. Farmers and workers, shopkeepers and mechanicals, servants and train drivers, upstarts in all their callings, the common people do not know how to govern and are unfit for office. Governing, it used to be alleged, is a business best left to the superior few. The gentry of Pennsylvania in their attack on self-rule are worthy heirs of the English tradition of contempt for the common people. The grounds are dubious, the assertion unsupported by reason or experience. Empty ideas repeated often enough enter into and shape sentiments and dispositions and influence action. The British Empire is said to have been built by graduates in classics from Oxford and Cambridge, who armed with minds trained by mastering Latin and Greek, the rigours of philosophy, and the sweep of history, could turn attention to any issue and had just the right qualities for governing a princedom in India, administering a backwater in Borneo, and keeping the peace among warring tribes in the hidden valleys of Papua New Guinea.[49] In constitutional affairs the claim for the superiority of the few is not their trained minds, rather their being members of a sector of society with superior skills by endowment of breeding and the possession of property, occasionally refined by but not dependent on a trace of education. Its members stand out from the masses as being superior in all spheres of life. The result is a 'great distinction of persons', proclaimed the opponents of the 1776 Constitution of Pennsylvania.[50] The effortless ease of a fortunate few, the prince and his court, the knights of the shire, the men of property, and the elected representatives, are marked with pride in the upper register of constitutional discourse in England, Pennsylvania, and elsewhere. Stripped of the imagery of the body politic, the natural right of a few to rule is hard enough to justify empirically, even in societies where social divisions are deep and the common people kept low. Where all are treated with respect, are reasonably educated, and have access to information and analysis due to the wonder of technology, the notion is untenable.

Practical decision-making has several parts: an issue, the options, the evidence, and the determination. Men and women make practical decisions as a matter of daily routine about matters of importance to them, family and property, work

[47] Weber makes the same distinction under *formal* and *substantive* justice: *Economy & Society*, pp 654–8.

[48] The literature is huge; for a range of robust approaches and opinions: *The Courts and the People: Friend or Foe*.

[49] AP Thornton: *The Imperial Idea and Its Enemies: A Study of British Power* (New York: St Martin's Press, 1985); George Orwell: *Burmese Days* (London: Penguin Books, 1944).

[50] Quoted in G Wood: *The Creation of the American Republic*, p 235.

and leisure, and endless others. The yeomen and yeowomen of Vacy Plains were in charge of much that affected them. They turned virgin land into farms well-run and profitable. They acted together to settle local issues, from building schools and churches to improving the roads. They engaged in local government at several levels, helped each other out at harvest and at lambing and in many other ways, and settled disputes among themselves. They argued about politics and the wider issues of the day. Some were elected to state parliament and local councils. Folk memories from old Europe of religious division lived on, more a curiosity than source of enmity, some bemused that others would not play tennis on Sunday, who in turn marvelled that some would not eat meat on Friday. Marriage across the lines was frowned on but tolerated. Another group, thinking both to be victims of superstition, repaired to the secrecy of the lodge to indulge in antics and rituals that aroused the amusement of others, while fuelling fantasy as to what went on. Nevertheless, in discussing and settling the common matters of daily life, all brought to bear the sociability and the solidarity needed for communal action. They were not well educated in a formal way but no one doubted their good sense on practical matters of economics, politics, and social life. The yeoman and yeowomen of Vacy Plains are not exceptions, the capacity for practical judgement being common to all levels of society. Between decisions in the course of private endeavour and those in the public sphere, whether of local concern or national, there is no barrier, no dividing line between people. To parade the process of governing as something apart for which just a few are fit, is to distort reality. Governing on whatever rung relies on practical decision-making of the same kind as in private and communal affairs, and of which all citizens are capable, rather than being the preserve of caste or class or coterie. When expert knowledge and specialist skills are needed, they are available in a form easily understood by all, especially now in the age of technology available to all.

Levelling tendencies The people's being unfit to govern is reason enough to keep them away from power, their unruliness makes it a positive duty. Charles Stuart in his reply to parliament on the eve of war, written by his advisers Culpeper and Hyde, exposes the 'wild humours' and unfortunate propensities of the people. One is their disposition to rise above their station and destroy 'all distinctions of families and merit' and end in dark equal chaos of confusion'. Another to 'destroy all rights and properties'. A third to disrupt 'the long line of noble ancestors' and in their place 'a Jack Cade or a Wat Tyler'.[51] A dark sentiment, at least eloquently expressed, compared with the vulgar invective noted earlier, but just as deadly.[52] The same sentiment motivated Ireton's plea at Putney that to give the vote to the

[51] Charles Stuart: *His Majesties Answer to the Nineteen Propositions* (1642) reproduced in *The Stuart Constitution: Documents and Commentary 1603–1688* (ed) JP Kenyon (Cambridge: Cambridge University Press, 1986), p 18.

[52] Discussion of the upper register: Chapter VI.

common men, the soldiers who had won the war, would be the end of property, its protection the purpose of a constitution. The grandees of Pennsylvania levelled the same claim against the common freemen. The longer the debate raged over the right constitution for a republican order, the deeper it delved into the foundations of constitutional authority. Liberty is the mediating concept, the oak in the forest that catches the eye, yet vigorous among its roots is a notion of equality. It is hard to avoid the foundation of equality, half submerged but as firm as a rock.[53]

Relations between the two, between liberty and equality, is at the core of self-rule. All freemen, by contrast with their slaves, are equal bearers of rights and have equal status as right-holders. That is the basis of republican discourse, the foundation of the constitutional order, where juridical equality defines a sphere within which all are equal.[54] Equal as a matter of constitutional entitlement to defend and protect rights. Trouble breaks out when we move from juridical equality to reality where all domains—social, economic, and political—are deeply unequal. The concepts are separate; juridical equality belongs to constitutional discourse, defines legal relations, but says nothing about other domains of social relations. However, just as the two domains of justice struggle to stay separate, the discourse on the two senses of equality cannot in the practical world be kept apart, the tension between them unavoidable. The tension sits at the centre of self-rule. A people equal as right-holders, and equal in governing themselves, is likely to be disposed towards equality in a substantive sense. On that ground rises the fear of levelling. A people vested with the power of government is likely to level a sceptical gaze on social and material inequalities. Disparities of property and wealth are due in part to former restrictions on the people's liberty to improve their lives. Now that the restrictions are removed and the people have equal liberty, the sentiments of substantive equality are aroused and dispositions form to ease economic inequalities. Such dispositions are resisted or at least moderated in the interests of social harmony. The risk however is there and the stakes are high, enough to incite the privileged few to condemn the multitude, to cast doubt on their ability and their authority, and to take all measures to remove their power to level.

To conclude The journey through the field of self-rule has been long but instructive. An idea that sounds natural and compelling in principle turns out to be hard to put into practice and beset by instability. It is not that the people doubt their ability to govern themselves; nor are they daunted by the instabilities and the practical obstacles to governing themselves well, both of which with energy and effort they could overcome. That is the point, the crux of misgivings about the demands self-rule would make on them. Good government is critical in contributing to well-being, but has to be kept in proportion. Personal endeavour and collective action within social relationships are the main sources of well-being and take up most of

[53] G Wood: *The Creation of the American Republic*, p 238.
[54] Discussed in detail in Chapter IX:9, 10, 11.

the people's time, energy, and effort. The concern is that the levels of engagement, vigilance, and censure needed to govern themselves well would distract from their own endeavours and detract from rather than enhance well-being. The question then is how to balance the two, being attentive to governing on the one hand, and pursuing personal and shared ends on the other. A solution starts to take shape based on ideas the people have picked up in passing through the various constitutional fields. The idea of themselves as *keepers* of the constitutional order, rather than the front-line functionaries, has stayed with them and seems promising. The other idea centres on the tools of engagement, vigilance, and scrutiny, the means by which to keep the functionaries to purpose, to make sure they govern well. The exacting demands of self-rule on the people's engagement in governing would be scaled back, while the means of vigilance and censure strengthened. Governing is left to officials with some engagement of the people, but their main task is to keep a check on quality. Just how that is achieved has to be worked out. One way is to hand authority to representatives and trust them to govern well; that has some advantages but major drawbacks, as we shall see in the next chapter. Another of more potential is to develop the notion of the people as keepers of the common good, the subject of the last chapter.

Notes: Chapters XII and XIII

Liberty as the aim of good government, including the people's ruling themselves

According to Francesco Patrizi: 'Nothing can be of greater importance in civil society than liberty, towards which the spirit of one's whole city should be turned': *The Founding of a Republic* (Prato, 1531) quoted in Q Skinner: *The Foundations of Modern Political Thought*, p 156. Machiavelli discusses liberty at length in *The Discourses.* Quentin Skinner provides an invaluable analysis of both writers.

I have suggested liberty is valued for two reasons, one as a quality of personhood, the other as instrumental to other social goods. As Paul Rahe points out, Machiavelli emphasises the *instrumental* value: 'cities have not grown either in domination or riches when not in a condition of liberty': *Against Altar and Throne*, p 55. Discussed in *Machiavelli's Liberal Republican Legacy*, (ed) PA Rahe.

Active or passive citizens

Adam Smith records: 'where the people had at first equal access to the magistracies, but finding it altogether troublesome resign'd it to the town council, who still continue to be possessed of it, and have the power of choosing their own members on a vacancy': *Lectures on Jurisprudence*, pp 226–7.

Upstarts

A word with a long history commonly used to describe a person who has risen suddenly from a humble position, often assuming an arrogant tone. The Lincolnshire rebels of 1551 considered Thomas Cromwell 'a social upstart' for his 'unwanted innovations': Zarat: *Origins of Democratic Culture*, p 53. On being banished by Richard II, Bolingbroke prepares for the life of 'A wandering vagabond, my rights and royalties/Plucked from my arms perforce and given away/To upstart unthrifts': *The Tragedy of King Richard the Second*, Act 2: 1: 119. While Joan of Arc thinks 'this upstart [Charles the Dauphin] is old Talbot's ghost': *The First Part of Henry VI*, Act 4: 7: 87.

Concept of a slave

The word *slave* comes into English from the Latin *sclavus* via old French *esclave* meaning 'a person who is the chattel of another'. A chattel has no juridical status, no legal rights. The Slavic people of central Europe acquired the name from marauding neighbours who sold them into slavery.

Between freedom and slavery

In accounts of liberty reference is often made to the *Codex* of Justinian where 'a fundamental distinction' is made between free persons and slaves. A person may be free in this constitutional sense, but be subject to all sorts of restrictions under specific laws. Which takes us back to the point in the text that the quantity and quality of liberty is determined by the terms of the constitution and the laws.

Non-arbitrariness

Liberty is sometimes defined as non-domination of one over another. In telling people what they may or may not do, law by nature affects liberty. On one view, presented as the republican view, liberty is lost only if the law is arbitrary. To act *arbitrarily* is to act on opinion, capriciously, or without constraint, while to have arbitrary power over another is to *dominate* the other, which means to have 'commanding influence over': *Concise Oxford Dictionary*, p 58. Arbitrary power is one way of interfering with liberty but there are plenty of others. Laws stated in clear terms can interfere with liberty. Philip Pettit, casting liberty as non-domination, explains that liberty is not lost by law if it pursues 'the common interests of citizens' and 'in a manner that conforms to the opinions received among the citizenry': *Republicanism: A Theory of Freedom and Government* (Oxford: Oxford University Press, 1997), pp 36–7.

This takes us back to the foundations of constitutions and the relationship between rulers and ruled. To limit justified restrictions on liberty to laws that 'conform to the opinions of citizens' is problematical, because it would limit drastically the power of governments to govern. Across the sweep of history, the making of laws conforming to opinion is a rare event. Princes are not normally restrained by the opinions of citizens, and the representative few are there to *form* rather than *conform to* opinion.

That law serve liberty and conform to the sentiments of the people is the aim of the people ruling themselves. They soon realize that sentiments range widely and choices have to be made among them, to the benefit of some, the loss to others. They would reject the idea that laws are for that reason arbitrary. This brings us back then to the dilemma of how to reconcile being free with being governed. The problem is that the coordinated action, of which government is uniquely capable, supplies social goods the people want; yet, whatever the form, governing restricts liberty.

The advantage of self-rule is not to eliminate the loss of freedom common to any form of rule. That would render rule impossible. It is rather to lessen the loss of liberty in two ways.

First, each person has a say in setting the rules, in influencing the content of the rules, offering options and contesting alternatives. The expectation is that as a result the laws are moderate and respect liberty. The people's having control of the law-making process would enable the expectation to be met. Secondly, laws respecting liberty, while a major gain of self-rule, is not enough. The process of applying the law opens the way to loss of liberty by the actions of officials. A system of self-rule enables the people to keep close watch over officials and guard against liberty being abused in application. A watch more exacting than that allowed in other forms of rule. Self-rule for these two reasons has the potential to protect and preserve liberty in making and applying law, not absolutely but better than other forms of rule.

Quentin Skinner raises a variation: 'You will be rendered unfree if you merely fall into a condition of political subjection or dependence, thereby leaving yourself open to the danger of being forcibly or coercively deprived by your government of life, liberty, or property'.[55] Discretion in the hands of officials increases the risk of subjection, and may be a means of domination of one over another.[56]

55 Q Skinner: *Liberty Before Liberalism* (Cambridge: Cambridge University Press, 1998), p 69.

56 The risks are analysed in DJ Galligan: *Discretionary Powers*.

The solution often proposed is to govern through clear and settled rules. It is a false solution. Liberty lost by the application of rules, even rules fairly and accurately applied, is still a loss of liberty. Rules remove or reduce the uncertainty of discretion, but leave intact the loss of liberty imposed by the rules themselves. Rules may even be a more serious threat to liberty than discretion that allows consideration of factors banned by rules, some for the bad, some for the good: see the discussion in my *Discretionary Powers*. In condemning Claudio to death, the acting-governor Angelo applied strictly the letter of the law. In the face of Isabella's pleas for mercy, Claudio defended his actions by claiming the law allowed him no discretion to soften or suspend the terms: W Shakespeare: *Measure for Measure*. In protecting liberty, form matters but substance matters more. The conclusion must be that any form of government, including self-rule, no matter how benevolent and well-conducted, both protects and restricts liberty.

Processes and outcomes

For classification of procedures and the relationship of each to outcomes: J Rawls: *A Theory of Justice* (Oxford: Clarendon Press, 1972).

XIV
Rule by Representatives Re-presented

1. Entering the field of rule by representatives

The images of princely rule and self-rule in the background, the people enter the field of rule by representatives. Having brushed against this form of rule before, they notice it falls somewhere between princely rule and self-rule, as if somehow to make up for the shortcomings of each while lacking the coherence of either. That is cause for caution. The people have come to realize constitutional authority relies on paring back hopes of perfection and, instead, promoting compromise and moderation. They are aware that rule by representatives is linked to the discourse of democracy, not the pure form of self-rule but rule by a few whom the people elect. The few rule, while the people decide who they are to be, have some influence on their actions, and, with an election never far away, have some means for holding them to account. So stated, the relationship is straightforward: the people elect the leaders, who govern, and who may be removed at the next round of election. What puzzles the people is the representative part; what is gained by presenting relations between people and rulers in the language of representation. The people have reason to be wary. They learnt from observing princely rule how the representative element is used to keep them away from the process of governing, not to engage them. The prince claims to represent the people, although the people have no say as to who the prince is and slight influence on his actions. The people have seen how, with the passing of power to an elected few, *representation* stays on board with no certain purpose. The effect seems to be to keep them in their place, demanding restraint and support while limiting the scope for engagement, vigilance, and censure.

Representative rule in modern dress is born of the union of self-rule and princely rule, inheriting traits of both. The parents are not natural partners. Each leaves its imprint on the off-spring, representative rule, the one vesting plenary power in a few, the other keeping alive the idea of the people deciding their own well-being. The hope is the tension be tamed enough to satisfy the people and to enable government to be both effective and responsive to their interests. The justification is that an assembly of representatives few in number is able to act wisely and decisively, compared to an unwieldy aggregate of the people, while at the same time being attentive to the people. Whether in practice an alliance of the few and the many is capable of coordinating sentiments, dispositions, and actions to

Keepers of the Common Good. D.J. Galligan, Oxford University Press. © D.J. Galligan 2024.
DOI: 10.1093/9780198907398.003.0014

create good government is contingent on several factors. Failure is common due either to the elected few losing touch with the people, or to the people advancing too vigorously their own interests causing conflict and division. Sometimes the two combine to end in government competent, respectful of the people's interests, and dedicated to the common well-being. The contingencies on which the balance hangs are revealed and evaluated in the final chapter.

The aim in this chapter is to enquire more closely into, and to grasp more securely, the nature and appeal of rule by representatives. The account is brief because this form of rule has appeared before and much squeezed under it is better viewed from other standpoints.[1] The matters for now are to show the social base of rule by representatives and to enquire into the provenance. That leads to two lines of enquiry, one running down from princely rule, the other reaching up from the people ruling themselves, the meeting of which results in representative rule. The next step is to scrutinize the familiar form and to see how it fits into social relations between the people and representatives in contemporary conceptions of rule. The question is whether, after the search for meaning and efforts to expose the essence, and taking account of its leading role on the constitutional stage, the concept of representation adds to the understanding of relations between the people and rulers.

The answer swings back and forth between two theories. On one, the *agency* theory, representatives act as agents on behalf of the principal, the people, presenting or re-presenting their interests in the process of governing. The people are in charge but for practical reasons delegate portions of power to agents. On another, the *substitution* theory, the few stand in for the people, on more exuberant versions even assume their identity and acquire their power, so that the actions of representatives are the actions of the people. The purpose of both theories is to show that the people are both the source and the holders of constitutional authority, which they exercise through representatives. To the two accounts, each semantically subtle, there is an alternative, blunt and pedestrian, that has no need for the concept of representation, except in a weak and metaphorical sense, yet displays accurately the relationship between the many and the few. The few chosen by the people rule; the people accept being ruled; then find ways of getting the few to rule well. On this account, by contrast with agency and substitution, no pretence is needed of the people being in charge and ruling themselves. The task now is to examine the three approaches to rule by the few, to cast doubt on two, and to lay the foundations for the third, the subject of the final chapter. Let us begin with a working model as a point of reference.

[1] For the several meanings drawn from the texts of constitutions, see Chapter VI; for the place on representation in the keepers' model, see Chapter XV.

2. A model of rule by representatives

First The people, the source of constitutional authority, elect leaders who have plenary power to govern.

Second The duty of the leaders is to govern for the common good, the good of all and the nation as a whole. Being 'wise, patriotic, and lovers of justice', the elected leaders know the common good.[2]

Third The separation, or 'partition' of powers among the legislative, executive, and judicial agencies contributes to good government.[3]

Fourth The secondary agencies of government, mainly absent from the discourse, are instituted by and accountable to the primary legislative and executive agencies, while kept within the bounds by the courts.

Fifth The relationship between the people and leaders is defined by and confined to election. The commitment to justice means the people have access to the courts.

Sixth Elected leaders listen to the voices of the electors, but are not bound by them, and exercise independent judgement in governing.[4]

Seventh Beyond voting and having access to justice, the representative model neither requires nor provides a fuller or wider role for the people. They are likely in practice to have some scope to engage in the processes of governing, be vigilant, and deliver censure, although that is not a condition of the model.

Eighth The people are expected to exercise self-restraint, support the institutions and processes of governing, acquiesce in and, indeed, consent to their actions.

A pattern of opinion, a set of sentiments and dispositions among the people takes shape. The people value rule by the few for several reasons. A small assembly is able to act firmly and decisively; has the ability to decide the common good and the power to achieve it; while being linked to the people through the electoral process. Other reasons may be added. Rule in the hands of a few is a solution to some of the instabilities of the people ruling themselves, while lessening the risks of princely rule. Most reassuring of all is the assumption that the few know the common good, have unique insight into what constitutes good government, and the power to act accordingly.

The model is likely to be frowned on for not making reference to *representation* and playing down the *democratic* dimension. The idea of the people governing themselves through representatives, instead of defining the relationship, is absent. The model looks instead to the social context and the practical reality

[2] Words of James Madison: *The Federalist No. 10*, p 45.

[3] *Partition* is Madison's term: *The Federalist*, p 163.

[4] Leaders are not to be instructed by the people, although there are a few exceptions, see Chapter VI:5.

of government being entrusted not to the people, but to a few leaders, backed by the agencies. That the people elect and may remove the few at the next election falls far short of the people's ruling themselves in any serious sense. Even if the people manage to have influence, the power to make decisions and to take action remains with the few. On this practical even mundane approach, election is a means, a useful means, for appointing rulers and having some influence on the conduct of rule. Supposing we were to describe the ruling few as *representatives*, the question would be what is added, what otherwise hidden quality of relations between people and rulers is revealed by *representation*. There are two approaches, the *agency* and the *substitution*, the purpose of each to show that the plenary power to rule stays with the people, who are ruling themselves through representatives. On the *agency* approach, the people appoint by election the few as agents to act on their behalf; on the *substitution* approach, representatives stand in for the people.

Some deny even the status of agents, preferring to regard the elected few as servants of the people.[5] Let us settle on agency as broad enough to cover the idea of the few employed or retained by the people to do certain tasks. The relationship is one of principal and agent. The principal authorizes the agent to work on its behalf, while the agent reports back to the principal. Election is the mechanism for appointing and dismissing agents. Among the problems with this account, two stand out. The elected few neither look like nor behave as agents of the people. They claim and in practice have plenary power to govern. They make law and decide policy; create and control the machinery of government; and do all that is needed within the discretionary space to govern. The other problem is the roles are reversed: the agent has power over the principal instead of the opposite. Between elections and subject to any constitutional conditions, the elected leaders have authority over the people to decide their well-being, to define their rights and to impose duties. That an agent have such power over the principal is not only unusual but odd, enough to throw into doubt the relationship. The language of agency could have merit in keeping elected leaders down to earth by reminding them an election is never far away; but as description of the relationship fails.

The other attempt to insert representation into relations between the people and the elected few is framed as *representative democracy*, a notion of uncertain meaning, loosely defined as the people ruling themselves through representatives.[6] A lot hangs on that word *through*, which is best construed in this way. The many create a relationship with a few by which the few act in the name of the many. The relationship is not just the delegation of power by one to another for practical purposes. It is that but more, a mystical union whereby the few substitute for, in some

[5] The constitution of South Korea refers to elected leaders as 'the servants of the people': see Chapter VI.

[6] Madison refers to the advantages of 'the substitution of representative' for the people: *The Federalist No. 10*, p 47.

sense become the people, so that their actions are the actions of the people. The union allows plenary power at an abstract level to stay with the people, while at a practical level passing to the few the task of governing. Substitution of one for the other catches the sense of the relationship. The submerged subjunctive allows the actions of representatives to be treated *as if* they were the actions of the people. By the act of electing, the people are presumed to authorize the few to act for them and in their name, not as agents, but *as if* they were themselves the people. Having settled the relationship at the abstract level, the people still have to confront the reality of power being in the hands of a few. The power to elect and dismiss now has a second function as a practical measure, a way of holding the elected to purpose. A constitutional field designed in this way unites the mystical and the mundane, on one hand representatives being the people, on the other hand fallible functionaries tempted by appetite, prone to incompetence, and misrule. How the two live side-by-side, the two domains of discourse be reconciled, the tension eased between elected leaders being the people, and yet answerable to them, remains a mystery. One solution is to remove the mystery by doing away with the answerability part and freeing the representative to rule unshackled.[7] The lessons of princely rule still fresh in their minds, the people are wary of unshackled leviathans and hold fast to the notion that, despite fancy fictions about representation, plenary power is in the hands of a few, who have to be kept under watch.

How we end up with three different conceptions of representative government, each claiming to be coherent even compelling, has to be explained. One has no room for representation, except in the sense that the few govern on behalf of the people, while for the other two the concept is essential in showing how, despite appearance and practice, the plenary power to govern stays with the people. That means a brief encounter with the history of each, tracing the origins, the social relationships, and the matching discourse. The enquiry takes two paths. One starts with rule from below, the people ruling themselves, out of which leaders emerge, who soon aspire to be more than one among many, more than agents or delegates, to acquire plenary power and become a substitute for the people. The other path starts with rule from above, the prince who represents the whole, the nation, the realm, and the people. The real people, as opposed to the abstraction, exert influence, agitate for more say, and gain a foothold in the constitutional field. Princely rule gives way to rule by a few elected by the people. Social relations between rulers and ruled, the few and the many, are recalibrated to give life to the awkward offspring rule-by-representatives. Perhaps not so awkward after all. Despite the mixed parentage and uncertain identity, there are signs of the offspring escaping its origins and maturing into a coherent and appealing concept of rule, an idea to return to as the chapter ends.

[7] This approach Thomas Hobbes favoured.

3. Ascending from the people ruling themselves to rule by representatives

The first path ascends from the people ruling themselves to end in rule by representatives. The people delegate power to a few as a practical measure to ease the burden of self-rule. The Abbé Sieyès describes it as government by proxy. Persons, each with a natural liberty, associate to form a common will for the pursuit of common purposes. As the numbers grow and the people spread out, a simple measure is to delegate to a few the power to act for the whole.[8] It is not a surrender of power, rather the assignment of just enough to enable a select few to govern. The reasons are practical. The people lack the time and probably the skills to govern themselves. Delegation of rule to a few means the business of governing is left to those who have the ability and the time, while the people are free and safe in advancing well-being through their own efforts. They retain the power to revoke the assignment to officials and to alter the terms. There is, however, at the core of this pleasing account a tension. Tension between the people holding onto plenary power and the few adding to their own. The tension is brought out by following through the image of the people cooperating for common ends and noting the traps along the way.

Adam Smith traced the path from the people ruling themselves to rule by a few.[9] Association begins with families of hunters who live independently and decide matters of common interest as they occur. The age of shepherds follows; the concept of property emerges; mutual dependence grows. Assemblies of the people convene to settle disputes and determine matters of concern to all, guided by custom and founded on consensus. No sense of governing as a distinct social process is yet evident. That cannot last. Some families are more prosperous than others; inequalities grow. The need for laws beyond custom and consensus to protect property and maintain disparities becomes pressing; institutions form. The community as a whole remains in control of order, peace, and security; but over time leaders emerge and agencies with executive, judicial, and administrative powers appear and acquire power. Still within the common assemblies and under their control, but a seed of disharmony has been sown. Competing ideas begin to appear; different discourses are born, the logics leading in different directions. From the people's point of view, the assembly of common membership is still the centre of authority, the agencies mere conveniences, means to ends settled by the assembly. By contrast, agencies once created acquire their own character

[8] Abbé Sieyès: 'What Is the Third Estate?' in *Sieyès: Political Writings* (ed) M Sonenscher (Indianapolis, Cambridge: Hackett Publishing, 2003), pp 134*ff.*

[9] A Smith: *Lectures in Jurisprudence*, pp 201*ff.*

and weave around themselves a discourse to match and justify their place. They incline towards autonomy and independence, partly in order to be effective, partly from sentiments of superiority. A superiority cultivated by ownership of, or close links to property and the power and status it confers. Add time, the time to engage in the processes of governing, which for most is ruled out by the daily demands of meeting needs and improving lives.

Between the community and the agencies of governance a balance was found and kept. The society of Anglo-Saxon England is admired for succeeding over centuries to do just that. In admiration, no one rivals Obadiah Hulme whom we met in Pennsylvania as the inspiration of the Constitution of 1776. The intention was that Pennsylvania reproduce Anglo-Saxon England between the waning of Rome in the fifth century and the conquest of William in the eleventh. To the Saxon tribes descending from northern Europe we owe, according to Hulme, the English constitution as a form of government 'far superior to the Greek and Roman commonwealths'.[10] Superiority lies in 'the principles upon which the elective power is conducted'. The power of election is to allow the people, dotted across the country and remote from each other, to form a legislative body 'commodiously fit for action', and to which every man by election consents. Election satisfies the natural rights of each man to govern himself and to achieve 'truth and justice' without regard to riches or poverty. And because it is impracticable in large communities for each man to act for himself, he gives up a portion of liberty in return for the gains common action offers. The solution is 'to delegate his power in trust to some other person to act for him'.[11] The 'elective power of the people is the first principle of the constitution'. Yet, the freemen of Anglo-Saxon society were cautious. They knew 'the degenerating principles of mankind', in particular 'that power makes a vast difference in the temper and behaviour of men'.[12] Hulme concludes: 'For this reason, they never gave up their natural liberty, or delegated their power, of making laws, to any man to make, for a longer time than one year'. In summary, although for practical reasons the community assigns powers to persons for specified purposes, the conditions are so stringent it may reasonably be concluded the community continues to rule itself. The freemen of Pennsylvania adopted the same approach, but their efforts were in vain.[13] The trouble is the balance between the people staying in charge of governing, and delegating power to a few, is unstable and prey to ambition, for the reasons set out in the previous chapter. The balance, hard enough to sustain at local levels, becomes more fragile as nations form and grow. The cracks of division appear and widen, the few soon claim to know best what is good for all, while the prince awaits summons to return and restore strong rule.

[10] O Hulme: *An Historical Essay*, p 3.

[11] *Ibid* p 5.

[12] *Ibid* p 6.

[13] For a more complete account, and perhaps more measured of the Anglo-Saxon constitutional order: JEA Joliffe: *The Constitutional History of Medieval England.*

4. Between the people ruling themselves and princely rule

The Levellers took a different route to reach much the same conclusion about relations between the people and rulers. To the Anglo-Saxons and the freemen of Pennsylvania, government grows out of relations among the people as a practical solution to a practical problem. The Levellers, confronting a system of rule entrenched from on high, start at the opposite end. James I is plain: the king governs; he is 'above the law as both the author and giver of strength thereto'.[14] The king's power as head of the body politic is absolute in the way the head of the family is absolute, or was in the seventeenth century. He deals with his subjects as he wishes. He has 'the power of directing all the members of the body to that use which the judgement in the head thinks most convenient'.[15] In civil kingdoms, the king chooses to rule according to law, which he makes, and restrains his power to suit. His son Charles I later was forced to concede that law-making is a joint activity of the king, the house of peers, and the commons; but it is not a sharing of rule. The king takes counsel from the two chambers and listens to their advice, but the plenary power of rule is his. The elected chamber guards the liberty of subjects, while the peers are 'a screen and bank between the prince and the people'.[16]

Despite the fine words and noble sentiments, reality for the Levellers was lethally different. Having suffered abuse of rule by all three, king, peers, and commons, the Levellers worked backwards to build a competing constitutional order. Power over the people cannot appear from nowhere and float about freely. It must be for a purpose, the purpose portrayed in the imagery of the body politic and enlisted to justify the king's authority. It is held on trust to sustain the good health of the body politic, the well-being of each organ. If trust be broken, authority loses purpose and lapses. Power lapsed reverts to its original source, the people, who are sovereign and the source of government. In place of power descending from on high, it now ascends from below.[17] An alternative constitutional order unfolds. Memories of that pre-constitutional hinterland of ideas are revived, social relations between the people and representatives redefined, leaving no room for king or nobles who claim authority by birth and inheritance. Only the House of Commons as the elected chamber is qualified to govern. Its own status however is in question. Parliament's claim to represent the people as a substitute for them, to be their embodiment, and therefore detached from them, is a myth to dismiss. The Levellers deploy a different language, invent a new set

[14] King James I of England: *True Law of Free Monarchies* (1598) in *Constitutional Documents of the Reign of James I 1603–1625* (ed) JR Tanner (Cambridge: Cambridge University Press, 1960), p 14.

[15] King James' Speech to the Parliament, 1610 in *Constitutional Documents*, pp 15–16.

[16] *The King's Answer to the Nineteen Propositions* (18 June 1642) in *The Stuart Constitution: Documents and Commentary* (ed) JP Kenyon (Cambridge: Cambridge University Press, 1986), p 19.

[17] The idea of power ascending from below or descending from on high is examined more fully in: W Ullman: *A History of Political Thought: The Middle Ages* (Baltimore: Penguin Books, 1965).

of concepts; parliamentarians are now agents of the people or to be more precise their servants.

At this point, the discourse of the Levellers meets that of the Anglo-Saxons. The mystical image of representation is discarded, representatives demoted. Far from the lofty notion of becoming the people, they are now agents or servants elected to serve the well-being of the people, 'to provide for their welfare and freedoms'. And for no other purpose.[18] The use of agents and servants is a practical measure and nothing more. The people are relieved of the burdens of governing by allowing a few agents to govern on their behalf. The powers of agents are to be limited and monitored. The terms are to be stated in *An Agreement of the People* signed by all who are eligible to vote.[19] The transition from rule by the prince embodying the realm, to the few as substitutes for the people, ends with the people ruling themselves through agents and servants. That is how the proposal was interpreted. The logic may be sound, the sentiments endearing and compelling. The transition, however, never took place, the new order neither tried nor tested. Parliamentarians were soon back in the chamber, not as agents and servants of the people but their substitutes. The old order was restored and a touch of polish added, the king's head removed, and kingship abolished, the nobles neutered. The ruling few called themselves representatives and were sworn to act for the good of the nation and the well-being of its members. They were elected by a small sector of society and were neither dependent on nor answerable to the people as a whole.

The Levellers were edged out and soon forgotten. The constitutional order trundled along carving a path between two poles. One the people's demand for recognition as the sovereign body, the source of constitutional authority, and for fuller engagement in government. The other efforts to maintain the myth that authority somehow has another source. Not that it descends from on high as the Stuarts contended, but has its origins in the common good, once known by the prince, now claimed by parliamentarians. At the same time they know the need to adjust to a changing social order, to listen to the people's demands for wider suffrage and pay more attention to their well-being. The solution devised by the elected few sitting in the commons' chamber was to invest themselves with sovereignty. And so, as noted earlier, the doctrine of the sovereignty of parliament was invented and still stands, although a critical bit is left out, the full doctrine being the *sovereignty of the people* in parliament. The people's being present in parliament through their representatives has consequences. If parliament be the people, then its actions are the actions of the people, the people as an abstract whole. Since the people are present in parliament there is no constitutional place for them outside parliament, no social relationship between the real people and

[18] *England's Miseries and Remedies* (author uncertain; thought to be Sexby) in *Divine Right and Democracy* (ed) D Wootton (London: Penguin Books, 1986), p 276.

[19] *On the Agreement of the People*: *Divine Right and Democracy*, p 283.

the representatives other than a small percentage having the right to vote. The meaning of representation descends from that of princes embodying the realm and being head of the body politic. And so we have arrived at that other, earlier sense of representation, its origins far distant from the real people.

5. Descending from princely rule to rule by an elected few

According to Obadiah Hulme the old English constitution came to an end with the conquest of William the Norman in the eleventh century. The Norman is condemned for replacing a constitutional order in which the people governed themselves, with one based on the will of the king. The power of one replaces the communal power of the whole. Hulme's contention is only partly true. Communal government of the Anglo-Saxon kind continued at local level, while the king's power, even if absolute in principle, was soon encased in a discourse of ideas and concepts drawn partly from Anglo-Saxon society, and partly from canon law and the legacy of Roman law. The king's authority came from the community and had no purpose other than to serve the community. Just what community means here and how it is the source of authority, are matters much discussed and deceptively subtle.[20] The point for now is how the idea of the community as the source of authority could be exploited to explain and justify princely rule. How could it come about that, as John Watts explains: 'The royal dignity and majesty were primarily sustained—by the communal power of his satisfied subjects'.[21]

Two ideas supply the answer, one that the community as a whole is a distinct entity, the other that the prince is the means, the vehicle by which the interests of the whole are realized.[22] Notice the move from the concrete to the abstract: the people in all their colours become one entity, the prince moves from being a person with power to become a symbol of the realm. The purpose of the double abstraction is profound. The good of the community relies on the prince, whose authority is for the sole purpose of protecting and advancing the good. Arthur Monahan explains how these secular ideas have their origins in the church and canon law, and originally in Roman law. The community becomes a corporate entity, the *universitas* of Roman law on whose behalf the proctor acts.[23] The proctor is defined as a person 'able to embody, represent, function in place of another',[24] which may be a person or a corporation. The idea of the prince as the vehicle to the good of the

[20] Several texts of particular use are listed in the Notes.

[21] J Watts: *Henry VI and the Politics of Kingship* (Cambridge: Cambridge University Press, 1996), p 29.

[22] *Ibid* p 30; also Susan Reynolds: *Kingdoms and Communities in Western Europe*, 900–1300.

[23] AP Monahan: Consent, Coercion, and Limit: The Medieval Origins of Parliamentary Democracy (Kingston and Montreal: McGill-Queen's University Press, 1987), pp 114ff.

[24] *Ibid* p 114.

community is ambiguous. It could mean the prince as a vehicle driven by, and so under the control of the community. The correct meaning is that the prince is the means, the sole means, through which the communal good, the interests of all, are known and acted upon. Between the two there is such unity and harmony that the community is able to act only through the prince.

The way is open for two more acts of abstraction. One introduces *representation* into the constitutional field. Just as the proctor represents the *universitas* of the Church, the prince is the representative of the corporation, or *universitas* of the people. And just as a modern corporation acts only through the directors, and the Church only through the pope and the bishops, so the community acts only through the prince. The other abstraction, now familiar, is bold in ambition. The prince as proctor represents in the sense that he becomes or embodies the community; the people as an abstract whole is represented by the prince as proctor. Social relations between the people and the prince are transcended to become an abstract relationship between the symbol of the people, and the symbol of the prince as its embodiment. The prince representing the people in this special sense entered secular constitutional discourse in pre-modern Europe and stayed for centuries. Princes were enabled to rule as the representative of the people, but without entering into a social relationship with the people, beyond 'fearful duty'.

The idea eventually fades, the discourse loses its force, fresh reasons have to be found for power being in the hands of one or a few. Consent, the old warrior wandering about the field, so far unwanted, is called into service.[25] If the prince or the few constitute the people, consent is not needed, has no place in the discourse. When ideas of embodiment fail to convince, consent is drafted to rescue the relationship. The people are now the real people, the aggregate of persons. They enter a relationship with the ruling one or few based on consent. Consent as a fiction takes its place in the field. The people act *as if* they had consented to surrender their natural power to the prince or the few in return for protection. Among ways of construing the fiction of consent, two stand out. On one count the people agree among themselves that the actions of the prince or the few be deemed to be their actions. On another the people enter into a contract with the prince or the few in which they consent to being ruled.[26] The one or the few rule as they wish, while the people, despite the ingenuity and the illusion, are left where they were, out in the constitutional cold. However, the power of the people could no longer be ignored and the constitutional field had to be redesigned. The people's directly ruling in the Anglo-Saxon sense was out of bounds and the few were still in charge. But the relationship had changed. The power of the people to select and dismiss rulers by election gave birth to the idea of the people ruling themselves through representatives. Representatives depend on the people for election but once in office have the

[25] For an account of consent, see Chapter VI.

[26] The first approach is associated with Hobbes, the second with Locke.

plenary power to rule and are not under the mandate or instructions of the people. The precise nature of the relationship was left vague, the distribution of power between the many and the few open to interpretation. Weighing on one side was the idea of the few knowing best what is good for the whole, on the other side the people's knowing their own well-being and wanting the power of rule to be being used for that purpose. We have seen how the Italian city-states strove to define the relationship in the thirteenth and fourteenth centuries, and how the striving continued across Europe and beyond in the seventeenth and eighteenth centuries. Out of such efforts emerged a notion of rule by representatives to take its place in the constitutional order.

Among the routes to that destination two stand out. For one let us return to the Abbé Sieyès where the tension is now in the open. Society begins with 'individual persons seeking to unite' to advance the well-being of each by coordinating the actions of all. This 'first epoch' gives way to a second in which persons unite to form a common will. Power follows the common will and so 'resides in the whole'. The meaning is not clear; how an aggregate of wills becomes a common will is not explained, nor how tensions between them are resolved. The third epoch resolves the uncertainties by entrusting government to representatives. The tension deepens. The community retains the right to will but 'entrusts the right to exercise that power to someone else'. The master stroke follows: the representatives decide the common will. Sieyès writes: 'it is no longer a *real* common will that acts, but a *representative* common will', which means the power to decide the common will passes from the community to representatives. The cycle is complete, the power of the people passed to representatives. Neither Sieyès nor his admirers notice how a practical measure to ease the burdens of the people ruling themselves, ends in a new paradigm of constitutional authority, a reordering of the relationship between the people and representatives, where the representatives rule, the power to elect representatives the only trace left of self-rule. In moving from its origins in the people ruling themselves to rule by representatives deciding the *common* will, the new order connects to and takes meaning from earlier ideas of rule descending from above. Poised between the people ruling themselves and rule by representatives, the exact position uncertain, the Sieysian form of rule leaves the people perplexed.

The other route offers a more pragmatic way of explaining the new constitutional order, while keeping the few in charge. Put simply, the few rather than the people know what is for the good of all and can be relied on to work for it. 'It may well happen that the public voice, pronounced by the representatives of the people, will be *more consonant to the public good* then if pronounced by the people themselves, convened for the purpose' (italics added). The words of James Madison, a continent apart, stated the sentiment implicit in but left unsaid by Sieyès, while echoing voices heard in parliament. The sentiment entered the constitutional field to define the design, sometimes called representative democracy, at other times republican rule.[27] The people observing the new dispensation, while relieved to be rid of talk of *wills*, common or representative, are uneasy. The pragmatic account hides an ambiguity. On one reading the reason for the few ruling is to replace with firm and decisive rule the divisions and weaknesses associated with the people ruling themselves. The quality of rule is contingent on many factors. The few do their best to deliver good government but make no claim to special knowledge of the good of the whole, a view Edmund Burke made immortal.[28] On another reading, one closer to both Madison and Sieyès, is the idea descending from on high and embedded in images of substitution, that the few know what is good for the whole, have insight into the common good.[29] The people note the difference and resolve to keep it in mind in settling on a form of rule.

Rule by representatives in contemporary form weds the two ideas noted, one agency the other substitution. The two pole positions sit awkwardly together, one descending from the ruler acting *as if* he were the whole, the other ascending from the people as a community in charge of its affairs.[30] The balance between the two depends on the distribution of power, the people on one side, the elected few on the other. The more representatives act as substitutes for the people, the more power they have; while the more they are held to be agents, the more say to the people. That power shifts about in this way is critical to understanding the relationship, and in turn representative government. That the constitutional order be built on such shifting sands seems a sign of lamentable confusion. However, on closer look there is a defence. The mobility of power within the relationship, at times favouring the few, at other times the people, can be a strength. Some matters call for firm and decisive action by the few, others are best settled under the influence of the many, while most come somewhere in between. The unstable alliance between the two, the legacy of princely rule on the one hand, enduring fragments of self-rule on the other, is the appeal of rule by representatives, the reason for revising opinion of the oddly-shaped offspring.

6. Conceptions of representation

The words representation and representative are not as settled or as straightforward as they seem. The verb to represent came into English in the fourteenth century from the French *representer*, a corruption of the Latin *repraesentare*, more faithfully followed in Italian as *rappresentare*. The English *to represent*, a transitive verb, has two meanings only loosely related. The more common is to bring

[27] J Madison: *The Federalist No. X* in *The Federalist*, p 45.
[28] On subtle differences between Burke and Madison, see Notes.
[29] Madison makes reference to the substitution theory: *Federalist No. 10*, p 47.
[30] For a different but compatible account of ascending and descending theory, see W Ullman: *A History of Political Thought.*

something to mind by presenting an image or symbol. That painting of Rafaello represents an unknown young woman by bringing her to the mind of the viewer. In the theatre actors not just bring to mind but become the character. It is a short step to the proctor becoming or embodying the Church, or in a secular setting the ruler becoming or embodying first the realm, then the nation, later the people. The verb has another meaning less obvious but real. *Represent* is a contraction of *re-present*, meaning to present something again. By subtle extension, to present something again covers the case where one acting for another presents something on behalf of the other. It seems to match the language of agency, where the agent presents or re-presents the case of the principal for some purpose.

Constitutional discourse has absorbed both senses of representation. Let us reverse the order and start with one presenting or *re-presenting* the interests of another for a stated purpose. By a mild act of imagination the relationship between the people and the few may be seen in this way. In Anglo-Saxon society, the original purpose of appointing some to official positions was to have the interests of all present in the processes of governing. The Norman prince ruled, but took advice and counsel from several sources, one the knights from the shires who presented the interests of local communities. The knights had no say in rule; their duty was to put before the king matters to take into account in ruling. The knights were described as *representatives* just in the sense they presented or re-presented the interests of communities to the king.[31] The idea dusted and updated fits and helps to explain rule by representatives. The elected few are responsible for presenting the interests of the electors in the process of governing. Although not bound by instructions, the few are appointed by a community, sometimes small and defined, at other times large and loose; but still a community whose members want their interests to be known and to count in the decisions of officials. It is easy to see why the elected few are thought of as agents or even servants, the status preferred by Adam Smith and the Levellers. However described, the idea is the agent or servant presents the interests of the principal or master to the process of governing. Stating the relationship in this way exposes the fallacy. The image of politicians as our servants is attractive but too crude.[32] Presenting or re-presenting the interests of electors is part of their function, an essential part, but not the whole; they must also decide. And as we saw on first entering the constitutional field, there is more to deciding than tallying up interests, more to it than shepherding the interests of the flock into the decision-process.

That leads back to the other meaning, the idea that representatives act for the whole. Putting aside the more outlandish images of substitution, acting for the whole has two parts. One is that the few stand in for the people, have plenary

[31] The practice and the meaning of representation are well-described by Susan Reynolds: *Kingdoms and Communities in Western Europe.*

[32] Too crude despite being later endorsed by Adam Smith: *Lectures on Jurisprudence.*

power in their name and on their behalf. The other part is the few know the good of the whole, the people collectively, and act to achieve it. That is more than and different from acting for particular interests of persons, groups, and sectors. The idea of the good of the whole, the common good, we have seen to be embedded in constitutional discourse. An article in the *Manchester Guardian* in 1883 called for 'A fresh method of election by which representatives shall be made to reflect with greatly increased accuracy the wishes and opinions of the whole of the electors'.[33] Representatives *reflecting* the wishes and opinions of all electors suggests representation is more than presenting or *re-presenting* the interests of persons, groups, and sectors. Presenting such interests is the first stage of a process of deliberation and decision. At the second stage the few decide, and in deciding *reflect* with *greater accuracy* the common good. This is the other dimension of representation, another term in relations between the people and representatives. Representatives do more than present, deliberate on, and settle competition among interests; they are alert to, and have a duty to act for the good of the whole. That means taking account of particular interests, then deciding the good of all, the common good, or whatever other term captures the interest in the whole shared by all. Being responsible for the whole is easily construed as representing the whole and a short step away from becoming the whole. Whether anyone now would want to take the step is doubtful. The relationship is well-described as one of substitution in the practical sense that the few govern on behalf of the people.

7. The people's opinion of rule by representatives

In entering the field ruled by representatives the people are of two minds. They are eager to learn how the shortcomings of princely rule and self-rule are made good, while being cautious of the claims made earlier for rule by representatives.[34] The lines of descent are now clear and understood. The first begins with the ruler who represents the people as a whole, knows the good of the whole, and rules for that purpose. The second is based on the people knowing and being in charge of advancing their own well-being. After noting the openness of the concept of representation, tracing the source of several meanings, and marvelling at the subtlety, sometimes sophistry of each, the people are ready to assess the merits of rule by representative in designing the constitutional field. Hacking through the undergrowth of claims and sifting through the sands of meaning, the people arrive at several conclusions.

The first is the practical appeal of rule by a few. The people have learnt how a system of government contributes to their well-being, while governing well takes

[33] *Manchester Guardian* (22 October 1883).
[34] See Chapter V:3.

time and effort, is complicated, and requires certain skills. It divides into two parts, one to make decisions and take action on a daily basis, the other to oversee government agencies. The people expect not perfection but that rule be moderate in content and tolerably efficient in action. They realize there is no necessary link between who governs and good government, whether the prince, the few, or the people themselves. Some matters are best left to the strong leader, others entrusted to the people, while most are safe enough in the hands of the few, subject to safeguards. Secondly, it dawns on the people that a distinction has to be made between practical reasons for conferring authority on a few, and believing the few know the common good and how to reach it. They have seen how that idea comes from earlier forms of rule, how it found its way into republican discourse and survives in contemporary versions of representative democracy. The idea under scrutiny turns out to be dubious in principle and lacking evidence in practice. The reason for conceding power to a few is partly to have firm government and partly on that base to build good government. A third conclusion is that, among the conditions of good government, relations between the people and the ruling few are critical. Vesting authority in a few is a step towards good government but only a first step. Where the risks are high and there is no certain path to success, the people's power of influence is needed, nudging officials towards good government, the quintet of measures the means, restraint and support in one hand, engagement, vigilance, and censure in the other. How the means are best used and how effective are variables; how the discretionary space where much of governing goes on can be brought within reach has to be considered.

The last matter for the people is *representation*, whether the concept is needed and adds to understanding, or could be dropped from the discourse without loss. Does the concept reveal anything about the relationship between the people and the ruling few? The form of rule is neither simply rule by a few nor the people ruling themselves. It is a distinct form of rule with no certain name. To call it representative democracy, harmless enough at one level, misleads at another. The use of 'representative' as an adjective qualifying 'democracy' is not accurate, the relationship not being one of self-rule modified, the people ruling themselves through representatives. The people make no pretence of ruling themselves, but concentrate instead on selecting rulers, influencing their actions, and holding them to account. *Representation* is not wholly discarded but keeps a minor place inherited from its parents, agency and substitution, both of which leave their mark. The elected member is to some degree an agent in presenting the interests of electors to the processes of governing, although what that means and the nature of the relationship between the elected member and the constituency, are highly variable. The other parent, substitution, is present in that the elected members do stand in the place of the people, do what the people ideally would do themselves. Traces of both parents live on, but as long as not mistaken for their offspring, do no harm. In the meantime, that rulers be elected by the people, while not enough to satisfy the people, is a base around which to construct a more complete and dense relationship between the people and rulers, and a more satisfactory sense of constitutional authority. From being the ugly duckling of dubious parentage, rule by the elected few has the potential to grow swan-like into a form of rule to which the people are drawn. A form where they and the few have a role in the processes of governing, while keeping the few under the eye of the people and their influence. The verb to *keep* and the concept of *keeping*, having already caught their attention, now point the way to a fresh approach to the constitutional field, into which they now enquire.

Notes

On rule by representatives

From a large body of literature, the following I have found especially useful, while many others not mentioned have been instructive.

The sociological side

Max Weber: *Economy and Society* (Volume 1).

Pierre Bourdieu: *Language and Symbolic Power*, Chapter 8.

Accounts historical and theoretical

Quentin Skinner holds first place as a guide to the many strands of rule by representatives, among whose writings the following are a foundation: Q Skinner: *Foundations of Modern Political Thought* and *Visions of Politics*. See also the essays in: *Republicanism: A Shared European Legacy* (eds) M van Gelderin and Q Skinner.

H Pitkin: *The Concept of Representation* (Berkeley: University of California Press, 1967).

B Manin: *The Principles of Representative Government* (Cambridge: Cambridge University Press, 1997).

Founding ideas of the American republic

A Hamilton, J Madison, and J Jay: *The Federalist* is the base on which I have drawn, the contributions of James Madison in particular. The leading contemporary source is Gordon Wood: *The Creation of the American Republic*. Additional sources historical and theoretical are referred to in Chapter XII in considering the ideas around the Italian city-states of the thirteenth to fifteenth centuries.

Tension within rule by representatives

The tension noted in rule by representatives between rulers and the people is present between the prince and the nobility. Described by Harrington as 'a wrestling match between King and nobility and inherently unstable'. Discussed by John Pocock in *The Machiavellian Moment*, pp 387*ff*. Harrington found similar instability in 'the ancient constitution' which meant mainly Anglo-Saxon society, contrary to that of unity and coherence presented by writers like Obadiah Hulme. The tension is normally deplored and the search launched for a form of government without it. That was the appeal of the body politic; the organic whole left no room for unresolved tension. Pocock proposes a 'perfect partnership of all citizens and all values' as the only way to avoid a few ruling in the name of the many: *The Machiavellian Moment*, pp 71*ff*.

The people are sceptical of such notions as 'perfect partnerships'. The alternative is to value the instability, the conflict among persons, groups, and sectors, as a route to good government. That is the basis of Machiavelli's view of a well-functioning republic: considered at length in the *Discourses*.

Abbé Emmanuel Sieyès

Sieyès' account of representative rule is a point of reference in later discussion: E Sieyès: 'What Is the Third Estate' in *Sieyès: Political Writings* (ed) M Sonenscher: *Sieyès: Political Writings*.

For commentary: JK Wright: 'The Idea of a Republican Constitution in old Regime France' in *Republicanism: A Shared European Heritage*: (eds) M van Gelderen and Q Skinner.

Community as the source of authority and the delegation of power to leaders

Obadiah Hulme: *An Historical Essay on the English Constitution: an Impartial Inquiry into the Elective Power of the People, from the First Establishment of the Saxons in this Kingdom* (London: Edward and Charles Dilly, 1771; reprinted in Gale Print Editions). Adam Smith left an account of the origins of societies, the nature of Anglo-Saxon society, and its demise. A major theme is the gradual shift of power, legislative, executive, and judicial, from the people and their localities to the central government: *Lectures on Jurisprudence*, pp 254–61.

Other notable writings on community: Arthur Monahan: *Consent, Coercion, and Limit*; Susan Reynolds: *Kingdoms and Communities in Western Europe 900–1300*; John Watts: *Henry VI and the Politics of Kingship.*

John Warr's opinion of Anglo-Saxon society is rather different from Obadiah Hulmes'. After noting that Roman law applied throughout England and Scotland, Warr writes: 'till the subversion of this state by the Saxons, who made so barbarous a conquest of the nation, and so razed out the foundation of former laws, that there are less footsteps of the civil law in this, than in France, Spain, or any other province under the Roman power': *The Corruption and Deficiency of the Lawes of England Soberly Discovered: Or Liberty Working up to its Just Height* (1649) in *Divine Right and Democracy*, p 154.

The Levellers

The Levellers regarded parliament as 'a representative body of the people'. Representatives are 'but the servants' of the people to 'provide for their welfare and freedom'. A representative body is needed because 'by reason of their numbers' the people cannot do 'in their own persons without hazard both of confusion and desolation': *England's Miserie and Remedie* (1645) in *Divine Right and Democracy*, p 276.

The idea of representatives as servants of the people has foundations in constitutional discourse long before the Levellers. On one strand of discourse the king was no more than 'a supreme magistrate' whose power flowed from, was entrusted by, the people, who served 'as their attorney', and whom they could turn out in the same way as a servant could be turned out: Smith: *Lectures in Jurisprudence*, pp 397*ff*.

John Lilburne and Richard Overton warn that the people must 'exact an accounting from their servants and, if not satisfactory, to recall power into their own hands': *The Out-cryes of Oppressed Commons: A Warning for All the Counties of England* (1647). See further: Blair Worden: 'Republicanism, Regicide and Republic: The English Experience' in *Republicanism* I, p 30.

Madison and Burke

James Madison's account is summarized as follows. Due to the diversity of interests, democracy leads to factions, some of which then control government to the cost other interests. The solution is 'refine and enlarge the public views, by passing them through the medium of a chosen body of citizens, whose wisdom may best discern the true interests of the country, and whose patriotism and love of justice will be least likely to sacrifice it to temporary or partial considerations'. It 'will not be denied that' the few, not the people, are better able to discern the 'public good'. The advantage of 'the substitution of representatives' is their 'enlightened views and virtuous sentiments': *The Federalist No. X* (1787). Madison goes on to warn against 'interesting too strongly the public passions' by referring 'constitutional questions' to the people: p 258.

Madison rejects the idea of 'an actual representation of all classes, by persons of each class' as 'altogether visionary'. Instead, 'merchants, members of the learned professions, and the landed interests' are capable of representing all sectors of society: pp 166–7.

Edmund Burke

'Parliament is not a *congress* of ambassadors from different and hostile interests, which interests each must maintain, as an agent and advocate, against other agents and advocates'. Parliament is 'a *deliberative* assembly of one nation with *one* interest, that of the whole—the general good' as opposed to 'local purposes' and 'local prejudices'. Members of parliament exercise 'unbiased opinion, mature judgement, enlightened conscience' and so 'ought not to be sacrificed to the electorate': *Speech to the Electors of Bristol* (1774).

The ground shared by both is: (i) there is a common good, (ii) which is best decided by the elected few. Then follows a subtle difference: for Madison the few are able to 'discern', that is, know and define the common good. Burke's few, being less self-assured, try to *work out* what is best for all rather than *know* the 'general good'.

XV
The Keepers of the Common Good

1. Re-imagining the constitutional order

This study began with David Hume's noting the ease with which the people submit to rule, adding that 'it is on opinion only that government is founded'. The people although submitting have their own opinion, stand a step apart, and view the constitutional order with a critical eye. Hume later replaced *submission* with *acquiescence*, a softer term signifying compliance with conditions. That the people's opinion, sentiments and dispositions count, subtly but critically opens a crack in the constitutional fortress allowing the people to slip through to enter a field where they have some share in and influence over cultivation. This seems to be what Hume had in mind. On one hand the people judge it to be in their interest to gain 'the general advantage of government', even if the benefits are basic; on the other hand they realize the field opens up avenues for advancing interests. From this point of entry, my aim has been to show how submission and opinion come together, how the people submit to rule, while in the conduct of rule their opinion counts. Or more simply, how the constitutional order is capable of providing government that is both effective and responsive to the people, the process guided in Hume's words by *moderation* to reach in Vico's words *equilibrium*.

Early encounters with the peasants of Gagliano showed how a community, despite living in conditions of privation, could stand back from the constitutional order, view it with a critical eye, and condemn it as *inauthentic* and *illegitimate*. How the peasants came to such judgement, the reserves on which they drew, is the question central to constitutional understanding. The search for an answer, Adam Smith holding the lantern for Vico deep in thought, led back to a foundation of human endeavour, grounded in humanity and civility and rendered in practice as well-being. The next step was to consider the constitutional order as one kind of collective action towards that end. Then to identify and separate two registers of constitutional discourse, one generated by that foundation of purpose, the other emerging in the course of history to justify the system in place, based partly on the benefits brought to the people, partly on fictions. The focus then moved to the experience of the people in confronting the constitutional order. Several patterns of opinion appear, prompting metaphors of a fortress on one side, freedom on the other, a field in between. Each metaphor rests on a form of rule, the fortress associated with princely rule, freedom with the people ruling themselves, the field less settled and open to ideas for cultivation. Each form of rule serves aspects of well-being, one promising security and protection, the other celebrating liberty

Keepers of the Common Good. D.J. Galligan, Oxford University Press. © D.J. Galligan 2024.
DOI: 10.1093/9780198907398.003.0015

by allowing the people to be in charge of their affairs, the third drawing on both to mark out a new direction. Each form promotes in the people a matching opinion. Princely rule is viewed as a safe port in a storm, self-rule the ultimate harbour. When the storm passes the people want more than security; at the same time they learn to resist the siren call to rule themselves. They conclude that in matters of constitution as in all forms of social endeavour there is, sadly, no port of perfection. There remains one harbour to enter, a port beckoning and offering 'fine merchandise'. Rule by representatives, holding itself out as a refuge from the rigours of princely rule and relief from the risks of self-rule, combines two ideas, the people being in charge of their affairs, while rule is in the hands of a few, the representative part bearing signs and a legacy of princely rule. The people know the power to elect and dismiss rulers, and the influence it gives them over the course of governing. But doubts remain. They are sceptical of *representation*, partly due to its origins in a fiction, partly because it entrusts plenary power to a few, and partly because the relationship between people and representatives is left uncertain, and anyhow is not enough itself to keep rulers to purpose or to ensure sound rule. The representative relationship applies only between the people and the elected few, leaving the agencies and officials, the empire of government largely outside its scope. At this point the journey ends, the anchor dropped, rule by representatives the final harbour spruced and started to show its appeal, tarred to hide its faults.

The people know better, leave behind the call of the sea, the search for an all-weather harbour, and return to the tedium and turmoil of the field intent on improving the yield. The signs are there of a fourth pattern of opinion, a fresh way of understanding how the people approach the constitutional field. The task now is to draw out the pattern, the sentiments, and dispositions of the people on which it rests; show the historical evidence; then assemble the keepers' model. It is neither princely rule nor self-rule nor representative rule, although the influence of each is evident. It is inspired by and has origins in the theory of human endeavour and collective action on which this study is based. Several features stand out. The model begins with the power of the people to elect and dismiss leaders, from which follows the potential to influence how they govern. Next to notice around and below the elected leaders are many sites of power, legislative and executive, administrative and judicial, each capable of serving one or other aspect of the people's well-being whether protection, welfare, or enablement. In assessing the sites of power, the people notice the different functions and structures. The purpose at some sites is to apply settled standards to persons and situations; at others to decide matters within defined zones of discretion. Both sit on the surface but reach down to the deep discretionary space around each site, especially prominent at the highest levels of government, in which much of governing takes place and with which the people have limited scope to engage, be vigilant, or to censure.[1] The need for such

[1] Analysed in Chapter V:3.

a space, an undefined zone of discretion in the conduct of government, the people acknowledge. Their aim is not to fill the space with standards but to watch over it, exert influence on its use, and urge explanation and justification for actions taken within it. At the high levels of governing, the people's capacity to influence action is backed by the power of election and dismissal; at the sites below, they rely on the practical measures of engagement, vigilance, and scrutiny, framed by the power to withdraw support and relax self-restraint.

'The herd without a keeper strayed', words of Walter Scott, catch the spirit of the concept.[2] Keeping watch prompts the concept of *keepers*, they who have 'charge, care, or oversight of any person or thing; guardian, warden, or custodian'.[3] The people are the keepers of the common good who watch over those with power to make sure it be used properly. The keepers have an open role, an undefined and unlimited authority to find ways and means of keeping government to purpose. They accept the power of officials then take measures to prevent them from straying. Within the bounds the few may graze but beyond they must not stray. And so the title: *Keepers of the Common Good, the Keepers* for short.

2. A fourth pattern of opinion

Priding himself on always putting the 'Weal of the Publick' over his private ends, James I went on to proclaim himself 'to be ordained for the procuring of the Wealth and Prosperitie of his People'.[4] Ordained to decide the common good and enforce it, the people grateful and supportive. On this pattern of opinion the people accept the prince's assurance and consider their well-being safe in his hands. By 1642, Charles I facing war and a hostile House of Commons, was forced to redefine relations between king, elected chamber, and the people. Government is 'trusted to the king'. The elected chamber 'was never intended for any share in government or the choosing of them who should govern'; but it is 'an excellent conserver of liberty', words on which much hangs.[5] *Liberty* was used broadly at the time to mean well-being more generally.[6] In conceding to the elected chamber a role in conserving well-being by keeping watch over government, the prince had crept out of the fortress to enter the field bearing a fresh pattern of opinion to plant. In those few words the king, ably advised by Culpeper and Hyde, in redefining social relations between the ruler and the ruled, catches the spirit of the keepers' model. The people through elected parliamentarians now have a place, a *share* Machiavelli called it, in

[2] W Scott: *Lady of the Lake* (1820) Chapter III:IX.

[3] *Keeper* as defined in the *Oxford English Dictionary*.

[4] Quoted in Chapter VII:4, now for a different reason.

[5] Charles I: *His Majesty's Answer to the Nineteen Propositions of Both Houses of Parliament* in *Divine Right and Democracy* (ed) D Wootton (London: Penguin Books, 1986), p 171.

[6] The wider meaning of *liberty* is plain in Warr's *A Spark in the Ashes*.

the constitutional field, not to govern but to keep government to purpose.[7] Notions of well-being remain constant while the means change; no longer left to the sole judgement of prince but now engaging the people. The most daring prince knows it prudent to take notice of the people's opinions; indeed parliament originated in knights bearing news from the towns and shires of their needs and wants. The people themselves found ways of influence, some such as addresses and petitions eventually gaining legal status, others informal, from minor displays of dissatisfaction to serious matters of protest, resistance, even rebellion. The difference is that the king's admitting the people into the constitutional field, until then barred as outsiders, enabled them to take active part, confined and constrained, but of high potential in securing well-being.

As princely rule gave way to rule by the elected chamber, relations between parliamentarians and the people moved to the centre of the constitutional field. The path of princely rule split into three. One ended in rule by elected representatives on whom the people are disposed to rely, either as their substitutes or simply as wise. Another path led to the people ruling themselves, with a matching opinion that well-being is best served by their being in charge, the fate of which we have witnessed. The last of the paths, pegged by King Charles but left for others to level and pave, marks a pattern of opinion, a set of dispositions embedded in history but barely acknowledged by rulers and bound to be frustrated. If government is to serve the people's well-being, the people need to be on the inside, able to exert influence on rule, keep it under watch, and hold it to account. They neither govern nor aspire to govern but have a role in keeping government to purpose, to protecting and advancing their well-being. This pattern of opinion invoked to prop up princely rule became, ironically, the foundation of modern constitutional fields where the people have a place secure and integral to cultivation. The efforts of the people over centuries to have their needs and utilities known and respected by leaders and officials, viewed through this frame of reference, take on a new meaning and coherence otherwise missing. Simple but profound: the people, no matter how lowly they be in the social order, have a place in the constitutional field that allows them to find ways of having their well-being acknowledged, secured, and advanced by government, whatever the form. On this empirical understanding of human action, Vico constructed the natural law of peoples, those maxims of common sense on which human action rests in all fields of endeavour, including the constitutional.

Adding to the irony, the Levellers, prominent among Charles' critics, viewing rule from below not above, advocated a pattern of opinion similar to his. Not to

[7] N Machiavelli: *The Discourses*, pp 111, 225. On the similarity of the king's words to Machiavelli's, see Notes.

prop up princely rule but to force the elected chamber, emerging as the seat of power, to govern for the well-being of the people, their 'liberty, peace, and safety'; to advance 'their wele' not 'their woe'.[8] By 1647, the Levellers held the House of Commons to be 'the sole institution of government', but in need of instruction. They had no intention of overthrowing government, without which there would be 'confusion and desolation'. Nor do the people aspire or intend to govern themselves. If government were 'to take care of comfort and contentment', the people would not only acquiesce but give positive support.[9] Men would enlist voluntarily and there would be no need to press them into service. The people would be 'all well-minded' and show 'true English confidence' in government. Officers of government, being the servants of the people, their power is 'but deputative and of trust'.[10] Elected leaders are not substitutes for the people let alone become them. They are representatives just in the sense that, coming from the towns and shires, they can make known and ensure respect for local notions of well-being. The people enter the constitutional field with a foundation of ideas and values, a concept of fundamental law based on 'right reason and equity', prior to and by which to judge all that takes place with the field.

Noting the danger of power, the Levellers see the election of leaders as a way of having influence on how they govern. A free press is necessary 'to know the voice of the people' and to keep them informed. Only then are the people able 'to grow impatient of their thraldom and shake off their yoke' and all forms of oppression.[11] The results of government conducted under the watch of the people for the well-being of all, is a nation of 'absolute freemen' and 'a just, plenteous, and powerful nation'.[12] These elements together constitute an approach to the constitutional field, witness a pattern of opinion among the people well-stated as their being *keepers of the common good*. The same pattern of opinion drawn from the sentiments and dispositions of persons and groups across time and place, plainly witnessed in rebellion, is grounded on two notions. First, *purpose*: peoples precede nations and have an innate common sense, a notion of well-being, of civility and humanity, with which to guide their lives and the institutions they build or confront. Second, *means*: the processes of government, the means by which to cultivate the constitutional field to serve well-being, are most effective if the people are able to engage, be vigilant, and impose censure, while exercising self-restraint and giving support.

[8] J Lilburn: 'England's Birthright Justified' in *The Leveller Tracts 1647–1653* (eds) W Haller and G Davies (New York: Columbia University Press, 1944), pp 270, 306.

[9] R Overton and W Walwyn: *A Remonstrance of Many Thousand Citizens* (1746), p 10.

[10] *A Warning for All the Counties of England* (24 March 1647).

[11] *Remonstrance*, p 8.

[12] *Ibid* p 12.

3. Keepers' model and social foundations

The keepers' model of constitutional order may now be constructed.

First The people confront a constitutional order and a system of government already in place, in the formation of which they only occasionally have a say.

Second The purpose from the people's perspective of the constitutional field, and each site of power within it, is to protect and advance their well-being, for which each agency needs a degree of autonomy and independence in deciding and acting.

Third Social relations between the people and officials at all levels and sites are defined and guided by that same purpose.

Fourth The means available in keeping power to purpose, and managing the risks, are to engage, be vigilant, and impose censure, the manner and extent at each site to match the nature and function.

Fifth The power to elect and dismiss leaders is valued principally for the influence it allows the people over the course of governing. The people eschew ideas of a special even mystical bond whereby officials become them.

Sixth The people accept the need for a balance at each site between the influence of the parties whose interests are affected, and the duty of officials to act for the good overall.

Seventh Aware of the discretionary space around each site of power, a space that deepens as power increases, and knowing the need in governing well, the people find ways of watching over it, while realizing much will remain out of reach.

Eighth Fictions have no place in the model, although knowing the tendency of fictions to form within social relationships, the people are on guard. The fictions of sovereignty, consent, and representation they regard not as a sign of their power, but the opposite, the draining away of their power to officials.

Ninth Acknowledging the processes of governing to be imperfect and the scope for influence limited, the people's expectations are moderate. Even to achieve reasonable regard for their well-being across the sites of governing requires determination and effort on their part, tempered with patience and persistence, seasoned with realism.

The keepers' model prompts further reflection from the people's point of view. Strong rule of the kind provided by the prince sometimes serves their ends, but is not a sound basis for permanent rule. They are drawn by the idea of being in charge of their own affairs by ruling themselves, but know the instabilities are real, the risks high. The prudent course is to be alert to cracks and crevices in the processes of governing into which to insert elements of self-rule. As for rule by representatives, the notion of handing over power to a few who are inclined to regard the people as a dangerous faction, and anyhow claim to know what is best for them, is unappealing. Nevertheless, the people see sound reasons for entrusting government to a few leaders, over whom the power of election gives them influence. Much of governing takes place amid the network of agencies, from the low administrative to the high judicial, whose members are not elected. How to hold the agencies to purpose, and the processes suited to the task, are issues the people face. The case for government is plain and the potential utility of the many sites of power a useful, even necessary addition to personal and collective action. The people know about power from experience within social relationships; they see the benefits while aware of the dangers. The more power the more the potential benefits, yet the more likely misuse and the graver the consequences. Another reflection leads back to the foundation from which the people approach the constitutional order. The hinterland of well-being, the sentiments and dispositions encountered among the peasants, made plain in the lower register of discourse and witnessed in rebellion. The people so grounded are able to stand back from social institutions, the constitutional order included, to view them with detachment, uncover the foundations on which they rest, and assess their potential contribution to well-being. Finally and critically, the people approach, engage with, and watch over the constitutional field and all sites within as a means to civility and humanity, to their well-being in all its forms. So equipped and enlightened, the people as keepers of the common good confront the processes of governing.

The constitutional order and the place of the people acquire new meaning, a fresh understanding simple, subtle, and of consequence. Simple in having a standpoint from which to view the constitutional order as a means to the well-being of all, the goal to make sure it be used for the purpose. No more 'idolising of the form' of rule as if there were a right form, a sure means to sound outcomes.[13] Substance replaces form and fictions fade, the stress falling instead on outcomes, on getting results, and making use of whatever means are available, formal and informal. Subtle but seminal in redefining the relationship between the people and officials. Election is no longer a symbol of representation, a process by which the few substitute themselves for the people, leaving the people themselves powerless. Election backed by dismissal is a practical measure by which the people decide from time to time who holds the power of leadership, from which follows power to have influence on their actions.

Most notably, the constitutional order acquires a unity, coherence, and social foundation otherwise missing. Viewed through the frame of the keepers' model, all sites of power and the agencies attending are for the common purpose of the people's well-being. Each agency at each site contributes by protecting or advancing a portion of well-being from minor to major. A few main sites are

[13] Words of John Warr: *A Spark in the Ashes*, p 34.

normally provided for in the constitution itself, but most are created by the elected leaders. On one approach, unity and coherence are gained by linking agencies to the electoral process. The agencies are instituted and empowered by, and answerable to the elected leaders, and through them to the people as electors. The link upwards to the electoral process accounts for only part of the place and power of the agencies of government. A distinction is to be drawn between *authority* and *function*. The authority of agencies flows from above, but the function of each, the practical use of authority is left to the agency to settle, in some cases at the margins, in others at the very centre. The keepers' model guides the process along two main lines, one concerning function, the other defining relations between agency and persons with an interest. The function at each site is to serve an aspect of well-being, outlined by the parent law but largely left to the agency to work out and define more fully, which often includes designing the process. The agency tends to acquire a degree of autonomy and independence, not as a departure from constitutional propriety, but as a necessity in achieving purpose. Attention to purpose leads naturally and smoothly to the foundation of social action, the concern for the well-being generally, and how within a specified space it may be advanced. Two sets of social relationships follow, the one between agency officials and elected leaders, the other between the agency and persons whose interests are affected, whether one, a few, or the people as a whole.

Administrative law, the law covering agencies and processes, of developed legal systems provides evidence to match the keepers' model and how it works in practice. Each administrative agency has its aims and method; each forms relations with those whose interests are affected. When placed within the keepers' frame, the underlying unity and coherence, the need for a degree of autonomy and independence, are plain. Approaches and processes shift and change, reasons and justifications range, all dedicated to protecting or advancing an aspect of well-being. A sphere of discretion is needed to cope with the variables, deal with competing interests, and reach a defensible outcome. Discretion has a second role, to guard the wider public good, the well-being of the people more generally. Both issues are present at each site of administrative power, the one immediate and pressing, the other in the background, often silent but on call when needed to defend the good overall. The model has special appeal in clarifying the place of courts in the constitutional field. The courts occupy an awkward position, expected to be independent in judging, but not connected or accountable to the electoral process. On the keepers' approach, independence enables the courts to serve well-being by applying the law and doing justice. Justice according to the law leads to and cannot be separated from being responsive to the principles underlying the rules, which means being ready to reach down to the deeper precepts of social life and relations. Not to bring about 'the full-blooded pursuit of social justice' but to be at least responsive to the sense of justice implicit in the rules, founded on and flowing from the well-being of the parties.

A final point is the place and power of interested parties at all sites of governing, from applying rules at one end to making high policy at the other. A place ranging from being on the margins to close involvement, with many points in between. Involvement means more than being engaged but extends to being vigilant, keeping watch; and where warranted being censorious, some forms common to all sites, others moulded to fit the site. The people's engaging with leaders continues throughout the term of office; they exert influence and expect explanation and justification for actions taken. Continuing engagement is in marked contrast to the people who, once having voted, are deemed to acquiesce in whatever be decreed. The keepers' model is able to cope with elements of the standard forms of self-rule, princely rule, and representative rule. All fit within the framework of common purpose, one granting the people final say on some matters, another allowing special measures to maintain safety and security, the third inserting an element of genuine representation into relations between people and leaders.[14] While resisting the appeal of ruling themselves, yet confident that on some matters well-being is best served by their having the final say, the people are alert to opportunities. Similar reasoning applies to vestiges of princely rule. The tendency to concentrate power in the hands of leaders with only weak constraints does not normally serve the people's well-being, although on occasions exceptional measures are needed. The people accept the need, while aware of the risks and alert to the case for added vigilance. Representation has a place with the keepers, modest but valued. The elected leaders do sometimes *present or re-present*, speak on behalf of and act to advance the interests of the people, or a sector or segment of them, in the processes of governing.[15]

This account of the people's approach to the constitutional order prompts further comments. One is to note that while some goals of government are settled and reasonably objective, well-being as it would be construed by an impartial observer, others are variable and subjective to the people's preferences, their sentiments and dispositions, their perception of interest. Government is valued for having at each site officials empowered to settle the matter, to have the final decision as to the common good. Another point to note is the limits of process in guiding decisions and actions, leaving much to the discretion around each site of power. Discretion is triple-sided: one at the margin of standards; a second marking a subfield of power; a third leading deep into the space around power. How to confront each side, how to guide it towards the common good is an issue for the keepers. Reflection on discretion summons up the two faces of power, one bright the other dark. One a resource enabling action for the peoples' well-being, the other a mount of wanton will to be tamed; a mount menacingly unruly when ridden by a few. Finally, the people as keepers have learnt from other forms of rule, particularly princely rule

[14] See Chapters XIII and XIV.

[15] On *representation* as *re-presentation*, see Chapter XIV.

and self-rule, the merits and drawbacks of each; they have looked behind the fictions of representative rule to redefine the power of election and to salvage a modest sense of representation.

The keepers' model is cautious about form, the idea that if the right form were found good government would follow. That is why the form of rule has drawn so much attention. If one form of rule fails to honour the common good it must be changed, a better form found. Jack Cade thought his replacing the king, his mouth becoming the parliament, would be the perfect form. His followers were few. The Levellers concluded that rule by one or a few is bound to betray the common good, the fatal defect the people's exclusion from the processes of rule. Some like the freemen of Pennsylvania took that to mean the only safe form is the people's being in charge. Then the path runs out, the discourse stifled. Other forces more powerful gathered and a different constitutional discourse was invented, recovered partly from medieval theories of representation, partly from notions of a republic, and partly to maintain a certain social order. Rule by representatives was born and launched and stooped to conquer, until that goliath of constitutional discourse met its match in the keepers of the common good. Or, borrowing the wisdom of John Warr, 'true reason is a great traitor to the outward form', its overthrow inevitable, 'for 'tis the perfection of the shadow to expire into the substance'. Eschewing form in favour of substance, seeing 'counterfeit reason is the ape of the true',[16] the keepers display the common sense proclaimed by Vico, anchored in civility and humanity, to achieve 'the perfection, equity, and reason' of the constitutional order.[17]

4. The common good

When the commons of Kent rose in rebellion in 1450, the 'common weale' was their guide and the anchor of their actions.[18] Behind the leader Jack Cade, a murderous villain, lay a worthy cause and a constitutional vision. The rebels in invoking the common weal went straight to the foundation of authority. The purpose of rule is the common weal or good, which means the well-being of all, here that the commoners' rights however few be respected. The common good may seem an unsound base on which to build a constitutional order; an open concept, some say an empty concept; but a concept to which all forms of rule lay claim and give content. Despite the fickleness and the promiscuity, the common good remains critical to relations between the people and officials. To be clear in defence, the common good is the frame defining the purpose of the relationship, to which the sentiments and dispositions of parties supply the content. The two registers of discourse help in understanding. Both claim the common good, which each interprets in its own

16 'ape' means mimic.
17 J Warr: *A Spark in the Ashes*, p 36.
18 See Chapter IX:5 for a fuller account.

way. The upper register to preserve the settled social order, while the lower register finds meaning in a deeper, unadorned, even primitive, sense of the purpose of human endeavour. Despite the upper register vaunting its virtue and dominating discourse, a segment of the people willing no longer to tolerate oppression, rebel. Lacking arms they need grounds, and for that they look back to origins, to recover and revive the foundation of social relations, never wholly forgotten but forced to the shadows. On that foundation the common good is based and given meaning, not as a normative concept, but a concept framed in experience and embedded in the sentiments and dispositions of the people.

The common good of the keepers' model has two elements, the one familiar and conventional, the other unheralded but critical. That the well-being of the people constitute the common good is the conventional part; that the people determine the content of their well-being the critical. The prince as head claims to knows the good health of the body politic and all its organs; members of parliament to know what is good for those for whom they are substitutes; the slave-owners of Virginia best able 'to discern the true interests of their country'.[19] By contrast, according to the keepers, the people themselves are the judges of their own well-being. Intent on advancing civility and humanity, guided by purpose, the people give meaning and content to the concept. Some aspects are shared in common, others contested, resolution left to the tug-and-scramble of social life. However complex and contested, the people themselves are the final arbiters of their own well-being, hence the common good. On that foundation the lower register of discourse is based. The people so equipped enter the field, approach each site of power as a potential means to well-being as they know it, and direct their efforts to cultivation. Success is unpredictable and variable; but the purpose is constant and the spirit unbowed, the power of the lower register never exhausted and the sense of well-being innate a perpetual inspiration. The constitutional order viewed in this way becomes a field of endeavour, a potential source of well-being, meeting needs and advancing utilities by protection, welfare, and enablement; the task of the people as keepers to see that it does.

Alert to Warr's warning against idolising form, we now attend to process and its place in governing. Process fends off the fate of form by being tied to outcome; not free-standing or an end in itself but the means by which to reach a given outcome. The outcome sought determines the process; as outcomes vary processes follow. Processes are formal or informal, the one tied to legal relations between people and officials, the other referring to informal action to influence the use of power. The aim is to show the link between process and outcome, and the practical limitations. The main kinds of process across the sites of governing, each defined by outcome, are threefold: electing officials; deciding policy either to deal with a specific issue or to set standards for the future; applying standards to cases.[20] Each merits a

[19] J Madison: *The Federalist No 10*, p 45.
[20] Chapter V.

treatise of its own and all are much analysed. My aim here only to show how each process fits the keepers' model, how the people as keepers use process in cultivating well-being. Let us reverse the order: first applying standards; then moving to areas of defined discretion; merging into the residual space; finally electing and influencing leaders.

5. Processes of governing: adjudication

Adjudication is the process of applying settled standards to a situation where the issue, usually, is to decide how someone is to be treated. The aim is to reach an accurate outcome based on evidence and findings of fact, interpreting and applying the standards to the facts, *rectitude* as Bentham named it. Adjudication serves well-being by doing justice and respecting rights. Justice in the sense of giving what is due according to the rules, which entails upholding rights arising under the rules. Justice in this individualized sense ranks high in the order of well-being, for Hume the ultimate 'purpose or object' of government,[21] the lack a ground of censure.[22] The people share the sentiment of justice and the value, and support the concern for *due process* to ensure accurate outcomes, while respecting certain other values.[23] Several concerns call for further reflection. First, they know the process of adjudication is imperfect, mistakes are made and justice denied, showing the need for additional processes for detection and correction. Secondly, doing justice according to the rules serves well-being in a clear and compelling sense. Thirdly, the rules are settled at prior sites of defined discretion, where deeper notions of justice enter the process, sometimes settled and shared by the parties, at other times a matter of contention. The keepers expect diverse and competing notions of justice to have been aired and argued, and taken into account in the course of setting standards. Fourthly, we have noted how interpreting and applying the standards engages with the contextual contingencies where ideas of substantive justice reappear around the edges, ready to enter and bear influence.

The responsibility of courts in delivering justice, where they stand between the two spheres, are issues much debated and contested. At one end, rules are applied narrowly and strictly, at the other end the rules merge into deeper principles. Between judges being 'the mouthpieces of the law', and delivering justice in a more profound sense, more moderate approaches are open. In settling on a point somewhere between the poles, the keepers are guided by several factors, here to be noted rather than investigated. First, they accept the courts' primary duty is to do justice to the parties by applying the rules, giving what is due, honouring

[21] See Chapter I:2.
[22] See Chapter IX:3–6.
[23] Considered at length in my *Due Process and Procedural Fairness*.

expectations. Secondly, considering the uncertain line between the justice of the rules and justice around the rules, the courts need guidance in marking a course between them. Among the factors to consider, two have most weight. One is the relationship between courts and other agencies of government, especially the legislative and executive, how power is distributed among them and the contribution of each in achieving the common good. The keepers know the functions of each, how design follows function, and not least the competing accounts of the judicial process. Alert to the imperfection of social institutions in serving purpose, the keepers are cautious about doctrines of strict separation of agencies according to function. The other factor guiding the courts is the need to be robust in having resort to notions of justice implicit in the rules. The compass of experience points to the propensity of courts, historically, to go beyond strict rules, to put aside form in favour of equity, and touch on deeper ideas of justice. The reign of Henry VII was notable but not unusual in creating courts authorized to reach beyond the rules of law to notions of equity. An approach leading inexorably to the hinterland of ideas and values native to peoples and at the core of the lower register.[24] The common people, seeing how their well-being was served, flocked to the courts. The lesson of history is the capability of courts to contribute to well-being by taking a broad approach to their place in the constitutional order. And, finally, as administrative agencies have spread and the functions widened, many are engaged in adjudicating, the same issues arise: respecting due process, finding a balance between rules and discretion, and between conceptions of justice.

6. Processes of governing: defined discretion

Defined discretion refers to a space at each site of power where the outcome is left to the judgement of officials. The keepers know the need for zones of discretion in protecting interests, providing benefits, and enabling the people to improve their lives.[25] The risks being well-known, the issue is how to be confident the common good is served. Two features guide action. One that the agency pay attention to those whose interests are affected; the other that, in deciding, the agency have a sense of the common good more generally. How to meld the two is the measure and the mystery. Since the outcome is not set in advance, the focus is on process, structuring the discretionary space with a process guiding officials to a justifiable outcome. On some matters the purpose is plain and undisputed: defending the nation and dealing with emergencies, coping with natural disasters and plagues or the threat of civil war. On other matters, interests are affected in different ways, with disagreement among persons, groups, and sectors as to which interests count and

[24] See Chapter XI:7.
[25] The discussion under self-rule is relevant here: Chapter XIII:6.

the comparative value, and difference of opinion as to the merits of potential outcomes. Out of this clash of interests and opinion, officials assess comparative worth and judge what serves best the general well-being. It is not quite Adam Smith's all-out-scramble but a process structured by procedures and guided by values and principles. Some interests are protected against others, some are consigned weight in the decision-process. Many still are left to face each other unprotected, relying on reason in hope of persuasion, all contending to serve overall well-being.

The study of administrative law and process shows how defined discretion is handled in practice and how it fits well within the keepers' model. Each area of discretion is designed for a purpose, although the contours and the content may be open to argument. The agency adds structure and the issues are identified to guide submission and argument. Parties with an interest are entitled to engage, although what amounts to an interest and whether it qualifies, is for the agency to settle. The parties are heard, their arguments and supporting evidence recorded; deliberation follows. The process is at times enriched by the agency's stating potential outcomes, the reasons, and costs and benefits of each, the parties invited to comment. The agency makes the final decision and states reasons backed by evidence; explains and justifies the outcome and the selection among competing interests, the process conducted and overseen by officials trained for the purpose.

The outcome still relies on discretionary judgement, but the rigour of the process may win the parties' support. Several comments are due. First, this approach assumes that while consensus may be reached in some zones of discretion, more typically interests compete and notions of well-being are in contest, making plain the need for the agency's power to reach down to the foundations of purpose. Secondly, the limitations are plain: process lays the path to an outcome but the agency settles the destination. No matter how rigorous the process, how serious the deliberation, the outcome turns on a residue of discretion. Thirdly, the character of the agencies and the nature of their task ranges from amateurs armed with simple good sense, to others who are experts in the subject, across a spectrum from economics to science and technology. Fourthly, the approach applies at all levels and sites across government. Where matters complex or contentious are in issue, whether locally, regionally, or nationally, the keepers' model envisages a parallel process of rigour, of deliberation and debate, informed by evidence and expert knowledge where needed, resolved for reasons stated and justified.

The logic of the keepers' model, plain and compelling, is likely to be met in practice to varying degrees. The people share a realism, a seasoned scepticism, a common sense understanding that processes, however exacting, often fail in securing sound outcomes, judged by the common good and the well-being of the parties. Restraint and support remain intact, despite disappointments and setbacks, unless the interests most valued, held most critical to needs and utilities, be neglected or abused, rekindling memory of the natural law of peoples and a native sense of constitution. Officials may act to calm discontent by taking account of less conventional sentiments and dispositions of persons, groups, or sectors, presenting or re-presenting them in processes of decision-making. The social order of uneven power and disparity of resources among persons, groups, and sector bears on the discretionary process in two ways, one concerning entry, the other unevenness within. Some find it hard even to enter a process, despite the potential effect on their interests, while those who make it may be daunted by the dominance of select persons, groups, or sectors, and fumble and stumble in making a case. Adjustments can be made to open entry to all affected, measure taken to modify the imbalance. The people bow to reality and know such adjustments make only moderate difference. They know the constitutional order is designed not to transform social relationships but to install a system of government that can cope with and take measures to work within and on occasions modify the reality.

7. The deep discretionary space and the limits of process

Around the sites of power, select spaces are structured by an adjudicative process, others are left to the defined discretion of officials. The line between the two is not strictly drawn, discretion on the margins of standards merging into discretion at the centre.[26] Beyond the reach of both the discretionary space remains and deepens. The deeper it goes, the more resistant to being structured by process, the more distant the people, and the more uncertain relations with officials, who use the space as they think fit, at times openly often in secret. Some matters are best dealt with away from the public gaze, considered and decided in confidence; others because officials prefer the freedom the space confers, freedom from disclosure, whom to engage with, and the ends to advance. Avenues of engagement are on some issues open to all, on others confined to certain persons, groups, and sectors. Engagement is occasionally direct but more likely to be indirect, while often there is none at all. The people's interest is that the deep space be used for their well-being, the practical issue what means they have to engage, be vigilant, and deliver censure. They remain on the lookout for ways to extend the reach of process by engaging with officials and having influence, by encouraging deliberation, explanation, and justification. They are vigilant in watching over the actions of officials within the space, while attentive to forms of censure, from criticism at one end to legal remedies at the other. Ambition is tempered by worldly wisdom, the realization that much of governing, even the crucial parts, is destined to be conducted deep-down in the discretionary space, out of sight and beyond process. The people know efforts to engage, be vigilant and censorious are rewarded only

[26] See Chapter V for a description of the discretionary space.

moderately, while accepting that without restraint and support on their part even the best government will 'totter and shake'.[27]

A glance at how other forms of rule handle the deep discretionary space offers guidance. Princely rule projects an image of the leader who, being virtuous and wise, knows and is guided by the common good at all sites and levels. Informal avenues of influence appear but are narrow and precarious. The contrasting image of the people ruling themselves, engaging in processes and deciding outcomes, has no fear of the discretionary space because the people themselves are in charge. A noble idea marred by reality, by competing opinions about how best to advance the well-being of all, turning the deep space into a site of tugging-and-scrambling. Rule by elected representatives is more promising, although relations between electors and elected have to be clarified, ideas from the past reckoned with and refined. On one discourse representation signifies the transfer of power from the people to leaders, whether by becoming them or by the wise and worldly few knowing what is best for them. The one is regarded as quaintly diverting, the other although dressed as common sense shows a distrust of the people and leaves unstated the exact nature of the relationship. The keepers accept the spirit of Burke's rebuke against instructing their elected representatives, and the need for leaders to have power to be in charge of, and decide the major matters of governing. Nevertheless, between the people's abdicating power at one end, and their being in control at the other, relations with elected leaders have to be given content. On that turns the keepers' approach to the deep discretionary space.

Election frames the relationship and moderates what happens within. The people elect the leaders, who are not mere agents to be instructed, but hold plenary power to lead and oversee the processes of governing. The leaders give content to the discretionary space, partly by deciding all issues themselves, and partly by delegating power to other agencies with instructions and guidance as to its use. The leaders control the flow of information to the people; they decide the scope for the people's being engaged, bound to be narrow, and settle the processes. The question for the keepers is how to enter the deep space of the constitutional order, at first sight as forbidding as the real deep space, and have influence within it. The answer begins with the power of election and then considers other avenues of influence, ways of keeping watch, and measures of censure. The narrow scope for formal processes prompts attention to informal ways of influencing the discretionary space. The means are many, some within the constitution and the law, some outside. The Levellers were among the many who placed high value on a free press, while freedom of speech and expression are linked historically and conceptually to keeping officials and agencies under watch. Public protest follows and takes many

[27] The words of Reverend Henry Meriton: Chapter VIII:3.

forms. All have a central place in the keepers' constitution, although here we must be content to note the use and the utility, well-documented elsewhere.

8. Midsummer in Athens and a quarrel in Rome

Peter Quince's imagined musings as he prepares to present the play on the occasion of the duke's wedding we have heard.[28] The fear of being hanged for roaring too loudly and offending the ladies we have witnessed.[29] Then there is the ridicule of the royal spectators, the mean dismissal of the mechanicals in mounting a play, who are said never to have 'laboured in their minds till now', the giddy comments as the play goes on. The words of the play threaten no disorder, incite no disaffection. How then can it be right that the mechanicals be mocked by the duke and his circle? Much effort had gone into writing and staging the play to show, as good citizens, their loyalty and respect for the duke in marking his wedding. The occasion is marred and relations between prince and mechanicals corrupted by the courtiers' licence to belittle the players and ridicule the play. Although the prince's power is entirely personal, he is not a tyrant, indeed shows regard even affection for his subjects. When Egeus counsels the duke not to permit the play, he insists it go ahead. 'I will hear that play;/For never anything can be amiss/When simpletons and duty tender it'.[30] Even the simpletons in their 'tongue-tied simplicity' are able to show loyalty and discharge to the duke their 'fearful duty'. 'Fearful duty' is the critical concept. The duke's concern for his subjects is real, but within a relationship where he rules and citizens obey without question. The power of rule is personal to the duke, subject to his wishes and whims, influenced by giddy courtiers as well as counsellors. The mechanicals have no voice. No voice in the decision as to who rules, no voice in the channels of influence, no settled way of having their interests considered and counted. The duke neither answers to them nor accounts for his actions. Quince's instincts are right. A relationship of 'fearful duty', of absolute power vested in the ruler, can be used to advance the well-being of his subjects, or just as readily to oppress them, all at his will. Between fearful obedience and outright rebellion there is no middle ground, just a discretionary space in which the duke has all the power. The mechanicals may gaze but have no power to act, no power in the space between obedience and rebellion.

If Quince's curiosity had led him to look for answers elsewhere, the story of Coriolanus would have caught his attention. The consuls of Rome rule with the support of the senate. The people have no say in how they are ruled but do have a voice in election. Coriolanus, nominated to be consul by the senate and

[28] Peter Quince first appears in Chapter VII:1.
[29] *Midsummer Night's Dream*, Act 1: 2: 71–2.
[30] *Ibid* Act 5: 1: 77.

endorsed by the nobles, has to be confirmed by the people. It is a power 'but a power we have no power not to do'[31] declares one citizen, the convention being that the people acclaim the candidate proposed. Coriolanus is popular with the people for his bravery in defending Rome, for 'what he did before Corioles'.[32] 'All tongues speak of him'; 'prattling nurses let their babies cry' while they praise him;[33] the 'commons made a shower and thunder with their caps and shouts' as never seen before.[34] Nevertheless, Coriolanus has to put on the white gown, subject himself to the gaze of the plebs, and show his wounds. He is a worthy candidate but a proud man, who had earlier sworn that if nominated for consul he would never put on 'the napless vesture of humility' nor show 'his wounds to the people, beg their stinking breaths'.[35] His lack of love for the people is palpable, 'leaves nothing undone that fully discover him their opposite';[36] 'their affections a sick man's appetite'.[37] Ambition tempers revulsion and Coriolanus comes before the people, clad in the white gown, 'the gown of humility', the customary gown to show the candidate's suitability to rule.[38] They accept that if he 'show us his wounds and tell us his deeds' they must 'tell him their noble acceptance';[39] 'if he would incline to the people' there was never a nobler man.[40] The citizens are to come before Coriolanus and 'give him our own voice with our own tongues'.[41] He refuses to show them his wounds as convention requires but has done enough to earn their voice of approval. One citizen sounds a note of caution: 'You have not, indeed, loved the common people',[42] yet adds his voice in the 'hope to find you our friend'.[43] So confirmed, Coriolanus makes his way to the senate-house.

Events take a dramatic turn. The citizens meet the tribunes who are the 'tongues o'th' common people'.[44] Needled by the tribunes, second thoughts surface. Coriolanus mocked them, flouted them, used them scornfully, and refused to show his wounds as custom decrees. Once he had their voices, he had no further use for them. One tribune reminds the plebeians that when Coriolanus was a 'petty servant to the state' and had no power, he was their enemy who 'ever spoke against

[31] *The Tragedy of Coriolanus*, Act 2: 3: 5.
[32] Act 1: 10: 62.
[33] Act 2: 1: 203*ff.* A *malkin* is an untidy servant.
[34] Act 2: 1: 263.
[35] Act 2: 1: 230–3. *Napless vesture* means threadbare clothing.
[36] Act 2: 2: 20.
[37] Act 1: 1: 176.
[38] The white gown is the symbol of the candidate's having the right qualities to govern. *Candidate* comes from *candid* which means in Latin *white*. The candidate wears the gown to show his whiteness suggesting a cleanness or purity of character. Which in turn suggest an ability to transcend personal feelings and traits and rule impersonally.
[39] Act 2: 3: 6.
[40] Act 2: 3: 39.
[41] Act 2: 2: 45.
[42] Act 2: 3: 93.
[43] Act 2: 3: 104.
[44] Act 3: 1: 23. Reminiscent of the House of Commons as depicted by King Charles.

your liberties/ and the charters that you bear/i'th' body of the weal'. If he were in power, he should 'still remain fast foe to th' plebeii/your voices will be curses to yourselves'.[45] What they should have done, adds the other tribune, is 'plucked/either his gracious promise which you might—have held him to'. Or if that 'galled his surly nature,/-So putting him to rage' then you should not have elected him.[46] Did you not perceive, Brutus the tribune asks, the contempt with which he solicited your votes? That augurs not well for the future. He will use the power of the consul to crush you and leave you with 'no more voice/than dogs that are as often beat for barking'.[47] The citizens are aroused and resolve to revoke the election.

On hearing the news, Coriolanus lets forth a stream of invective against the people; his true view of the constitutional order pours out. His sentiments towards the common people, if hedged before, are now in the open, raw and brutal. He has 'shed his blood' for them; now he shall use his lungs 'to coin words till their decay against those measles', the people. When rebuked by Brutus for such contempt, Coriolanus turns on the tribunes. Brutus is abused as the 'horn and noise of the monster's', the people of course the monster. Coriolanus goes on to warn of the confusion when 'two authorities are up, neither supreme'. The people in denying support for him are 'The cockle of rebellion, insolence, sedition'. Where the people had power, as in Greece, they 'nourished disobedience' and 'fed the ruin of the state'. When asked by Brutus why the people should elect him to speak for them, to be their voice', Coriolanus admits his true fear. To give them voice is to abandon reason, for the people will soon claim to be 'the greater poll', the superior power. The authority of the consuls will count for nothing and the rabble will soon 'Break ope the locks o'th' senate and bring in/the crows to peck the eagles'. 'Gentry, title, wisdom' will fall in the face of 'unreasoned actions', the actions of the mob.[48] The 'multitudinous tongue' will then 'lick the sweet', the power of the state, 'which is their poison'.[49] All will end in ruin. The citizens arrive to be told by the tribunes they are about to lose their liberties. What is the city but the people, asks the tribune Sicinius, to which the citizens shout as one 'The people are the city'. Coriolanus has one last retort: 'That is the way to lay the city flat/To bring the roof to the foundation'.[50] Such words are treasonous. Coriolanus is arrested, charged, threatened with death, before being banished to become Rome's sworn enemy.

[45] Act 2: 3: 176*ff.*
[46] Act 2: 3: 190*ff.*
[47] Act 2: 3: 215*ff.*
[48] Charles I's fear of the people is expressed in language remarkably similar to that of Coriolanus.
[49] Act 3: 1: 69*ff.*
[50] Act 3: 1: 203–4.

9. The power of election

Whoever rules has to gain the restraint and support of the people. Duke Theseus fostered the sentiment of 'fearful duty', while attending to their well-being, enough to sustain the disposition of support. Henry VII gained loyalty by setting up courts of easy access and wide jurisdiction to hear the people's complaints and deal with their grievances. The loftiest of princes is keen to know what the people are thinking, their opinions and their expectations. Few outdo Richard Plantagenet in ruthlessness as he plots and murders his way to kingship. Yet, with the severed head of Hastings before him, removed for being a traitor, Richard is desperate to know what the people think in order to avoid censure, 'the censures of the carping world'.[51] Buckingham is sent to explain to 'our duteous citizens'[52] the reasons for a killing. On his return Richard hears with dismay that 'when bid them that did love their country's good/cry "God save Richard, England's king!"', 'they spake not a word'. More of Richard's deeds on the road to rule we need not chart. Enough to note his concern, verging on obsession, that the people know and approve his actions. A concern shared by every ruler, and strong enough to shape the course of constitutional history; proof of Hume's axiom that rule depends on the opinion, the sentiments and dispositions, of the many, partly to guide the direction it takes, partly to adjust and cope where unfavourable. The English parliament, as we have noted, grew out of the king's need to know of opinion across the realm, to be informed of the people's aspirations as well as their grievances, and to have counsel on how to meet them.[53] The power to elect members of parliament lay in the future, but election when it came had its origin in the need for leaders to know and respond to the opinion of the people.[54]

Empowered by election, the people are no longer beggars at the rulers' door or feet for their shoes. The mild tones of supplication are replaced by the voice of authority, the fearful modesty of subjects by the confidence of citizens. Election redefines the relationship. The people's expectations are raised and they find ways of influencing the course of rule no matter who rules. Election raises the level. The people expect more, which the rulers for their part have good reason to meet. Instead of being outsider the constitutional field, the people are partners in its cultivation on terms to be settled within the frame of election. Leaders retain the power to rule, remain masters of the discretionary space, but now pay attention to the voices of people in a manner never imagined by the most benevolent prince.

[51] *The Tragedy of King Richard III*, Act 3: 5: 66.

[52] *Ibid* Act 3: 5: 63.

[53] On the origins of parliament, see JR Maddicott: *The Origins of the English Parliament 924–1327* (Oxford: Oxford University Press, 2010).

[54] The knights and burgesses, at first summoned by the king, are later elected and become representatives of the local constituencies, and hence is hatched the notion of the elected members standing for and later becoming the people.

The power of the people shows in several ways. Election defines relations at two levels, locally between electors and candidate, nationally between electors and the political party. The one gives the people influence over the local representative, the other over leaders of the party. Even if the choice of candidate be limited, the people's power to choose, to accept or reject one or another, frames and defines the relationship between them. Election backed by the power of dismissal enables influence, one in obtaining commitments in advance, the other in guiding action in office, a third in demanding reasons for action. The sequence of action within the relationships begins with the people's engaging with candidates to determine their fitness to govern and to obtain undertakings as to the use of power in office, some relating to local interests others the general interest.

Candidates for office are expected to show their fitness to govern for the people's well-being. To be a candidate is to be *candid* about one's character. The relationship is no longer command and obedience softened by the benevolence of the prince, the duke, or the consul. The relationship is now on terms and conditions over which the people have some say. The plebs are rebuked for not having used their power to 'pluck' from Coriolanus a 'promise' to protect their liberties and their weal. Such a promise becomes a condition of election to which the consul is held, a ground for keeping him under watch and subject to censure. He has shown proof of his ability to govern; has humbled himself to stand in the market-place to show he has nothing to hide and much to give. Yet, the warning signals sound. He cannot stoop to show his wounds and makes no pretence of respect; his earlier declaring his love for the people as the love he bears 'the rotting carcasses of dead men' cause for suspicion.

The power of election is not yet spent. Ways of engaging, being vigilant, and imposing censure acquire a firmer base and last through the term of office. Engagement begins with candidates putting themselves before the people, showing their qualities, and giving undertakings. After election other forms of influence develop, some aimed at undertakings being honoured, others on the prospect of dismissal next time round. Engagement opens avenues of vigilance, of keeping leaders and their actions under scrutiny, from which follows the power to insist on explanation and justification, the most virile offspring of election. The power of censure completes the sequence. Richard Plantagenet abhorred but had to heed 'the censures of the carping world', the common people. Censure can be mild disapproval, rising to unfavourable criticism or reprimand, ending in dismissal.[55] How the plebs of Rome would hold to his promises a consul who dismisses with contempt their 'giddy censure' is not clear.[56] Formal processes were lacking, blunt force the last resort, as depicted in another encounter in Rome between the people

[55] 'To you, Lord Governor,/Remains the censure of this hellish villain./The time, the place, the torture': *Othello,* Act 5: 2: 177. *Censure* a capacious concept.

[56] *The Tragedy of Coriolanus,* Act 1: 1: 259.

and the assassins of Julius Caesar. Passionate in support of Caesar, the plebs seek revenge. Mark Antony, disclaims his 'power of speech' and denies intention to incite. Yet, the crafty venom of his words is enough 'to stir men's blood', 'to move the stones of Rome to rouse and mutiny'.[57] Enough to incite the people to force Brutus and Cassius to flee Rome, burn their houses, and beat up Cinna the poet as a suspect. Not the ideal way of holding leaders to account but the only one open. Between obedience and riot the people now have other options. Election changes the relationship and enables the people to devise forms of censure across the range, from the mild to the manly. The next election looms and the leaders who refuse to explain and justify their actions in governing risk retribution.

The advice of Polonius to his son Laertes commends itself to the keepers: 'Take each man's censure,/but reserve thy judgement'.[58] Let leaders be censured, but remember they have to govern, and in governing settle matters of all kinds, many within the discretionary space. Good advice, and essential in calming passions and moderating the disposition to engage and to influence. The keepers' aim is not to remove discretion by imposing a rigid grid, an iron cage of rules and restrictions, an impossible undertaking anyhow. The aim is to reach a median between the people's power to keep government to its true purpose, its first intent, and the power of officials to put that purpose into practice. The median is a metaphor, not a fixed point to be found and made permanent. A metaphor that tries to capture relations between the people and officials, whether elected by the people or appointed by the elected, the content of which is ever variable according to events and practical judgement. The well-being of all the guiding purpose, the power of election framing the relationship, the processes of engagement, vigilance, and censure are the means by which the people give content and structure to the conduct of government, the means by which to exert influence in the deep discretionary space.

10. The power of gaze[59]

Vincentio, the duke of Vienna declares his love for the people, but adds he does 'not like to stage me to their eyes'.[60] He admits being 'staged to their eyes', being under their gaze, is a valued practice; but he does 'not relish well/Their loud applause and *aves* vehement'. Nor does he think the leader who does to be 'of safe discretion'. In a few words the Duke touches on two ideas critical to good government: the leader cannot avoid being under the gaze of the people; but the wise leader stands back a pace, keeps a distance from the applause and the *aves*, the signs of devotion. Both

[57] W Shakespeare: *The Tragedy of Julius Caesar*, especially Acts 1: 2 and 3: 1.
[58] *The Tragedy of Hamlet*, Act 4: 1: 7.
[59] 'A lover's eyes will gaze an eagle blind': W Shakespeare: *Love's Labour's Lost*, Act 4: 3: 310.
[60] W Shakespeare: *Measure for Measure*, Act 1: 1: 68.

add to and deepen relations between people and leaders, both are commended by the keepers. Remember the shame of Lady Eleanor paraded under the 'giddy gaze' of the people. To keep under gaze is to have certain power over, as the drama of Coriolanus portrays. Against all his instincts, Coriolanus submits to the gaze of the people, wearing the gown of candidness to show his fitness to rule. *Candour or whiteness*, the critical concept, has a value of its own.[61] The *oracular paradigm* developed by JE Green in an original and admirable analysis, centres on the leaders who are watched.[62] The people watch, and have the power to decide the setting and the terms of watching.

A stranger reading the daily headlines or hearing the morning news would be led to think the power of government were vested in one person, the leader. Not only autocrats of dubious credentials, but prime ministers and presidents duly elected are held personally responsible for matters of high policy and major importance. The prime minister is presented as if he or she were not just the leader of government but government itself. The leader who gains control of the political party, dominates other elected officials and the executive; instructs administrative agencies, even putting the courts at risk. Most of all, the leader cultivates a direct and special relationship with the people. When the prime minister wields her handbag in Brussels, the home crowd cheers. When she takes a hard line in international affairs, promises to sort out immigration, and attacks the opposition as soft-headed, ratings rise. When promises are made to look after the sectors most loyal, to give them jobs and improve their lot, ratings soar. The combination of the two, power within the constitutional field and a special relationship with the people, marks a type of leadership. A kind not confined to autocrats with no place in a diverse society of elections and protected rights, but common to nations of all kinds, even the most democratic.

Election gives rise to a special relationship between electors and leader, creates a distinct authority, and confers a unique 'legitimacy'.[63] Weber calls it *plebiscitary authority and plebiscitary democracy*. Knowing the people have the power to depose as well as appoint, leaders have an incentive to win their support, best done by cultivating their loyalty. Leaders speak to the people directly, appeal to certain sentiments and dispositions, fuel their fears then douse the flames with promises. Impatient of settled standards, processes, and agencies, the parties prefer direct encounter and distinct understandings. On Weber's account the plebiscitary relationship has origins in *charisma*, defined as 'a compelling charm which inspires devotion in others'. Persons so endowed have qualities rendering them exceptional. At first linked to religion and the supernatural, charisma extends to secular

[61] *Ibid* p 138.
[62] JE Green: *The Eyes of the People: Democracy in an Age of Spectatorship* (Oxford: Oxford University Press, 2010).
[63] M Weber: *Economy and Society*, pp 241*ff*.

leaders who boast abilities in which the people come to believe. That is the basis of the relationship, not an 'ethical, aesthetic, or any other point of view'.[64] Belief in the qualities is the first step; confidence in the holder's capacity to deliver on promises the second; delivery in practice the third. At the extremes, followers become fanatical, allowing emotion rather than calculation to shroud the process. What goods are promised and whether they are delivered is viewed through a prism of loyalty to the leader, obscuring even prevailing over the reality, the leader's true ability to deliver. When the truth dawns that actions have not matched promises, the relationship is at risk and the leader disposed of without ceremony.

In more moderate forms charisma and emotion give way to practical factors. The leaders exploit their status and make promises the people expect them to deliver. A touch of faith remains, faith in the leader's being able to meet promises, faith often clouding practical judgement. The relationship's being direct and personal does not conform to, is prone to transcend, the relationships defined by the constitutional order, to weaken or even render them irrelevant. A unique kind of authority forms. The influence of privileged sectors lessens in favour of others more widely drawn, including the lower, normally subdued and subservient, now in league with the leader.[65] This kind of leadership we have seen to be common, even inevitable in social relationships. At one end are the Jack Cades who exude charisma, enough to inspire blind loyalty in their followers; at the other end are elected leaders who, lacking charisma, see their interests served by cultivating the people or certain sectors directly. Election fosters the relationship and tightens the bond.[66] The issue for the keepers is how to cope with plebiscitary authority, how to accept the inevitable and contain the consequences. But first there more to be said about the concept of gaze and its place in the relationship.

On the *oracular paradigm*, building on Weber's concept of plebiscitary democracy, the voice of the people is separated from their gaze.[67] The *vox populi*, the people struggling to be heard and their interests advanced, is well-documented in constitutional discourse. Having leaders under their gaze adds a dimension, flourishing in the field but outside official discourse. The occasions of gaze range widely, from prime minister's question time and to defending a decision, from the searching interview to the public enquiry, and many more, some formally staged, others spontaneous. The recognition of gaze as an element of the relationship is a notable contribution to social understanding. The value lies in identifying a source of power, subtle but substantial, of the people over leaders. The nature of the power, at first sight elusive, is best clarified by considering the two perspectives, the people's and the leader's. The gaze of the people can be passive or active: passive

[64] *Ibid* p 242.
[65] *Ibid* p 244.
[66] Weber's reasons are set-put in the Notes.
[67] *Ibid* p 153 contains a lucid summary.

in listening to explanation and justification; active in conveying approval or disapproval. The leader experiences gaze in several ways: sensations of discomfort; pressure to explain and defend action; a chance to display personal qualities. The leader under gaze, like Lady Eleanor, feels the force of disapproval, sometimes signalled by silence, often augmented by speech. Being under gaze, leaders feel pressure to account for their actions, defend what they or their government have done. Although the wise duke Vincentio could not bear 'to be staged' to the people's gaze, he admitted the good—'though it do well'—the value of gaze in holding leaders to purpose. The 'loud applause and *aves* vehement' that he did not relish could well be replaced by the opposite, cries of shame and condemnation. If the power of gaze signals approval, it may equally register disapproval. There is a more positive side. Being under gaze allows the leader to explain and justify what has been done and how the people benefit. A quality especially valued in accounting for actions within the discretionary space, from which the people are largely barred.

Gaze has a further function of encouraging leaders to have and to show 'the personal traits', the distinguishing features needed to rule well. To show they are capable of 'discipline and determination', the traits needed to govern for the well-being of all.[68] Discipline shows control of personal traits; determination suggests defining and shaping the traits to serve purpose. Virtue has gone from the discourse, replaced by personal traits as the guide to good government, although quite which traits is debatable. Personal traits are linked to the sentiments and dispositions aroused by a leader's interest in ruling for the well-being of the people. To be candid, to display one's whiteness, is a metaphor for being fit to rule, a sign of having the traits or features that seem to be needed in governing, at least good faith and an impartial concern for all, an honourable record and a capacity for self-restraint. Gaze may induce leaders not only to show, but actively to cultivate, character and the necessary traits.

The place in the keepers' model of the plebiscitary relationship between the people and leaders can now be assessed. All peoples try to keep watch over leaders no matter how remote or ruthless they be. If leaders are candid in the sense suggested the task is made easier. A leader's disposition to submit to gaze and be candid is strengthened and made more compelling when joined to the people's power to elect and dismiss. Against the backdrop of election being never far away, the power of gaze continues and intensifies through the term of office, forcing leaders to be open about what they have done, what they intend to do, and the reasons. As election looms, the power of gaze peaks. On the record of candour, the continuing account of sentiments, dispositions, and action, the people are able to judge the suitability of candidates for re-election. If the record is wanting, or the signs for the future discouraging, the candidate may be rejected as the plebs of Rome rejected

[68] *Ibid* p 151.

Coriolanus. Next is to note how gaze, the means to candour, has ties to engagement, vigilance, and censure. The people's being able to gaze on leaders is a form of engagement, subtle but potentially effective, a form the leader finds hard to escape. Vigilance, from the Latin verb *vigilare*, means to watch. Gaze as watching is a form of vigilance, encouraging the leader to defend actions; enabling a record to be compiled and a reckoning planned. Gaze opens avenues of censure, from criticism to complaint to defeat at the next election. As Buckingham, sent to account to the commons for the beheading of Hastings, soon learnt, silence itself can be 'carping censure'.

11. Gains and losses of the plebiscitary relationship

That the leader be under the eyes of the people, Duke Vincentio commended, even though being 'staged' and acclaimed by 'loud applause' did not suit him. Nor he added as he left the stage should it suit the 'man of safe discretion'.[69] The reasons, left unstated by the duke, are plain. The leader who welcomes the applause and the *aves* enters a relationship with the people that tends to break free from the constraints of the constitutional field, obscuring even abandoning relations within it. Leaders know the power of direct appeal to the people and are inclined to encourage it. Even the British prime minister, the first among equals, the chairman of cabinet the collective committee of government, constitutionally confined, is tempted and on occasions succumbs to the power of direct appeal to the people. One prime minster believed he was the key to electoral success; another was condemned for her 'neglect of cabinet government'; a third openly displayed his 'plebiscitarian traits',[70] his being inclined to bypass parliament, appeal directly to the people, and cultivate a special bond. All milder versions of the plebiscitary impulse, but enough to show the potential risk, the tendency to cross the constitutional boundary, leaving behind the institutions and standards, the guides and constraints laid down for the conduct of government.

Gains and losses result. Among the gains two stand out. One, the leader supported by the people directly and vocally feels not only empowered to act decisively, but is emboldened to be daring, to take measures stretching the boundaries, avoiding the processes of governing and the risk of opposition. The shadow of princely rule in the background, the appeal of rule firm, direct, and unopposed is hard to resist, now with the authority of the people directly conveyed. Another gain follows. Among the leader's strongest supporters are likely to be groups and

[69] *Measure for Measure*, Act 1: 1: 66–70.

[70] Discussed in EC Hargrove: 'Evolving Executive Authority in Anglo-American Democracy: Coping with Leadership Dispersal' in *Dispersed Democratic Leadership: Origins, Dynamics, and Implications* (eds) J Kane, H Patapan, and P 't Hart (Oxford: Oxford University Press, 2009).

sectors who normally find themselves on the margins of the field and who struggle to have a say in cultivation, their voices if heard, unheeded. The fast track to engaging with leaders, the short cut to influencing action, for them has compelling appeal.

Among the losses, some grave others moderate, several are notable. First, the prime minister who bypasses cabinet lacks the counsel and judgement of colleagues, the moderating effect of diverse opinion and deliberation, a loss constitutional endeavour over centuries has tried to avoid. The same tendency applies to the civil service, a source of reasonably detached and often specialized counsel and advice, backed by evidence. The case of the prime minister, one of many, some more drastic, is commonly encountered across nations. Constitutional constraints get in the way and are set aside; and as the power of the leader grows, the easier to set them aside. The standards and values of the constitution are replaced by the relationship between leader and followers, direct and unpatrolled by outside influences. Secondly, plebiscitary power tends to appeal to sectors of the people rather than the whole. The wider the appeal the stronger and more justifiable the power of the leader. But power is not fussy and ambitious leaders are content, as long as it keeps them in office, to win the loyalty of select groups or classes. Loyalty is buttressed by singling them out as special, having both qualities and needs that separate them from the rest. As the bonds between leaders and followers tighten, a gap opens up between them and the people as a whole. Government is skewed to benefit believers to the neglect of the rest. The third and most serious loss follows: the common good of all, the well-being of all persons, groups, and sectors is sacrificed to benefit some. The keepers are cautious. John Warr's warning about form overtaking substance has been turned upside down. Substance stripped of form is as unwelcome as the opposite. The keepers see the social forces inclining towards plebiscitary authority and the need to make provision. If the relationship between people and leader flourishes, they want to know the consequences? Does it make the discretionary space more unruly, less amenable to structure and standards? Or does it potentially give the people more influence over leaders? In the practical settling of these matters at the various sites of governing, the keepers are guided by common sense and experience, the need to find a balance between form and substance.

12. Journey's end

The journey has been 'long, full of adventure, full of knowledge'. Launched by Hume's observing opinion to be the foundation of government, the journey led to the barren land of Gagliano to gather the wisdom of the peasants. Then continued to other lands, other peoples, in search of the Ithaca of constitutions, guided by Smith and Vico, and others who went before or came after, Warr's warning a compass in avoiding the shoals of form to the sacrifice of substance. 'Hosts of cities have been visited—to learn and learn from those who have knowledge.'[71] It has not been hurried and has lasted, literally, long years. And just as the poet cautioned against expecting too much of the Ithaca of life, the same applies to the people's place in the constitution. The conclusion is modest. No Ithaca of form is to be found; no grand harbour to enter and anchor; no fine theory to encompass all. The people know their well-being, celebrate civility and humanity, and the many ways the constitutional order can contribute. The hoped for harbour, the port of perfection, does not exist; instead just a field, rough and untamed, fertile but fickle; a field of many sites of power from the high to the low, the critical to the casual; a field the people strive to cultivate, success as dependent on conditions, some controllable others not, as the real field on the seasons. Expectations are moderate, founded on the wisdom of common sense; on knowing the promise and the potential, while heeding the limitations, the imperfections, and the dangers. The means to realize expectations, equally, are moderate, success variable, achieved only by keeping watch over the field, engaging in the processes, being vigilant, and capable of censure, while showing restraint and giving support. That is the Ithaca of constitutions, the purpose of endeavour. Let the poet Cavafy have the last word:

> And if you find her poor, Ithaca has not defrauded you.
> With the great wisdom you have gained, with so much experience,
> You must have understood by then what Ithacas mean.

Notes

Keepers' Model

Among the many scholars who, without adopting the name, touch on or present an approach similar to aspects of the keepers' model of constitutional authority, Pierre Rosanvallon stands out: *Democracy Past and Present* (New York: Columbia University Press, 2006) and *Democratic Legitimacy: Impartiality, Reflexivity, Proximity* (Princeton and Oxford: Princeton University Press, 2011). Just three points briefly to note. First is the shared emphasis on the function of 'independent authorities', or in my term agencies at the many sites of governing, in contributing to the well-being of the people: *Democratic Legitimacy*, p 101. Secondly, Rosanvallon's writings may be read as an unravelling of the upper register in order to revel the real relations between the people and officials. Thirdly, his account is framed in terms of *democracy*. On the ground that the concept of democracy, while

[71] CF Cavafy: *Ithaca* in *The Complete Poems of Cavafy*, p 36.

central to political discourse, is on the edges of constitutional discourse, democracy has not been the focus of my analysis.

Keepers and democracy

However, a notion of democracy could be constructed from the keepers' model. *Demos,* the *people* + *cracy,* rule of = *democracy,* rule of the people. A perfect case of *form* separate from and prevailing over *substance*, or in John Warr's words *idolising form.* The keepers' model starts with substance, that is, the purpose of rule. *Well-being* is the purpose, the people the best judges of what constitutes well-being. The issue then: what are the means, the practical measures to serve the people's sense of well-being. Form elbows in, slanting the search towards form, a search for the right form, leaving substance to lag behind. Ruling themselves is the obvious form, but the risks are high. Rule by representatives removes some of the risks of self-rule, but has its own defects as a form serving well-being.

The keepers' approach abandons, indeed bans, the search for a defining form, settling instead on practical means for keeping power to purpose. Form, if insisted on, splinters into several ways and means by which to advance the people's well-being. All are in the hands of the people, the *demos* themselves. Each contributes to the process. The splinters acting together have the potential to ensure purpose is served; but success is contingent and dependent on numerous factors. *Democracy* on the keepers' approach is anchored in *substance* not *form.* The people, the *demos,* at the centre, the good of the *demos* the guiding purpose is reached, not by finding the right form, but by practical measures working together to harness rule to purpose.

Machiavelli and the keepers

In writing of the grandeur of the Roman Republic, Niccolò Machiavelli relates how the nobility, fearing rebellion by the people, granted 'the populace a share in the government; the senate and the consuls retaining, however, sufficient authority for them to be able to maintain their position in the republic', that is, to govern: *The Discourses* (London: Penguin Books, 1970), p 111. The people being the natural 'guardians of liberty', it is 'reasonable to suppose will take more care of it' than the nobles: p 116. The words are almost the same as those of Charles I, quoted before, conceding the House of Commons, the elected chamber, be 'excellent conservers of liberty', but not to govern: see p 4. Machiavelli put the same idea well: 'Rome mobilized the power of the people' but without undermining government.

Machiavelli went on to argue (i) that in order to protect liberty the people have a share in governing, rather similar to that of the House of Commons in 1642; (ii) that 'squabbles between the populace and the senate should, therefore, be looked upon as an inconvenience which it is necessary to put up with in order to arrive at the greatness of Rome': pp 123–4, a sentiment with which Charles would not have agreed. By 'share' is meant not to govern, but to have a place in the constitutional field, again similar to that proposed by the king. Machiavelli goes on to explain that the reason 'that made Rome servile' to the dictators was 'the loss of authority of which the citizens were deprived': p 194. Machiavelli's approach to the people and their place in the constitution, fits well the keepers' model. For further discussion: B Crick: *Introduction* to *The Discourses,* pp 11–71 and F Raab: *The English Face of Machiavelli: A Changing Interpretation 1500–1700* (London: Routledge & Kegan Paul, 1965).

Discretionary space

Discretionary power is a subject much discussed. KC Davis: *Discretionary Justice* (Baton Rouge: Louisiana State University Press, 1969) is the pioneering study and good place to start. The ideas in the text are discussed in more detail in my *Discretionary Powers: A Legal Study of Official Discretion.*

The people and the parliament

The Levellers chart the gradual development of relations between the people and parliament in the seventeenth century. The corporate concept of the people is replaced by the real people and their real needs and utilities. The evolving sense of parliament having authority from the people is shown in the questioning of various practices: monopolies, tax, prerogative power, and seizure of property: *England's Birthright Justified* in Aylmer, pp 57–8.

Sentiments of the people

Among many studies of the sentiments of the people towards the constitutional field, the following are recommended:

L Diamond and MF Plattner (eds) *How People View Democracy* (Baltimore: The Johns Hopkins University Press, 2008).

SN Soroka and C Wlezien (eds) *Degrees of Democracy: Politics, Opinion, and Policy* (Cambridge: Cambridge University Press, 2012).

J Kane and H Patapan (eds) *Good Democratic Leadership* (Oxford: Oxford University Press, 2015).

Taking note of and sustaining opinion

In Hamlet's words: The prince 'may not -/Carve for himself, for on his choice depends/The sanity and health of the whole state;/And therefore must his choice be circumscribed/Unto the voice and yielding of that body/Whereof he is the head': *The Tragedy of Hamlet*, Act 1: 3: 19.

Power of election

Weber on the power of election over leadership: 'the risks of recall or failure of re-election make it impossible to pursue a strictly objective course of decision and administration, without regard to such consequences': *Economy & Society*, p 270.

Political theorists of democracy cling to the notion that the people are ruling themselves. The people, unable themselves to discharge the functions of ruling, elect officials and confer on them the power to rule as their representatives. The principal purpose and power of election is to appoint representatives, who then stand in for the people, or even become them. The people then are ruling themselves through representatives. The mysteries and problems of that logic are discussed in Chapter XIV. That the people are ruling themselves through representatives explains why less attention is given to the need to influence representatives, keep them under scrutiny, and exert influence during the term of office. Among the many adherents to this logic, JS Mill is an early advocate, RA Dahl a more recent: *On Democracy* (New Haven and London: Yale University Press, 2000), especially pp 93–5.

On leadership

J Kane, H Patapan, and P 't Hart (eds) *Dispersed Democratic Leadership: Origins, Dynamics and Implications* (Oxford: Oxford University Press, 2009).

The emergence, nature, and power of the modern political leader: discussed by Weber: *The Profession and Vacation of Politics*, pp 311, 324. On the power of the leader over the cabinet, the parliament, and the party: pp 324, 350–1. On the conditions necessary to nurture and sustain leadership: *Economy & Society*, pp 263*ff.*

On the keepers' model, relations between the people and elected leaders is distinctive and shares some common ground with Weber's account. Drawing on the concept of plebiscitary authority and plebiscitary democracy, he writes: 'The tendency is for electoral positions to become autocephalous spheres of authority': *Economy & Society*, pp 268–9. *Autocephalous* means independent spheres of authority. Within the sphere: 'The leader (demagogue) rules by virtue of the devotion and trust which his political followers have in him personally': p 268.

The keepers acknowledge that as a feature of the relationship, but want to know more, in particular, what happens within it and the power of the people to influence it.

Joseph Schumpeter gives an account of the place of the people in *Capitalism, Socialism, and Democracy* (New York: Harper & Brothers, 1942). The primary role of the people is to elect the leaders, to 'produce a government'. This replaces the idea of 'the classical theory of democracy' that their role is to decide 'political issues': p 269. To understand how 'democratic politics' serve the social end, we 'must start from the competitive struggle for power and office and realize that the social function is fulfilled, as it were, incidentally': p 282. The struggle for power and office is what really matters. The people as voters do not decide, indeed are incapable of deciding policies, while the notion of a common good is fanciful. Outcomes are arbitrary and chaotic. The justification is not that an ethical good is served but 'an unqualified confidence in democratic forms of government as such': p 253.

Several comments. (i) The election of leaders by the people is central to the keepers' model, although there is much more to the relationship than bare election. Having elected leaders, the people have power to influence, scrutinize, and control them. Limited powers but nevertheless important in structuring the relationship. (ii) The social end for the keepers is the well-being of the people, the question for constitutional design is how best to get there, the means. The keepers are keen social observers and know the nature of leadership, the struggles that go on amongst potential leaders, the processes by which leaders are produced, and the limited capacity of those who win. They know too well the unruliness of power and the risks. Yet, measured against other options and allowing for the risks, conceding power to a few seems to be the best means to the well-being, although riddled with imperfection. (iii) That the people are incapable of deciding courses of action, choosing among options, judging a good idea from a bad, is an old record worn out rather than reinforced by repetition. That they do not normally initiate policy is not to be confused with their good sense in judging policy and assessing the merits. (iv) To hanker after a settled sense of the common good is to retreat to the safety of the upper register where all is established and all to be preserved. Once we leave that safe harbour the seas are choppy, the passage uncharted, and shallow shoals a constant worry. But the destination is known, the well-being of one and all the compass. For further comment on Schumpeter: JE Green: *The Eyes of the People*, pp 171–7.

Plebiscitary leadership

Weber on plebiscitary leadership. A few points to note additional to the text. References are to *Economy and Society*.

Plebiscitary democracy is defined as a 'variant of charismatic authority'. It 'hides behind a legitimacy that is *formally* derived from the will of the governed'. The leader (demagogue) rules by virtue of the devotion and trust which his political followers have in him personally': p 268.

Plebiscitary leadership is dependent on the 'confidence of the ruled': *Economy & Society*, p 267. The relationship tends to be based on 'a highly emotional type of devotion to and trust in the leader'. This favours the type of person who 'is most spectacular, who promises the most, or who employs the most effective propaganda in the competition for leadership'. [269] Plebiscitary leadership—scorns rules etc admin—Loyalty depends on 'promoting the material good of the followers': p 269.

The role of persons and elites accumulating political power in their own hands is well-discussed. Perhaps the best known is: JA Schumpeter, *Capitalism, Socialism, and Democracy* (London: George Allen & Unwin, 5th edn 1976).

Under the gaze of the people

JE Green's *ocular model* has three main elements: (i) the objects of gaze are the leaders: 'the ocular paradigm recognizes *the leaders who are watched*' as the object of popular power: p 128; (ii) the people's power of gaze is separate and different from the power of having their voices heard: p 128; (iii) the people use this power to control not the outcomes of the political process but *the means of publicity*, 'the conditions under which leaders appear on the public stage': p 129.

A cautionary tale about gaze. Shakespeare's King Henry IV, usurper to the throne, presents a rather different account of the people's gaze: *The History of Henry IV*. The king rebukes his son, the future Henry V, for giving up his rightful place at court and instead 'becoming a companion to the common streets' where he has 'Enfeoffed himself to popularity'. 'Being daily swallowed with men's eyes,/ they surfeited with honey, and began/To loathe the taste of sweetness, whereof a little/More than a little is much too much'.

When he appears among the common crowd he 'Afford[s] no extraordinary gaze'. Yet, the king continues, it is the *extraordinary gaze* that 'is bent on sunlight majesty', 'which shines seldom in admiring eyes'. To be extraordinary, gaze must not become too common or too often, or the people will become 'with his presence glutted, gorged, and full'. The king contrasts his own demeanour as 'being seldom seen', so when he does appear it is 'like a comet—that men would tell their children "This is he"'.

The power of gaze

According to Lord Biron: What the people see can be more important than measured judgement: 'He's loved by the distracted multitude/Who like not in their judgement but their eyes': Claudius speaking of Hamlet: *The Tragedy of Hamlet*, Act 4: 3: 4.

Giddy

Shakespeare uses *giddy* to describe the people as perceived by members of the upper register. Others in addition to Lady Eleanor's lament at being under 'the giddy gaze'.

Coriolanus shows his contempt for the 'giddy censure' of the commons: *The Tragedy of Coriolanus*, Act 1: 1: 259. Richard Plantagenet notes that 'many giddy people flock to him': *Richard Duke of York*, Act 4: 9: 5. Giddy here means fickle or inconstant as in 'giddy Fortune's furious fickle wheel': *The Life of Henry V*, Act 3: 6: 26.

Cast of Characters from the plays of William Shakespeare

W Shakespeare: The Complete Oxford Shakespeare (eds) S Wells and G Taylor (London: Guild Publishing: 1990)

All Is True: Henry VIII (Henry VIII): Queen Catherine

The First Part of Henry VI (Henry VI Part I): Richard of York, Gloucester, Suffolk, Lady Eleanor

The History of Henry the Fourth (Henry IV Part I): King Henry IV

The First Part of the Contention of the Two Famous Houses of York and Lancaster (Henry VI Part 2): Jack Cade

The Life and Death of King John: Philip the bastard

The Comical History of the Merchant of Venice (Merchant of Venice): Bassanio, Shylock

The Merry Wives of Windsor: Page

A Midsummer Night's Dream: Duke Theseus, Peter Quince, Tom Bottom, Egeus,

Measure for Measure: Vincentio Duke of Vienna, Angelo Acting-Duke of Vienna, Isabella and Claudio

Pericles, Prince of Tyre (Pericles): Pericles, three fishermen

The Tempest: Caliban, Prospero, Ferdinand

Troilus and Cressida: Ulysses

The Tragedy of Coriolanus (Coriolanus): Coriolanus, Menenius, Tribunes Brutus and Sicinius, Citizens

The Tragedy of Hamlet, Prince of Denmark (Hamlet): Hamlet, Polonius, Laertes, Grave-digging Clown, Claudius

The Tragedy of Julius Caesar (Julius Caesar): Julius Caesar, Mark Antony, Brutus, Cassius, Cinna

The Tragedy of King Lear (King Lear): King Lear

The Tragedy of King Richard the Second (Richard II): King Richard

The Tragedy of King Richard the Third (Richard III): Philip the Bastard, King Richard, Buckingham

The Tragedy of Macbeth (Macbeth): Macbeth, Macduff, Malcolm

As You Like It: Touchstone

Love's Labour's Lost: Biron

Other references

The Tragedy of Othello (Othello)

Two Gentlemen of Verona

Bibliography

Acemoglu, D and JA Robinson: *The Narrow Corridor: States, Societies, and the Fate of Liberty* (London: Penguin Books, 2019).

Aquinas, T: 'De Regimine Principum' in J Mathias (ed), *Politica Opuscula* (Turin: Marietti, 1948).

Arato, A and Z Miklosi: 'Constitution Making and Transitional Politics in Hungary' in L Miller (ed), *Framing the State in Times of Transition: Case Studies in Constitution Making* (US Institute of Peace Press, 2010).

Ascheri, M: *Storia Politica e Sociale della Repubblica di Siena* (Siena: Betti, 2000).

Aylmer, G: *The Levellers in the English Revolution* (New York: Cornell University Press, 1975).

Axelrod, R: *The Evolution of Cooperation* (London: Penguin, 1984).

Baker, K: *Inventing the French Revolution* (Cambridge: Cambridge University Press, 1990).

Ball, T and JGA Pocock: *Conceptual Change and the Constitution* (Lawrence Kansas: University Press of Kansas, 1968).

Baron de Montesquieu: *The Spirit of the Laws* (published in 1748, published in English in several editions, translated by Thomas Nugent, Introduction by Franz Neumann) (New York: Hafner Publishing, 1949).

Bassani, G: *Il giardino dei Finzi-Contini* (*The Garden of the Finzi-Contini*) (Milan: Mondadori, 1976).

Baxter, R: *A Holy Commonwealth* (Cambridge: Cambridge University Press, 1994).

Benner, E: *Machiavelli's Prince: A New Reading* (Oxford: Oxford University Press, 2013).

Beramendi, V and others: *Direct Democracy: The International IDEA Handbook* (International Institute for Democracy and Electoral Assistance, 2008).

Berlin, I: *Vico and Herder: Two Studies in the History of Ideas* (London: Hogarth Press, 1976).

Blount, J: 'How do Constitutions Matter: Popular Representation in the Drafting Process' (Workshop: How do Constitutions Matter, Foundation for Law Justice and Society, Oxford, 29 June 2012).

Bourdieu, P: *Language and Symbolic Power* (Cambridge, MA: Harvard University Press, 1991).

Bowsky, W: *Un comune italiano nel Medioevo: Siena sotto il regime dei Nove (1287–1355)* (Milano: Il Mulino, 1986).

Braddick, MJ: *State Formation in Early Modern England c. 1550–1700* (Cambridge: Cambridge University Press, 2000).

Braudel, F: *A History of Civilization* (New York: A. Lane, 1994).

Bromwich, D: *The Intellectual Life of Edmund Burke* (Cambridge, MA: Harvard University Press, 2014).

Brown, W: *Undoing the Demos* (New York: Zone Books, 2015).

Bull, H: *The Anarchical Society* (Oxford: Oxford University Press, 1977).

Burke, E: Speech to the Electors of Bristol at the Conclusion of the Poll (1774) in *The Works of the RH Edmund Burke* (London: HG Bohn, 1854) 446–8.

Burke, E: 'Speech at Mr Burke's Arrival in Bristol' in I Kramnick (ed), *The Portable Edmund Burke* (London: Penguin Books, 1999).

Butt, D: 'Judicial Independence and Transformative Constitutionalism' in DJ Galligan (ed), *The Courts and the People: Friend or Foe?* (Oxford: Hart Bloomsbury, 2021).

Camus, A: *La Peste* (London: Methuen, 1959).

Canovan, M: *The People* (Cambridge: Polity Press, 2005).

Chekhov, A: *Uncle Vanya* (London: Heron Books, 1969).

Clark, M: *Medieval Representation and Consent* (New York: Russell & Russell, 1964).

Dahl, R: *How Democratic is the American Constitution?* (Yale University Press, 2001).

Damaska, M: *The Faces of Justice and State Authority* (New Haven: Yale University Press, 1986).

Danford, JW: *Getting Our Bearings: Machiavelli and Hume* (Cambridge: Cambridge University Press, 2009).

Davenant, C: *Essays Upon Peace at Home and War Abroad* (London: Printed for James Knapton, at the Crown in St Paul's Church-yard, 1704).
Davis, KC: *Discretionary Justice* (Baton Rouge: Louisiana State University Press, 1969).
Defoe, D: *Some Remarks on the First Chapter in Dr Davenant's Essays* (Washington: A. Baldwin, 1704).
Dessìi, G: *Paese d'Ombra* (Milan: Mondadori, 1972).
Diamond, L and MF Plattner: *How People View Democracy* (Baltimore: The Johns Hopkins University Press: 2008).
Dobson, RB: *The Peasants' Revolt of 1381* (London: Palgrave, 1983).
Durkheim, E: *The Division of Labour in Society* (London: The Free Press, 1984).
Dworkin, R: *Taking Rights Seriously* (London: Duckworth, 1978).
Eliaeson, S: *Max Weber's Methodologies* (Cambridge: Polity Press, 2002).
Elias, N: *The Civilizing Process* (Oxford: Blackwell, 2nd edn 2000).
Elkins, Z, T Ginsburg, and J Melton: *The Lifespan of Written Constitutions* (Cambridge: Cambridge University Press, 2009).
Ellickson, R: *Order Without Law: How Neighbours Settle Disputes* (Cambridge, MA: Harvard University Press, 1991).
Elster, J: *The Cement of Society* (Cambridge: Cambridge University Press, 1989).
Elton, GR: *The Tudor Constitution: Documents and Commentary* (Cambridge: Cambridge University Press, 1960).
Etzioni, A: *The Common Good* (Cambridge: Polity Press, 2004).
Evans Pritchard, E: *The Nuer* (Oxford: Oxford University Press, 1940).
Ferguson A: *An Essay on the History of Civil Society* (Cambridge: Cambridge University Press, 1995).
Filmer R: *Patriarcha and Other Writings* (Cambridge: Cambridge University Press, 1919).
Fortescue J: *On the Laws and Governance of England* (Cambridge: Cambridge University Press, 1997).
Foucault M: *Discipline and Punish: The Birth of the Prison* (London: Penguin, 1991).
Foucault M: *The History of Sexuality: The Will to Knowledge* (London: Penguin, 1998).
Galligan, DJ: *Discretionary Powers: A Legal Study of Official Discretion* (Oxford: Clarendon Press, 1987).
Galligan, DJ: *Due Process and Fair Procedures: A Study of Administrative Procedures* (Oxford: Clarendon Press, 1997).
Galligan, DJ: 'Authoritarianism in Government and Administration: The Promise of Administrative Justice' (2001) 54 *Current Legal Problems* 88–105.
Galligan, DJ: *Law in Modern Society* (Oxford: Clarendon Law Series Oxford University Press, 2007).
Galligan, DJ: 'The Paradox of Constitutionalism or the Potential of Constitutional Theory' (2008) 30 *Oxford Journal of Legal Studies* 343–67.
Galligan, DJ: 'Legal Theory and Empirical Research' in P Cane and H Kritzer (eds), *Oxford Handbook of Empirical Legal Research* (Oxford: Oxford University Press, 2010).
Galligan, DJ: 'The Indirect Origins of the Juridical Constitution' (Law and Society Annual Lecture, University of Oxford, 15 June 2011).
Galligan, DJ: 'The People, the Constitution, and the Idea of Representation' in DJ Galligan and M Versteeg (eds), *Social and Political Foundations of Constitutions* (New York: Cambridge University Press, 2013).
Galligan, DJ, 'The Levellers, Arbitrary Power, Representation, and the Constitution' in DJ Galligan (ed), *Constitutions and the Classics: Patterns of Constitutional Thought from Fortescue to Bentham* (Oxford: Oxford University Press, 2014).
Galligan, DJ: 'The People, the Levellers, and the Constitution' in DJ Galligan (ed), *Constitutions and the Classics: Patterns of Constitutional Thought from Fortescue to Bentham* (Oxford: Oxford University Press, 2014).
Galligan, DJ: 'Concepts the Currency of Social Explanation of Law: A Review of the Later Work of William Twining' (2015) 35 *Oxford Journal of Legal Studies* 373–401.
Galligan, DJ: *Magna Carta: A Mess of Pottage, A Beggarly Thing* (London: Lecture to American Bar, 2015).
Galligan, DJ: 'On Constitutional Authority' (Valedictory Lecture, Wolfson College Oxford, 2017).
Galligan, DJ: *Putney Debates* 2019 (Foundation for Law Justice & Society: *fljs.org*).
Galligan, DJ: 'Ally or Enemy, Friend or Foe' in DJ Galligan (ed), *The Courts and the People: Friend or Foe?* (Oxford: Hart Bloomsbury, 2021).
Galligan, DJ: *Courts and the People, Friend or Enemy* (Oxford: Hart, 2022).

Galligan, DJ and M Kurkchiyan: *Law and Informal Practices: The Post-Communist Experience* (Oxford: Oxford University Press, 2003).
Galligan, DJ and M Versteeg: *Social and Political Foundations of Constitutions* (New York: Cambridge University Press, 2013).
Gelderen, M and Q Skinner: *Republicanism: A Shared European Heritage* (Cambridge: Cambridge University Press, 2002).
Gentles, I: 'The Agreements of the People 1647–1649' in M Mendles (ed), *The Putney Debates of 1647* (Cambridge: Cambridge University Press, 2001).
Giddens, A, *The Constitution of Society* (Cambridge: Polity Press, 1984).
Giddens, A: *Politics, Sociology and Social Theory* (Cambridge: Polity Press, 1997).
Gierke, O: *Political Theories of the Middle Age* (Cambridge: Cambridge University Press, 1987).
Ginsburg, T, Z Elkins, and J Blount: 'Does the Process of Constitution-Making Matter?' 5 (2009) *Annual Review of Law and Social Science* 201.
Goetsch, J: *Vico's Axioms: The Geometry of the Human World* (New Haven: Yale University Press, 1995).
Goldsworthy, J: *The Sovereignty of Parliament* (Oxford: Clarendon Press 1999).
Goodin, RE (ed): *The Theory of Institutional Design* (Cambridge: Cambridge University Press, 1996).
Gough, JW: *Fundamental Law in English Constitutional History* (Oxford: Clarendon Press, 1955).
Green, JE: *The Eyes of the People: Democracy in an Age of Spectatorship* (Oxford: Oxford University Press, 2010).
Greenblat, S: *Will in the World* (New York: WW Norton & Co, 2004).
Gregory, E: *A Modest Plea for the Due Regulation of the Press* (London: R. Sare, 1698).
Guicciadini, F: *Discorso di Logrogno* cited in JGA Pocock: *The Machiavellian Moment* (London and Princeton: Princeton University Press, 1975).
Haller, W and G Davies (eds): *The Leveller Tracts 1647–1653* (New York: Columbia University Press, 1944).
Hallett, W and G Davies (eds): *The Leveller Tracts 1647–1653* (New York: Columbia University Press, 1944).
Hamilton A, J Madison, and J Jay: *The Federalist* (London: JM Dent, 1971).
Hampshire, S: *Thought and Action* (London: Chatto and Windus, 1959).
Hanson, RL: 'Democratic Republicanism as the New American Hybrid' in T Ball and JGA Pocock (eds), *Conceptual Change and the Constitution* (Kansas: Kansas University Press, 1988).
Hardin, R: *David Hume: Moral and Political Theorist* (Oxford: Oxford University Press, 2007).
Hardin, R: 'Why a Constitution?' in DJ Galligan and M Versteeg (eds), *Social and Political Foundations of Constitutions* (New York: Cambridge University Press, 2013).
Harre', R and PF Secord: *The Explanation of Social Behaviour* (Oxford: Basil Backwell, 1972).
Harrington, J: *The Commonwealth of Oceana and a System of Politics* (1770) (ed) JGA Pocock (Cambridge: Cambridge University Press, 1992).
Hart, HLA: *The Concept of Law* (Oxford: Clarendon Press, 1961).
Hill, C: *The World Turned Upside Down: Radical Ideas During the English Revolution* (London: Penguin, 1972).
Hill, C: *Change and Continuity in 17th Century England* (London: Nicholson, 1974).
Hindle, S: *The State and Social Change in Early Modern England, 1550–1640* (Basingstoke: Palgrave, 2002).
Hobbes, T: *Leviathan* (ed) N Malcolm (Oxford: Oxford University Press, 2012).
Holbach, P-HT: *Systeme social ou principes naturels de la morale et de la politique* (Paris: 1773).
Holmes, S: *Benjamin Constant and the Making of Modern Liberalism* (New Haven and London: Yale University Press, 1984).
Holt, JC: *Magna Charta* (Cambridge: Cambridge University Press, 3rd edn 2014).
Hume, D: *The History of England* (1778) (Indianapolis: Liberty Fund, 1983).
Hume, D: *Essays Moral Political and Literary* (Indianapolis, Liberty Fund, 1985).
Hume, D: *Treatise on Human Nature* (ed) LA Selby-Bigge (first published 1739) (Oxford: Clarendon Press, 1988).
Humphrey, L: *The Nobles, or of Nobility* (London: Thomas Marshe, 1563).
Ihalainen, P: *Agents of the People: Democracy and Popular Sovereignty in British and Swedish Parliamentary and Public Debates 1734–1800* (Leiden & Boston: Brill, 2010).
Initiative and Referendum Institute, 'A Brief History of the Initiative and Referendum Process in the United States' (I&R Quick Facts) (2006) <www.iandrinsinstitute.org> accessed 7 August 2013.

Joliffe, JEA: *The Constitutional History of Medieval England* (London: Adams and Charles Black, 1961).
Judson, M: *The Crisis of the Constitution: An Essay in Constitutional and Political Thought in England 1603–1645* (New Brunswick: Rutgers University Press, 1949) (Paperback 1988).
Kantorawitz, EH: *The King's Two Bodies: a Study in Medieval Political Theory* (New Jersey: Princeton University Press, 1981).
Kelly, MRLL: 'The Coronation Oath' (Doctoral Thesis, Macquarie University, 2010).
Kelman, HC: 'Compliance, Identification, and Internalization: Three Processes of Attitude Change' (1958) 2 *Journal of Conflict Resolution* 14–32.
Kenyon, JP: *The Stuart Constitution: Documents and Commentary* (Cambridge: Cambridge University Press, 1986).
King Charles I: *The King's Answer to the Nineteen Propositions* (London, 1642).
Knighton, H: *Chronicon Henrici Knighton* collected in Dobson, RB (ed): *The Peasants' Revolt of 1381* (London: Palgrave, 1983).
Knights, M: *Representation and Misrepresentation in Later Stuart Britain* (Oxford: Oxford University Press, 2005).
Krause, S: *Montesquieu's Science of Politics: Essays on the Spirit of Laws* (eds) DW Carrithers, MA Mosher, and PA Rahe (New York: Rowan & Littlefield, 2001).
Kronman, AT: *Max Weber* (London: Edward Arnold, 1983).
Law, D: 'The Myth of Imposed Constitutionalism in Japan' in DJ Galligan and M Versteeg (eds), *Social and Political Foundations of Constitution* (New York: Cambridge University Press, 2013).
Levi, C: *Christo si è fermato a Eboli (Christ Stopped at Eboli)* (Firenze: 1943; London: Penguin, 2000).
Lilburne, J: *England's Birthright Justified* (London: Larner's Press, 1645).
Locke, J: *Two Treatises on Government* (ed) P Laslett (Cambridge: Cambridge University Press, 1960).
Lockwood S: *Sir John Fortescue: On the Laws and Governance of England* (Cambridge: Cambridge University Press, 1997).
Lottini, G: *Avverdimenti Civili* (Bologna: G Mancini, 1574).
Lukes, S: *Power: A Radical View* (London: Macmillan, 1974).
McCloskey, D: *Bourgeois Equality: How Ideas, Not Capital or Institutions, Enriched the World* (Chicago: University of Chicago Press, 2016).
MacCulloch, D: 'Kett's Rebellion in Context' (1979) 84 *Past & Present* 36.
Machiavelli, N: *The Discourses* (London: Penguin Classics, 1987).
Maddicott, JR: *The Origins of the English Parliament 924–1327* (Oxford: Oxford University Press, 2010).
Manin, B: *The Principles of Representative Government* (Cambridge: Cambridge University Press, 1997).
Mann, M: *The Sources of Social Power* (Cambridge: Cambridge University Press, 1986, 2012).
Marshall, MG and BR Cole, *Global Report 2017: Conflict, Governance, and State Fragility* (Centre for Systematic Peace USA, 2017).
Meriton, H: *A Sermon Preacht at the Cathedral Church in Norwich* (London: Printed for W. Battersby and John Place, 1696).
Meuwese, A: 'Popular Constitution-Making: The Case of Iceland' in DJ Galligan and M Versteeg (eds), *Social and Political Foundations of Constitutions* (New York: Cambridge University Press, 2013).
Micraelius, J: *Syntagma historiarum ecclesiae omnium* (Naples: Sumptibus J. Lüderwaldi, 1644).
Monahan, AP, *Consent, Coercion and Limit: The Medieval Origins of Parliamentary Democracy* (Kingston and Montreal: McGill-Queen's University Press, 1987).
Najemy, LM: *Corporatism and Consensus in Florentine Electoral Politics, 1280–1400* (Chapel Hill: University of North Carolina Press, 1982).
North, D: *Institutions, Institutional Change and Economic Performance* (Cambridge: Cambridge University, 1990).
Offe, C: *Modernity and the State: East, West* (Cambridge: Polity Press, 1996).
Oman, CWC: *The Great Revolt of 1381* (Oxford: Clarendon Press, 1906).
Ostrom, E: *Governing the Commons: The Evolution of Institutions for Collective Action* (Cambridge: Cambridge University Press, 1990).
Parker, H: *Observations upon Some of His Majesty's Late Answers and Expresses* (London: n.p., 1642).
Pease, TC: *The Leveller Movement* (1923) (London: Nabu Press, 2012).
Piaget: *The Moral Development of the Child* (New York: The Free Press, 1965).
Pitkin, H: *The Concept of Representation* (Berkeley: University of California Press, 1967).

Plamenatz, J: *Man & Society* (London: Longman, 1963).
Pocock, JGA: *The Machiavellian Moment* (Princeton: Princeton University Press, 1975).
Pompa, L: *Vico: A Study of the New Science* (Cambridge: Cambridge University Press, 1990).
Post, G: 'A Roman Law Theory of Consent' (1950) 26 *Wisconsin Law Review* 67.
Post, G: *Studies in Medieval Political Thought: Public Law and the State, 1100–1322* (Princeton: Princeton University Press, 1964).
Postema, G: *Bentham and the Common Law Tradition* (Oxford: Clarendon Press, 1989).
Pothill, D: *Protecting the People's Voice: Identifying the Obstacles to Colorado's Initiative and Referendum Process* (Independence Institute, 2009).
Prest, W: *William Blackstone and the Free Constitution of Britain* (Oxford: Oxford Academic, 2014).
Rahe, P (ed): *Machiavelli's Liberal Republican Legacy* (Cambridge: Cambridge University Press, 2006).
Rahe, PA: *Against Throne and Altar* (Cambridge: Cambridge University Press, 2008).
Rawls, J: *A Theory of Justice* (Oxford: Clarendon Press, 1972).
Renner, K: *The Institutions of Private Law and Their Social Functions* (London: Routledge & Kegan Paul, 1949).
Reynolds, S: *Kingdoms and Communities in Western Europe 900–1300* (Oxford: Clarendon Press, 2nd edn 1997).
Rollinson, D: *A Commonwealth of the People: Popular Politics and England's Long Social Revolution, 1066–1649* (Cambridge: Cambridge University Press, 2010).
Rosanvallon, P: *Democracy Past and Present* (New York: Columbia University Press, 2006).
Rosanvallon, P: *Democratic Legitimacy: Impartiality, Reflexivity, Proximity* (Princeton and Oxford: Princeton University Press, 2011).
Rosen, L: *The Anthropology of Justice: Law as Culture in Islamic Society* (Cambridge: Cambridge University Press, 1989).
Rosenberg, RAJ: *Book of Samuel: The Jewish Study Bible* (Tanakh Translation: Oxford University Press, 2004).
Rosenn, KS: 'Conflict Resolution and Constitutionalism: The Making of the Brazilian Constitution' in Miller (ed), *Framing the State in Times of Transition: Case Studies in Constitution Making* (Washington: United States Institute of Peace Press, 2010).
Sajó, A: *Limiting Government: An Introduction to Constitutionalism* (Budapest: CEU Press, 1999).
Salisbury, John of: *Polycraticus* (12th century) (ed) CJ Nederham (Cambridge: Cambridge University Press, 1990).
Schevill, F: *Siena: The History of a Medieval Commune* (New York: Harper & Row, 1909).
Schmidt, D: *Citizen Lawmakers* (Temple University Press, 1989).
Schofield, P: *Utility & Democracy: The Political Thought of Jeremy Bentham* (Oxford: Oxford University Press, 2006).
Schumpeter, J: *Capitalism, Socialism, and Democracy* (New York: Harper & Brothers, 1942).
Schwartz, D: *Culture & Power* (Chicago: University of Chicago Press, 1987).
Scott, J: *Corporations, Classes and Capitalism* (London: Hutchinson, 1979).
Sieyès, A: 'What is the Third Estate?' in M Sonenscher (ed), *Political Writings* (Indiana: Hackett Publishing Company, 2003).
Skinner, Q: *The Foundations of Modern Political Thought* (Cambridge: Cambridge University Press, 1978).
Skinner, Q: *Liberty Before Liberalism* (Cambridge: Cambridge University Press, 1998).
Skinner, Q: *The Foundations of Modern Political Thought* (Cambridge: Cambridge University Press, 1998).
Skinner, Q: *Visions of Politics: Renaissance Virtues* (Volume II) (Cambridge: Cambridge University Press, 2002).
Slack, P: *Poverty and Policy in Tudor and Stuart England* (London: Longman, 1988).
Smith, A: *Wealth of Nations* (London: G. Bell and Sons, 1925).
Smith, A: *Lectures on Jurisprudence* (delivered 1762–63) (eds) RL Meek, DD Raphael, and PG Stein (Indianapolis: Liberty Fund, 1978).
Smith, A: *The Theory of Moral Sentiments* (first published 1759) (London: Penguin Books, 2009).
Sonenscher, M (ed), *Sieyès: Political Writings* (Hackett Publishing Coy, 2003).
Spitz, J-F: 'From Civism to Civility: D'Holbach's Critique of Republicanism' in M van Gelden and Q Skinner (eds), *Republicanism: A Shared European Heritage* Volume II (Cambridge: Cambridge University Press, 2002).

Stourzh, G: 'Constitution: Changing Meanings of the Term from the Early Seventeenth to the Late Eighteenth Century' in T Ball and JGA Pocock (eds), *Conceptual Change and the Constitution* (University of Kansas Press, 1988).

Strayer, JH: *On the Medieval Origins of the Modern State* (Princeton: Princeton University Press, 1970).

Stretton, T: *A Social History of England 1500–1750* (ed) Wrightson K (Cambridge: Cambridge University Press, 2017).

Stuart, C, King Charles I: 'The King's Answer to the Nineteen Propositions (1642)' in *The Stuart Constitution: Documents and Commentary* (ed) JP Kenyon (Cambridge: Cambridge University Press, 1986).

Stubbs, W: *The Constitutional History of England in Its Origin and Development* (London: Forgotten Books, 1878).

Syme, R: *The Roman Revolution* (Oxford: Clarendon Press, 1939).

Tanner, JR: *Constitutional Documents of the Reign of James I* (Cambridge: Cambridge University Press, 1960).

Thompson, JB: *Language and Symbolic Power* (Cambridge: Polity Press, 1991).

Tierney, B: *Religion, Law, and the Growth of Constitutional Thought 1150–1650* (Cambridge: Cambridge University Press, 1982).

Ullman, W: *A History of Political Thought: The Middle Ages* (London: Penguin Books, 1965).

van Gelderin, M and Q Skinner (eds): *Republicanism: A Shared European Heritage* (Cambridge: Cambridge University Press, 2002).

Vico, G: *New Science: Principles of the New Science Concerning the Common Nature of Nations* (first published 1774) (London: Penguin Books, 1999).

Villani, M: *Cronica di Matteo Villani* quoted in Najemy Walsingham, F: *Historica Anglicana* (ed) EM Thompson (Rolls Series, 1874), reprinted in Dobson: *The Peasants' Revol.*

Voigt, S: 'The Consequences of Popular Participation in Constitutional Choice—Towards a Comparative Analysis' in A van Aaken (ed), *Deliberation and Decision* (Ashgate, 2003).

Warr, J: *A Spark in the Ashes: The Pamphlets of John Warr* (eds) Sedley S and Kaplan L (London and New York: Verso Books, 1992).

Watts, J: *Henry VI and the Politics of Kingship* (Cambridge: Cambridge University Press, 1996).

Weber, M: *Economy and Society* (eds) G Roth and C Wittich (Berkeley, London: University of California Press, 1978).

Weber, M: 'Parliament and Government in Germany' in P Lassman and R Spiers (eds), *Political Writings* (Cambridge: Cambridge University Press, 1994).

Weber, M: 'The Profession and Vocation of Politics' in P Lassman and R Spiers (eds), *Political Writings* (Cambridge: Cambridge University Press, 1994).

Whaley, D and T Dean: *The Italian City-Republics* (London: Longman, 4th edn 2010).

Whitehead, AN: *Adventures of Ideas* (London: Collier-Macmillan, 1933).

Whitley, R: *Diary of Roger Whitely* (Oxford: Bodleian Library, 1685).

Widner, J, 'Constitution Writing and Conflict Resolution: Data and Summaries' (Princeton University, 2006) <www.princeton.edu/power/data/> first posted 2006, accessed 11 September 2012.

Winch, P: *The Idea of a Social Science in Relation to Philosophy* (London: Routledge & Kegan Paul, 1958).

Winthrop, J: *History of New England 1630–1649* (ed) JK Hosmer (New York: C Scribner, 1908).

Wittgenstein, L: *Tractatus-Philosophicus* (London: Routledge & Kegan Paul, 2nd edn 1971).

Wolin, S: *Tocqueville: Between Two Worlds* (Princeton and Oxford: Princeton University Press, 2001).

Wood, A: *The 1549 Rebellions and the Making of Early modern England* (Cambridge: Cambridge University Press, 2007).

Wood, G: *The Creation of the American Republic* (University of North Carolina Press, 1969).

Wootton, D: *Divine Right and Democracy: An Anthology of Political Writing in Stuart England* (London: Penguin, 1986).

Worden, B: *Republicanism, Regicide and Republic: The English Experience* (Cambridge: Cambridge University Press, 2002).

Zagorin, P: *Rebels and Rulers 1500–1660* (2 volumes) (Cambridge: Cambridge University Press, 1982).

Zaret, D: *Origins of Democratic Culture* (Princeton: Princeton University Press, 2000).

Table of Constitutions and Acts

Instrument of Government (1810, 1949, 1974, 1975, 1991)
Constitution Act (1982)
Albanian Constitution (1998)
Basic Law for the Federal Republic of Germany (1949)
Commonwealth of Australia Constitution Act (1900)
Consolidated Version of the Treaty on European Union (2010)
Consolidated Version of the Treaty on the Functioning of the European Union (2010)
Constitution of Colombia (1991)
Constitution of Costa Rica (1949, 1989)
Constitution of Denmark (1949)
Constitution of Finland (2000)
Constitution of Greece (1975, 1986, 2001, 2008)
Constitution of Ireland (1937)
Constitution of Japan (1946)
Constitution of Luxembourg (1868, 1948, 1998, 2007)
Constitution of Malta (1964)
Constitution of Montenegro (2007)
Constitution of Romania (1991, 2003)
Constitution of the Commonwealth of Australia (1900)
Constitution of the Czech Republic (1992)
Constitution of the Federative Republic of Brazil (1988, 1995, 2006)
Constitution of the Federative Republic of Brazil (1988, 1995, 2006)
Constitution of the Federative Republic of Nigeria (1999)
Constitution of the Fifth Republic (1958, 1962, 2008)
Constitution of the Italian Republic (1947)
Constitution of the Kingdom of Norway (1814, 2007)
Constitution of the Kingdom of Norway (1814, 2007)
Constitution of the Kingdom of the Netherlands (1983)
Constitution of the Oriental Republic of Uruguay (1830)
Constitution of the Oriental Republic of Uruguay (1830)
Constitution of the Principality of Andorra (1993)
Constitution of the Republic of Angola (2010)
Constitution of the Republic of Argentina (1853, 1994)
Constitution of the Republic of Bulgaria (1991)
Constitution of the Republic of Cameroon (1972)

Constitution of the Republic of Chile (1980, 2005)
Constitution of the Republic of Guatemala (1985, 1993)
Constitution of the Republic of Honduras (1982)
Constitution of the Republic of India (1950, 1970)
Constitution of the Republic of India (1950, 1970)
Constitution of the Republic of Korea (1948)
Constitution of the Republic of Lithuania (1992)
Constitution of the Republic of Moldova (1994)
Constitution of the Republic of Nicaragua (1987)
Constitution of the Republic of Poland (1997)
Constitution of the Republic of Serbia (2006)
Constitution of the Republic of Serbia (2006)
Constitution of the Republic of South Africa (1996)
Constitution of the Republic of Turkey (1982)
Constitution of the Slovak Republic (1992, 1999, 2001)
Constitution of the Slovak Republic (1992, 1999, 2001)
Constitution of the Ukrainian National Republic (1996)
Federal Constitution of the Swiss Confederation (1999)
Federal Constitutional Law of Austria (1920, 1929, 1945)
Fundamental Law of Hungary (2011)
The Belgian Constitution (1994, 2007)

Index

For the benefit of digital users, indexed terms that span two pages (e.g., 52–53) may, on occasion, appear on only one of those pages.